INVISIBLE CITY

INVISIBLE CITY

THE ARCHITECTURE OF DEVOTION IN SEVENTEENTH-CENTURY NEAPOLITAN CONVENTS

HELEN HILLS

OXFORD
UNIVERSITY PRESS
2004

OXFORD
UNIVERSITY PRESS

Oxford New York
Auckland Bangkok Buenos Aires Cape Town Chennai
Dar es Salaam Delhi Hong Kong Istanbul Karachi Kolkata
Kuala Lumpur Madrid Melbourne Mexico City Mumbai Nairobi
São Paolo Shanghai Taipei Tokyo Toronto

Published by Oxford University Press, Inc.
198 Madison Avenue, New York New York 10016

www.oup.com

Library of Congress Cataloging-in-Publication Data
Hills, Helen.
Invisible city : the architecture of devotion in seventeenth-century Neapolitan convents / Helen Hills.
p. cm.
Includes bibliographical references and index.
ISBN 0-19-511774-3
1. Monastic and religious life of women—Italy—Naples—History. 2. Convents—Italy—Naples.
3. Church architecture—Italy—Naples. 4. Aristocracy (Social class)—Italy—Naples.
5. Naples (Italy)—Religious life and customs. 6. Naples (Italy)—Church history. I. Title.
BX4220.I8 H55 2002
271'.9004573—dc21 2002025272

1 3 5 7 9 8 6 4 2

Printed in the United States of America
on acid-free paper

To airy nothing

An earthly habitation

and a name

ACKNOWLEDGMENTS

The research for this book took me to some wonderful places and introduced me to some remarkable people. I am grateful to everyone who helped during the course of the work and who afforded me this extraordinary privilege.

I am indebted to many institutions and individuals who made the research for and writing of this book possible. A J. Paul Getty Fellowship in the History of Arts and the Humanities (1998–99) and a Faculty Fellowship at the Institute of Arts and Humanities at the University of North Carolina at Chapel Hill (Spring 1996) provided me with the leave from teaching and administration to undertake substantial parts of the necessary research and writing. Prolonged final stages of work on proofs were undertaken during an AHRB Matching Leave Award (2001–2), for which I am deeply thankful. I am grateful to the University of North Carolina at Chapel Hill and to the University of Manchester and to my colleagues at both institutions for the opportunity to take advantage of those research leaves.

Research trips to Italy were financed largely by the University of North Carolina at Chapel Hill, which granted me University Research awards in 1995 and 1996 and a Junior Faculty Development Award in 1993. Two Small Grants from the British Academy in 1998 and 2000 were also invaluable. I am pleased to acknowledge this generous institutional support.

My debt to those who have helped me in southern Italy grows ever greater.

For invaluable help in Naples, I am deeply grateful in particular to Cesare De Seta for practical help, for putting me in touch with other scholars in Naples, and for generously letting me use his superb maps. Giuseppe Galasso unhesitatingly shared his profound knowledge of Neapolitan history and provided useful guidance. Nicolo Spinosa and the staff of the Soprintendenza per i Beni Artistici e Storici di Napoli afforded me assistance, plans, and access to churches and convents. I should also like to thank Architetto C. Pasinetti for providing access to useful plans and photographs.

Numerous librarians and archivists assisted me throughout the course of research. Staff at the Archivio di Stato in Naples were unfailingly helpful. I should like to thank them and the photographic staff there in particular. I am also indebted to the services of staff at the Archivio di Stato and the Biblioteca Nazionale and Biblioteca Communale in Palermo. Wonderful treasures turned up in the Biblioteca di Stato and the Biblioteca della Società Napoletana di Storia Patria in Naples, where I was always assisted to the full. Writing this book would have been impossible without the efficiency and helpfulness of the librarians and staff at the British Library and Warburg Institute. Francois Quiviger was particularly kind in providing very prompt and full assistance to my many bibliographical questions.

Various parts of the book were first presented in seminars or conferences in Britain, Italy, and the United States. Comments and questions offered then spurred me on, often in unforeseen ways. The Group for Research on Medieval and Early Modern Women, composed of some inspirational scholars from Chapel Hill, Duke, and North Carolina State Universities, was particularly challenging. I thank everyone for their suggestions. Graduate students at Chapel Hill kept me on my toes. This book is strengthened by the work we did together.

I was spurred on by friends and colleagues to assume greater intellectual courage at crucial stages. In particular, I should like to thank Joseph Connors, Mary Pardo, Marcia Pointon, and Mike Savage, who helped me more than they knew.

Several scholars, already heavily burdened with other demands, generously read and commented in full on substantial parts of this book. I thank especially Tommaso Astarita, Joseph Connors, Mike Savage, and John Pinto for their many very insightful suggestions and sensitive criticisms. Although I was unable to pursue all their wonderful suggestions, this book is greatly improved by their help.

Sarah Böck-Cormack, in the most difficult circumstances, dedicated precious hours to improving particularly wretched prose. Others who provided timely advice or help are Aloisio Antinori, Francesco Benigno, Giuliana Boccadamo, Sofia Boesch-Gajano, Caroline Bruzelius, Peter Burke, Gaetana Cantone, Stan Chojnacki, Teresa Colletta, Simon Ditchfield, Louise Durning, Penelope Gouk, Barbara Harris, Frances Huemer, Martin Kemp, Arthur Marks,

Genoveffa Palumbo, Mary Sheriff, Tom Tweed, Richard Wrigley, and Gabriella Zarri. I thank them all most warmly.

For their advice on translating Latin, Italian, and Spanish, I am indebted in particular to Tommaso Astarita, Mary Pardo and Anna Vio, who helped me toward a much closer understanding of many documents. Their suggestions rendered my translations much more elegant and accurate. Margaret Günsburg, Shayne Mitchell, Spencer Pearce, Cristina Pecoraro, Rosalba Piazza, Nino Recupero, Roger Ling, Nigel Townson, and Dino Vizzini also always cheerfully gave assistance with translating and interpreting a host of documents. My thanks to all of these kind people. All errors remaining are mine.

Generous assistance with all manner of practicalities was unstintingly given to me by Cristina Pecoraro, Pasquale Nania, and Dino Vizzini. They were also among the first people who helped me to see beyond first impressions of the Italian South. I am always grateful to them.

Joyce Berry commissioned this book, and Susan Ferber zealously guided it through production. It is enhanced by the color plates made possible by a generous Weiss/Brown Publication Subvention Award from the Newbery Library, Chicago, in support of outstanding works of scholarship on European culture. At the last minute, Krys Chandler helped me secure a Small Grant from the University of Manchester Faculty of Arts Research Fund to meet unforeseen expenses with the black-and-white figures. The Mark Fitch Fund also subsidized these costs. The farsightedness of these institutions permitted me to include images here which are necessary to the book's argument and which are not well known. I should also like to thank Jerry Blow at Chapel Hill and Anne Perrett, Michael Pollard, and Derek Trillo at the University of Manchester for their photographic expertise, on which I heavily relied. In Naples, Massimo Velo undertook requests for photographs of archival plans or church altarpieces with good humor and expertise.

Genoveffa Palumbo kindly helped me to find ideal accommodation in Naples. Tessa Addenbrooke was unfailingly supportive. Staying with her during research trips to London libraries always left me reinvigorated. Lynda Jessup, Peter Higginson, Sherryl Kleinman, and Dee Reynolds gave encouragement at critical junctures. Murph and Bill Parkinson provided a refreshing point-of-view, and Isambard Hills-Savage helped to keep it all in proportion. Without the expert child-care of Carole Sharp and her family, this book would have taken even longer. Frederick Hills, Eva Rainbow-Hills, and Margaret and Denis Savage helped with child-care when we were stuck.

Finally, my deepest thanks go to Mike Savage for his unwavering understanding and support, emotional, intellectual, and even practical, which have sustained me at every stage of this book's genesis and realization.

Manchester, 2000

CONTENTS

INTRODUCTION *Convents and Conventual Life in Early Modern Italy* 3

1 Cittadelle sacre *and the Politics of Conventual Urbanism* 19

2 *Virginity and Enclosure* 45

3 *Dowries and Daughters* 62

4 *Living Like Ladies: Conventual Patronage* 90

5 *Convents and Conflict: Conventual Urbanism in Naples* 120

6 *Conventual Optics of Power* 139

CONCLUSION *Conventual Architecture as Metaphor for the Body* 161

Notes 183

Glossary 229

Bibliography 231

Index 253

INVISIBLE CITY

INTRODUCTION

Convents and Conventual Life in Early Modern Italy

Nowhere is the social significance of female aristocratic convents more evident than in baroque Naples. Shaped and defined by religious institutions and princely palaces, the city is scoured by narrow crevasses of sunless streets, lined with looming convents and monasteries, sealed to the outside world like sheer dark cliffs. From afar, the dominance of religious institutions is immediately evident. From Castel Sant'Elmo, the Angevin castle rebuilt in the sixteenth century, high to the west of Naples, the city cascades dramatically and unevenly down the slopes to the sea like a huge ruptured open-air theater. Conventual belfries and belvederes thrust into the air, jostling to gain advantage in this tilted city; church domes hover with a calm confidence over the chaos of crowded rooftops; and green rectangles in monastic cloisters form oases of disciplined nature amid seething buildings and bustling streets. But at street level, conventual architecture professes little overt interest in the city over which it has such dominance. It is a strangely introverted world, in which these powerful institutions turn their backs on passersby. Dark street frontages of volcanic pozzolana stone are relieved only by occasional grand doorways, rusticated windows, or a fleeting glimpse into a cloister, dappled by the shade of lemon trees. In the seventeenth century those dark walls separated the frenzy, heat, and noise of street life from the cool and protected environment, princely and religious, on the other side. Increasingly, into the urban fabric female convents inserted their massy presence. The number of convents swelled dramatically through the seventeenth century, until squares, streets, and whole neighborhoods were dominated by them. Only the conventual churches, glowing with gilt and inlaid marbles, festooned with frescoes, or pristine in exquisite white stucco, allow the outsider in, and, in sharp contrast to their unyielding exteriors, envelope the visitor in a sensuous intensity of color, shape, and sound, while hinting at the concealed presence of the nuns themselves, behind latticework grilles and gilded screens.

This urban concealment and advertisement reveal the contradictions in which aristocratic female monasteries were deeply enmeshed in early modern society. They proudly linked and abashedly straddled poverty and inherited splendor, the public and private, religious and secular, rules of strict enclosure and the exigencies of familial politics, God and temptation. They housed women from the most privileged classes in Italian society, who often had little control of their own destiny and were sometimes forced into convents against their will; women who, willing or unwilling inmates of convents, managed through art and architectural patronage and ambitious urbanistic projects to assert their own transformative view of their world. These paradoxes are expressed, defined, and resisted in all aspects of conventual life, most evidently both in the urban strategies adopted by convents and in the architecture and decoration of conventual complexes and their often sumptuous churches.

Conventual power was exercised not simply through physical dominance. The concept of the city itself was intricately connected to the idea of unseen virgins praying for its protection. Ruling-class power, too, was maintained by their existence: aristocratic familial strategies were decided in relation to, and made possible only with resort to, female convents to house their surplus female progeny. Thus convents reached their tentacles into many areas of Neapolitan life, even those apparently remote from convent walls. This book explores the connections between the visible and advertised aspects of conventual life, between their imposing buildings and fabulous churches and the invisible issues of virginity, dowries, and spiritual holiness. It investigates the relationship between the architecture of female aristocratic convents in early modern Naples and the bodies they were built to house, seeking to link architectural discourse not simply to that of social hierarchy and exclusivity, but to the anxieties and unspoken fears circulating in the shadows of those discourses.

Scholarship concerned with conventual life has tended to move in two divergent directions. Broadly speaking, scholars have concentrated either on conventual life, the varied roles of convents and their inmates, more or less ignoring the architecture that both gave shape to and articulated these activities; or they have turned to the architecture, reading it in relation to religious devotion within the convent, again stopping short at the convent wall, or at ascribing it to a single individual, an "exceptional" female patron whose patronage is portrayed as innocent of the muddy compromises of familial and urban politics.[1] Much current scholarship continues to focus on individual artists, architects, and even artist-nuns.[2] Fascinating though such studies are, they tend to approach art and architecture as the inspired product of exceptional individuals, artists, and patrons, rather than as the product and shaper of broader social forces, in relation to meaning and power. Here I seek to expose architectural patronage and form as not inevitably arising from given specific historical, material, and religious conditions, but as necessary for, or useful to, certain groups of people, always politically and socially motivated, intent on ensuring that they were not obscured by rival aristocrats, religious orders, or convents in the specific and changing—often uncomfortable and awkward—historical circumstances in which they found themselves. Architecture thus assumed urgent political purpose and consequence.

Three principal nodes in the construction of identities through urbanism and architecture dominate this book. First, the familial identities of the nuns, daughters of feudal aristocrats whose position was increasingly threatened as a result of Spanish colonization, or of rich and ambitious bureaucrats carving out careers at the Spanish viceregal court. Second, their class identities: nuns accepted by aristocratic convents were often noble and rich, accustomed to considerable economic freedoms and privileges. Third, religious identities: nuns were both wives of Christ and members of powerful religious institutions, subject to the demands of the ecclesiastical hierarchy.

The ramifications of virginity in relation to spirituality, masculine honor and shame, and social status make it a highly sensitive issue, justified and protected by multilayered and often paradoxical claims. Art historians have not yet interrogated the evidence of the built environment to ask how virginity is marked architecturally. This book illuminates how noble virginity was constructed and shaped by the built environment, examining how enclosed aristocratic nuns in seventeenth-century Naples used urbanism and architectural patronage to rearrange the spaces in which they spent their lives to articulate new versions of old accounts of virginity and monacation, and the resistance they met with.

This book focuses unapologetically on southern Italy, the Mezzogiorno. Traditionally regarded as backward and ignorant, as trailing northern and central Italy, especially Rome, economically, socially, and politically, the south is also seen as lagging behind culturally and artistically.[3] This produces a tendency to overlook cities south of Rome. But Naples has been blessed with excellent researchers especially within that city, whose work on urbanism and social history, in particular, now permit an approach to architectural history which attempts to link form to political meaning.

Art historians of early modern Italy have too long preferred to focus on the "centers" of artistic production, particularly Rome, Florence, and Venice, which produces a dangerously distorted view of the relationships between artistic production and identity in this period. It misses the chance to consider the relationships between artistic production, colonization, and gendered identities in Europe—as Naples was part of the huge Spanish empire between 1503 and 1734. Rome, by contrast, was an overwhelmingly—anomalously—male city, as center of the ecclesiastical hierarchy of the Catholic Church. One would expect the Eternal City to house large numbers of male and female monasteries, but the unprecedented domination during the baroque period of other cities, especially Naples, by religious orders requires explanation—an explanation which, in turn, affects our easy assumptions about Rome.

The most important characteristic distinguishing southern Italy from central or northern Italy is the combination of Spanish rule with feudalism. While political and administrative power were increasingly centralized at court, the aristocracy in Naples retained greater feudal power, institutions, and privileges than anywhere else in Italy, apart from Sicily and Sardinia. Well over three-quarters of the land and between two-thirds and three-quarters of the population of the early modern Kingdom of Naples were subject to feudal jurisdiction.[4] Whereas in northern Italy and northern Europe feudalism was in decline during the seventeenth and early eighteenth centuries, the reverse was true in Sicily and Naples, with a concomitant impact on conventual expansion, urbanism, and art patronage.[5]

In 1503 the Spanish government established itself in Naples through the viceregal court. This represented considerable political change for Spain and the Kingdom of Naples, and it also marked an important change in the political, economic, and social character of the city of Naples, as these areas of life were brought, through the viceregal court, more directly than ever before into the orbit of Spanish control. Most significantly, the Spanish Crown was secure enough to limit the political power of the Neapolitan aristocracy; it favored the social ascent of new families, Neapolitan, Genoese, and Iberian in origin, merchants, financiers, and officials of the Crown. While the Crown was willing to curb aristocratic political power, it pursued no policy of curtailing the economic and social privileges of the feudal aristocracy, especially outside the city. On the contrary, those privileges increased significantly, provided that Naples functioned within the Spanish imperial system as the Crown saw fit.

Naples and Sicily served an important strategic military function for the Spanish but were undependable allies. Above all, their support was indispensable in countering Turkish attack. After the decisive victory against the Turks at the battle of Lepanto in 1571, the Kingdom of the Two Sicilies remained an important source for men and resources, but the Spanish directed their energies northward to the defense of Spanish Flanders and Milan. For a brief interlude after the revolt of Masaniello, Naples was a republic, ruled by the duke of Guise in 1647–48. Otherwise it was governed from the viceregal court in Naples until 1707. Between 1707 and 1734 Austria ruled both Naples and Sicily, but in 1734 they returned to Spanish rule as a result of military conquest by Charles of Bourbon, son of Philip V of Spain. The Spanish Bourbons maintained uninterrupted rule until 1806.

GENDER, SOCIAL CLASS, AND ARCHITECTURE

This book approaches female convents and their churches as particularly fertile sites for investigating the relationship between gender, social class, and architecture in early modern Europe. Monastic architecture was central to the social construction of difference between religious men and women, and even between men and women in general. Religious identities, personal mobility, and sexuality were maintained through space, boundaries, and architectural adornment. Architecture constructed the habitus which connected common interest groups. Convents were connected to the aristocracy through their material culture, to particular families through sites and bequests, but above all they were connected to the habitus of aristocratic women. This is architecture designed and built for female patrons, to enhance female religious devotion and to foster the separation of women from men and from the competing demands of the world, and it was used almost exclusively by women—itself a remarkable fact in a field where information about audiences and users is notoriously hard to come by.

On the face of it, the female convent church, whose patrons and audience were predominantly female, seems a likely place for the production of female, even feminine, design driven by women's needs, desires, and aspirations. This book investigates the appearance, urban siting, decoration, and the religious, social, and political functions of female convent churches in seventeenth-century Naples, including their functions as depositories of profound social disequilibria. Femininity is analyzed in terms of virginity and social class, the driving forces of class politics and aristocratic survival, and the significance of dowries to show that, far from being an explanation of convent architecture, the complex construction of upper-class virginal religious devotion is interrogated and redefined by convent architecture itself.

This book, therefore, starts with a discussion of the role of convents in the economic and social arrangements of aristocratic families. I then turn to the evidence of the internal decoration of convent churches in order to illuminate some of the central preoccupations and contradictions in conventual life. How is it that female virgins came to occupy such visible and prominent spaces in early modern Naples? Why did the grilles and grids through which they engaged with the outside world receive such attention and emphasis? Who was looking at whom, and with what political effects in terms of power and resistance?

The formulation of this book assumes that women of early modern Italy were subject to, and indeed complicit in, many of the pressures of patriarchal society; but it also postulates that women were not passive foils on which men could simply project their needs and ideals of womanhood, but were instead active shapers of their lives, capable of conforming to or resisting stereotypes. The intersection of the privileges of social rank and the disadvantages of gender is central to the book's conception. This study is, therefore, designed to shed light on the operations of class-gender dynamics in relation to early modern Neapolitan convents and their significant urban presence. In convents, architecture, urbanism, and belief systems cross paths; here, investigation into the early modern city, identities, and issues of social class intersect.[6]

Active participation in religious life allowed women access to power which was in other spheres closed to them. Indeed, it gave them access to a "public" space at a time when such spaces were generally inaccessible to women. The constraints on that access, arising in part from its definitions derived from Christian exegetes and tradition, form an important part of this study. Convents represent the public face of a sanctioned female group. Access to a public space crucially allowed women to put on a public face. I examine those facades and faces convents and their inmates assumed.

CONVENTS AND URBANISM

Conventual buildings not only shaped the environment in which nuns lived, they also played an important part in shaping the cities in which they stood. Naples was a city dominated by convents, a state of affairs which provoked opposition and alarm in some quarters. I examine the impact on the city of the formidable presence of convents in its midst, asking why they were opposed or supported and by whom, and what impact such a presence had on the nature of images of the city. I also investigate the urbanistic strategies adopted by convents and religious orders; how they purchased property, including aristocratic palaces, in order to build splendid new buildings; which areas they favored and why; and the nature of rivalries and conflicts between convents in relation to property disputes, vying for land or access, and struggles over views, unobstructed skylines, and protected enclosure that was not overlooked by neighbors, whether secular or religious. The same urban politics that shaped exteriors also invaded interiors. The politics of urbanism continued behind closed doors—or on both sides of closed doors—and contributed to the nature of interior space, its handling and decoration.

Part of the crucial significance of convents was that conventual communities were able to articulate a public, recognizable presence in the city. Female presence, whether institutional or individual, in the early modern city was religious. But what was the nature of that "religiousness" in terms of conventual architecture? A second and related question is more difficult: how does the built environment shape who looks at whom and how, in what guises, and with what effects? To answer this question, I draw on ideas about metaphor, although I resist a simple collapsing of the built environment into metaphor alone (itself as problematic as the untheorized "reality"-representation model long abandoned in the wastelands of art history).

GENDER AND RELIGIOUS PRACTICE

Of course, female religious orders did not function alone as important patrons of architecture and art. The Catholic Church was a dominating presence in early modern Italy. Ecclesiastical institutions in general were the leading patrons of the arts, as they had been since the fourth century. But it was through female religious orders that women had greatest access to institutionalized forms of power, including art patronage.

The conventional wisdom grew up that Protestantism was beneficial to women because it sanctified the family, instituted divorce, and admitted women to the priesthood of all believers.[7] By contrast, Catholicism was presented either as continuing in the same mode as before the Reformation or as restricting women's lot. Certainly the Church marginalized women. Secular clergy were necessarily male; women were excluded from the service of the altar and from handling ceremonial vessels. They were barred from the priesthood by church law and discouraged from the eremitical life by social custom. The struggles of the Council of Trent have been seen as resulting in rigid control over female spirituality, stricter regulation of women in convents, renewed emphasis on virginity, and general narrowness and orthodoxy.[8] Scholars increasingly argue that the prestige of consecrated women suffered a reversal even before Trent, between 1500 and 1530.[9]

Despite this picture of uniform ecclesiastical repression, the general consensus is that in convents women were freer, more independent, and better educated than in any other sphere open to them; and it is generally taken as concomitant of that assumption that the buildings which housed them would reflect these qualities of institutional autonomy, spiritual devotion, and religious dedication.[10] "No institution has ever won for the lady the freedom of development that she enjoyed in the convent in the early days," claimed Emily James Putnam, herself the future president of a women's college, in 1910.[11]

Indeed, it has become customary to view the conventual system in stark terms, either idealized as a place of comparative freedom and independence for women or stigmatized as a place of imprisonment. The former approach tends to promote readings of conventual architecture as sign of obedience, conformity, and religious observance (their quiet halls, simple, whitewashed corridors, and private cells; their churches which emphasize eucharistic devotion) and to assume an identity between an institution and a coherent power system. The latter presents them in scandalous terms, in which their architecture becomes incidental and tends to be ignored—as centers of pent-up sexuality, passionate romance and intrigue, enclosures whose walls were only ever really intended to be straddled during spicy late-night assignations and furtive wooings. The reality was more complex and contradictory, as medievalists have shown by relating church decoration programs not only to female religious devotion but also to their urban and social contexts.[12] Instead of framing the investigation in terms of negative and positive, it is more useful to think in terms of process, to examine how nuns shaped their own lives and how they interpreted what historians have tended to see as the conflict between family and convent, the opposition between the secular and the divine.[13] Recently, Daniel Bornstein, rejecting what he sees as the received wisdom "which holds that women were pawns manipulated by men in the sociopolitical game of marriage alliances, and that those who were too ugly or too expensive to marry off were dumped in whatever convent would take them," offered instead his vision of women as "constant consumers of the sacred."[14] This muddying of the waters has been very useful, but Bornstein's notion of women as consumers of the sacred, even as possessing "sacred charisma," as exemplary consecrated virgins, perhaps does not go far enough.[15] The relationship between female spirituality and high birth was long-standing and significant. Women were much more likely to be accepted as candidates for beatification and canonization if they were of high birth, as Pierre Delooz, Donald Weinstein, Rudolph Bell, Jean-Michel Sallmann, and other scholars have demonstrated.[16] However, while noble birth and good social connections were almost indispensable in recruiting powerful sponsorship and support for a potential female saint, they were incidental, not intrinsic, to the actual performance of female saintliness. Indeed, female sanctity often assumed the form of self-abasement, social humiliation, and the repudiation of worldly privilege. It is my contention that institutional spiritual holiness was understood, at least within convents themselves, as necessarily enhanced by upper-class blood. In other words, upper-class women actually enhanced sacredness, even produced it, because of, and not despite, their noble blood. This, in turn, affected the architecture and urbanism of aristocratic convents and, consequently, the entire city. As a whole, it should perhaps be seen as part of the "aristocratization" of conventual life after Trent.[17]

Given that women were social dependents, their concurrence with their fathers' choices does not mean that they would have chosen convent life for themselves. Indeed, some signal women actively rebelled against the system and against their father's wishes.[18] Nevertheless, the vast majority of conventual inhabitants were acquiescent in their fate; and it is unthinkable that this would have been so had many nuns been outraged at the system leading to their enclosure and at the conditions of their lives inside. In order to explain their acquiescence, we must appreciate the degree to which convents were presented to young women as the most natural and respectable pathways available to them, the considerable overlap for women between the nature of aristocratic and conventual life, and the degree to which convents were institutionally relatively attractive, affording opportunities unavailable to ambitious women in other spheres for the exercise of authority and ambition and for the exploration of piety.

Marriage and producing heirs remained the principal alternative to religious life.[19] This was not necessarily more attractive than being shut up in a convent. Indeed, several of the women most prominent in founding and governing Neapolitan convents rebelled against the marriage match planned for them by their families, or, during or after an unhappy marriage, sought fulfillment or tranquillity in an environment which afforded them greater protection from familial claims.[20] In any case, the dangers of childbearing, the subordination of wives to husbands, and the restrictions of female domestic life, familiar to aristocratic women, doubtless lent the shady cloisters a certain attraction.

Many of the same interests served by confining daughters in convents were also sought through marriage, with comparable restrictions on women's agency. Marriage partners were selected principally to advance the political and economic interests of the patrilineally defined family. The head of the family (usually the father) sought the most advantageous marriage available in order to enlarge the family's estates, raise its social standing, and strengthen the political influence of the clan. Their dependence on the dowries provided by their fathers meant that daughters rarely had much choice in the matter.[21] Daughters could carry patrilineal property, but they could rarely possess it. The fear of wives with rich dowries exerting excessive influence over their new households prompted male writers to caution future bridegrooms about the dangers of trying to net too good a catch. Thus Giuseppe Passi, in his book *Dello stato maritale*, published in Venice in 1602, quotes Aristotle's dictum that "wives dominate men because they have a large inheritance."[22] Furthermore, once married, women found themselves subject to their husbands legally and financially.[23] The Venetian Moderata Fonte (1555–92), a respectable widow, harshly criticized marriage, underscoring the loss of property and rights that accompanied it: "By taking a husband . . . one becomes a slave . . . and in losing one's freedom, one loses also the control of one's things, placing everything within the dominion, and according to the will, of him who has been bought. . . . think what a beautiful thing it is to marry. . . . you lose your possessions, you lose yourself, and you acquire nothing in the end except children who only give you trouble, not to mention the tyranny of a man who dominates you according to his desire."[24] Instead of marriage, Fonte advocates chastity, or *virtù*.

Although institutions known as *malmaritate* did exist for unhappily married women, for aristocratic women the shame and loss of status to their blood family made this a last resort. Even the lot of widows was often determined by their deceased husband's family, and few enjoyed great freedom of choice.[25] In short, the interrelation between sexuality, economics, and politics meant that women were not free whether marriage or the convent had been chosen for them.

If marriage produced often difficult limitations, a more independent life as a prostitute was unthinkable for an aristocratic woman; fiercely stigmatized, it was also an unattractive option to women of lower social classes. Prostitution loomed as the most desperate fate for unmarried women without financial support. Hardly a tract on women and their behavior fails to warn of the degradation and damnation of this way of life, especially in the eyes of the Church. Establishments designed to prevent females from turning to prostitution did exist, having been founded in the larger cities by sixteenth-century reformers and supported by benefactors.[26] They were hideous, highly regulated institutions, combining all the disadvantages of conventual life with those of poverty and social degradation.[27]

If the alternatives were not inherently attractive, it is vital to remember that life in the convent was not necessarily uncomfortable or austere. Not only was conventual life socially respectable, but it gave women a unique opportunity to enhance their spiritual lives and their relationship with God and offered considerable compensations in terms of human comforts, too. This is not to say that women were necessarily content in convents, still less that they did not have resentments and reservations, but rather that their choice of respectable conventual life over the loss of respect is significant. There were, after all, vast numbers of women who did make their own livings in seventeenth-century Italy. Hard though it would have been, aristocratic daughters could have chosen that way of life. The fact that they chose to retain the spiritual, material, political, and social advantages of conventual life indicates that this life had its compensations and that their habitus and a desire to retain their class privileges played an important part in their acquiescence.

Female religious orders provided shelter, support, and a holy or respectable way of life, and women joined religious orders in formidable numbers. Monastic life was one of the few ways in which women could gain institutional recognition within the Church. In one crucial area it could even be argued that the Church was "feminized."[28] "Mystical conquest" was spearheaded by women and had far-reaching effects, reaching deep inside the church hierarchy and affecting spiritual guides and religious leaders.[29] Yet even as it was feminized, the Church was also "aristocratized." Social rank was as important as gender: access to prominent conventual positions was overwhelmingly restricted to women of high birth. Although the male orders accepted their female counterparts, they tended to treat them with suspicion, and the major orders took pains to safeguard themselves from any drain—especially economic—that the female orders might represent in their regard.[30]

It is important, however, not to overstate either case. Indeed, an adequate explanation of female patronage in convents cannot arise from an analysis of the immediate reasons why women were there in the first place. As art historian Marilyn Dunn has emphasized, women of the patrician class had little choice about their futures, regardless of whether that choice involved preference for marriage or the convent.[31] What is needed, instead, is an awareness that their patronage was undertaken in relation to material, spiritual, and sociopolitical circumstances and also helped to shape the very circumstances in which they found themselves. As Bornstein writes, "Discerning the power of these pawns requires acute insight and careful attention to nuance—and paradox."[32]

GENDER AND ART PATRONAGE

Nuns were not timid patrons, at least in the baroque period. There is nothing self-effacing about the artwork they commissioned. It is bold, expensive, fashionable, and unforgettable. The relative uninterest in female convents as institutional architectural patrons stemmed from a widespread assumption that convents were passive institutions beholden to male superiors within the ecclesiastical hierarchy. It is frequently presumed that nuns did not make key choices about the works commissioned for their convents. Other problematic assumptions follow from this. To assume that nuns had no experience of art outside their convent or that male intercessors, confessors, or *mezzani* always made the critical links and the crucial decisions is a mistake.[33] Conventual walls were extremely porous. Although girls as young as twelve might begin their engagement with enclosure, contact with their family was maintained until they were at least sixteen. Nuns involved in commissioning artworks came from rich and aristocratic backgrounds, precisely the class that was most active in commissioning artworks in the secular world. They did not lose their aristocratic *mentalité*, their cultural formation and skills, simply as a result of taking the habit. Further, their contacts with the capable and well-connected ruling-class world were not severed by monacation. Secular men and women, especially noblewomen, came and went, to and from the convent, not infrequently on a regular basis, so some nuns were able to hear news of art and architectural commissions outside and keep up with extraconventual issues. Moreover, nuns who joined convents as widows could draw on a lifetime's experience to act as effective patrons and could share their expertise or knowledge with other nuns and the conventual community. Finally, the idea that to commission art was somehow to trespass in a secular sphere is bound to modern notions of art and its functions and does not receive contemporary expression.

What is needed now is a different sort of feminist strategy that retains a concern with social history and with gendered patronage, but that locates these within contested fields of discursive formations. How did certain people and groups enter into spaces of representation, which spaces did they enter, and why? How did architects sanction the presence of groups of rich and well-connected religious women in the heart of the city? What relationships were constructed between convent and city, and between convent exteriors and interiors? In other words, how did architecture shape the social coding of sacred space? While any discussion of this group of aristocratic female patrons cannot do full justice to the subtleties, the rich psychological variations, and the infinitely complex texture of the constituent parts of their individual identities, it is important to consider them as a group, rather than as separate studies of exceptional women.

While contextualization is crucial, it must never become seamless. A social history of art which seeks to contextualize artistic production sometimes risks making art apparently inevitable. That is to say, the more seamlessly art is seen in relation to the contexts in which it was produced, the more we lose a sense of contingency and unpredictability with regard to the production of those objects, as well as to their precise appearance, their curious fashioning, and their stylistic handling. Too often that sense of contingency and surprise is retained only by recourse, to greater or lesser degree, to the notion of the "genius," by emphasizing the intervention of the individual, the gifted artist, or the extraordinary patron. In this book I seek to expose the architectural patronage and urban ambitions of convents and their workings not as inevitable, arising effortlessly out of specific historical material and religious conditions, but as necessary for, or useful to, groups of nuns, religious orders, and familial power interests confronting precarious social conditions. I want to hold on to the (self-evident) truth that a building produces a new space and makes possible an alteration of social relations rather than simply perpetuating or articulating an existing arrangement. As Marilyn Dunn has pointed out, patronage by women was a common phenomenon, not an exceptional occurrence.[34] And yet studies of early modern patronage generally fail to establish (or even to show much curiosity about) patterns or trends in the way art was commissioned, collected, or valued by different individuals or groups.[35] Studies of female art patronage tend to limit the complexity of their subjects by emphasizing gender in isolation, as if their subjects were somehow female before all the other aspects of their manifold identities. Such an approach flattens its subjects, eclipsing the significance in particular of family and social rank with the risk that the complexity of motives attributed to male art patrons, including interconnections between their piety, their desires for social distinction, their political ambition, and their familial status, is replaced by reducing female patrons primarily to gender.

A reluctance to acknowledge the degree to which art patronage is not simply the product of social and political privilege, but actively helps to maintain that privilege, is aggravated in the case of religious art, whose patronage is often explained as prompted by "female piety." While female piety and religious conviction are crucial aspects of women's ecclesiastical patronage and cannot be reduced to political or other motivation, the assumption that piety is separate and primary, causal in relation to ecclesiastical patronage, needs to be examined. Piety, isolated in itself, neither explains nor determines. An analysis of piety reveals it to be more complex and less socially neutral than a simple model of piety-as-cause implies. Artistic activities, such as the patronage of churches and chapels and their decoration, sometimes formed important impetuses to nuns' spiritual lives.[36] Piety is anticipated, delayed, and traversed by social currents and therefore needs to be analyzed in relation to them. A failure to undertake this task condemns us to a continuing neglect of the forms that religious patronage produced, in favor of a superficial concern with iconographies.

Reluctance to analyze female patronage politically is exacerbated in relation to aristocratic women. Scholars (especially non-Italians), apparently spellbound by patrons who are both aristocratic and female, have tended to interpret their actions as exceptional and individual rather than as class-based. The relationship between piety, participation in conventual patronage, the careerist ambitions of specific female patrons, and their place within the wider social and political structure of the city must be analyzed in relation to their high social rank.[37] We need to think of women more sociologically, to relate those who were successful in determining specific architectural and artistic outcomes, and the precise chosen form of those artistic creations for which they were in part responsible, to broader dynamics within society and to the other women whose very presence often made possible the prominence of the few. The successes of the few must be interpreted in relation to their social rank and economic standing, to urban and familial politics, and to social constraints.

Recent work which rightly seeks to illuminate women's roles, strategies, responses to opportunities, challenges, and obstacles has sometimes obfuscated the limitations on their room for maneuver. In part this is a consequence of the focus on individual exemplary women. Being quick to celebrate individual achievement may risk obscuring the limitations regularly enforced and imposed on women by systems of property ownership, ecclesiastical structures, and familial and theological discourses. The policing of convents through episcopal visitations early received scholarly attention, and more recently the advantages convents presented in terms of surveillance of females to powerful dynasties have been illuminated in terms of urban politics by Elissa Novi Chavarria in particular. This book reads conventual architecture also in terms of these limitations.

Conceiving of the convent as sacred center, focused on the institutional imprimatur it received from the religious order and ecclesiastical hierarchy responsible for its organization, has led to the assumption that its meanings were largely predetermined or generated from above by the ecclesiastical hierarchy. While a convent apparently emanated an intrinsic religious significance of its own, it also provided a ritual space for the expression of a range of sometimes conflicting perceptions and meanings which nuns, their families, and visitors brought to the convent and imposed upon it. Convent walls enclosed a multitude of competing religious, social, and political discourses, sometimes differing only slightly, while at others radically diverging.

The chapters in this book represent some of those competing voices. Chapter 1 explores the context for the rapid spread of convents in seventeenth-century Naples and the politics of conventual urbanism, showing how the divisions within the Neapolitan aristocracy and their grip on urban power through the Seggi fostered conditions in which the convents housing their daughters flourished, almost untrammeled.

Virginity, hooked as it was into the theological heart of monasticism and into the center of the system of familial honor, is explored in chapter 2. Notions of virginity, an apparently timeless concept, are actually historically specific and had precise consequences in seventeenth-century Naples. It is vital to grasp how the maintenance, protection, and celebration of virginity, central to the conventual economy of perfection, were fused and confused with discourses of aristocratic honor.

Chapter 3 demonstrates the consequences for convents of the pressures on aristocratic patrimonies—especially those of the feudal aristocracy—and the particular strategies they adopted to preserve them, above all the exploitation of primogeniture and entail. Convents became an easy solution to a difficult problem, providing secure and respectable houses for daughters who could not be married without dangerously dispersing aristocratic fortunes. For the new bureaucratic nobility, patronizing a female convent on a lavish scale afforded the opportunity for familial social advancement both through the attendant urban, ecclesiastical, and religious distinction (the promise of the afterlife hovering glamorously over every bequest), and through the close contact between their daughters and those of dominant urban families within the convents. The money lavished on female convents cannot be understood apart from the crucial role they assumed within the economy of family honor and fortune of both the feudal and nonfeudal aristocracy.

Chapter 4 focuses on patronage within convents, showing not only how significant were conventual dowries to the program of conventual expansion in seventeenth-century Naples, but also how crucial were the powerful familial connections (and wealth) rich daughters brought with them.

Convents were among the most powerful and ambitious actors on the urban stage in baroque Naples. Chapter 5 explores their urbanistic strategies for dominance, their exploitation of "the vertical city," and their rivalry. It argues that by the 1770s the discourse of urban expansion and dominance had altered significantly. Frankly self-serving and paradoxically introverted advertisement emphasizing the religious significance of convents for the city and the self-sacrifice of individual well-born nuns gave way to claims which emphasized the well-being of the city as a whole.

Chapter 6 analyzes the optics of power within convents and their churches to show how their architecture exploited the ambiguities and contradictions of nuns' social and religious identities to project nuns to center stage. In particular it seeks to connect the development of the nuns' choir to the apotheosis of virginity and to the increased—and gendered—veneration of the Eucharist.

This book analyzes the intersections between gendered identity and architecture, as well as the tensions between institutional claims to poverty, humility, and architectures of exclusion and social exclusivity; between the institutional demands of a religious order and aristocratic familial ambitions and privileges; and between the ideals of virginity, purity, and self-sacrifice and the advertisement and encouragement of their transgression, inherent even within the discourses articulating those ideals. In short, this book investigates the relationships between conventual institutions and their architectural and urbanistic representations, leading us to consider those convents in relation to gendered identities, religious vocation, and aristocratic familial politics.

Conventual architecture is unusually redolent of the operation of power in space. We are familiar with the idea that techniques of power are invented to meet the demands of production in the broadest sense.[38] I wish to extend such a notion to include the production of religious devotion and to consider that production as significantly spatial. I analyze conventual architectural organization in terms of the politics of sight, and the relationship between flesh and stone, uncovering the connections between the clothing of bodies and the layered cloaks applied to the walls that housed them, their unclothing, and the fear of their nakedness. Architecture is approached as metaphor, specifically the architecture of aristocratic female convents as metaphor for the body of the aristocratic female virgin nun. Conventual architecture relies not only on separation, exclusion and hierarchies of access. It also depends to an unusual degree on what Foucault termed "the optics of power"—the control of sight lines, the deliberate granting or stinting of visual access, and carefully contrived asymmetrical viewing patterns. This book analyzes conventual architecture in relation to the optics of power.

I

Cittadelle sacre and the Politics of Conventual Urbanism

"What has happened is that the religious houses, even when their origins were quite modest, may then come to occupy an entire district from one end to the other, until it reaches the edge of the built-up area; and as it is difficult to find in Naples a street without a monastery in it, if nothing is done about such a grave and ruinous abuse, in this way the regulars will in the long run be able to buy up the entire city."[1]

This is the cry of alarm of Neapolitan lawyer and reformist historian Pietro Giannone, in his *Istoria Civile del Regno di Napoli* of 1723, at the creep of religious houses, male and female, over the urban fabric of Naples.[2] Although Giannone's claims were hotly disputed at the time, the situation was striking enough to provoke comment from non-anticlericals, and from foreign visitors, too.[3] In his 1692 guide to Naples, Celano's remarks on the preponderance of religious houses, especially female convents, reveal his regret and disapproval. After describing the Dominican church of Gesù e Maria, he writes, "From this church, going down, the street known as the graveled street of Gesù e Maria: in this street, on both sides, there used to be beautiful and grand palaces; today they have almost all been converted into conservatories for nuns."[4] Significantly, Celano reserves his criticism for the less distinguished female religious institutions; when commenting on the old aristocratic convents, his tone is full of pride. Francesco Peccerillo felt so strongly about the superabundance of religious buildings that he wrote a whole book on the subject in 1719. His irritation sometimes caused him to exaggerate the problem: "Every quarter, every square, every corner, either is a church or belongs to the Church."[5] But his analysis was to the point. That the new buildings were superfluous to need added insult to injury: "The glory of God consists in the proper and timely worship of old churches, not in the superfluous and ambitious building of new ones."[6] In 1614 Bacco claimed that the population of Naples totaled 327,961 of which the population of monasteries and other restricted institutions accounted for 18,028.[7] When Gilbert Burnet, the Scottish historian, visited Naples in November 1685, he estimated that there were over one hundred religious houses there, that the number of ecclesiastics was 20,000, and that Naples held about 2 percent of all religious residents in Italy.[8] Both inside and outside the city walls, the concentration of monasteries and convents was remarkable, if not exceptional.

This chapter discusses the nature of this dramatic phenomenon, its causes, and the opposition to it, as well as the reasons for the failure of that opposition. Crucial here are Neapolitan urban politics, the civic administration of the city, the power of the aristocracy, the Seggi, and their relationships to ecclesiastical power, as well as the divisions within the aristocracy that gave rise to specific forms of conventual sponsorship. Having painted a picture of the relationships between aristocratic influence and conventual institutions, the chapter turns to examine the ensuing urbanistic competition between religious houses, demonstrating how rivalries were played out through building, focusing on the production and meanings of the "vertical city."

DOMINANCE OF NAPLES BY RELIGIOUS HOUSES

Churches and monasteries multiplied in our city, such that from now on it is no longer possible to keep a detailed and exact count of them," Giannone observed.[9] Naples was indeed a city abounding in churches and monasteries, male and female (Plates 1, 2). In the city the number of female convents rose from 25 in 1591 to 37 by 1650.[10] These ranged across religious orders and included 11 convents of the Franciscan order, 7 Benedictine, 6 Augustinian, 6 Dominican, 2 Capuchin, and 1 of the Regular Canonesses of the Lateran.[11] In addition several conservatories became convents, such as SS. Bernardo e Margherita (1643) and S. Monica (1646).[12] At the same time, the number of inhabitants also increased in most religious houses. The populations of female religious houses surged between the late sixteenth century and the devastating plague in 1656, when death swept through Naples, killing 50,000, and although they never picked up as rapidly thereafter, they resumed growth.[13] This increase was fairly even across religious orders, but with growth concentrated among the Augustinians and Spanish nuns, while the Franciscans retained numerical superiority. New and old religious orders eagerly consolidated their hold on the city.[14]

In 1640 Ottavio Beltrano, a Neapolitan historian, cited figures for the population of Neapolitan religious houses. Among the female foundations, S. Chiara was the grandest and most populous, with 350 nuns, followed by 176 Augustinian nuns at La Maddalena.[15] Quite a large proportion of female convents housed about 100 nuns: the Dominican convents of S. Sebastiano (100), La Sapienza (88), S. Caterina da Siena (80), and La Concezione (120); the Franciscan convents of S. Francesco (100) and S. Maria Donna Regina (100); Benedictine nuns at S. Marcellino (100) and S. Maria Donna Romita (100); and Spanish nuns at the Concezione in S. Giacomo (80).[16] In addition, there were a large number of women in institutions established for converted prostitutes or to protect young women or widows: the Convertite all'Incurabili (Pentite) (180), the Convertite Spagnuole (120), the Illuminate (80), the Convertite of S. Giorgio (50), and the conservatory of widows in S. Maria Guarita (30).[17]

Although these numbers are high, Naples does not head the league tables for high conventual populations.[18] Nevertheless, their impact on the city fabric was particularly marked, largely because of the institutionalized nature of local aristocratic power within the city, in the form of the Seggi, as we shall see. Indeed, it was the visible urban impact of religious houses in Naples that provoked the outcry from Giannone and the astonishment of strangers.

As the numbers of religious institutions increased and their populations swelled, their buildings steadily enveloped more of the city. Nuns exploited their aristocratic status and contacts in buying up property. Old families were displaced as convents spread, with even aristocratic palaces purchased for the foundation or expansion of religious houses.[19] Indeed, the frequency with which nobles put palaces up for sale afforded convents eagerly snatched opportunities for purchase.[20] The foundation of the new convent of S. Maria di Betlem in 1646–50, for instance, involved the purchase and occupation of a palace and its gardens.[21] The process of converting palaces to institutional use bore its most striking fruit at the Gesù Nuovo. Having purchased the Palazzo di Salerno, the Jesuits began converting it into a church in 1584, using stones of the facade and some of the interior walls. They also acquired a whole complex running along via Sebastiano as far as Port'Alba, bordered on the other side by the Cisterna dell'Olio.[22]

The aggressive process of conventual urban encroachment is dramatically illustrated in the area north of the Gesù.[23] In Lafréry's map of 1566, the block of S. Antoniello, with its western side on via Costantinopoli, is still an orchard, apart from a few small buildings and the odd palace (Figure 1). Donato Bertelli's map of 1570 shows a situation not greatly changed, with large gardens surrounding princely residences. But by 1653 Stopendael's map shows the effects of the process described by Pietro Giannone (Figure 2). Even aristocratic palaces have been enveloped in a complex arrangement of churches and cloisters. The Jesuit church has taken over the Palazzo di Salerno, and the connected college is joined to the monastery of S. Sebastiano. Further up the via S. Maria di Costantinopoli, in the area formerly occupied by the palace of the prince of Conca, a vast block has been transformed into a complex arrangement of churches and cloisters belonging to the convents of the Sapienza and S. Antonio (Figure 3).[24] The devouring of whole city blocks by religious houses was dramatic, and although more concentrated and visible in certain parts of the city, it was widespread throughout old Naples. The same pattern—conducted at greater or lesser speed—occurs for the richest as well as the more modest convents, from the Sapienza to S. Giuseppe dei Ruffi, from the Croce di Lucca to the Cappuccinelle. Thus secular buildings metamorphosed into religious institutions as religious houses transformed vast tracts of the city into their own image. Palaces and civic buildings, gardens and orchards were swallowed up and replaced by churches, dormitories, and refectories or sequestered into private cloisters. Blank walls pierced occasionally by tiny windows typified huge swaths of the urban fabric.

Although there were more male religious houses than female, the part female religious orders played in this process was considerable. Theirs was the power that could twist building restrictions around; theirs was the wealth that, in a period of escalating prices, could buy up whole blocks.[25] Indeed, female religious houses probably gained licenses for building more easily than their male counterparts, because of their high numbers of noblewomen.[26] The old city housed all the grand aristocratic convents. The area south of Spaccanapoli bordered by via Monteoliveto and Corso Umberto housed a number of distinguished aristocratic convents, including S. Maria Donnalbina, S. Chiara (which alone, in size, resembled "half a city"), S. Maria Donnaromita, SS. Marcellino e Festo, and S. Maria del Divino Amore;[27] to the north of Spaccanapoli, fringed by via Pessina to the west, piazza Cavour to the north, and via Poerio to the east, were the convents of S. Gregorio Armeno, the Croce di Lucca, S. Maria del Gesù (Gesù delle Monache), and the Sapienza.[28] The less socially prestigious convents and conservatories were usually built in the newer areas of the city, especially the northwest, which was dominated by conservatories and monasteries from the start.

Some of the newer areas of the city, seen as morally precarious for women, were under particular pressure from female religious institutions.[29] This was true of the Olimpiano, which, from the early seventeenth century into the eighteenth, was home to large numbers of prostitutes.[30] By the early decades of the eighteenth century the salita Pontecorvo housed no fewer than five convents, established as part of a concerted attempt to improve the moral nature of the neighborhood.[31] Three of these, the Cappuccinelle, the Maddalena, and the Periclitanti, were founded as modest conservatories. The Cappuccinelle had its origins in 1585 when Giovan Luca Giglio and Eleonora Scarpato "began by getting some girls to enter, gathering them throughout the city, exhorting them to take the aforementioned [monastic] habit, and to attend at set hours to say office and other prayers, in imitation of the Capuchin fathers."[32] The Maddalena, founded in 1605, housed poor girls, and the Periclitanti, established in 1674, was dedicated to "protecting the honor of those damsels who were increasingly ensnared by wolves."[33] Celano refers to the girls of the Periclitanti as "the damsels who through poverty are at risk of losing their honesty."[34] The convents' presence did not, of course, automatically guarantee the disappearance of the prostitutes. A record of 1721 shows that even fifty years after the Cappuccinelle's foundation, and despite work to rectify the layout of at least three alleyways where prostitutes had lived, "they continued to live behind the lane [where] our convent and church [stand]" in houses which were or had been the property of nobles.[35] Nonetheless, female religious institutions helped render an insalubrious area of the city more respectable, not simply by housing and reforming the lives of women and girls who either already were or were in danger of becoming prostitutes, but by furnishing a physical urban presence of respectability. Female convents and conservatories symbolized the moral probity of the city as a whole.

Cittadelle sacre: FORTRESS CITY

In some areas, religious houses were so tightly packed that almost no secular dwellings existed. Instead *cittadelle sacre* or conventual enclaves were formed.[36] A *cittadella* was a little city or small fortified area within a city, often used to instill obedience on recalcitrant citizenry.[37] This was the case in the area of S. Maria di Costantinopoli, where the monasteries of S. Agnello, S. Gaudioso, S. Andrea delle Dame, S. Patrizia, and S. Maria Coeli swallowed up the gardens and houses indicated on Lafréry's mid-sixteenth-century map, to the extent that by the mid–seventeenth century, not only had the gardens completely disappeared, but no buildings other than religious houses existed in that area (Figure 1).

Like the aristocratic palaces they emulated, convents were indeed defensive structures.[38] The metaphor of the fortress occurs persistently in contemporary descriptions of religious institutions. In his seventeenth-century account of the Baiano, for instance, Francesco Paolo Caracciolo describes the walls: "on leaving on the right the church of S. Chiara, one begins to explore the city which is indicated to us by big black palaces, high walls, similar to those of fortresses, which hide convents and gothic churches capped by bell towers which leap into the skies.[39] Francesco Peccerillo seizes on the same metaphor in his criticisms of the spread of religious houses in Naples: "it is not necessary . . . for a religious order to have, like princes with their strongholds, a place in every quarter of the city."[40]

Convents' unpierced walls and stolid occupation of entire blocks earned them the epithets of military architecture. Adopting aristocratic urbanistic strategies, many religious institutions pursued the policy, expressly articulated by the Jesuits, to "create a block" (*fare l'isola*).[41] It was this process, of course, that so alarmed commentators like Giannone, creating as it did highly visible signs of the command over the city enjoyed by the religious, with their impenetrable institutional blocks, apparently impermeable to lay interests, indeed, beating the nobles at their own game.

The advantages of standing as an "island" were emphasized in a manuscript account of the history of the Franciscan convent of the Consolazione, illustrated by a plan of the convent as a block (Figure 4). Referring to arguments advanced in 1624 in support of doubling its size to house eighty nuns, rather than forty:

> by making this outlay for the aforementioned expansion, this convent would remain in a block [on its own], subject to no one, airy, and free from all overshadowing; and more than that, in it there would remain a garden 140 *palmi* long and 76 *palmi* wide for the nuns' recreation, and for the same outlay, having workshops with vaulted rooms built all around the block outside the enclosure, as required in the Reform, would bring in from about 400 ducats profit that would come in each year in rent.[42]

Conventual occupation of blocks was defensive, designed to protect conventual institutions from being overlooked or in other ways compromised by contact with the rest of the city, including other convents; and it was aggressive, allowing convents to transform their vulnerable extroversion into a source of income.[43] Even public thoroughfares were consumed by conventual expansion. In expanding to meet the demands of formal enclosure, the conventual complex of S. Patrizia swallowed up the entire vico de' Sanguini.[44] The particularly prestigious Benedictine convent of S. Gregorio Armeno incorporated the via della Campana into its house in 1638 and opened another near the bell tower of S. Lorenzo. Likewise, despite strong protest from the inhabitants of the quarter, the new convent of Divino Amore swallowed the via di Pistaso in 1659.[45]

While fortress architecture protected religious inmates, it also produced an urban environment in which dominant institutions turned their backs disparagingly on city streets and thoroughfares, declaring institutional indifference to the cities that sustained them. Even the ambitious urbanist Benedictine nuns of SS. Marcellino e Festo indirectly acknowledged that proximate religious houses could produce a dangerously introverted urban environment with blind alleyways, which provided ideal hiding places for lurking villains and sealed the plight of their victims behind blind, dark walls. Arguing against a new street that the Jesuits proposed should be built near them, the nuns warned that it would attract wrongdoers and that "there would be no hope to the citizens of any help or longed-for rescue from people close at hand, there being on both sides the walls of the college and of the convent."[46] But this conscientious civic concern did not extend to curtailing their own urbanistic ambitions, nor was it successful in halting the new road.

The insularity achieved through occupying such fortress blocks guaranteed greater autonomy to the convent and greater control over its inhabitants, over visitors, and over contact with the outside world. But it was also symbolic. A fortified island represented enclosed virginity unequivocally, and massive towering walls occupying an entire block signaled an urban power to be reckoned with (Figures 4, 5). Religious houses hoped to persuade rich and powerful nobles to send their offspring to such grand institutions.

By the mid–eighteenth century, practical considerations were the least of it. Even when the number of their inhabitants had declined or was exiguous, convents sought to build. Thus in 1758 the Neapolitan convent of the Periclitanti, which housed merely four nuns, purchased a group of houses opposite its monastery for expansion, despite the opposition of the nearby Cappuccinelle who pointed out to the Curia in 1755 that "the monastery does not need to be enlarged today, nor is it possible to say that the nuns are pressed for space there having been that many [four] for the space of 45 years."[47] Occupying urban space had become primarily a means of representing urban power.

The dramatic increase in the number of convents added to an already difficult situation of congestion, overcrowding, and inadequate road, water, and sewage systems. As the religious orders bought up more land and property within the cities, the housing crisis grew more acute, provoking dissent and protest. In the Parliaments of 1609, 1611, and 1619, the municipality appealed to Philip III to prevent the insatiable encroachment by the most powerful religious orders of land and property.[48] Worse, the government favored the religious houses in their voracious building, while denying seculars the right to build houses in the suburbs. A tax on the purchase of lime payable within the city was waived for religious, provoking bitter protest from Parliament.[49] Further, legal support existed for religious institutions to sweep away the houses of seculars and replace them with religious institutions. To anticlericals like Giannone, old laws had been twisted inappropriately to advantage the religious:

> They extend even in these times to the acquisitions of the churches the fantastic teachings of our doctors, who ill adapting the ancient rules to

present times, twisting the meanings of the laws that they have not understood well, and paying no attention to the circumstances of the times or to the change in the state of things, driven by rash and ill-intentioned piety, with their pens they fostered to the utmost such acquisitions, and they were entirely inclined to extend the ways and the reasons, to the notable detriment of civil society, and to the most serious damage to sovereignty over one's own property.[50]

In 1629 the Sacra Congregazione dei Regolari in Rome issued a letter to the Neapolitan *Vicario* of the nuns laying out a series of measures to curb expenditure on dowries, monacation parties, and the like within convents, and including a rather feeble aside that the *Vicario* must moderate their spending on "splendid and sumptuous buildings."[51] In theory nuns found to be disobeying these instructions could be excommunicated or deprived of active and passive voice, but in fact attempts to curb building were half-hearted.

Anticlericalism strengthened after Masaniello's revolt. The politicization of the clergy looked shamelessly self-serving. The struggle between Jesuits and Theatines after 1648 for rewards for their support of Spain further weakened the social and political authority of the Neapolitan clergy, aggravated by indecorous behavior during the plague of 1656. Anticlerical feeling consequently grew. During the procession of San Gennaro's blood in May 1660, the nobles from the Seggio of Montagna displayed their lack of respect for the priests, acidly observing that "despite so much plague, they have remained plentiful."[52] Moreover, it was well known that the economic interests of the Church often flew in the face of local interests. "The religious have impoverished in this Kingdom," declared Fuidoro, "and more precisely in our city of Naples, the majority of the people, as a result of the donations they procured during the past plague to their monasteries and [which], afterward, most rigorously were upheld by their royal delegates against the true successors or creditors, and, may it please God, that they did not in this way greatly endanger the honor of those to whom the things rightly belonged."[53] He fumed about the treasures which the religious continually transferred from Naples, for the Tribunale della fabbrica of St. Peter's, through the nunciature, or otherwise.[54]

Given the reluctance of the Church to take remedial action, writers like Francesco Peccerillo urged the monarchy to take action, describing at length the deleterious situation and the diminution of monarchical power that it represented: "in their hands [the wise gentlemen of the royal Collateral Council] lies the remedy for many ills, and their great justice and prudence recognize the time and way to bring this about."[55] But nothing was done.

Monasteries enjoyed compulsory purchase powers until their aggressive exploitation of them provoked a petition to Philip III to relax building restrictions on private citizens. Nonetheless, compulsory purchases persisted throughout the seventeenth and early eighteenth centuries, thwarting private attempts to resist conventual expansion. For instance, in 1681 the convent of S. Monica made an offer on a house adjacent to existing convent buildings. Its owners and occupants, the widow Candida Gaudiosi; Orsola Gaudiosi, a virgin *in capillis*; and Rev. Felice Antonio Gaudiosi, heirs of Domenico and Aniello Gaudiosi, their father and uncle, rejected the offer, but the convent's lawyer appealed to the Sacra Congregazione, which obliged the Gaudiosi to make the sale.[56]

Religious institutions alone could effectively block the restless expansion of convents. Only the stubborn refusal of a convent to cede land thwarted the progress of the Jesuits' aggressive building program. Peccerillo, virulently opposed to female convents, bemoaned the situation: "it was not possible for the Jesuits at the Casa Professa to obtain a few *palmi* of space, which the nuns of S. Sebastiano had in excess, in order to place the main altar of [their] church symmetrically as befits the dignity of that church."[57]

The few instances when convents were defeated in urban struggles by nonregulars involved singularly well-connected individuals and families. Giannone cites one such defeat to demonstrate the degree of corruption in the higher echelons of the Church:

> In the famous lawsuit which Cardinal Filomarino our Archbishop filed against the nuns from the monastery of Donna Regina . . . it was claimed by the Archbishop that the nuns should be forced to sell him certain houses they owned facing his palazzo (even though there ran between them a public road) for the purpose of demolishing them in order to enlarge a vast court there, since the one there already was not broad enough to allow a six-horse carriage to enter with ease. The Cardinal di Luca, who, being at the time a lawyer in Rome, took up the nuns' defense, was stupefied by the arrogance, and with his plea . . . refuted all that had been pled by him to the contrary. But, to what good! the decision went in the Archbishop's favor, the houses were demolished and razed to the ground, and so the square was amply extended, so that now coaches and six can have comfortable and easy access to and from that palace.[58]

Thus an intersection of ecclesiastical and secular urban power politics determined who held sway in urbanistic interventions. In this case, the Franciscan nuns were defeated by the Cardinal Archbishop himself, but more usually it was the religious institution that enjoyed greater political influence and triumphed.

The situation in Naples of official inertia and reluctance to alienate vested interests contrasts with that in Paris, where monasticism was seen as an incumbrance to the monarchy because of the economic drain it represented. In about 1666 Colbert wrote to Louis XIV, "the monks and nuns not only fail to do work that would be for the common good, but also deprive the public of all the children that they would be able to produce."[59] He saw pensions and dowries as a potential aid to improving the situation: "it would perhaps be good to render the vows of the religious a little more difficult, even to take up again the custom of dowries and pensions for religious."[60] The king shared at least some of his misgivings and ordered that no new communities should be established without his permission, and that religious houses should spend their capital rebuilding cloisters, abbots' lodgings, and monastic quarters.[61]

Monarchical attempts to directly curb religious institutional power in Paris indicate that conventual dominance in Naples must be understood in relation to much wider concepts of the role and significance of the state and monarchy, as well as the importance of economic development in a city, rather than in narrow terms of religious issues alone. We shall return to this point.

The dramatic increase in the number of religious houses in general and of female religious houses in particular must be understood in relation to Naples's rapid population growth. During the second half of the sixteenth century and throughout the seventeenth, the city of Naples experienced a population explosion, with the result that seventeenth-century Naples was Europe's second most populous city (after Paris). Scholars disagree as to precise figures, but all concur that the number of inhabitants soared. At the end of the fifteenth century immigration had swelled the population of Naples to about 100,000 (at a time when the population of neither the Kingdom of Naples nor of the Mediterranean world was increasing). By the end of the sixteenth century, following a boost in population due to immigration from the countryside in the second half of the century, the city's population was probably in excess of 240,000.[62] In 1630 G. C. Capaccio, Secretary of the city, estimated the population at 300,000, but that figure represents only citizens of Naples.[63] In the following two decades the economic crisis in the Kingdom and increasing fiscal and feudal pressures greatly increased the flow of immigrants to the city.[64] By the middle of the seventeenth century the urban population reached over 400,000, probably around 450,000.[65] The terrible plague of 1656 devastated Naples's population and aggravated pressures on the city's infrastructure, killing about a quarter of the population, with the result that there were so many corpses on via Toledo that carriages had no choice but to run over them.[66] In good times and bad, the size of the population was burdensome to the city's development.[67]

Despite repeated attempts by the state to regulate the influx of people, prompted by alarm about the abandonment of agriculture and potential disorder in the city, nothing was achieved. Despite the glaring inefficacy of restrictive regulations passed to prevent population growth, few attempts were made to address the problems caused by the escalating population and overcrowding unequaled in any other European city.[68] Pozzolana, the unusually light volcanic stone used for building in Naples, intensified the density of the population by allowing buildings to rise to five or six stories, "something one sees in no other part of the world."[69] Higher buildings were an inevitable consequence of the prohibition of new building near the city walls and in the suburbs and hills surrounding the city (even though such prohibitions were honored more in their breach than in their observance).

For G. C. Capaccio, the popular class was a threat. The Neapolitan plebe was, he claimed, "the most indiscreet and undisciplined" in the world, "a base mendicant and mercenary people . . . ready to undo every good aspect of the finest republic."[70] This sense of menace was aggravated by the city's incapacity to regulate economic activity among manufacturers, merchants, or financiers. Most commercial activity lay in the hands of foreign merchants, above all the Genoese, and although the capital was much more developed economically and socially than the rest of the Kingdom, it remained backward in international commerce and finance.

Rapid population growth would not have created such a problem for Naples had it not occurred within a city tightly circumscribed by Aragonese defensive fortifications and city walls, designed both to protect the city from attack from Muslim corsairs or the French fleet and to ensure control over the population within (Figure 9). Pedro Alvarez de Toledo, viceroy of Naples between 1532 and 1553, temporarily ameliorated the problem by enclosing an additional fifty hectares within a new city wall, embracing the hill of Pizzofalcone, the suburb of Chiatamone, and part of the Chiaia district.[71] Improvements were made in the water supply, sewage system, and street paving; the port and arsenal were revivified; and the Courts of the Sommaria, Vicaria, and Regio Consiglio were concentrated in the modified and extended old Castel Capuano, thereby centralizing the judicial and administrative instruments of government in the east of the city. To protect Naples from marine attack, the Aragonese seawalls were fortified and moved seaward. Invasions from the interior were guarded against by a new city wall on the hillside.

Civil unrest, or anti-Spanish revolt, also preoccupied Pedro de Toledo. To help suppress revolt quickly and effectively, he organized both castle building and improved communications within the city. In 1537 Pedro Luís Scrivá, a military engineer, was appointed to rebuild Castel Sant'Elmo, which occupied an unrivaled logistical position, perched high to the west of, and overlooking and visible from, the whole city. Its defensive function, expressed by its impressive bastions and moat, were complemented by a garrison and cannons able to level the city. In the shadow of Castel Sant'Elmo, a dense grid of streets, known as the *quartieri*, or barracks, meaningfully emphasized in contemporary city maps, was built to house the Spanish garrison. Above all, the new wide via Toledo, cut uncompromisingly straight between the Royal Palace and the northwestern edge of the city, allowed rapid response to civil unrest from the adjacent garrison and stamped viceregal authority indelibly on the city. This street, soon lined by aristocratic palaces, rapidly accrued viceregal, military, and aristocratic authority as a ceremonial thoroughfare, functioning as a symbolic hinge between the old city and the part newly opened to its west (Plate 2).

Determined to retain control over the expanding population and to improve the city's defense, the Spanish Crown periodically ordered the viceroys to forbid construction outside the city walls.[72] These measures were ineffective, however, because they were bypassed by powerful families and religious houses that were able to afford the fines incurred or avoid them completely. Meanwhile, building continued inside the city walls, leading to some of the tallest buildings and worst overcrowding of early modern Europe.

Many of the factors that drew other groups to the city also attracted female religious orders. The attractions of Naples were considerable to rich and poor. In 1594 Francesco Mercaldo, Medicean agent in the Kingdom, observed that the rich were drawn to the city by the attraction of "living quietly and without harassment from the officials that there are throughout the Kingdom."[73] Certainly the city's economic allure was hard to resist. Whereas inhabitants of the Kingdom were subject to both state and feudal taxes, including a stiff tax to pay for Spanish military expenditure, residents of the city of Naples paid only municipal taxes and were exempt from other dues. Together with subsidized grain, this enticed immigrants from all over southern Italy.

Naples was a political and administrative center where the viceroy resided as representative of the Spanish Hapsburg monarchy, and it was the capital of a large state, the Kingdom of Naples. Bargains struck to ensure the support of the Neapolitan baronage for the Aragonese and then the Hapsburgs strongly increased the tendency toward juridical and fiscal privilege enjoyed in the capital.[74] The Crown adopted the "strategy of the capital" to maintain a strong and loyal center, very much under viceregal control (as opposed to the feudal control of the provinces), by concentrating its bureaucratic machinery and compelling most nobles to demonstrate their fidelity by their presence at the viceregal court. The Spanish Crown encouraged aristocrats to move into Naples, away from their independent power bases in the kingdom. In 1629 Bacco lists 57 princes, 83 dukes, 121 marquises, and 73 counts living in the city.[75] The aristocracy was lured to the city. Aristocrats prized their city palaces particularly highly. Indeed, their haste to entail them before anything else indicates the degree to which the family palace represented social prestige and familial identity and pride.

For the rich, educated, and ambitious, proximity to the seats of political, judicial, and ecclesiastical power was vital. Pedro de Toledo's determination to exercise control over the city prompted his policy of attracting the feudal aristocracy to the city. Here, as in Sicily, Spanish viceregal policy deliberately uprooted nobles from their traditional seats of power—their provincial stronghold castles, where they could act independently from and even in opposition to Spanish government—and brought them to Naples to be under the surveillance of the Spanish viceregal court.[76] Concomitantly, the court promoted the interests of bureaucrats and financiers. The number of high-ranking officials and bureaucrats directing and staffing hospitals, the army, fortifications, the fleet, and customs, and the number of midlevel officers, businessmen, and entrepreneurs, swelled markedly in this period.[77] At the other end of the social scale, Naples offered "abundant opportunities for work at any time."[78] For the poor, opportunities for employment were far greater than in the countryside, especially because of Naples's flourishing commercial port.[79]

The overcrowding, competition for space, fear of the Neapolitan plebe, and the political necessity of maintaining a presence within the capital prompted a building spree among secular and ecclesiastical magnates and institutions. The traditional aristocracy and the new nobility, high-ranking functionaries of the Spanish state, vied with each other within the city, in building splendid palaces.[80] "In effect," writes Labrot, "the viceroys relinquished the city to these powerful families, shrewdly directing their aggression toward competition for prestige and the magnification of their own sense of honor."[81] Building to magnify their honor was a major preoccupation for aristocrats. It is this aristocratic model that religious institutions assumed.

Given the city's problems of overcrowding and an overburdened infrastructure, why were religious orders, especially female religious orders, allowed to expand old convents or set up new ones on such an unprecedented scale in the seventeenth and eighteenth centuries? An increased religiosity, spurred by the "Counter-Reformation" or by Trent, has traditionally been seen as the primary cause.[82] There are, however, a number of weaknesses in such arguments, even if we set aside the continuing controversy among historians as to whether or not Trent or the reform of Catholicism resulted in increased religiosity. In particular, such an account fails to explain why the increase in religious houses was particularly marked in certain cities. Nor does it explain why the increase in numbers was particularly acute among female convents in prestigious city-center sites and among aristocratic, rather than plebeian, women.

There are indications that the city's rapid expansion actually advantaged Neapolitan religious houses in economic terms. Their incomes during the first half of the seventeenth century were unusually high and during the years before the anti-Spanish revolt and the plague of 1656 were higher than at any other time during the seventeenth century.[83] Neapolitans were quick to contribute money to religious institutions for a variety of motives. Pietro Giannone claimed that bad consciences often lay behind acts of apparent piety.[84] Implacable anticlerical that he was, he claimed that churches and monasteries profited considerably from family feuds, as testors left their goods to the Church to spite their families.[85] He argued that the plague was a blessing in disguise for religious institutions, as its depredations were so profound that the city had been left almost emptied.[86] After plague swept through the city, leaving a wake of death and illness, many people, he claimed, had no one to leave their property to, so instead they bequeathed it to churches and to religious.[87] A heightened sense of the fragility of life and awareness of the proximity of the next world also served to make such bequests particularly attractive at this time: "to this contributed in no small part the teaching, put about by monks themselves, and well rooted in these times, that if those who have robbed in life leave their goods to the Church in death, they will settle all their accounts with God."[88] The years immediately after the plague may indeed have been years of cheap property and easy expansion for city dwellers, private or institutional, but this situation did not last long; soon pressure for land in the city grew intense and hostility to religious institutions mounted correspondingly.

While dubious motives doubtless prompted some bequests, there were also many who made bequests to churches in good faith. There were also broader causes of these phenomena. The Spanish government and the church hierarchy encouraged religious orders to settle in Naples. During the second half of the sixteenth century Catholic orthodoxy became a determining element of the ideological base on which the Hapsburg monarchy in Madrid depended. The weakness of Spanish power meant that viceroys needed the moral and economic support of the Church. No fewer than five viceroys of Naples during the seventeenth century were also cardinals.[89] Fearing heresy and public disorder, they turned to religious orders to help combat them.

Viceroys supported church building, sometimes making substantial personal bequests, and pushing the aristocracy into ever greater emulation.[90] The scale of viceregal intervention is exemplified by Viceroy Gaspare de Bracamante Peñaranda (1659–64), about whom Giannone declared, "there hardly existed a holy place that did not receive from him ample and generous alms."[91] Peñaranda's patronage included several female religious institutions. He contributed generously to the completion of building the *romitorio* of suor Orsola and to the expansion of the Carmelite convent of S. Giuseppe in Pontecorvo.[92] Indeed, he was particularly munificent in support of various branches of the Carmelite order, perhaps because of their Spanish origins. He supported the Carmelite monks in the restoration of their monastery and in its separation from the *torrione* of the Carmine, so that monks would not be troubled by the Spanish soldiers who lived there, and he contributed to the cost of building their monastery in the Chiaia. In addition, he supported building the churches of S. Maria del Pianto and S. Niccolò al Molo, and he ensured support for churches dedicated to the Immaculate Conception by encouraging popular devotion for that belief.[93] In short, viceregal support of religious institutions within Naples was everywhere evident.

Religious institutions could also exploit another fault line in Neapolitan politics, namely disagreements between the viceroy and the archbishop over their jurisdiction. Ascanio Filomarino's tenure of the archbishopric (1641–66) was particularly significant in this regard. Unpopular with his contemporaries, his independence and his ambitious concept of ecclesiastical jurisdiction provoked conflict with the Viceregal Palace and resentment among the orders who found the Capuchins preferred to them. When he and his court failed to don mourning dress after Philip IV's death in 1665, and when he failed to visit the viceroy to make his condolences, there was an irreparable break between Cardinal Filomarino and Viceroy Oñate (Iñigo Velez y Tassis de Guevara, count of Oñate; 1648–53).[94] Ecclesiastical jurisdiction was the ostensible cause of their dispute, aggravated by a clash of temperament between two punctilious men, but underlying it was the viceroy's lack of trust in the cardinal, whose behavior during Masaniello's revolt had been at best ambivalent.[95]

The cardinal's efforts to discipline female convents provoked deep hostility, especially from those able to exploit their royal patronage to resist the archbishop's scrutiny.[96] Count Oñate was determined to reduce clerical immunity and privilege; the Roman Curia and the Neapolitan archbishop were equally determined not to cede an inch. In short, divisions within the aristocracy, fractures within the Spanish government, and tensions between them meant that there was no united opposition to the encroachment of the city by religious houses.

Seeking to explain the increase in the number of female convents in terms of relaxation of the initial rigors of the Counter-Reformation Church—rigors that might have deterred potential nuns—ignores the increased stringency within post-Tridentine female convents, compared to their pre-Tridentine counterparts; and it does not account for the continued flourishing of female religious institutions throughout the seventeenth and early eighteenth centuries. In fact, the spread of convents throughout Naples was largely driven by aristocratic responses to a changed political situation, forging and reinforcing a powerful aristocratic-religious nexus. Economic and social factors, particularly the changing situation of the aristocracy affecting marriage dowries, are crucial and will be discussed in chapter 3. Under the Spanish, Naples was increasingly an aristocratic city. The strong presence of convents is one aspect of that. Conventual building habits were profoundly aristocratic in inspiration, pattern, and form. Just as aristocrats, encouraged by the Spanish Crown, moved into the city and displayed their status by lavishly building, rebuilding, and decorating their fortress-style palazzi, so convents seized upon prime sites in the city and undertook expensive building programs of expansion and decoration.

Crucially, the Neapolitan nobilities, both feudal and bureaucratic, supported the emergence of the urbanistic hegemony of aristocratic religious houses, because of the vital role those houses played in perpetuating or strengthening aristocratic power. Stronger viceregal government produced political bureaucrats eager to consolidate their power in the city, while the old feudal aristocracy had to adopt new strategies to counteract their loss of direct political power at court. The promotion of new families through government service and the increasing power of royal tribunals compelled landed aristocrats to move to the cities, adopt a court-centered life, and devise new ways of making their presence and influence felt, especially in relation to the new power groups within the city.

The dramatic increase in the number of convents and of nuns housed within them was a direct result of a survival strategy seized upon by the old feudal aristocracy. Many nuns were in convents not as a result of enjoying a religious vocation but to suit family politics; it was a respectable way for aristocratic families to avoid paying extravagantly expensive marriage dowries. Of course, this situation had long existed and was widespread, but it was aggravated by changing monarchical policies in the Spanish Kingdoms of Naples and Sicily after 1503. Whereas feudalism remained largely unchallenged in the Kingdom of Naples, in the capital itself the old aristocracy came under direct pressure from new families, both those promoted by the Crown and those who profited from new systems of government, finance, and trade. The monarchy promoted new families (mostly Neapolitan, Genoese, or Iberian in origin) responsible for discharging its financial and administrative tasks; and new families ascended in society through the growth of bureaucracy, finance, and trade (again these international merchants and bankers were mostly foreigners).[97] These new families chose to settle permanently in Naples. The result was that the old feudal aristocracy, ousted by the new bureaucratic creatures, lost its accustomed direct access to political power. The Spanish government in Naples sold jurisdictions, fiefs, and titles to Neapolitans, Iberians, and others, especially the Genoese. This made it possible for bankers, lawyers, merchants, magistrates, and financiers to become aristocrats. The old feudal aristocracy held on to its privileges in the face of this new threat. Membership of the Neapolitan patriciate was closed, and by the early sixteenth century that patriciate, which dominated the city of Naples, strengthened its connections with powerful provincial barons to form a single elite group. Most of the patriciate acquired fiefs, and most of the dominant barons became members of the city's patriciate.[98] In short, the old feudal aristocracy retained its power by maintaining its feudal strengths and extending them to the city through careful marriage and political alliances with the patriciate. To compensate for this, feudal aristocrats sought to increase their economic and social powers through the aggressive extension of their feudal privileges.[99] Feudal laws, traditions, and institutions remained key in determining family status and alliances wrought between Neapolitan families; those same traditions were exploited by aristocrats to expand or maintain their patrimonies.[100] Most important, the old aristocracy, in the teeth of these new threats, adopted new strategies in its determination of lineage and inheritance to safeguard its political and economic power with far-reaching consequences. Marriage was limited—to only one son in each generation in some families; entails were established; opportunities afforded through litigation were cunningly exploited; and dowry funds were set up. Aristocrats therefore adopted a policy of ruthlessly increasing entails, limiting marriage, and enclosing surplus daughters in convents in order to preserve their feudal patrimonies. In turn, the Spanish government was willing to preserve, even to increase, the powers and privileges of the feudal aristocracy, provided that the Kingdom discharged its responsibilities, particularly its military and bureaucratic offices, within the Spanish imperial system.[101] Moreover, if the Court proved to be more permeable to the new aristocracy, the feudal aristocracy held sway in the upper levels of the Church in Naples. This was so much the case that even at the end of the seventeenth century a well-established lawyer, Francesco D'Andrea, discouraged his nephews from becoming ecclesiastics because the top jobs simply would not be open to them.[102]

Although they were driven by different needs and had different strengths and weaknesses, new and old families not infrequently adopted similar strategies for clan and family enhancement. Some of the oldest families in Naples—the families of Carafa, Orsini, Ruffo, Pignatelli, and di Capua—together with some of the new feudal Neapolitan elite—the Cardinez, de Guevara, Montoija de Cardona, and Ravaschieri families—linked their status to the elaboration of a family strategy among all members of their lineage focused on loyalty to the Crown and on a privileged relationship to ecclesiastical institutions, both regular and lay.[103]

The fate of religious institutions, especially of female convents, was intimately bound up with the degree to which Naples remained a city of localities. Its peculiar system of government, the aristocratic Seggi—and, increasingly, the relationship between the court, the aristocracy, and the Seggi—deeply marked the city's development. An administrative structure developed under the Angevins, the Seggi functioned as administrative, judicial, and social machines, such that government was, in effect, largely in the hands of a narrow oligarchy.[104] Neapolitan town government was based on a class division between the nobles and the people. The nobility was divided into five administrative districts, known as Piazze (squares), or Seggi or Sedili (seats), while the people were represented by only one Piazza, the Seggio del Popolo, established in 1495 (Plates 1, 2). Of the Seggi, the two most important, with the highest concentration of aristocratic families, were those of Capuana and Nido, while those of Porto, Montagna, and Portanova had considerably less social standing and political influence.[105] Membership was restricted to aristocrats resident in Naples and by the late fifteenth and early sixteenth centuries, new rules made it very difficult for new families to join.[106] City government was in the hands of a college of seven Eletti (Elect), one for each of the six Piazze, with two representatives from the Montagna with one vote between them; the Eletto of the People's Piazza was selected from a group of candidates by the viceroy.[107]

There were many who were neither citizens nor members of a Seggio, including hundreds of noble families of greater and lesser importance (known for this reason as *fuori Seggio*), among them recent arrivals from the province, those recently ennobled, and about one-half to two-thirds of the non-noble population (including well-to-do merchants and the numerous urban poor). The feudal nobility, moreover, prevailed in the General Parliaments of the Kingdom, and when these ceased to be called after 1642, feudal grandees increased their pressure to be accepted into the Seggi that assumed the principal functions of the Parliaments.[108] In order to resist the pressure, particularly of the new nobility and the professional and merchant classes which represented most of the ascendant social energy in the city, the noble Piazzas obtained agreement from Philip II that no new members could be admitted to the Piazzas without royal license and the full agreement of all the nobles of the Seggio in question. This suited both the citizen nobles, who retained their exclusive edge on power, and the Crown, which was the major beneficiary of the continuing discord between the noble groups.[109] As Chavarria has observed, the mid-sixteenth-century policy of *serrata* and of oligarchic closure effected by the Neapolitan patriciate exacerbated tensions within the noble class, including their struggle over the control of ecclesiastical spaces.[110]

The city Seggi were the real strongholds of the urban patriciate, which, usually in cooperation with ecclesiastical hierarchies, struggled to control the government of female conventual institutions from the top down. Crucially, it was the Seggi who elected the committees in charge of the administration of buildings, streets, and fountains.[111] And the Seggi participated in the recruitment of nuns, in spite of the determination within some convents to order their own affairs.[112] Convents were consequently regulated either directly by the Seggi or indirectly by the Seggi's dominance over city affairs. The Seggi could intervene to safeguard conventual interests from attack, but they could also regulate conventual affairs from behind the scenes. Certain Seggi tended to dominate specific aristocratic convents located in the districts they administered. The leading families of the Seggi of Capuana and Nido, the Minutolo, di Sangro, di Somma, Capece, Bozzuto, and some of the branches of the Brancaccio and Carafa families, preferred the convents of S. Patrizia and S. Gregorio Armeno for their daughters.[113] From Angevin times, the principal noble families of the city had forged close links with S. Patrizia, especially through generous bequests to procure burial there.[114] Pope Paul III issued a brief in 1545 authorizing the nuns of S. Patrizia to choose six knights from the Seggio of Capuana and five from the Nido Seggio, from which would be nominated the four governors of the monastery, two from each Seggio, to administer its estate, either supporting or replacing the abbess.[115] Other members of the same two Seggi, the Piscicelli, Loffredo, and Giudazzo families, sent their daughters to S. Gaudioso. Meanwhile, S. Maria Donnaromita absorbed the daughters of old noble families (Galluccio, Sersale) that had suffered a degree of relative declassment.[116] Some families managed to place their daughters in the oldest monasteries of the Seggio, thereby renewing their connections with their place of origin, and some placed their daughters in new monasteries, thanks to the patronage accorded to novices by older nuns related to them through collateral branches of the family.[117] Noblewomen from the Seggio of Porto, including the families of Gennaro, Strambone, and d'Alessandro, took the veil at the convent of S. Maria Donnalbina, while S. Potito was the favored convent for the Rocchi, Rossi, Sanfelice, and Sorgente families from the Montagna Seggio, and from 1619 of the Muscettola of Leporano, a family that had joined the Seggio relatively recently.[118] Significantly, the relationship between the Seggi, specific churches, and the protection of young women was intimately connected in one of the Seggi's older rituals. Before meeting in the Seggio, nobles would attend their church, known as *estaurita* (from the Greek for "cross"). On Sundays a cross wreathed in palms was placed in front of the Seggio's church to which people gave alms. Those alms were spent on the poor of the quarter, on the church, and on "setting up [marrying] poor maidens."[119] In short, the activities of the Seggi had traditionally bound locality, church, and the respectability of vulnerable women together, a dynamic which increasingly focused on the major convents.

The lax discipline of female convents and the desire to gain control over their vast fortunes and property led to enormous problems and resulted in legislation from city government—in Naples as in other Italian cities.[120] The aristocracy took advantage of female convents to reinforce their hold on city politics and to benefit socially and economically by doing so. Nobles determinedly asserted their prerogative of governing the city. Their claims to ancient rights—real or assumed—of jurisdiction over female monasteries, and their attempts to nominate governors and to determine the recruitment of nuns, formed an integral part of the consolidation of power, based on a restricted clan, that lay at the heart of the Neapolitan Seggi. Aspiring social groups and the ecclesiastical hierarchies had to grapple with this agglomeration of privileges acquired of old by the Neapolitan patriciate, and with their system of control of sacred spaces reinforced during the early modern period.

Nobles sought to safeguard the interests of both monasteries and their own Seggio and to bind the two institutions tightly together through lavish conventual endowments. Typical in this regard is the stipulation, attached to Alfonso Caracciolo's bequest of 700 ducats in 1543 to the monastery of S. Maria d'Agnone, that "the Monastery may not take women to become nuns except for nobles of the [Seggi of] Capuana and Nido," that the abbess should be as closely related as possible to Caracciolo himself, and that nuns from the Caracciolo family should have their dowries reduced to only 100 ducats.[121] In this way, by exploiting his position in the Seggio, Caracciolo attempted to secure the future good standing of his unmarried kinswomen with minimum investment.

Seggi exercised direct financial and administrative control over female convents. Thus during the 1560s, the nobles of the Seggio of Montagna secured control over the convents of S. Arcangelo a Bajano and S. Maria degli Angeli by assigning Vincenzo Sanfelice and Giovan Francesco Poderico, respectively, as financial managers.[122] Between 1560 and 1568 Marino Ruffo became *deputato*, or representative, of S. Maria della Misericordia, and Camillo Sanfelice took the same position at the Vergini; both men belonged to the Seggio of Montagna.[123] Female convents were not uniquely subjected to this form of control: the male houses of S. Maria della Sanità (Benedictine), S. Severo, and S. Lorenzo (Franciscan) came under similar control from the Seggio of Montagna between 1622 and 1625.[124] Sometimes a Seggio sought to curb the power of religious institutions over which they had no authority. In 1628, for instance, the Seggio of Montagna determined that the convent of S. Gregorio Armeno, having received the much prized head of St. Gregory of Armenia, should receive no more of his relics.[125]

The close ties between aristocratic Seggi and female convents meant, of course, that while convents' interests might often be secured and sheltered by aristocratic intervention, conventual autonomy was seriously limited by aristocratic interests. On the one hand, female convents enjoyed special privileges because of their important protectors. The aristocratic Benedictine nuns of S. Gregorio Armeno, for example, received permission in 1638 to build on public land to enlarge their monastery.[126] On the other hand, conventual interests were sometimes sacrificed to those of the clan. The identification of certain noble houses with monasteries through locality (the Seggio) indicates not only the need and ambition of nobles to determine local politics within the Seggio and their identification with the Seggio to which they belonged, but also allowed them to reach beyond the local in both secular and religious terms. Aristocratic influence in conventual organization and politics transformed their localized power into richer currencies—urban power and spiritual power.

Aristocratic attempts to increase their control over convents were erratic, sometimes forceful, and usually unpopular within convents. Neapolitan nuns had grown accustomed to relative liberty and to administering their own revenues.[127] They frequently resisted—though not always successfully—imposition of more rigid controls, including government by representatives of the Seggi. Therefore, prioral elections and the chance to cash in on a share of ecclesiastical revenues became subject to sharp contention between monasteries, nobility *di piazza* and *fuori piazza*, and ecclesiastical hierarchies. The struggles within the convent of S. Arcangelo in 1519–20 clearly reveal these tensions. In 1519 the lawyer Alberico Oliva brought a lawsuit to the civil tribunal of the Archiepiscopal Curia against nuns Camilla de Feulo, Margherita Rossi, Giovanella da Notario, and Ludovica Bonet for an outstanding professional fee of 50 ducats.[128] In 1518 the reigning abbess, sister Violante Coppola, died and the nuns split into two camps over the election of her successor, with Elisabetta Gambacorta and Camilla Carmignani on one side and Camilla de Feulo, Margherita Rossi, Giovanella da Notario, and Ludovica Bonet on the other. The lawsuit was concluded in 1520, with Oliva being awarded his claim, to the delight of the nuns who had supported de Feulo's candidacy.[129] Struggles for power within the convent between competing aristocratic families continued. In 1526 the abbess Camilla de Feulo, notoriously pregnant, was accused of sacrilege and adultery and of having squandered the monastery's patrimony. Those nuns who had supported her election now turned against her, and their attack was directed and amplified by deputies from the Montagna Seggio, Galeazzo Cecinelli and Marino Stendardo, who were nominated as procurators of the monastery by the group opposed to the abbess.[130] Camilla de Feulo pleaded that she was victim of a conspiracy by nuns opposed to her and by some nobles of the Montagna Seggio, who had usurped her economic control of the monastery and the exercise of her elected duties. The Curia punished her crimes of sacrilege and adultery by depriving her of office and those revenues she received in her private capacity.[131] The politics of the Seggio, therefore, spilled over to determine conventual affairs.

Sometimes nuns resorted to force majeure to rebuff external intervention in their affairs by the Seggi. In the early 1550s, at their instigation, the Vicario granted relatives of the nuns of S. Festo permission to reform the conventual statutes and to bring the convent under the governance of the Nido Seggio, in whose area the monastery stood. However, these plans came to nothing, because the soldiers sent by the viceroy to enforce them were confronted by a furious abbess and nuns defending their independence with stones and sticks.[132]

Attempts by the papacy and the Neapolitan Curia to reform female religious institutions were therefore limited by the politics of the city's noble Seggi. In Naples the reform of female monasteries generally began with monasteries of recent foundation, such as the Sapienza, S. Andrea della Dame, S. Maria in Gerusalemme, S. Maria del Gesù delle Monache, and, at the beginning of the seventeenth century, SS. Trinità and S. Giovanni Battista.[133] The admittance of nuns was largely brought under the control of the city's political institutions, and the observance of the Tridentine decrees offered families greater guarantees for the protection of the honor of their daughters.

Where reform took place, it was fashioned to suit the interested noble Seggio. Thus the suppression in 1563 of the convents of S. Agata and S. Agnello proceeded without provoking particular opposition. The goods of these two convents "for the greater seemliness and honesty and for the good governance of the nuns" were sold on 28 February 1567 in the presence of two nobles of the Porto Seggio, and the money made was assigned to the convent of Donnalbina, which had accepted the nuns from the suppressed convents and whose finances were directed by delegates from the same Seggio.[134]

Just a few years later, however, the suppression of the convent of S. Arcangelo a Baiano, achieved by the zealous determination of Cardinal Burali d'Arezzo, aroused an irrepressible outcry.[135] The arrangements for the resulting redistribution of nuns to other Benedictine monasteries throughout the city enraged the nobles of the Montagna Seggio, who thereby lost control over the administrative affairs of S. Arcangelo, which they had gained only a few years earlier with the appointment of Vincenzo Sanfelice to direct its finances in the 1560s.[136] Resistance also came from the nuns of S. Gregorio Armeno, who—perhaps in support of the Montagna nobles—refused to accept the nuns from S. Arcangelo into their convent, on the grounds that their constitution prevented them from accepting nuns who were not nobles from the Nido or Capuana Seggi.[137] Noble interests therefore were decisive in promoting or thwarting convent reform.

Rivalries between Seggi extended to ambitions to benefit from convents' religious and symbolic power. This was one of the reasons why the Seggi sought to determine the character and populations of those convents most closely associated with them. Their interests extended beyond social and financial control to their spiritual resources. Thus the control and distribution of relics held by convents condemned to suppression became the subject of conflict. The arrangement whereby the archbishop assigned the miraculous relic of the blood of St. John the Baptist to the nuns of S. Gregorio was, for instance, contested by the nobles of the Seggio of Montagna, who claimed that the monastery of S. Potito had the right to its custody.[138] In their petition for the relics sent to Gregory XIII in 1580, the members of the Montagna Seggio made an explicit spiritual claim to decide the fate of conventual property: "the distinction of the five *quartieri* and districts is held dear in every respect, in which the five Seggi which represent the said city have their basis, with [their] various boundaries defined and separated, where reside the *cavalieri* who are distinguished in every detail of honor and prerogative, both in temporal and in spiritual matters."[139] This episode, which also typifies the divisions within the nobility and demonstrates the degree to which conventual fortunes depended on their powerful backers within the Seggi, ended with the relics being definitively assigned to the monastery of S. Gregorio Armeno. When a papal brief issued on 26 February 1581 sanctioned the control by a group of noble families of the Seggi of Capuana and Nido of a cult which was attracting widespread popular support, the prestige of that convent was undoubtedly raised in the eyes of the Neapolitan populace, and the primacy and prestige of the aristocracy associated with S. Gregorio Armeno were also conspicuously reaffirmed.[140]

Occupying key locations in various quarters of the city, female monasteries exercised important religious and social roles. They gathered up daughters excluded from the marriage market and destined for the cloister and whose families were associated with the Seggio where the monastery stood, and they acted as mediators in relation to the sacred, through prayer and the offices recited by the nuns. They functioned like banks effecting miraculous exchange. Blood, daughters, money, and the sacred could be exchanged one for another in a ceaseless striving for influence, security, power, and social and spiritual redemption.

The city of Naples was the prime site for the foundation and extension of female convents. One might imagine that sites far from urban unrest and potential defilement would have offered greater appeal to nervous noblemen seeking to safeguard the honor of their daughters and the good name of their families. Yet while sons often traveled far afield, daughters were usually kept close to their parents in the city. The aristocratic urban model, the power and influence of the system of government provided by the Seggi, and the fact that a city convent provided greater opportunities than a rural one for families to keep a close eye on their daughters and on their adopted institutions, made this option particularly attractive to the baronage.[141]

An urban site was safer, more easily supervised, than a rural one, as Alberti had identified many years earlier: "I will not find fault with a nunnery that lies within a city, nor would I praise one sited completely outside. Although the isolation of this latter would ensure that there were fewer disturbances, anyone who wanted to enter for criminal purposes would have more time and freedom, since there would be no bystanders to watch, whereas in the former, the presence of many witnesses and onlookers would discourage any crime."[142] The watchful eyes of the vigilant crowd were substituted for the watchful eye of the "vigilant guard" in the city's self-policing mechanism. While men's minds had to be protected in rural monasteries, women's bodies had to be safeguarded from contamination, even if that meant courting the very disruptions from which men had to be distanced. Women's religious worth was equated with the purity of their bodies and, consequently, their architectural confinement and its site were treated as its metaphor.

A city convent was attractive to families for other reasons, too. A convent in the capital offered higher status and better social contacts than one located in the provinces. Paternal pressure to persuade daughters to move to the city could be intense. Vittorelli's account, published in Naples in 1743, of the life of sister Maria Cecilia, is informative in this regard. Throughout much of her life as a nun, Teodora Caracciolo, a nun in the Augustinian convent of S. Giuseppe in Martina, faced intense persuasion from her father, Francesco Caracciolo II Duke of Martina, to move to the prestigious convent of Donnaregina in Naples, where two of the duke's sisters, Isabella and Teodora, were already established.[143] Her father roped in Padre Giuseppe Guevara, a Theatine who had been the girl's confessor, to persuade her of the city's attractions. Guevara wrote to Teodora commending the size, sumptuousness, and magnificence of Donnaregina, its very noble and religious character and that of the lady nuns therein.[144] His emphasis on the mundane attractions of Donnaregina, rather than on its spiritual life, indicates that that convent was most readily associated with such pleasures and that pursuit of the same was likely to determine a young nun's choice of institution. In this instance such arguments fell on deaf ears, as Teodora replied that "she found all the delights [of Donnaregina] in that small convent of Martina, and that this alone seemed to her bigger than the city of Naples."[145] Frustrated, the duke resorted to offering her financial inducements of 500 scudi per annum if she would only become a nun at Donnaregina. His efforts reveal that securing his daughter in a convent offering great social cachet was worth much to him. Meanwhile, Teodora's mother wanted her to become a nun in Rome, presumably for similar reasons.[146] But their daughter resisted these blandishments, steadfastly remaining in Martina. That Vittorelli uses this to boast of Maria Cecilia's superior religious commitment indicates the rarity of her choice.

If city sites were more easily policed by nuns' families and ecclesiastical authorities alike, occupying an important city site afforded female convents considerable advantages. Above all, such positions allowed convents to operate centripetally in the city, drawing into their orbit influential magnates, aristocratic families, and rich endowments through the charisma of aristocratic virgins. Thus aristocratic convents came to function in a mode diametrically opposed to monasticism's early relationship with the urban patriciate.[147] Early modern female aristocratic convents situated in the city provided women with cultural centers unparalleled elsewhere. Here, outside the domestic sphere (albeit tempered by familial, dynastic and class concerns), they could exercise institutional, financial, and political power and intervene in city politics. They were socialized, educated, and politicized to a degree unequaled anywhere else.

This chapter has shown how the process by which female convents grew in number and influence within the city of Naples was complex and intricately connected with other developments, including viceregal strategies within the city, the ambitions and anxieties of both feudal and nonfeudal aristocracy through the structure of the Seggi, and a continuous process of compromises between ecclesiastical and secular powers. No simple picture emerges. Female religious institutions were powerful and became a conspicuous urban presence, but they could not get their way at will, even in small matters. They were often swept along by tides more powerful than themselves, such as when they were dragged in the slipstream of the Seggi. But they did sometimes triumph over distinct aristocratic interests and over male religious institutions. The interplay between gender and social rank within the city was too complex to allow a simple formulaic hierarchy to emerge in their regard.

In the organization, governance, and reform of female convents, the urban aristocracy of Naples played a crucial role, both in exercising their broadly common interests and in their rivalries and divisions, including the resistance of the urban nobles to the provincial nobility and to nobles *fuori piazza*. The emergence of powerful courtly nobles and bureaucrats mitigated the divisions among the aristocracy of the Seggi. Their presence and influence prompted both the generally divided great families to unite in opposition, and urban nobles to resist the provincial nobility and nobles *fuori piazza*. Against the divided and semiautonomous branches of the Seggi nobles, there developed a new identity of rank, based on the claim of belonging to a supranational elite.[148] The presence in the Kingdom of Naples of high functionaries and soldiers of Spanish origin, of Genoese and Flemish bankers and merchants, their full integration into the imperial system, and the necessity of forging new alliances with those crucial centers of power—the court in Madrid on the one hand and the papacy on the other—propelled the leading Neapolitan families onto an international stage. It is precisely in this context that the fervid building, both secular and ecclesiastical, of the period in Naples must be understood.

Thus, even as the dynamics of Neapolitan city politics served to bring convents under the sway of the Seggi, so they also elevated them to key positions in urban power struggles, thereby also affording them significant influence and, at least in some instances, remarkable autonomy. The divisions within the Neapolitan elite also allowed convents to find backing and support from a wide range of patrons and to play one off against another. Moreover, as the elite grew in ambition, so did its eagerness to control conventual spiritual power, which in turn posed convents both greater opportunities and sharper problems. Much of that conventual spiritual power lay in the significance of virginity. It is to this that we must now turn.

2

Virginity and Enclosure

I want . . . to dwell on the constitutive connection between the sexual and the social body.
—THOMAS LAQUEUR,
Making Sex: Body and Gender from the Greeks to Freud

The maintenance, protection, and celebration of virginity were central to the conventual economy of perfection. Virginity required certain provisions even as it bestowed spiritual and social blessings. The conventual task was to safeguard and honor virginity to allow virgins to dedicate themselves to God. Virginity and its blessings were not, however, as straightforward as they might appear at first glance.

Man and woman's original innocence is fundamental to the monastic economy of perfection; indeed, the vein of speculation of Christian gnostics over the status of sexuality in Eden is ultimately the source of the ideal of virginity in later Western monasticism.[1] To understand virginity, one must start at the Beginning, since the notion of virginity crucially refers to the perfection of creation and the innocent life of humankind in Eden.[2] The patristics and important commentators on the Fall as recounted in Genesis held that prelapsarian humans were created virginal like the angels, that sin does not constitute human's first ontological status, and that sexuality is a direct result of their sin: "sin does not define what it is to be a man; beyond his becoming a sinner there is his being created."[3]

There were, of course, disagreements among the Church Fathers over the nature of sexuality in Paradise.[4] However, they shared the quondam aspect of an understanding of virginity: the Fall is associated with an original transgression of a distinctly sexual nature (though some associated it with the body and sexuality itself, others with the sexual act, and Augustine not with sex but with the loss of control by the mind over the body). Gregory of Nyssa, the Greek Church Father of the fourth century A.D., and John Chrysostom (d. 407) regard prelapsarian Adam and Eve as leading lives like those of angels, in a state of asexuality and angelic innocence. If they had not sinned, God would have created more humans in exactly the same way as He created them and the angels.[5] In the gnostic economy, all the evils of human life are explained in terms of a single primal transgression; the prelapsarian existence was asexual and free from death. The corollary to this is that creatures free of death had no need of sexuality.[6] Sexlessness, immortality's sign, became its prerequisite. According to the gnostic notion, sexuality produces life because it is the cause of death; therefore, just as sexuality is linked with death, so asexuality is connected to life. Thus Gregory of Nyssa claimed that the virgin or monk (*monos*) is the soul redeemed from the duality of bodiliness to return to the monism of heaven; and John Chrysostom argued that life without death can only be achieved by renouncing sexual activity.[7] Ambrose (339–97) and Jerome (c. 341–420) regarded death as an inevitable outcome of marriage, and Chrysostom went so far as to claim "where death is, there is marriage. But virginity does not have this companion. It is always useful, always beautiful and blessed."[8]

While Christian gnosis viewed the material world as inevitably stained, the Western tradition saw it as the creation of God, and therefore good, although corrupted by the Fall.[9] Augustine, foremost in the Western tradition, agreed with the Eastern Church Fathers that Adam once had *apatheia*, or stoic immovability that was part of angelic life, but he interpreted *apatheia* not as ontological asexuality but as suspension from desire.[10] There was no lust in Paradise because there was no need of it. The body and soul were in harmony with the will, which was not the maimed thing that it soon became.[11] But intercourse to humankind in its fallen state was a shadow of death: sexuality mocked the will and betrayed a primal dislocation.[12] The significance of Augustine's thinking for Western notions of virginity is immense. His position manages to combine the notion of sexuality as part of the original human condition with prelapsarian virginity (Eve would have remained a virgin because she did not feel lust). Despite Augustine's emphasis on the loss of control (lust) rather than sexuality itself as denoting the Fall, the notion that the Fall was sexual remained strong and nourished a belief in later centuries that sexuality was sin.

Monasticism kept virginity alive as a vital component of Christian living. Central to monasticism was the equation of virginity with the ontological state of human nature before the Fall, derived from the Fathers of the Eastern Christian gnostic tradition.[13] Virginity, then, is equated with the angelic life, freed from sexuality and physical death. The association of sexuality with physical death gave rise to the idea that people leading a life of virginal perfection attain or even surpass the angelic mode of existence.[14] Ambrose claims, "in holy virgins we see on earth the life of the angels we lost in paradise" and quotes Matthew 22:30: "They neither marry nor are given in marriage, but are like the angels in heaven."[15] For Methodius, virginity is an "angelic transformation" of the human body.[16] Medieval monastic literature refers frequently to the notion that the life led by a cloistered monk anticipates that of an angel in heaven.[17] The superiority of human virgins over angels lies in the fact that humans have to struggle with the problems of the flesh from which the angels are gloriously free.[18] The practice of virginity in this life not only anticipates but brings closer the return to asexuality of creation.[19] The idea that those who lead a life of virginal perfection could reach the way of being of the angels was the most remarkably persistent idea arising from the association of sexuality with physical death. This, too, was fed by the quondam aspect of Christian millenarian thinking that supposed that at the millennium all would be as once it was. Thus Ambrose claims, "in holy virgins we see on earth the life of the angels we lost in paradise."[20] Indeed, there were claims that monastic life actually outshines the *vita angelica* because humans have to resist fleshly desire. Chrysostom and Cyprian articulate this notion precisely.[21] Virginity was the most essential prerequisite for a life of perfection in Christianity. Moreover, since virginity was the shortest route to heaven, not just for humankind but for the cosmos, the Fathers keenly urged virginity to men and women.

For women the implications of virginity were even greater than for men. Christian dogma produced a concept of female virginity whose social significance went way beyond that of vestal virgins and was founded on the mystery of the Incarnation. Ambrose articulates this notion clearly: "the strongest and most powerful motive that we can have to maintain virginity, the highest praise that we can accord it, is that God was born to a virgin."[22] For the early Christian philosophers, a physical and tangible embodiment of virginity was essential to conceive of the birth of Christ as miraculous. They evoke material virginity through metaphors: seal, closed door, cloister, wall. Without the *porta clausa,* the coming of Christ would be not a mystery, but a natural birth. Mary's unique state as virgin and mother required a clearly defined concept of real virginity. Although patristic writers resisted the idea of the anatomical basis of virginity, they used it metaphorically in relation to Mary. Thus, commenting on Ezekiel 14:2, "porta haec clausa erit et non aperietur," Ambrose saw Mary as the door through whom Christ will enter the world.

In the view of many churchmen, women could only transcend their unhappy corporeal state by pursuing a life of sexless perfection. Virginity dominated and defined the perception and conception of the female religious far more than it did for men.[23] Patristic writers praise virgins for having repudiated their own sexuality and even for becoming "male" or "virile."[24] Moreover, the equation of virginity with human nature before the Fall fed into the early popular eschatological belief that the millennium would be a return to what once was and to a period of asexuality, a belief that had a learned counterpart in Gregory of Nyssa's interpretation of Galatians 3:28 that "there is neither male nor female" in the resurrected Christ.[25] Virginity suspended the sexual divide between male and female. John, Christ's closest disciple, was a virgin; the intimate association of Christ, Mary, and John, all three saved from death by assumption or dormition, indicates the value of that "hermaphroditic virginity" as a superhuman, divine, and angelic state.[26] This hermaphroditic virginity, probably derived from the gnostic rejection of procreation and death articulated by Gregory of Nyssa, is not the same as the negation of sexuality, which had to be directed toward heaven. In this category are the "brides" of Christ and the virginal Christian mystic.

The patristic writers first associated female chastity with comportment.[27] Since women inclined more readily than men to lust, gluttony, and other temptations of the flesh, they should cling tenaciously to the rational control of the body, especially through chastity and *modestia*.[28] A virgin, notes St. Ambrose, should model herself on the Virgin Mary and observe *dignitas, gravitas,* and similar qualities in her comportment. During the Italian Renaissance men and women were expected to observe the same standard, *modestia*. That standard was by origin classical, yet it was one which the Middle Ages and Renaissance linked to the Christian ideal of chastity and thereby associated particularly closely with women.[29]

Crucially, the Christian patristic definitions of virginity emphasized the intentional and moral aspect of integrity and sexual abstention.[30] Chrysostom, who composed more treatises on asceticism and marriage than any other Greek-writing Father, extends his claim that true virtue must be more than simple abstention from evil to embrace virginity.[31] He defines virginity as sanctity of the body and spirit and argues that virgins must be chaste not only in body but also in mind, in order to be ready to receive the divine Spouse.[32] For Chrysostom, virginity has a fixed and brittle nature. Of St. Paul's statement "neither does a virgin commit a sin if she marries" (1 Cor. 7:28), Chrysostom argues, "he is not speaking of a girl who has renounced marriage, for it is apparent to all that she has sinned in an unforgiveable way."[33] While we live on earth, humankind struggles to be as angelic as possible through virginity, which can permit virgins to take Christ as their Bridegroom in heaven.[34]

Female virginity is, therefore, an absolution in its quondam nature. Female monasticism is the resurrected life of the gospel whereby women are freed from the twofold curse on Eve of childbearing and subordination to men. The benefits of virginity were defined in relation and, increasingly, in opposition to those of marriage. During the first few centuries after Christ, marriage came to be regarded as inferior to virginity. St. Paul clearly states that celibacy is preferable to marriage: "If a man has a partner in celibacy and feels that he is not behaving properly toward her, if, that is, his instincts are too strong for him and something must be done, he may do as he pleases; there is nothing wrong in it; let them marry. But if a man is steadfast in his purpose, being under no compulsion, and has complete control of his own choice; and if he has decided in his own mind to preserve his partner in her virginity, he will do well. Thus, he who marries his partner does well, and he who does not will do better."[35] 1 Corinthians 7:34 was frequently quoted to emphasize the value of virginity over marriage: "the unmarried woman or virgin is anxious about the affairs of the Lord, how to be holy in body and spirit; but the married woman is anxious about worldly affairs, how to please her husband."[36] "A nun tries to please God, a married woman the world," argued Leander of Seville, "a nun preserves the integrity of the virginity with which she was born, a married woman is corrupted by giving birth."[37] No one advocated virginity more ardently than Jerome, who regarded marriage as polluting and child-rearing as repulsive.[38] Jerome's letters to Roman aristocratic women, urging them away from marriage and toward chastity, were particularly influential in early modern Italy.[39] Significantly, both Augustine and Jerome allowed married women to compensate for their own loss of integrity by dedicating their daughters to virginity; in them is preserved and attained what has been lost in a wife.[40]

The debate about whether virginity is a state of the body or of the soul continued long and hard. Antique medicine, with its insistence on the unruptured hymen (*signaculum*) as proof of feminine virtue; early modern medicine; and patristics answered the question differently. Ambrose, Augustine, and Cyprian argued against the practice of manual checks on virginity. Not only are such checks fallible, says Ambrose, but they insult the virgin and risk producing the very effect that is investigated. Just as he argued for a sexuality for Adam that could be freed from lust, Augustine makes a clear distinction between physical and spiritual chastity, arguing that rape without the slightest consent of the victim does not remove the *sanctitas* of the girl, because chastity is a virtue of the soul (*virtus animi*). Augustine does not pit chastity of mind against the integrity of the body, but links the *sancta voluntas* with the *sanctitas corporis* which derives from it, because the body receives orders from the mind and is not autonomous. Therefore, if the mind gives evidence of a fixed will, then the body, too, will remain holy; what destroys virginity is desire. After Augustine, the notion of virginity as a pure state ultimately defined by the will persisted among theologians. Thomas Aquinas largely follows Augustine and gives a negative response to the question "Does virginity exist in the flesh?" For him chastity lodges in the mind, not in the flesh.[41] Aquinas is particularly clear on this issue:

> Consider a complete sexual act at three levels. The first physiological, namely the breaking of the body's reserve. The second psychological, or of body and soul together, namely the orgasm of sensory pleasure. The third is solely from the soul, namely the intention of reaching that delight. Of these the first is incidental to morality, which takes into account only what directly relates to the soul. The second is like the material in which the moral act works, for sensory passions are the medium for moral virtue. It is the third that is completed by the moral form, for reason supplies what makes an act moral.
>
> Well then, since virginity is defined in terms of moral integrity, the unbroken hymen is incidental to it, the immunity from the pleasures of orgasm is like its material, whereas the purpose of perpetually abstaining from this pleasure gives it completion and meaning.[42]

Onofrio Zarrabini, regular canon of the Augustinian order in Venice, echoed St. Augustine in 1586, distinguishing between virginity and corporeal innocence, arguing that although humans are born with material virginity, this is not equivalent to the state of perfect virginity: "to be truly virgin it is not enough to have virginal flesh; but it is necessary that one's mind be free from any sort of carnal desire."[43] If virgins are sacred (and their sanctity stands for much more than their utility as reproductive organisms), then female sexuality is evil and treacherous. Female virginity must, therefore, be vigorously upheld. This was particularly the case because of the unredeemable character of virginity. "Although God can do all things," writes Jerome, "He cannot raise up a virgin after she has fallen."[44] Although God can restore the virginal mind to its integrity, He cannot restore the uncorruption of a virgin's body once she has carnally known a man.[45] However, Zarrabini does grant that if a woman who is no longer a virgin should recover her resolution to live perpetually a virgin, she can be so rewarded in the next life.[46] At their best, therefore, virgins on earth are like the angels in heaven in terms of resisting the weaknesses of the flesh, while resembling the first humans in earthly paradise.[47] The significance of the preservation of the hymen, present, albeit deemphasized, in *Summa theologica*, assumed ever greater emphasis, so that beyond theological circles, virginity was regarded as the preservation of corporeal integrity.[48] The logical consequence of freeing the notion of virginity from the *signaculum* was that all parts of the body were susceptible to corruption. Thus Methodius of Olimpus argued that it is ridiculous for virgins to preserve their sexual organs from contamination if they do not also control their tongue, sight, hearing, and touch—in short, each and every part of the body where a desire can occur.[49] These ideas are perhaps nowhere expressed more fully and clearly than in female monastic *clausura*.

Virginity did not necessarily require enclosure. After Jerome, degrees of continence below conventual virginity were evaluated and promoted.[50] An ecclesiastical treatise on the role of women, written by Agostino Valier, bishop of Verona discerns four separate "laudable states" among women. Virgins living in convents as brides of Christ were ranked highest; they were followed in descending order of importance by nuns resident outside convents or unmarried women (*le dimesse*), widows, and married women.[51] Widows could contribute to discipline by showing themselves unassuming in the habit, dedicated to the aid of young people in danger and to the teaching of Christian doctrine. Bishop Valier introduced a fourth state, that of the *dimessa* or "humble woman," a virgin in the home, promoted also as of great advantage to their families, the Church, and the city.[52] Valier was building on medieval models of virginity in which women, such as Mary of Oigniers and Elizabeth of Hungary, achieved the spiritual rewards of virginity despite marriage and motherhood.[53] The Roman noblewoman Caterina Ginnasi, niece of Cardinal Domenico Ginnasi, belonged to Valier's fourth category. Refusing to marry, she devoted herself instead to a "devout and spiritual life." Her epitaph in S. Lucia in Rome describes her as the "nonsterile virgin who is fertile in virtues."[54] She was commended by her uncle, shortly before her death, for living like "a religious woman in seclusion, alien to worldly pomp, who would die as an angelic virgin even if outside the cloister and thereby bring special glory to his house."[55] Even women who were not nuns could bring honor to their family, provided that they were clearly virgins.

Churchmen promoted female celibacy in order to alleviate some of the problems of forced monacations. Zarrabini defined virginal, marital, and widowed states of virginity, reserving special praise for those virgins who live in their own houses: "Blessed are you, then, who persevere in such a noble state amidst the uproar of the world. . . . Your room is heaven, your word is divine contemplation, and your Spouse is Christ."[56] For Zarrabini virginity is nobler than other forms of chastity (albeit not more noble than the other virtues): "There are three sorts of chastity: the pudency (*pudicitia*) of the married, the continence of widows, and the chastity of virgins, which we maintain is more excellent than the other two. . . . For who can deny that it is much more noble and excellent to scorn any sort of carnal pleasure than only one particular sort?"[57] Zarrabini does not, however, regard virgins as a homogenous group; they are divided not only by where they live, and whether they live enclosed lives or with their families, but more crucially by innate characteristics: "There are many virgins; but in truth they are very different among themselves; since some are stupid, others wise, some live in houses of the world with their relations, and others allow themselves to be enclosed voluntarily in holy convents."[58] Virginity itself is insufficient, in Zarrabini's eyes, to guarantee celestial union with God, regardless of whether the virgin lives in a convent or not. For him the key issue is the quality of the dedication to a virginal life, since, to God, "the humility of the conjugal state is always more welcome than haughty virginity" and "all virgins are stupid who serve virginity not for glory or love of immortal God, but rather for mundane glory, and to be admired, praised and celebrated by human mortals."[59] Significant here is both the acknowledgment that virginity was socially respected and the warning that female pride would undermine all the benefits that virginity might bestow.[60]

Zarrabini advises virgins living in the outside world to protect their virginity. They should stay behind closed doors, avoid gossip, and talk of mundane matters; they should keep their eyes down, use modest words, eat with moderation, and drink little wine; and their ears and eyes should be closed to song, games, and musical instruments.[61]

Although virgins living at home were regarded increasingly favorably, civic and ecclesiastical authorities discouraged the more communal way of life adopted by semireligious women, such as beguines, *pinzocchere*, Sisters of Common Life, *beate*, and tertiaries.[62] The existence of such women confused the boundaries between clerical and lay and raised difficult questions with regard to inheritance and to institutional authority. In particular, the prestige of consecrated women, which had been growing during the early sixteenth century, seems to have been greatly diminished from about 1530. The prophetesses, female religious leaders who had been respected as living saints and *divine madri*, lost respect and support and were sharply excluded from public life.[63] The "living saints," who had assumed an important profile in pre-Reformation religious devotion, tended to cede in significance to saints who were oriented specifically to the next world, a tendency which formed part of the widening gulf between the sacred and the profane.[64] Certainly enclosure fostered a more introverted and exclusive role and sense of identity for nuns.

Virginity was desirable, but it was also dangerous. Convents served to restrict and regulate it by excluding some women (on the basis of class, economic means, and so on) and preventing access to virgins by others (with a few exceptions, based on social class, specially purchased economic privilege, or religious authority), while simultaneously advertising and celebrating their presence. Virginity could strengthen the social order, but it was also potentially threatening to it because of its inherent potential for transcendence. Protestantism dealt with this problem by abolishing the notion of chastity as a special mark of holiness while attacking the "diabolical superstition" that sexual abstinence could give rise to superhuman powers; by contrast, Catholicism reaffirmed celibacy for priests and tightened the rules governing the dedication to perpetual chastity of religious, while simultaneously strengthening its opposition to organized virginity for laypeople. This insistence served to keep sharp the distinction between ecclesiastical and lay states. Monasteries and convents played a crucial part in representing that distinction physically and ostentatiously. But the transcendent possibilities of virginity meant that virgins and the institutions that housed them occupied ambiguous positions within Catholicism and had to be carefully policed. This led to particular value being placed on those institutions which opened themselves most readily to external control.

TRENT, ENCLOSURE, AND DISCIPLINE

The Council of Trent marked a turning point for female convents. Trent resulted in unprecedented centralized control over female convents, the curtailment of liberties within them, and, above all, greater insistence on enclosure. Its attempts to ensure that all female orders would henceforth be enclosed had far-reaching and, in some cases, devastating consequences for female monasticism in Catholic Europe.

Ironically, the impact of the Council of Trent on conventual life was probably greater because it did not allow adequate time for discussion. Hurriedly, in the last session of the council in December 1563, deliberations turned to female religious orders and to enclosure "in a haste more similar to a flight than to a true and proper conclusion" without proper discussion or consensus.[65] The council was uninventive, relied upon the resuscitation of earlier rulings, and left a trail of ambiguity and uncertainty in its pronouncements affecting female orders. Pope Pius IV wanted to finish the council before his illness finished him; and his successor, Pius V, decided to abandon the publication of the Acts of the Council, as he feared controversy between the Molinists and the Thomists.[66] Issues discussed and determined ranged from financial provisions to administrative organization, from the election of abbesses to religious issues such as the frequency of communion to be adopted by nuns.[67]

The most important decree, however, was the renewal of the bull *Periculoso* (1298) of Boniface VIII, which required bishops to reinstate the strict enclosure of nuns (absolute prohibition against their leaving the convent, except in case of emergency) wherever it had been violate (*ubi violata fuerit*) and to preserve it wherever it was inviolate (*ubi inviolata est, conservari maxime procurent*).[68] This opened gaping uncertainties about the correct measures to be taken with the open monasteries where enclosure had never existed.[69] Furthermore, Trent relied on the well-worn ways of reforming female orders: there was almost unanimous consent that reform should be determined by the general superiors of the religious orders, who controlled most religious houses.[70] If nuns resisted, the military could be called in. Nuns needed episcopal permission to set foot outside all convents at any time.[71]

After the Council of Trent, conventual enclosure—physical separation—became the principal means toward discipline. Enclosure produces what Foucault calls "the protected place of disciplinary monotony," within which space and time can be organized to suit the needs of the institution, without reference to the world beyond that which is enclosed.[72] Indeed, enclosure became the focus and subject of ecclesiastical tests of conventual obedience. The respectability and prestige of convents were measured not by the degree of religious devotion pursued by nuns therein, but by the effectiveness of their enclosure, the symbol of their separation from the world, and the guarantee of the virginity of the disciplined bodies inside.

It was easy enough to pass the decrees, but their implementation proved to be a vexed issue.[73] The struggles which raged before and after the council throughout Italy focused on whether female convents were to be strictly vocational, part of the clerical order, as reforming bishops advocated, and answerable to the episcopacy; or whether they were to continue to provide the social function of harboring superfluous daughters.[74] That tension marks conventual architecture of this period.

The process of ironing out abuses and the strengthening of communal life was never completely successful. Much more successful were attempts to enforce strict enclosure, measures to isolate convents from the outside world. Architects steeped attention on the elements that became symbolic of enclosure: high walls, rusticated doorways, locks, bars, and turntable wheels (Figures 27, 28, 29, 30, 31, 40, 41). Desire to emphasize nuns' claustration was sharpened by its constant erosion in practice and by the contradictions and ambiguities inherent in nuns' positions. Enclosure brought with it new architectural demands: a refectory for communal eating; careful separation of lay and regular constituencies; parlatories; alterations to churches; and so on. Often these changes prompted large-scale building programs, which justified extending the monastic complex. Sometimes this resulted in the extension of gardens and courtyards, where in compensation for rigorous enclosure an image of the garden of Eden or of heavenly Jerusalem was created.[75]

Whereas before Trent, aristocratic women had been able to choose open convents, after Trent had, in effect, abolished them, they were compelled to live their lives under stricter regimes, despite not necessarily enjoying any religious vocation. In turn, this situation prompted a certain laxity in enforcing the rules in aristocratic convents. Thus political and social resistance to rigorous visitation could lead to less rigorous application of the rules.[76] More successful were attempts to enforce strict enclosure, which became the dominant theme of conventual architecture.

The contradictions of the system were everywhere apparent. In Naples the dispute over female convents, especially those under royal patronage, split the archbishops supported by Rome against the viceroys supported by Spain. Viceroy Olivares explicitly insisted that the pope must recognize that Neapolitan convents provided the means for impoverished Neapolitan families to maintain their family's honor. The viceroy's point was that the Church must adjust its ideal of convent life to social reality.[77] In short, the subordination of religious institutions to the requirements of the ruling classes was an intrinsic aspect of conventual life, even if it was rarely articulated explicitly.[78]

Despite its vagueness, Trent provided for sharp, even violent, enforcement of its decrees. But this did not mean that all convents were subject to draconian rules. It all depended on the nature of the bishop in charge. Even when a bishop was particularly vigilant, as Archbishop Filomarino was in Naples, nuns continued to enjoy considerable freedoms.[79] Subsequent synodal legislation shows that even with regard to enclosure, the most one could say was that its observance was only formal.[80] Nevertheless, generally speaking, Trent brought more regulation to nuns' lives (and, with it, opportunities for the privileged to circumvent stringent requirements). Strict convents remained strict (since abbesses retained day-to-day powers), while lax convents and open convents, previously administered by abbesses, became stricter in those dioceses with reforming bishops. Fidelity to religious profession and obedience to the authority of the Fathers became the foundations of the new discipline. Bishops became primarily responsible for good government of nuns. They assumed, sometimes ardently, the responsibility of visiting and reforming convents, often placing in the hands of nuns' relations the task of setting the finances in good order.[81]

In Naples, after Trent, visitations by Archbishop Alfonso Carafa and Cardinal Archbishop d'Arezzo, in particular, resulted in the closure in 1564 and 1577 of several lax or recalcitrant convents and the decanting of dedicated nuns to other convents of the same order within the city. The nuns of S. Agata were sent to S. Maria Donn'Albina; those from S. Benedetto were dispersed between several convents. In 1564 nuns from the Misericordia near the Porta di S. Gennaro, went to S. Arcangelo a Bajano, but this was suppressed in 1577 and nuns were further diverted to S. Patrizia, S. Gaudioso, S. Maria Donnaromita, and S. Gregorio Armeno.[82] In 1565 the Benedictine convents of S. Festo and S. Marcellino were united, delayed by ardent lobbying of protests to Rome by the nuns involved.[83] There can be no doubt that the Council of Trent's rulings on female monasteries, when rigorously applied, shocked nuns with their strictness and intransigence. Fulvia Caracciola, abbess at the convent of S. Gregorio Armeno in Naples, recorded that in 1568 seventeen nuns fled the convent because of the new restrictions.[84]

Ecclesiastical rules and fortified architecture were matched by internal regulation. Bishops and superiors of religious orders attempted to print and vulgarize the rules and constitutions that represented the principal structure of monastic discipline. Of the 266 examples of convent rules and constitutions published between 1497 and 1704, about 88 percent were printed after 1564; and of the 188 rule books published over the same period, only 23 were published before the Council of Trent.[85] Specialized spiritual texts for religious women exhorted respect for the rule and monastic vows, and modeled behavior around the notion of progress toward the perfect nun. *Alcuni avvertimenti nella vita monacale, utili et necessari a ciascheduna Vergine di Christo,* by the Franciscan Bonaventura Gonzaga of Reggio (1568), sought to instruct nuns "in few words" how they should conduct themselves "to walk properly in such a way to eternal life and to true beatitude."[86] He includes warnings about the necessity of constant good behavior: "You may never be sure that you are not seen, so that you should proceed in visible things with prudence, in touch with chastity and in everything else with modesty and discipline, as if the whole world were gazing at your actions."[87] But he adds that it is not in the eyes of the world that the nuns' behavior is truly measured, but in those witnesses of all actions, the angels, God, and the conscience: "whosoever ceases to do bad things, not through love of the good, but through fear of earthly punishment or loss of worldly honor, is not among the true servants of Christ, because this sort [of behavior] is more pleasing to men than to God."[88]

Preachers and confessors, trained and instructed by the diocesan Ordinaries, were charged with teaching regular observance and controlling its practice. In the circle of Borromaic reform in the diocese of Milan, one book in particular, *Specchio religioso per le monache* by Giovanni Pietro Barchi (1609), indicates the emphasis placed by ecclesiastical authorities on the "nun's career."[89] This is a taxonomy of sins related to slack observance of the rule, constitutions, and orders of superiors. Vested with the task of improving ecclesiastical discipline and themselves professionalized through a plentiful casuistical literature, the nuns' confessors acquired a role that had ever more to do with safeguarding the honor of the religious house and less and less to do with the individual conscience.[90]

This was not a new fusion. The etymology of *claustrum* is closure. For the great eleventh- and thirteenth-century thinkers, the interior of the monastery coincided with its exterior; the "inside" of the body of the monk was the "where" of peace, the *locus animae* which, in Augustine's words "non in spatio aliquo est."[91] The interiority elaborated by St. Augustine was not simply the identification of a place outside of space. That "place" was transformed through metaphoric praxis, since it can be spoken of only metaphorically. Exterior space therefore became a metaphor for interior space.[92] The convent became a metaphor for peaceful devotion and the exterior of the regular's body its sign. For women the sign of that devotion was their chastity; and the sign of that sign was the sealed convent wall, as the introduction to the 1671 statutes of the Franciscan convent of S. Maria Maddalena in Turin articulate: "So much did the Son of the Virgin like this virtue [chastity], that when he came to the world, he chose to be born to the purest Virgin that the human race boasted, and for this having to singularly shine in gestures, in words, and in behavior of enclosed nuns, whose exterior shows very often the interior, because it exactly preserves it, the following statutes are made."[93] Although theological discussions of virginity emphasized the necessity of purity of spirit, beyond theological discussion virginity was conceived physically, the hymen being the proof of feminine virtue, itself commensurate with family honor. Early modern convents occupied a position straddling both these worlds. While much emphasis was placed on humility of spirit among nuns, conventual architecture and regulations were principally concerned with protecting the state of virginity conceived physically, and with celebrating the attendant familial honor and collective angelic aspirations that followed from that.

Although all forms of virginity were valued, virgins in enclosed religious orders received highest praise.[94] Enclosed nuns were not subjected to tests of their virginity: their undertaking to exercise the moral qualities attributed to virginity—humility, purity, simplicity—substituted for physical examination. For the nuns of the cloisters, Zarrabini reserves the sweetest promises: "Virgins, to whom your Spouse says: Come my spouses, my doves, receive the crowns that I have prepared for you: those crowns, what else are they, o spouses of Jesus Christ, if not your holy virginity, that makes you the most precious crowns in the hands of the Lord God of the heavenly exercises?"[95] Virginity was, nevertheless, construed as a state which had to be consciously and constantly safeguarded. Zarrabini argued that St. Augustine's claim that virginity is "a perpetual meditation of non-corruption in corruptible flesh" did not imply that a virgin might think of nothing other than of her virginal state, but rather that her commitment to it must be unwavering.[96] Taking up the metaphor of the enclosed garden, Zarrabini urges virgins to tend their fruits: "there are stairs which are very easy to climb thereafter in the brightest parts of those stellated cloisters; where there are already prepared eternal thrones for you to rest in everlasting peace."[97] He recommends that veiled virgins should castigate their flesh by vigils, fasts, unremitting prayer, and deprecations.[98] Likewise, enclosed virgins should not be "like dogs who return to vomit," but should steer clear of men and sensual temptation, avoid sensual clothing, head ornaments, grand clothes, and lascivious perfumes.[99]

Female sexuality was regarded as the peculiar weakness to which religious women might most easily fall prey and, consequently, precisely that area which needed to be most closely guarded. Carlo Borromeo's influential discussion of confession, sin, and penitential practice, *Istructionum,* warns against female concupiscence, the corrupting qualities of women, especially their threat to priests' chastity. Since lust was more deeply ingrained in women than in men, Borromeo advises that contrition should be recognized and penance meted out unequally in their regard. When a male penitent confessed fornication, as soon as his mistress left his home he could be absolved. When a female penitent confessed the same sin, she should be refused absolution until she "displayed the true marks of her repentance . . . for several months."[100]

Virginity was at the heart of monasticism and therefore a principle upon which spiritual ideal the development of the institution has largely depended. Indeed, it was the monastic economy that preserved the ideal of virginity since in Augustine's thought virginity had no real raison d'être. Enclosure brought the Eastern ideal to the West institutionally, but it remained bound to the equation of virginity with the ontological state of prelapsarian human nature of the Fathers of the Christian gnostic tradition.

In early modern Italy, virginity was seen in relation to its opposite. Whereas for men the religious condition was perceived as liberation from marriage bonds, for women it was seen as replacing marriage to a husband with marriage to Christ.[101] The notion of the *sponsa Christi,* distinguishing the dedication of women to a religious life from that of their male counterparts, is central to female conventual spirituality and to the development of an erotic spirituality.[102] For women, the monastic profession emphasized the *consecratio virginum* and its symbolism referred to marriage nuptials. This is of particular significance in the context of nuns who were in convents largely to meet their families' needs to exercise control over their sexuality in order to protect the patrimony. The sexuality of young noblewomen in a society which operated a system of inheritance based on male primogeniture was always the focus of considerable anxiety and interest, whether they were inside or outside the convent.

The image of Christian virgins as brides of Christ is first recorded by Tertullian (*De oratione,* xxii) and dates from at least the third century. The idea derived from pagan gnosticism in which the metaphor of sexual union was frequently used to describe the relationship between the individual soul and the Godhead.[103] Chrysostom claims that celibate women will greet Christ as their Bridegroom when they die.[104] The notion of the bride was emphasized in the Solomonic literature of the Old Testament, particularly the Song of Songs, and this notion was established and amplified within the Christian gnostic tradition particularly by Origen, the Greek theologian of the early third century A.D.[105] Tertullian marks an important development in the bride metaphor, which was the narrowing of the idea of *sponsa* to mean a virgin woman.[106] This occurred because the Latin Fathers regarded the Bridegroom of the Song of Songs not as the gnostic word, as Origen had, but as the Man-God Christ. Part of this interpretation was an emphasis on Christ's humanity and, therefore, at least a concomitant acknowledgment of his sexuality.[107]

Already in the fourth century Ambrose noted that the rite for the consecration of virgins closely resembled that of marriage.[108] In the *Sacramentarium Gregorianum* the veiling of a virgin occurred in weddings both with Christ and with men. Between the tenth and twelfth centuries, the liturgy restricted the nuptial condition to consecrated virgins. Mystical marriage, which hitherto had represented the union of the soul and God, and the Church and Christ (that is, the abstract united with collective entities), became a personal union. Now the only real brides were those women who were nuns.[109] The logical consequence of this conception of the monastic profession for women as akin to marriage was that breaking the vow of chastity was treated as adultery.[110]

Control of female sexuality was a central function of post-Tridentine convents.[111] At the same time, spirituality became particularly sexualized. Ironically, although virginity was held in the highest possible regard, and thought of as superior to marriage, nevertheless it was the sexual content of the *sponsa* metaphor which was taken up to express the consuming passion of the soul's union with the Godhead. It put the marriage to Christ on an equal footing with human marriage, defining both as the same kind of relation. It followed logically that the union with a heavenly Spouse had far more to recommend it than marriage with a merely human one. One of the interesting consequences of these developments was an enhanced emphasis on the femaleness of the professed virgin.

That the emphasis on securing a respected and powerful husband in Christ undercuts vaunted Christian virtues, such as humility, does not deter writers of devotional literature for nuns from heaping up the virile attractions of the Christ Spouse. Thus in his treatise on the training of nuns, Leander of Seville: "virginity wins a special favor for itself in Christ in that a nun may claim as her Bridegroom one before whom angels tremble, whom powers serve, whom virtues obey, to whom things celestial and terrestial bow down."[112] Christ's blood is even described as a "dowry."[113] Leander's text emphasizes the importance of the *sponsa Christi* as an intercessor: "If you are acceptable to God, if you shall lie with Christ upon the chaste couch, if you shall cling to the embrace of Christ with the most fragrant odor of virginity, surely, when you recall your brother's sins, you will obtain the indulgence which you request for that brother's guilt."[114] What was intended allegorically for monks was open to much more literal interpretation by women (unshadowed by attendant homophobic fears).[115] The union between the asexual soul of the virgin and the Godhead rapidly became a union between female virgins and Christ, an emphasis which received extra impetus from developments in the courtly love tradition. Thus female virgins came to occupy a special place in the Christian-gnostic soul marriage and, significantly, the writings of female mystics from the twelfth century to the seventeenth emphasize the eroticism of their relationship with Christ.[116] The exaltation of the nun as Christ's bride gradually obscured the Christian-gnostic notion of the nuptials of the soul.

If the twelfth century was the critical period for the redefinition of the *sponsa Christi* concept and for the appearance of a sexualized Christ and a feminized and sexualized virgin bride, the sixteenth and seventeenth centuries saw the resurgence of these ideas, accompanied by a pronounced growth in female mysticism. The writings of St. Teresa of Avila were particularly influential in this regard:

> O soul beloved of God! Trouble not yourself; for, when His Majesty brings you here and speaks to you as delectably as He speaks to the Bride in the canticles,—using many such phrases (as I have said) as "Thou art all fair, O my love," to show the pleasure which He takes in her—it is to be supposed that at such a time He will not allow you to displease Him; rather He will give you what you cannot yourself provide so that He may take the greater pleasure in you. He sees that the Bride is lost to herself and enraptured for love of Him, and that the very strength of love has taken from her the power of understanding, so that she may love Him the more.[117]

Increased emphasis on the corporeality of Christ and on his physical torment encouraged women to return his love in kind, with terrible pain and suffering. Exemplary female religious invariably emphasize apparent loss of control over their own bodies, as the virgin offers Christ her body to hang on the same cross.[118] "See with your spirit, not with your head," Jesuit P. Ignazio Vittorelli urged cloistered nuns.[119]

In the post-Tridentine era, prompted partly by conflict with Protestant criticism and partly by renewed emphasis on the early Church, virginity once more became an important issue.[120] As Protestants denied its spiritual significance, Catholic thinkers were pushed into a reassessment of their understanding of virginity, along with other important precepts of their beliefs. Early modern churchmen relied heavily on biblical and patristic texts for concepts of virginity. The early modern Church advocated female chastity through sermons, confessions, pamphlets, and books, including the publication in 1562 of 800 copies of *De Virginitate Opuscula Sanctorum Doctorum Ambrosii, Hieronymi, et Augustini*, a selection from the Church Fathers' writings on virginity and one of the first publications of Paolo Manuzio's press in Rome—a clear sign of the support of churchmen.[121] St. Thomas's teaching, too, was reaffirmed by Catholic theologians of the Catholic reform. A highly significant development was the increasingly close alliance between the Eucharist, which played a crucial role in Catholic reform, and the concept of chastity, discussed in chapter 6.[122]

Virginity lay at the theological heart of monasticism, as well as the system of familial honor. While virginity in the home was increasingly supported, that in an enclosed convent was regarded as the greatest good, not just for the individual nun but for her family and indeed for her city. It allowed the individual nun to live the life of an angel and to make a heavenly marriage with Christ, which also fortified the city against evil. While a chaste wife or widow symbolized the exclusivity and inaccessibility of a family and functioned as its boundary marker, a virginal enclosed nun enhanced a family's honor and could represent social mobility. Virginity, therefore, constituted a value-made-body, or body as value, which served to emphasize the relationship between physical space and social space and to radicate the fundamental structures of a group in bodily experience. The link between aristocratic familial honor and virginity was forged by the system of conventual dowries. And it is to that system that we now turn.

3

Dowries and Daughters

My daughter! O my ducats! O my daughter!
— WILLIAM SHAKESPEARE,
The Merchant of Venice, II, viii, 15

Conventual urbanism and architecture were fashioned by the weft and warp of daughters and dowries. The dowry system, the heart of the social ideology of this period, lurks behind and within convents' high walls. It simultaneously generated the demand for conventual places for young women while excluding others, and it positioned daughters safely off-center in terms of inheritance while binding the fortunes of convents indissolubly to those of their inmates' families.[1]

When a woman married, her father had to provide her with a dowry, sometimes including land, that passed to her husband for the duration of the marriage. The dowry was not considered a female share in inheritance; on the contrary, it worked to exclude its beneficiary from inheritance.[2] Dowries guaranteed the honor of the entire family through the control of female sexuality. So central to the sexual economy was this system that, although complaints about excessive and escalating dowries were frequently made from the mid–fourteenth century on, the principle itself was never seriously questioned.[3] The dowry system underpinned a patriarchal system of property inheritance, but functioned paradoxically within it, buttressing women's dependence on men, while affording dowered women with a potential independence.[4]

Just as the tension between lineal and conjugal bonds was vital to the nature of domestic life and kinship organization of the urban patriciate, so the competition (or lack of it) between lineal and spiritual conjugal loyalties, between conventual women's relationships with their families (especially their fathers) and their spiritual marriage to Christ, was crucial to conventual life. At the very heart of these tensions lay the vexed question of the dowry. The dowry, embalmed in tradition, embedded in discourses of honor and respectability, was the grit in the soft flesh of the oyster and the pearl which both necessitated sacrifice and guaranteed virtue. A metonym for the wealth and social status of the bride's family, for the honor and good morals of the daughter, and for the social recognition accorded the family of the groom, a dowry functioned as the currency which could smoothly exchange the assurance of past good breeding for the promise of future wealth, respectability for cash, a woman for a bundle of property. These alchemical transactions transforming blood into property may appear to give women tremendous power and centrality in the system of exchange, but in fact dowries moved through women to position them off-center with regard to inheritance; they worked as lightning strikes a tree, a singular sudden blaze before the wood turns dark and burned.[5] While they served to guarantee the honor of women, they did so by safeguarding traditional notions of shame and dishonor through vigilant control of female sexuality.

Most upper-class women in seventeenth-century Italian society remained socially and financially dependent throughout their lives. Only upper-class widows, who were legally independent and possessed incomes from their jointures or dowers, enjoyed economic independence.[6] The fate of daughters was therefore tightly bound to the fate of familial fortunes. Thus the control of women, and of their sexuality in particular, through their incarceration in convents can be explained partly in terms of women's role as boundary markers and carriers of group identity—a role that was particularly important when their families felt undermined by political changes.[7] Policing nuns in convents protected the status of their families outside. In baroque Naples and Palermo the number of aristocratic nuns increased substantially just when feudal and nonfeudal aristocracies were striving to protect their own boundaries. To fathers, the disadvantage of the dowered marriage system was that it necessitated splitting up their lands. But they could conserve feudal property if they prevented their daughters from marrying and instead sealed them in convents. Commitment to virginity was allied to the dread of property dispersal.

The slippages and contradictions inherent in the marriage dowry system with regard to an earthly spouse also functioned in marriages to the heavenly Spouse. Like husbands, convents expected dowries in exchange for taking daughters off their fathers' hands and bestowing on them respectability and honor. Whereas earthly marriages ensured the production of heirs and the guarantee of lineage, heavenly marriages had to guarantee the absence of issue. Virginity was to the conventual dowry system what fertility was to the marriage dowry system. But whereas progeny were visible and childbirth often resulted in death, virginity was both invisible to the eye and an aid to life everlasting. In effect, the invisibility of virginity resulted in making virgins invisible. The promise of everlasting life that virgin nuns embodied was glimpsed only metonymically, through frescoed domes of saintly triumphs or heavenly gloria (Plate 3), the virgins themselves were sealed from sight, and virginity's public guarantors became high walls, exclusion, and secrecy.

THE ARISTOCRATIC BODY

The early modern southern Italian aristocracy was preoccupied with the acquisition and preservation of their status, power, and wealth, which involved complex and contradictory negotiations. They had to manage their revenues while sustaining high levels of consumption, an integral part of aristocratic identity; and they had to court the Crown and maintain their links with the state while striving to preserve as much of their independent social and economic power as possible. Many foundered, but others managed to exploit opportunities at the heart of these contradictions by devising inheritance and marriage strategies to protect their privileges. A radical change in noble strategies of succession was forged. As the feudal aristocracy encountered obstacles to their erstwhile hegemony, a new concern with legitimacy and purity of blood was spawned. Past blood legitimated present and future wealth and power, with the result that genealogists enjoyed a field day. Legal safeguards for patriarchy included tighter control on marriage and firm grips on inheritance.[8] The behaviors consequent from these strategies became the very definitions of aristocratic status.

Crucially, gender determined the transmission of social class. Women were the bearers of social status but did not possess it so as to be able to bestow it on others. If a noblewoman married a mere gentleman, an immediate loss of status ensued, as Giovan Battista de Luca warned in 1657, "the honorary status of the woman depends on the quality of her husband, so she is a sort of moon that receives all her light and splendor from the sun which is her husband."[9] The usual form of social mobility was for women of newly rich families to marry up. Very few daughters of high feudal families married men of the provincial nobility.[10] Such marriages provoked the sharpest criticism, and aristocratic families closed ranks to refuse new families entry to their most exclusive circles.[11] When Zevallos's scribe became a marquis, he was able to marry his daughters to representatives of the aristocracy, but his son Ferdinando "could not marry Neapolitan noblewomen and looked for a wife who was noble but foreign."[12] Although the Vaaz, a family of Portuguese speculators, managed to acquire the title of count, through the acquisition of numerous fiefs, they were barred from the sphere of the most prestigious feudal families.[13] Sixteenth-century treatises resisted cross-class marriage by warning prospective husbands of the risks of marrying a woman who was nobler or richer than they. Her social advantages, it was suggested, would encourage her to abrogate unrightful power to herself.[14] The woman's role in the patrimonial politics of aristocratic families was increasingly marginalized.

The loss of honor and status when an aristocratic woman married a man of lower birth meant that, except in unusual circumstances, aristocratic husbands were sought, but their escalating expense rendered cheaper conventual marriages ever more attractive.[15] If no aristocratic husband was available for an aristocratic woman, then she was seen as making a better wife for Christ than for a non-nobleman in this world: "when noblewomen cannot, because of the poverty of their house, be married to a gentleman equal to them, they choose instead the path of spiritual marriage and become nuns."[16] During periods of economic hardship, more daughters became nuns. The years 1620 to 1660 were particularly tough, and in that period two of the three daughters of both Giovan Battista, marquis of Brienza, and Carlo Caracciolo Sant'Eramo were placed in convents; while in subsequent years no women in the family became nuns.[17] Had more daughters married in this period, the high cost of husbands might have been disastrous for family finances.

Thus female sexuality occupied a central role within the political economy of the aristocracy. The embodied past determined the future. The aristocratic political order occurred through and was guaranteed by the body, by its protection, cultivation, and preservation from the dangers of contact with others, and above all by isolating the female body from others to retain the differential value of the class.[18] Thus the sex-gender system defined aristocratic class identity at its most vulnerable and most ardently defended point. Once the needs of a family had been met in terms of patrilinear inheritance and marriage, stringent circumscription of female sexuality and reproductivity occurred. Virgin daughters in convents thus both protected and represented the impregnable aristocratic body.

Historians of southern Italy have recently demonstrated how aristocratic clan and familial politics and their forging of dynastic connections changed significantly during the sixteenth and seventeenth centuries.[19] Strategies for survival frequently focused on daughters, leading to changes in policies on inheritance, marriage, and dowries when the aristocracy came under particular pressure.[20] Marriage might be limited to one son in each generation, and entails and dowry funds were established and exploited. The exclusion of daughters grew significantly as primogeniture and entail were used increasingly to restrict lineage, especially from the 1570s and 1580s.[21] Primogeniture and the marginalization of women from the circuits of transmission of feudal property led to profound changes in noble customs and in the overall strategies of aristocratic families. The process of formalization of privileges and rules, accompanied by ideological justifications, culminated in the second half of the seventeenth century.

The rules of feudal succession were negotiated between king and nobility over the *longue durée*. Broadly speaking, patterns of inheritance were established under Frederick II (1198–1250), partly by the "Constitutioni di Melfi" of the early thirteenth century and partly by political compromise between the monarch and the nobility.[22] The exclusion of women—so long as they were dowered—was sanctioned; a rule of preference for the eldest son was established; and practices for the transmission of property were strictly delineated.[23] Feudal succession was stringently vertical, with transmission along an ascendant line rigidly prohibited. Feudal property could be passed collaterally to a brother or to a brother's son who, in terms of rightful claim, enjoyed the same status as his father. Besides the distinction between descendant succession and collateral succession, a crucial distinction was established between *feudo antico* (ancient fief), which could be passed in both directions (to the son and his descendants or to a brother), and *feudo nuovo* (new fief), which was subject to immediate escheatment in the absence of a direct descendant.[24] The *Consuetudini della Città di Napoli* (1306) extended to nonfeudal (civic) claims much of the practice adopted under Frederick II, including the principle of excluding women (hitherto restricted to feudal property only).[25] They maintained the distinction between *bona antiqua* (inherited goods) and *bona noviter quaesita* (recently acquired goods) which existed in feudal constitutions, but they reversed the rules of transmission so that a testator could dispose freely of goods acquired directly (and therefore new), whereas with regard to inherited property, if the testator were male he could dispose freely of only half of it, and if female, of only one-tenth; the rest had to go to their sons, then to relatives in the ascendant line, then to other relations. In short, new property, which was not feudal by nature, was treated like a fief and was subject to feudal custom rather than to the normal heredity of Roman law.[26] Consequently, feudal settlements, the customary rights of the city of Naples, and noble dotal customs became mutually interdependent, although no standardized relationship existed between them.

Since Frederick's constitutions were riven with internal contradictions, practice was less systematic and exclusive of women than the principle. In particular, the principle of derogation, by which the monarch could authorize choices of succession, resulted in the practice of more or less private agreements being made between monarch and particular feudal families. The Angevin and Aragonese monarchies adopted this mode such that by the sixteenth century the division of feudal properties had become the norm. During this period, the key issues of exclusion of women and preference for the firstborn son created a forest of particular solutions that profoundly changed the framework of feudal inheritance. Males were preferred in inheritance to females, but women were not utterly excluded. If the original agreement granting the fief allowed the principle of female inheritance, then female exclusion was invalid.[27] This logic encouraged women, with the king's agreement, to buy up a fief again with a new investiture agreement. A daughter of a feudatory of *diritto franco* was also not excluded by a brother unless he personally had provided her with a dowry.[28] In these ways women were not entirely barred from inheriting feudal property until the sixteenth century.[29]

Similarly, until the sixteenth century all sons among leading Neapolitan aristocratic families, such as the Sanseverino, Caracciolo di Brienza, the di Capua of Altavilla, the Carafa, and the Ruffo, regularly inherited feudal property (although, of course, the best was usually bequeathed to the eldest son).[30] From the late fifteenth century, after the confiscations and conspiracies following the Angevin wars, the grand aristocracy actually managed to safeguard and extend their own feudal property.[31] Of particular significance in respect to dowries was B. Camerario's treatise, *Repetitio legis imperialem (sic) de prohibita feudorum alienatione* (Rome, 1558), which directly related feudal transmission to *assenso* (royal assent), which could not be ad hoc—"materia assensus est stricta"—but had to conform with the terms of investiture. Camerario argued that the formula "pro se et heredibus" used in feudal agreements implicitly made alienation of that property impossible and that the sovereign's assent could not authorize the assignation of a fief as dowry, or the division of a titled feudum, since the principle of indivisibility derived from the dignity that the exercise of feudal power conferred on the public good, the protection of the family, and on the prince's honor, and, therefore, "when it is divided it is not divided but corrupted."[32] If the king agreed automatically to the alienation of feudal privileges, he would lose control over the transmission of feudal property that only he could and should exercise. This rigorous reaffirmation of monarchical prerogative explains Charles V's agreement to the 1532 pragmatic, which allowed wider circulation of feudal property while at the same time strengthening his imperial control over the feudal system's mechanisms.

During the second half of the sixteenth century restrictions on feudal inheritance still endorsed by Charles V were overcome. In response to pressure from the indebted baronage, alienation of titled fiefs with revenues of more than 1,000 ducats was permitted in 1561, and in 1586 the distinction between *feudo antico* and *feudo nuovo* was abolished.[33] This had profound implications for the feudal nobility: fiefs were freed to the market and feudal succession was opened considerably. These changes prompted the aristocracy to protect their privileged position by closing rank. Just as during the fourteenth and fifteenth centuries the barons had responded to the monarchy's imposition of primogeniture against their wishes by systematically fragmenting their feudal property in order to spread the family lines and endow them all with noble property, now in the sixteenth century, in vastly different economic and institutional circumstances, having obtained almost complete freedom to convey and sell feudal property, the feudal aristocracy reacted by reaffirming primogeniture and limiting marriage among cadets, effectively reversing the practice of fragmentation of feudal properties.[34] These changes occurred at different speeds and to varying degrees from family to family. The Sanseverino family, for instance, was particularly precocious in adopting these changes, excluding women from inheritance in practice from the mid–fifteenth century and following strict endogamy in lineage.[35]

Exclusion of women was now more rigid and categorical than ever before. The *Prammatica 33 De feudis* issued in Naples in 1595 makes no bones about it:

> These most faithful city, baronage and kingdom recognize how easily estates and fiefs, titled as much as nontitled, acquired over great time, and through much exertion and service, are lost in a moment to their own families when the women succeeding to them marry into other families . . . they entreat Your Majesty to deign to qualify the present feudatories who in their fiefs and estates are able, whether in agreement whilst alive or by last will, to dispose of fees and titles to the benefit of that male of their families who at the time of the disposition will succeed, there not being a female in nearer degree, and likewise even if there are women in closer degree in a position to succeed.[36]

This new principle of exclusion of women from feudal inheritance represented more than a continuum within an established practice; it was a reinvigorated and ruthless response by the feudal aristocracy to threats to its powers.[37] That strategic restructuring of their inheritance practices had far-reaching social, economic, and political consequences, which impacted directly on aristocratic convents.

The establishment of the viceregal court in Naples in 1503 played a vital part in these changes. Thereafter, the old aristocracy in the city came under direct pressure from new families, both those promoted by the Crown and those who profited from new systems of government, finance, and trade. The monarchy tended to promote new families (mostly Neapolitan, Genoese, or Iberian in origin) to serve its financial and administrative needs; and new families ascended in society through the growth of bureaucracy, finance, and trade—mostly international merchants and bankers from outside the kingdom.[38] In the 1630s the Mezzogiorno was characterized by an intense commercialization of fiefs and offices, by Genoese bureaucrats and office holders striking root and by their progressive assimilation into the Neapolitan aristocracy, and by the intersection at their highest levels of business, finance, and political-administrative undertakings—which lent itself in particular to a "feudal offensive," aggressive acquisition or extension of feudal privileges.[39]

The old feudal aristocracy, ousted by the new bureaucratic creatures, sought to compensate for their lost political power by increasing their economic and social powers through the aggressive extension of their feudal privileges and by trading their name and status in the marriage market in exchange for hard cash.[40] Determination to maximize feudal privileges in turn led to significant new strategies in aristocratic clan and familial behavior. Before the mid–sixteenth century clans protected themselves through extension and fragmentation.[41] Great clans not only protected the families that constituted them, but they even promoted the proliferation of the number of families, an insurance policy in politically volatile times.[42] Most sons and daughters were married in order to extend or consolidate the maximum number of marriage alliances.[43] Thus in sixteenth-century Naples the Caracciolo family, one of the greatest and most powerful feudal clans, had more than forty families within its branches, having pursued a policy of "clan fragmentation" throughout the fifteenth and into the sixteenth centuries.[44] But this strategy was more or less reversed during the late sixteenth and seventeenth centuries, when clan fragmentation was replaced by consolidation.[45] Great clans closed ranks and adopted more rigid and formalized inheritance patterns in order to safeguard the patrimony, prestige, and purity of their families. Entails, limits to children's marriages, and legal limits to dowry prices proliferated during these troubled years.

Among the most effective tools in concentrating property and power within the family were primogeniture and entail.[46] Entails prevented the division of estates and the sale of princely seats, guaranteeing the succession of undivided patrimonies through the male line. Since the nature of the entail at its establishment was binding, the aristocracy used entails to tie their property of greatest value—economic or symbolic—closely to their family. Heirs could take benefit from property entailed, but they were bound to pass it to their successors in unaltered form. In Naples the aristocracy first imposed entails—from the late fifteenth century—on those aspects of the patrimony most crucial to familial tradition, prestige and social presence, such as the palace.[47] Multiple family households were common among the nobility in order to save the costs of running several households, and the consequent "centralization" on one seat inevitably linked that palace more intimately to the family name.[48] For example, Giovanni Caracciolo, count of Oppido, created an entail in 1546 on the Caracciolo palace in the Capuana district and added a series of injunctions against removing the escutcheons which adorned these buildings.[49] Thus entails were used to indicate a family's control and privatization of a space in a specific quarter of the city.[50] The Caracciolo's attribution to their palace of the capacity to embody noble values and family identity, the memory of ancestors, and the family's future cohesion indicates the multifaceted aspects of this noble family's sense of itself: feudal but also urban, with a centuries-old tradition of holding power in the Seggio.[51]

Rapidly, however, entails were used to protect whole estates. Some were even instituted by women. Before her death in 1628 Maria Ruffo, princess of Scilla, established in her will an entail of 150,000 ducats to protect from future alienations part of her feudal property.[52] This entail was directed to her daughter, Giovanna, to transmit it entire to her descendants, with the explicit exclusion of any daughters who either married outside the Ruffo clan or did not ensure that their successor would bear the Ruffo family name.[53] In the face of grave financial crisis, the Neapolitan aristocracy widely adopted similar protection of their feudal properties. In spite of the fact that feudal law regulated the succession of fiefs, Philip IV in a crucial change in 1655 allowed the aristocracy to establish entails on fiefs. Nor was it only the great noble families who pursued entails in this fashion. The lesser feudal nobility acted in the same vein, even in some cases engaging in this strategy rather earlier.[54] The agnatic entail thus assumed a meticulous structure, capable of regulating successive passages of property and prompting intense concern with genealogy.[55]

The extension of entails among the Neapolitan aristocracy was an economic and cultural response to the proliferation of enfeoffment that the market of fiefs had produced during the second half of the sixteenth century and the first decades of the seventeenth. After participating in a wave of speculation, the feudal aristocracy reaffirmed its identity as a closed social group and rejected, by individual choices that then became a general rule of rank, the freedom to alienate feudal land—that very principle it had long struggled for against the Crown during the fifteenth and sixteenth centuries.

Although lacking eighteenth-century wills' standardized formulas, wills in this period favored male primogeniture—though this was slightly less pronounced among female testators.[56] In the absence of males in all the lines indicated in a will, women were able to inherit property under certain conditions—namely by changing their surname to that of their eldest son or by paying inheritance to the firstborn male closest in degree in a line not indicated in the will.[57] Some women deviated from the strict system adopted by their male counterparts, even reversing the pattern of favoring the firstborn son. In 1663, for instance, Imara Ruffo, the widow of Giuseppe Spatafora, marquis of San Martino, nominated her firstborn son as particular heir and her cadet sons, Muzio and Pietro, as universal heirs, leaving her daughter, Camilla, the share of legitim.[58]

Noble families attended to patrimonial interests at the expense of individuals. Over and above safeguarding and strengthening noble prestige and protecting family fortunes exposed to the risks of the mechanisms of the market, entails were designed to stem growing debts and to prevent the ruin of a patrimony. As the system of primogeniture and entail determined the passage of goods to the eldest son only, his marriage assumed the greatest consequence. Good dowries concomitantly became assets more exclusive to eldest sons.[59] Aristocratic anxiety to avoid marriages below their social status even prompted the establishment of common dowry funds among families within a clan.[60] In turn, the concentration of grandiose dowries lured the aristocracy into planning for their recuperation, including marriage between parallel cousins or even double marriages between two brothers and sisters. Thus in the grand Neapolitan family of Ruffo di Scilla, Margarita Caterina (d. 1651) married her cousin, Giosia Aquaviva, and Maria, countess of Sinopoli, princess of Scilla, married her cousin Vincenzo Ruffo in 1590.[61] In the Carafa di Stigliano family, Roberta, second child of the first prince of Stigliano, married Diomede Carafa, count and later duke of Maddaloni, and Roberta's brother, Fabio, married Gerolama Carafa, Diomede's sister. Two generations later, two members of the same family married two other members of the Carafa family: Clarice, daughter of Antonio II, prince of Stigliano, married Ferdinando Carafa, duke of Nocera, while Clarice's brother, Marco Antonio, married Beatrice Carafa, daughter of the marquis of S. Lucido; the eldest son, Luigi II, prince of Stigliano, married Isabella Gonzaga, who was from the same family as his mother, Ippolita Gonzaga, and came with a stupendous dowry of one and a half million ducats.[62]

The new strategies adopted by the feudal aristocracy were most far-reaching in their implications for women. As primogeniture and entail became established practice and ever more widespread, the marginalization of women from the control of feudal property was consolidated. Generally speaking, entails excluded women unless they were part of the family or clan through marriage—and quite what that meant became ever more tightly restricted. In the early years of the seventeenth century, when Ettore Pignatelli requested admission for his daughter Giovanna, wife of Fabrizio Pignatelli, marquis of Cerchiara, to the agnatic entail founded in 1526, Philip III referred the decision to the Council of Italy, which responded by strengthening the legitimacy of the entailed succession of a son of a woman married into a family.[63] In 1720 a new pragmatic removed any chance of ambiguity. It ordered "the exclusion not only of the women in immediate line or of a man descending from such a woman even if she had married into the family but also the perpetual exclusion of women and their descendants."[64] Concomitantly, in that same year the baronage achieved the widening of feudal succession as far as the fifth degree. Thus women were increasingly excluded from inheritance even as feudal succession was broadened.

The practice of entail effectively limited dowries in number and sum, making marriage an option reserved for a minority of women among the richest and oldest feudal aristocracy.[65] Restricted dowries rendered prestigious marriages more difficult to achieve and the conventual option correspondingly more attractive. From the early seventeenth century to the first half of the eighteenth, marriage became increasingly restricted among the nobility to one son and one daughter. Thus when Giovan Battista Caracciolo died in 1620, he left debts probably higher than the value of his entire estate, and two of his three daughters became nuns.[66] Likewise, of the sisters of Carlo Ruffo (II), duke of Bagnara, only Maria Ruffo did not become a nun.[67] A skillful exploitation of both dowries and convents could thus be used to pass family property securely down the generations.

As dowries became more exclusive, they became more expensive. Between the mid–fifteenth and mid–sixteenth centuries noble dowries soared in value by five to six times.[68] Sums involved could be breathtaking. For instance, Diana Caracciolo Sicignano carried a dowry of 33,000 ducats to her marriage to Giovan Battista, second marquis of Brienza in 1590.[69] Three of the four sisters of Francesco Ruffo, duke of Bagnara, became nuns in Naples or Messina, which allowed Lucrezia to marry Gerolamo Alercon de Mendoza, marquis of the Valle Siciliana, with a dowry of 40,000 ducats.[70] In 1658 Cristina Gambacorta's magnificent dowry of 46,000 ducats strengthened the claims of her husband, Domenico, seventh marquis of Brienza, to the whole Brienza patrimony.[71] Using a dowry to buy or resecure a fief was sufficiently common by the eighteenth century for a formulaic clause—to the effect that the bride's family waived their rights over the dowry money—to be inserted in dowry contracts to bypass legal complexities when a dowry was put to this use. In itself, this also indicates how dowries were orchestrated increasingly to favor the groom and his family. Despite the warnings of prescriptive literature, in practice control over the woman's dowry in seventeenth-century Naples came to rest more and more in the hands of her husband's family.[72]

Dowries were proportional to the political and economic power of the future husband in relation to that of the bride's family: if he belonged to a grand and important family, the formation of the dowry involved the bride's entire family; whereas if he came from the lesser nobility, the dowry would be modest. In short, dowries were relational. Thus in the 1580s and 1590s the very grand Cantelmo and Tocco families gave their daughters an average of 30,000 ducats, while the di Capua family provided average dowries of 40,000.[73] The sums exchanged depended on the relative prestige of the two families involved, the relationship between them, the relative age of their noble status, and their patrimonies. For this reason daughters did not necessarily receive the same dowry as their mothers.[74] Generally, the great nobility gave dowries lower than they received. Between the early sixteenth and late seventeenth centuries the di Capua of Altavilla family received 343,800 ducats and assigned 290,000 in dowries; in the same period the Carafa di Bruzzano assigned a dowry of over 90,000 ducats in 1665 but received dowries in excess of 100,000.[75]

The exchange of name for cash by old aristocratic families is dramatically illustrated by the marriage in 1688 of Giuseppe Caracciolo, eighth marquis of Brienza, to Teresa, a daughter of nouveau riche Portuguese financier and bureaucrat Emanuele Pinto. Caracciolo was struggling to repurchase his alienated ancestral fiefs of Brienza and Pietrafesa and needed cash urgently. Pinto's family had grown rich rapidly during the later seventeenth century: in 1675 he had purchased for 46,000 ducats the Scrivania di Razione, an especially lucrative financial office charged with authorizing all government payments.[76] He was a member of the Royal Council, a knight of Calatrava, and in 1688 was ennobled as prince of Ischitella. His own marriage, to Geronima Capece Bozzuto, from one of the leading clans of the Seggio of Capuana, had helped make convincing aristocratic connections within Naples, and his daughter's marriage was intended to cement his climb.[77] Eager to be accepted into the highest echelons of Neapolitan aristocratic society, Emanuele paid a splendid dowry of 50,000 ducats for Teresa. For Giuseppe Caracciolo this was a welcome and tidy sum, as his entire patrimony was worth only about 200,000 ducats.[78] Even better was the fact that it came in hard cash, as this allowed him to purchase his alienated fiefs with the money earmarked for that purpose in Teresa's dowry.[79]

During the sixteenth and seventeenth centuries a shift occurred in the allocation of dowry money by grand noble families. The di Capua of Altavilla, for instance, received dowries of 79,800 ducats and gave dowries of 202,000 in the sixteenth century; in the seventeenth century, these figures changed to 264,000 and 80,000 ducats, respectively. In other words, their daughters' matrimonial alliances became financially less significant to grand noble families; those who were married received significantly smaller dowries than their counterparts of half a century earlier, and the increase in the number of women heading for the convent reduced dowry costs considerably.[80] The contraction of cadets' *vitalizi* and daughters' dowries between the seventeenth and eighteenth centuries shows how the weakest members of the noble families were made to bear the costs of the crisis in feudal income. While, for example, during the first half of the sixteenth century in the Carafa dei Maddaloni family in Naples, Count Tommaso made his second son, Roberto, heir to real estate to the tune of 18,000 ducats, by the beginning of the eighteenth century a cadet of the same family received a meager 280 ducats a year.[81] During the second half of the seventeenth and early eighteenth centuries, families frequently fixed a sum deemed suitable for all dowries.[82] Thus, for example, Bartolomeo di Capua established in 1691 that dowries in his family should not exceed 10,000 ducats "on condition that marriages be established with houses of the first order like our own" and that they should be raised from income and not from capital[83]—itself a capitalist, rather than a feudal, strategy. In 1665 Francesco Caracciolo fixed the dowry for his daughters who did not take the veil at 12,000 ducats, but his eldest son and heir, Petraccone, received a dowry of 60,000 ducats in 1662 from his wife, Aurelia Imperiali, daughter of the marquis of Oria. In turn, in his will of 1703 Petraccone reduced the limit on family dowries still further to a mere 4,000 ducats (presumably in addition to shares of dowry funds).[84] Likewise, while in 1616 Giovanna Ruffo di Scilla had a dowry of 100,000 ducats when she married Vincenzo Ruffo-Santapau, marquis of Licodia, and while in 1643 Maria Ruffo di Scilla carried the same sum when she married Francesco Domenico Carafa, half a century later in 1701 when Anna Maria Ruffo di Scilla married Carlo Ruffo, duke of Bagnara, the dowry was down to 36,000 ducats; and by 1703 when Enrica Ruffo di Scilla married Domenico di Somma, prince of Colle, the dowry was only 18,000 ducats.[85] Ironically, during the second half of the eighteenth century, the same families raised the limits on their dowry levels to the older, higher levels in an effort to seal off their social class from the emerging middle class.[86]

Just as the value of dowries changed significantly during this period, so did their composition. Up until the early sixteenth century, daughters, especially only children, received feudal property as part of their dowries. In the seventeenth century, however, renunciation of feudal property in marriage contracts became formulaic.[87] Likewise, the method of payment of dowries altered. During the early sixteenth century dowries were given in cash with at least one-third paid at the time of the marriage. The interval for paying the remaining sum was short, usually four to five years, in a few cases eight years. Thus dowries provided real opportunities for investment. From the late sixteenth century on, the percentage of the dowry paid in cash was reduced, dowries were composed of annual incomes in revenue or yields or credits which were often uncollectible or unrecoverable, and the period for repayment lengthened considerably. During the seventeenth and eighteenth centuries a clause was regularly inserted to protect the woman's family from having to guarantee the collectibility of a portion of her dowry.[88]

Increasingly, dowries were not paid in full. The Pinto Capece-Bozzuto family was shortchanged when their son married his cousin Giulia Caracciolo, daughter of the marquis of Brienza and Teresa Pinto. By 1755 they had received only 13,523 of the 39,000 ducats promised as dowry fifty years earlier by Giulia

Caracciolo's father.[89] Women usually paid the price for their father's failure to pay their dowries. Pasquale Caracciolo justified the complete absence of any bequest to his wife, Francesca Sersale, in his will of 1662: "for the space of 27 years I have spent much money at law to recuperate the dowry monies of the marchioness"; and in his will of 1683 Tiberio Ruffo bitterly bequeathed his wife "the unpaid dowries and this instead of inheritance."[90]

However, by the mid–eighteenth century conventions fashioned to protect family wealth sometimes proved to be counterproductive shackles. In 1757 the stranglehold of entail had become too much for Luigi Sanseverino, who brought an action against the vicariate in Naples, requesting, "notwithstanding the infinite debts" that burdened his patrimony, to dissolve the chains of entail so as to be able to marry his daughter Maria Francesca to Giuseppe Spinola with a dowry of 60,000 ducats, since the maximum figure of 15,000 ducats for dowries of women in the Sanseverino family, fixed by Giuseppe Leopoldo in his will in 1726 to allay the financial difficulties the family then faced, had become "too small and miserable for such a respectable magnate's house" and was seriously damaging the prestige of the Sanseverino.[91]

Aristocratic patrimonial politics marginalized women in other ways. Women's control over property and their children was sharply curtailed from the end of the sixteenth century, in parallel with the changes in the dowry system. During the late fifteenth and early sixteenth centuries, in addition to the restitution of the dowry *al dotario*, equivalent to one-third of her husband's feudal goods, a widow received particular bequests and the general usufruct of the patrimony of her husband. Together with members of her husband's family, a widow could steer the economic decisions regarding the family, both in her capacity as mother of their children and as executor of her husband's will. Control of the marital house, jewelry, and furnishings was usually hers. But from the late sixteenth century on, a new harshness in their terms to widows emerges in male wills. In his will of 1626 Luigi Vincenzo di Capua, for instance, stipulates that his wife might remain in the house only one year after his death. Widows' jewelry was frequently given to the eldest son or sold to finance the younger children, and specific bequests to widows disappeared.[92]

The changes in the nature of the dowry, its greater limitations, the diminution of the role of the *dotario*, and the progressive rigidity of men's wills indicate changed attitudes to women and reveal a conception of the family that was increasingly authoritarian, patriarchal, and patrilineal. Such formalized systems of inheritance tended to freeze a family's economic circumstances and block economic change, expressed ideologically in the seventeenth century as noblesse oblige. The maintenance of patrilineage was a mainspring of the identity of the Neapolitan aristocracy as a social group. By the end of the seventeenth century, male primogeniture and entail, as rigidly pursued by the richest and most powerful southern Italian families, allowed the old aristocracy to retain its social and economic primacy. While its numbers were much reduced as a result of the policy allowing only one son in each generation to marry, the old aristocracy successfully protected and consolidated its patrimonies.[93]

Although the burden of dowries was felt only in relation to female offspring, the growing emphasis on primogeniture meant that younger sons were also increasingly pushed into the Church (when the army was an inappropriate solution).[94] Fewer aristocratic offspring got married. Sons rarely married before the death of their father.[95] In short, there were fewer husbands to go around and fewer wives required. And convents could accommodate the shortfall with grace and purpose. The dowry system, therefore, produced both problems for the aristocracy in marrying their daughters and solutions for their safeguarding in convents.

THE CONVENTUAL SOLUTION

Convents allowed the maintenance of family honor, while saving the family purse. Convent dowries were obligatory, high, and rising. But they were not as costly as marriage dowries (which could represent five years' income for wealthy families), and they did not necessarily involve land. They obviated the need for lavish marriage dowries and the splitting up of estates, and they were socially acceptable, even prestigious, institutions. Not only did the family not lose financially, but it could gain in religious standing: a daughter's virginity, so theologically important, remained connected in the eyes of contemporaries with the family. A daughter could dedicate her prayers to the family. And once a daughter was married off to God, she was conveniently married for eternity, whereas a mortal husband did not necessarily solve the problem once and for all—though crucially, too, fathers could almost always remove daughters from convents if family fortunes changed. Solemn vows created comfortable security for both convents and families, because in canon law they were irreversible and excluded the nun from inheriting or bequeathing property and from valid marriage. Insistence on solemn vows and cloister therefore represented the most secure form of control possible.[96] In addition to meeting nuns' material needs, religious houses provided a social justification for their enforced celibacy and helped to police it. Thus convents converted potential loss into economic, political, social, and spiritual gain.

Aristocratic clans used special bequests to build support and solidify allegiance in specific convents to protect their family or clan at its most vulnerable points. The Caracciolo, for instance, aggressively exploited bequests to

Neapolitan convents to safeguard the present and future fortunes of their house. Alfonso Caracciolo, count of Brienza, left a bequest in 1543 of a 700 ducat annuity, payable from income received from the collection of the fish tax, to the monastery of S. Maria de Agnone "on condition that the said monastery may not accept women to take the veil except noblewomen from Capuana and Nido and that all nuns of the said monastery do not exceed the number 24 and six lay sisters and that the women of the Caracciolo family be not required to pay a dowry of more than 200 ducats."[97] In this way Caracciolo secured special low rates for his family, while ensuring the highest reputation socially for S. Maria de Agnone. Such actions represent the other side of the coin of the policy of pursuing entails and primogeniture. Caracciolo endeavored both to secure the protection of his family's reputation by providing for its women and to shore up the institutions that preserved their honor once they were outside the immediate protection of marriage and the family.

There was a fine balance to be struck in such attempts at social engineering. If they went too far, if concern with the family's most vulnerable points was seen to outweigh the prestige of the clan, or if concern for a daughter's well-being might prejudice that of sons, protest was vociferous. This occurred after the last count of Oppido in the line of the Caracciolo family died without heirs in 1630. He left his entire inheritance to the Annunziata on condition that from its income each year, 1,000 ducats should be put aside, and every three years the accumulated 3,000 ducats should be given as dowry to a daughter of the Caracciolo family; of the rest, 6 ducats a month should be given to poor cavalieri of the same family.[98] This upset members of the Caracciolo clan, who thought it unbecoming to the family's reputation, and they successfully petitioned Pope Urban VIII to change the conditions to establish a seminary for Caracciolo family sons.[99] Thus the precariousness of family prestige sometimes restricted the old feudal aristocracy's interventions in convents in ways from which the new bureaucratic nobles were free.

Socioeconomic, rather than religious, factors caused aristocratic conventual expansion at this date. The "conventual solution" was by no means confined to southern Italy. An astounding 50 percent of noble girls became nuns in twenty-seven Milanese noble families between 1600 and 1650.[100] In a sample of twenty-one Florentine patrician families between 1500 and 1799, 44 percent of daughters surviving infancy were placed in convents just before marriage age.[101] Indeed, there is some evidence to suggest that this practice was less pronounced in Naples than elsewhere. Based on his detailed study of the Caracciolo di Brienza, Tommaso Astarita argues that the Neapolitan aristocracy was "perhaps unique in only partially limiting the number of daughters who were allowed to marry." In his view, most daughters did marry: "among the many descendants of Domizio Caracciolo Rosso (d.1498) up to the early seventeenth century, it is possible to identify the lot of at least twenty women, only one of whom entered a nunnery."[102] But as Astarita acknowledges, the presence of a daughter in a convent is comparatively easily overlooked by genealogists.[103]

Convent records demonstrate that aristocratic families were regularly and well represented among the nuns (whether willingly or not). At least seven women in the Caracciolo clan in 1632 and at least twelve members of the Carafa family in 1710 were in Neapolitan convents.[104] Among the greatest Neapolitan families represented at S. Gregorio Armeno in the 1670s and 1680s were Lucrezia Pignatelli (abbess), Lucrezia di Sangro, Eleonora di Sangro, Anna di Sangro, Eleonora Carafa, Maria Capece Minutolo, Tommasa Carracciolo, Luisa Carracciolo, and Giulia Frezza.[105] Meanwhile, the list of abbesses at Donna Regina between 1525 and 1717 represents many of the greatest Neapolitan families, including the Carracciolo, de Rago, Loffredo, de Sangro, Carafa, Pignone, d'Aquino, Filomarino, Capece, Pignatelli, Spinelli, and Acquaviva.[106] In 1738 nuns at the Sapienza included sister Maria Domenica Carafa, prioress; sister Maria Serafina Arrezzo, deputy prioress; sister Maria Margarita Ruffo; sister Maria Costanza di Capua; and sister Chiara Maria d'Aquino.[107]

The dramatic increase in the number of convents founded during the seventeenth century must be understood in part as a response by noble families to threats to their economic and social privileges posed by the development of the modern state and, to a lesser degree, by inflation, as much as to any religious impetus provided by the Council of Trent. In fact, the surge in numbers of female and male monacations from the late sixteenth to the early eighteenth centuries among the nobility had no parallel among the non-noble class, the *popolari* (commoners).[108] The significance of convents for family fortunes meant that they experienced demands and pressures that militated against their spiritual mission, despite Trent's attempts to defeat secular concerns.[109] "The great obstacle to Tridentine uniformity was not individual backsliding or Protestant resistance, but the internal articulations of a society in which kinship was a most important bond," as John Bosay pointed out in 1970.[110]

Avoidance of marriage dowries by families and the benefits to convents of accepting young women from noble families meant that young girls received pressure from both institutions. When Nunzia Oriundo, a boarder at the convent of the Incurabili in Naples, wished to marry, she was opposed, for very different reasons, by both her brother-in-law and by nuns in the convent who did not wish her to leave.[111] Convent girls might be pushed hither and thither, at the mercy of their families both within and without the convent, as is clear from the case of Reparata, the sister of the duke of Atri. In 1662 the duke complained to the Sacra Congregazione dei Regolari that his sister, a boarder at S. Andrea, had been taken to another convent in order to explore her will ("per l'esplorazione della sua voluntà"). The duke suspected that she had been persuaded to become a nun by her aunts, who were nuns at that house. So the girl was moved to the convent of S. Gregorio, but the duke feared that even there she would be subordinated and abused, and requested her transfer to S. Maria Regina Coeli. This transfer probably never occurred, since in 1666 Reparata Acquaviva took the veil in S. Gregorio.[112]

Pacts exchanging comfort for spiritual intercession between fathers and their daughter-nuns were multifaceted. Explicitly on 21 January 1612, Francesco Villani agreed to pay his daughters, sister Maria Villani and sister Giovanni Maria (his daughter Cornelia), both nuns in the convent of S. Giovanni Battista, 36 ducats a year for life, and asked them—as if in exchange—to pray for his soul: "To . . . my two daughters with all possible affection I leave my paternal blessing, and I beg them to bless the memory of my soul in their prayers in which I have considerable faith because of the most holy choice that they voluntarily made with their lives."[113] Implicit here is the notion that his daughters' prayers are more worthy and likely to be efficacious because they had become nuns voluntarily. Spiritual returns could, therefore, be greater if a girl opted to become a nun of her own accord. One can imagine how subsequent pressure, more or less subtle, could result in a young girl's entering a convent, such that it would become impossible to distinguish her wishes from those of more prominent family members.[114]

Inevitably, the problems generated by the conventual dowry system spilled over the highest conventual walls. Forced monacation lurked like a guilty secret between aristocrats and clerics, always present because always denied. In his life of St. Asprenus, first Christian and first bishop of Naples, published in Naples in 1696 and dedicated to Archbishop Cardinal Cantelmo, Sigismondo Sicola naturalized female monachism by arguing that Neapolitan women had dedicated their lives to Christ before men had.[115] He expressed a certain sympathy for women "buried for life," but he justified enclosure in religious terms and describes their position as enviable: "[Those women] contained in those blessed walls open the doors of divine mercy. And it is also true that there is considerable martyrdom in a well-brought-up woman seeing herself enclosed within cloisters for ever, and she can rightly lament that she has been buried alive. But who does not know that that solitary life just as it renders her foreign to the scourges of the world, connects her uninterruptedly to the sweetnesses of Heaven?"[116] With these exclamations about their happy lot, any sympathy for nuns evaporates: "Most happy, then, o you heavenly seraphs, you purest white swans, you purest doves from the Empyrean, who, hatching Christian Virtue in your most chaste nests, know to produce shares of Paradise for your celestial Spouse."[117] Thus the rhetoric of the celestial Bridegroom also provided a ready justification for the practice of enclosure.

Like marriage dowries, conventual dowries were established relationally. Sometimes money mattered more to a convent than did a connection to a titled family; at others familial prestige allowed financial considerations to assume secondary importance. S. Francesco delle Cappuccinelle, for instance, eager for noble connections, made special provision for the duke of Montecorice. His daughter, sister Maria Illuminata dallo Spirito Santo (formerly Angiola Giordano), was the convent's first noble nun in 1700. In 1712 another daughter followed. Both paid dowries of 1,500 ducats. In 1721 the convent not only accepted two more of his daughters, but kept their dowries artificially low at the same figure and accepted payment in installments from income from rents on houses, because the duke could not pay in cash.[118] Very occasionally, even the most aristocratic convents accepted a woman without a dowry. Thus sister Patrizia Maiorana (Virginia Maiorana, the daughter of Carlo Maria Maiorana and Lucrezia Carafa), described as "poor" and "without dowry," was received at S. Giuseppe dei Ruffo in 1605.[119] Only rich convents could afford such risky strategies. Patrizia Maiorana lived to the ripe old age of seventy-two—forty-four years at the expense of her sister nuns.[120]

Sometimes dowries were transferable. Monies were transferred, for instance, from Giulia Caracciolo to Isabella Acquaviva at the convent of S. Gregorio Armeno in Naples in 1628.[121] In June 1628 Signore Carlo Brancaccio, in charge of the bonds established for Giulia Caracciolo, promised to pay 105 ducats annually to the convent of S. Gregorio to cover the cost of food for Donna Isabella Acquaviva. In addition, he promised 1,500 ducats for her dowry, 400 ducats for the cost of her monacation, and a further 400 ducats for the expenses of profession. Another 50 ducats were to be paid to her annually throughout her life. "Other promises" were also made, presumably pledges of small sums of money.[122]

It was usually in convents' interests to accept girls from rich backgrounds since legacies and gifts were always a possibility and they could, in rare circumstances, unexpectedly become heirs of family fortunes. In January 1636, for example, the convent of S. Francesco delle Cappuccinelle a Pontecorvo received a grand payment of 8,894 ducats, sizable in relation to that convent's finances, which was the inheritance of the deceased Marc'Antonio Brunengo della Riviera di Genoa and came to the convent through the persons of sisters Maria Arcangiola and Maria Teresa di Giuseppe, his daughters and heirs.[123]

High conventual dowries meant that female monastic houses often became very rich. This enhanced their attractiveness to aristocratic families, since it made them more exclusive environments and ensured that their daughters would live comfortably, even if not to the standard to which they were accustomed. Conventual dowries afforded noble daughters privileges within religious institutions and, in return, the system was jealously safeguarded by the aristocracy. Aristocratic opposition scuppered most proposed reforms. For instance, a proposal made in 1602 to change the system of earmarking dowries to a more communal dowry system in 1602, provoked consternation from the nobles, as Antonio Bulifon noted in his diary:

> And on 17 April the marquis of Bracigliano was sent from Naples as ambassador to father Cesare Miroballo, with 400 ducats a month, for the lawsuit that was pending with Cardinal Gesualdo about reforming the nuns, that is that women on entering a convent to become nuns, should be obliged to put their dowry [to the use of] the community; to which proposal the nobles objected, refusing [the idea] that the abundant dowries assigned to their daughters should be placed in common with small dowries issuing from non-nobles, which would result in nonmonacations in future.[124]

Although the Pope initially rejected Miroballo's appeal, the latter persisted and managed to stay the pope's hand on the matter. The reform was revoked and Miroballo's triumph was celebrated by the Eletti and the deputies of S. Lorenzo.[125]

CONVENTS AND THE NEW NOBLES

Just as convents played a crucial role in the strategies of lineal and financial centralization of the feudal aristocracy, they were exploited by the new nonfeudal nobility, though for different reasons. Depositing a daughter in a prestigious convent helped the new nobles to establish themselves socially; to gain closer contact with old aristocrats through their daughters, sister nuns in the same institutions; and even to accrue the respectability conferred by conspicuous patronage of prestigious religious institutions.

A particularly emblematic example of this strategic use of convents by the new nonfeudal nobility occurred at the convent of Croce di Lucca during the mid–seventeenth century, where Nicolò Giudice exploited the conventual system to advance his family, protect his name, and forge closer links with the highest social classes and the Church in Naples, both by placing his own daughters there and by patronizing it financially with particular élan.

Giudice was a particularly prominent member of the Genoese bankers and merchants who were central to the bureaucratic financial establishment of mid-seventeenth-century Naples.[126] He was from a rich Genoese family of merchants and bankers established in Naples, the son of Marcantonio Giudice, who bankrolled the Spanish monarchy and was rewarded by being executed on a charge of fraudulent bankruptcy. Perhaps his father's loss prompted Nicolò to abandon financial speculation and to diversify his economic investments—to include feudal landownership and employment in the bureaucracy—but he was not alone in embracing this strategy.[127] Whatever his precise motivation, the decision was shrewd, drawing together as it did the economic and social clout of feudalism with the political influence of professional service, and he rose rapidly up the social scale. In 1615 he received the office of Corriere Maggiore, head of the postal service of the kingdom, which furnished him an income of about 34,000 ducats a year and the credit and confidence of Viceroy d'Ossuna. This allowed Giudice to assume a visible profile in Neapolitan society and to rise to the highest ranks of the nobility. He entered the Order of the Knights of St. James in 1618, received the title of prince of Cellamare in 1631, and the next year became a member without salary of the Collateral Council.[128] An eye for the main chance, combined with social and political acumen, allowed him to make his mark financially at the viceregal court and in ecclesiastical circles. His work of mediation during both the Revolt of Masaniello and the French expedition of 1654, led by the duke of Guise, and his shrewd choice of marriage partners for his descendants all played a part.[129] He followed this success over the following years by buying up considerable feudal property in Puglia, which brought not only financial advantage but consolidated his social status, making him one of the leading figures of the kingdom.

But new titles, current political influence, and financial success were not enough. Giudice reinforced his success by extending it temporally, into the past (genealogically) and into the future (through ecclesiastical patronage), even to eternity. In the mid-1630s, he commissioned Genoese scholar Federico Federici to compile his genealogical tree for an official history of his family, to which he accredited noble origins. But this bid ran into the sands. Federici, currently engaged on a monumental history of Genoese families, believed in a strict equivalence between nobility and feudalism, and he retorted that the Giudice family originated from the coastal area and that it was not noble but *popolare*.[130] Giudice responded to this setback with his customary versatility. He simply turned to biographers willing to oblige him with the story he desired of an ancient family of illustrious origin and *pietas christiana*, securely rooted in the city, which had served the republic through government and military service. Thus his long-lived noble identity, equated with participation in government, was secured.

Next Giudice turned to the future and to the Croce di Lucca. Andrea Sbarra and Cremona Spinelli, husband and wife, originally from Lucca, had founded the church in 1534 in honor of the holy crucifix known as the Volto Santo, much venerated in Lucca.[131] They also provided money for a convent, and in 1537, in an adjacent residence, Observant Carmelite nuns began to settle.[132] The small community quickly became renowned for its piety and discipline, and by 1624 there were eighty resident nuns, keeping as many as six priests for divine service, together with minor clerks.[133] In short, minor nobility and bureaucrats with connections at court were well represented here, well before Giudice committed his money to the convent in 1643.[134] The strategic selection of sister Cristina de Stefano, from one of the most eminent families of the aristocracy of Salerno, as prioress in 1593 signaled the convent's ambition to improve its aristocratic connections.[135] By the time of Giudice's bequest, therefore, the Croce di Lucca was a convent on the rise, patronized by ambitious bureaucrats on the make, with a seemly aristocratic sheen.

The rebuilding of the convent began in 1643. Giudice's bequest was prompted by an invitation to help the nuns in their endeavor by Cardinal Filomarino, who shrewdly recognized the potential dovetailing between the interests of the ambitious Genoese and the convent. Between 1643 and 1653 the prince of Cellamare spent at least 72,530 ducats on the building and decoration of the convent; in all, through the purchase of houses and land, Cellamare spent over 77,000 ducats.[136] Of this the nuns repaid to him as much as 68,000 ducats. Giudice decided to resume his credit, in return for certain requests made quite unabashedly on behalf of his family, both inside and outside the convent. Between 1641 and 1650 five of his daughters, Aurelia, Elena, Isabella, Eleonora, and Maria, entered the convent, where their maternal aunt was prioress—well placed to protect their interests. The first four became nuns, while Maria remained a boarder (*educanda*).[137] Each girl received a dowry of 1,000 ducats and the special privilege of a private servant. These privileges, negotiated on the back of Cellamare's lavish patronage of the monastery fabric, and his sister-in-law's influence from within ensured his daughters prominent and protected positions within the convent. Advantages accrued to Cellamare's family outside the convent walls also. In terms of reaping honor, prestige, and respectability for his entire family, these were sure-sighted investments.

Giudice was not alone among men on the make in exploiting the Croce di Lucca for the social advancement of his family, but he was one of the most successful, as Carlo Celano's glowing account confirms:

> The prince of Cellamare . . . a cavalier of incomparable wisdom and of no ordinary reputation for his rare qualities, having a number of daughters, decided in his goodness to allow to the same daughters the honored choice of their condition. Some of them wished to marry and they were placed with suitable husbands from the first rank of our nobility, with respectable dowries. Aurelia, Maria, Elena, Eleonora and Isabella del Giudice decided that they wanted no spouse other than Jesus

> Christ and that therefore they became nuns here. . . . The Prince their father, in addition to the dowries and the generous life-long annuities [*vitalizi*] that he assigned them, for it to be known to the world that these four daughters had become nuns through religious fervor alone and not to save on dowries, had the monastery entirely rebuilt, spending more than 120,000 scudi in addition to the rich chaplaincies that he established there; and he would have spent more had there been need for more; so that this monastery is among the most beautiful and magnificent that exists, not only in our city, but throughout Italy, having been entirely rebuilt; and if one could see inside, it would be a marvel to each through its magnificence.[138]

Although Celano credits Giudice with giving 120,000 scudi, almost half of this sum comprised the dowries of the four Giudice nuns and payment for their servant. Even in this regard, Giudice achieved a handsome bargain. On the strength of recommendation of no less a person than Cardinal Filomarino, Giudice's third daughter entered the Croce di Lucca at the standard dowry rate and without loss of privileges (active and passive voice). In his recommendation, addressed to the Congregation of Bishops and Regulars, Cardinal Filomarino described the prince as a "very pious, prudent cavaliere, and one of the richest that the city possesses."[139] Clever self-presentation and a display of wealth, strategically focused, directly assisted Giudice's social rise. His good reputation, bolstered by Filomarino, was as decisive as any real facts of the matter. Moreover, part of Giudice's generous "gift" was no more than a loan. Between 1644 and 1650 the convent repaid 8,900 ducats to the prince of Cellamare in several installments, money which the convent received from the monacations of Angelica and Cecilia Lubrano, Violante Capece, and the daughter of the marquis of Taviano, Isabella de Franchis (themselves perhaps attracted by Giudice's investments).[140]

A slick operation, Nicolò Giudice's legacy accrued him considerable social prestige for comparatively little economic outlay. Indeed, the sum he paid was considerably less than that credited to him by later generations.[141] On the strength of his bequest, the prince negotiated generous terms from the convent for both his daughters and his wife. But Giudice was concerned not only with securing his own reputation and comfort for his family in this world; he was after no less a prize than eternal life, one of the most sought-after social privileges. To this end also he exploited his convent connections. Eleonora Palagano and Giudice's daughters, specifically as a result of his bequest, were allowed to nominate *in perpetuo* four chaplains for the celebration of four masses a day for the prince and his family, and the entire convent had to recite litanies, chosen by Cellamare, for his soul. To cement even closer ties between the convent and his family, he requested a tomb for himself and his descendants in the chancel and arranged for an inscription to be placed in the choir in memory of his good deeds for the convent, so that nuns could remember him in their prayers.[142] Although his choice of burial site indicates that Giudice lacked burial options of greater antiquity, it should be seen, like his constructed family tree, as part of his ambition to plant unmistakably aristocratic roots.[143] Even the prince's burial, therefore, formed part of his organization of his symbolic power, and his choice of its location ensured an elegant and spiritually distinguished resting place for his body, while binding his family name inexorably to the Croce di Lucca. In short, the convent bestowed religious charisma upon the prince's family.

Nicolò Giudice treated the convent of S. Croce di Lucca like a feudal appendage, as a dependence of his family palace. In disregard of all the rules of enclosure, his wife and members of her family visited each month, ate there, and circulated freely in the dormitories. For almost thirty years the convent was steered by members of his family. Between 1663 and 1693, with only a few brief interruptions, the position of abbess was occupied by Dianora Palagano, his sister-in-law, and Aurelia and Elena, his daughters. Many of Giudice's nieces, on both sides of the family, entered the convent, either simply as *educande* or to take the veil, when they invariably received the best positions.[144] Here, too, during the decades around Masaniello's revolt, side by side with Cellamare's daughters in the convent were daughters of some of the highest magistrates of the Kingdom of Naples.[145] Here, then, was one of the nodes of intersection of a crucial network of relations of business and clientelism with which Cellamare was linked.

In all this, Nicolò Giudice's wife, Ippolita Palagano, played a crucial but unsung role. Her marriage to Giudice in 1623 brought him vital feudal lands, prerogatives, and titles.[146] The daughter and heir of Lucio Palagano and Zenobia della Marra, she came from an old noble family of Trani, and her dowry included the fiefs of Corato, Cerignola, Casal di Mercurio, S. Antonio di Mercurio, S. Antonio, Pietrafesa, Candela, Rocca, Tito, Torre Santa Susanna, Acquaricca, S. Vito, and Cellamare. Ippolita brought Giudice the vital personal connections to the Croce di Lucca, since her sister, Dianora Palagano, was a nun at the convent, which she had entered as an *educanda* in September 1617, aged barely six. Although her dowry of 1,000 ducats was paid to the convent in effect only in 1645, her presence at Croce di Lucca formed the platform on which Giudice built.[147] Between them, Giudice and his wife secured the necessary familial, political, social, economic, bureaucratic, and spiritual substance to safeguard the future of their family.

Significantly, the family's fortunes continued to be tightly woven to the Croce di Lucca and, as certain branches accrued greater status, even to the grander convents of Donnaromita and S. Gregorio Armeno. Nicolò Giudice and Ippolita Palagano had fourteen children. One son followed a political career at the court in Madrid; the other in the Church in Rome. Domenico, their first son to survive infancy, followed his father's footsteps in pursuing a bureaucratic career, serving the Spanish Crown on various royal councils in Italy and Madrid, and at the courts of Paris and Savoy (Turin).[148] He married Costanza Pappacoda in 1653, the youngest daughter of Elena and Giuseppe Cavaniglia, prince of Triggiano and marquis of Capuruso. Two of their daughters entered the monastery of Croce di Lucca; two others entered the convent of S. Maria Donnaromita, under the protection of older nuns there from the Cavaniglia and Pappacoda families.[149] In other words, daughters were distributed to maintain the family's representation at Croce di Lucca, while strengthening social allegiances at another key convent, Donnaromita.

While his sons were sent away to make their name and broader fortunes in Rome, Madrid, and beyond, like most Neapolitan aristocrats Giudice kept his daughters close at hand. They all remained in Naples, and he did all he could to ensure that their lives would be as comfortable as possible and rebound as much religious and social prestige to the family. The daughters at Croce di Lucca both served and were served by Giudice's wealth and status. His other daughters, Cornelía, Zenobia, Chiara, and Teresa, married members of the prestigious Seggi of Capuana and Nido, each with an impressive dowry of 60,000 ducats.[150] Thus money was traded for social standing. Some of the daughters of these marriages entered the Croce di Lucca, under the care of their maternal aunts. Lucrezia, Laura, and Dianora Caracciolo, daughters of Prince della Villa and Zenobia Giudice; Agnese and Eleonora Pignatelli, daughters of the dukes of Bisaccia; and Zenobia and Chiara Carafa, daughters of Teresa Giudice and the duke of Noia, all entered the Croce di Lucca, making it a real stronghold for the clan.[151] Other daughters entered the convents of S. Maria Donnaromita and S. Gregorio Armeno.[152] The duke of Noia's remaining daughters became nuns at Gesù delle Monache, which, together with the Sapienza, represented a stronghold of the Carafa family.[153] Within a generation, the Giudice family had ramified their social success across the city.[154] Bound to the noblest Seggi and the Croce di Lucca, and linked to Naples's grandest convents, the family's pious reputation and its prestigious connections within Naples were secured for future generations. The grandiose Palazzo Cellamare (formerly Carafa di Stigliano) in the Chiaia district of Naples is the starkest sign of the success of the Giudice family. Antonio Giudice, prince of Cellamare and duke of Giovinazzo, acquired the earlier palace in 1696 for 18,000 ducats and immediately set about ambitious building works which resulted in the grandiose building we see today.[155] That palace was built, figuratively speaking, on the foundations laid by Antonio's grandfather, Nicolò Giudice.

The Croce di Lucca was particularly favored by men of similar background to Giudice, including the Zufia and de Franchis. Like Nicolò Giudice, they undertook a strategy of diversification in investments in feudal land, finance, and offices and sent their daughters to that convent.[156] From Cellamare's own circle, Cesare Lubrano, an able merchant and financial speculator who later gained the title of duke of Ceglie, smoothed the way into the Croce di Lucca for two members of his family by providing, in addition to the usual dowries, a contribution to the convent of 800 ducats each, various annuities totaling 428 ducats, and the promise of a further annuity should either of them come to hold the post of sacristan.[157] Gaining access to a convent was only the first stage in a strategy of securing lasting familial links to and influence within it.

Sometimes potentates' interventions were designed less to safeguard family interests than to promote specific social groups. Like Nicolò Giudice, Antonio Diez y Gomez, a Spanish bureaucrat with important offices at court, including that of Secretary of State and War, capitalized on his patronage of a female convent to achieve several interrelated aims. He used it to secure a position of respectability and security for his family in Neapolitan society; to promote his good standing with the Church and with God; to safeguard his soul; and he also deployed it to further Spanish interests in Naples. His bequests began fairly modestly in about 1712 when he arranged for some paintings to be given to the convent of S. Francesco delle Cappuccinelle a Pontecorvo. Here he set up a dowry fund of 70 ducats for a Spaniard or, failing that, a Neapolitan.[158] Some years later he arranged for the establishment in the same conventual church of two perpetual chaplaincies, once all four of his daughters were dead, to say 3,000 reliquiam masses for his soul and for those of his relations. He also left substantial property to the convent.[159] This bequest ensured special privileges for his family within the convent, as indicated by the fact that four of his daughters became nuns there between 1712 and 1725.[160] Like Nicolò Giudice, Antonio Diez y Gomez selected a comparatively new convent for his attentions. Unlike S. Chiara or the Sapienza, S. Francesco delle Cappuccinelle, which was founded as a conservatory in 1585, lacked a long history of connections with aristocratic and royal families. Indeed, the first recorded monacation of a noble's daughter at S. Francesco occurred only in 1700.[161] Diego y Gomez's relative social position at S. Francesco was therefore higher than it would have been at the grander convents and allowed him more visibly to mark its culture.

Conversely, S. Francesco delle Cappuccinelle benefited from accepting nuns of bureaucratic, Spanish, or Genoese origin. The Razionale of the Reale Camera della Sommaria, Giovanni Francesco Sebastiano, sent two daughters there in 1607, and two of his granddaughters followed in 1615.[162] The convent also inherited considerable sums from other Genoese families.[163]

The conventual system intertwined and made apparent the relations between blood, familial prestige, the dowry system, and social charisma. Insecurities and uncertainties about the nature of those relationships were directly responsible for Cellamare's spending money on the fabric and decoration of the monastic buildings themselves. Nowhere is this clearer than in Celano's claim that it was to show the world that his daughters had become nuns from religious conviction, and not to save on dowries, that the prince had the monastery rebuilt. Significantly, such a claim was necessary to counter any ready assumption that his motives had been economic. Cellamare's belief that spiritual commitment could be demonstrated by spending vast sums of money on a convent reveals the profound extent to which religious and secular values were confused and enmeshed. Paradoxically, the usual practice of protecting feudal privileges and money by ensconcing daughters in convents could lead nobles to flamboyant display of expenditure on convents in order to demonstrate that this was not their motivation. In short, Giudice's success was both partly derived from and spectacularly announced by his flamboyant patronage of the Croce di Lucca convent.

From the mid–seventeenth century, a group of men like Nicolò Giudice, aware of being part of an international elite but by origin outsiders in the Kingdom of Naples, carefully inserted themselves into Neapolitan society. Connected by numerous business and political ties, their lives were marked by the importance of the viceregal court, by their support of Madrid during the military emergency, by the display of their palaces, and by their careful support of particular ecclesiastical institutions. The behavior of this group was not rigorously determined by the logic of patrilineage, but, rather, worked for the prestige and honor of the whole family. The new nobility displayed a greater level of engagement with central political power, both through marriage alliances and positions within the state apparatus, than the old citizen patriciate, but in other ways their paths paralleled each other and even intersected. The exploitation of ecclesiastical positions and of female monasteries was shared by both groups. The new nobility here emulated the old established nobility, but they also perhaps more aggressively bound their family fortunes to those of the convents. What was undertaken by the old nobility to secure its position and prevent financial loss was undertaken by the new nobility to consolidate its position, raise its profile, and guarantee its name in the city and beyond. Convents were the lucky beneficiaries of patronage and attention from both (competing) groups.

At the heart of female monasticism was a fundamental contradiction. Conventual life fulfilled many social, political, and economic functions that had nothing to do with the theological underpinnings of virginity or with broader religious beliefs. Convents were particularly useful to aristocratic families, and especially to their heads, in providing a respectable solution to the problem of surplus daughters, particularly younger daughters, difficult wives, or widows. They allowed the patrimony to remain intact by circumventing the necessity of marrying off daughters and the concomitant necessity of lavishing upon them as marriage dowry family land and magnificent wealth. But convents also provided a thoroughly respectable alternative to marriage (avoiding the indignities and lack of respectability of the other principal alternatives to marriage, particularly spinsterhood or prostitution—and, of course, there were very few aristocratic spinsters, let alone prostitutes). Convents not only conserved family property; they also preserved family honor by protecting the chastity of daughters. In addition, they provided for daughters the opportunity of spending their lives in service to their blood family, by praying for their souls and by acting as their representative inside the convent, sometimes institutions of considerable political, social, and civic power.

Whether formally articulated or simply understood through practice, convents were either grand and aristocratic or more modest and nonaristocratic. The emphasis among the aristocratic convents on their social distinction tended to elide distinctions between high birth and spirituality. This startling elision between social rank and holiness, between the social world and the most radical and absolute form of negation of the world, had two notable consequences.[164] First, the confluence of noble and spiritual values meant that the aristocratic policy of placing surplus daughters in convents could be effected relatively painlessly to all concerned. Second, this confluence further disguised economic and social motivations behind monacations, making it always possible to present the social in terms of the holy.

While feudal aristocratic families tended to use convents to avoid loss of feudal prerogative, the new aristocracy, which had risen through service at court, exploited convents to safeguard their family name and honor and to increase their social and religious status. The sometimes startlingly generous bequests to convents made by this group should be understood in this light. In turn, those splendid financial gifts, along with dowries and *vitalizi*, allowed convents to build beautifully and richly. Convents played a crucial part in the rationalization and justification of the new practices of excluding daughters and bequeathing the patrimony to the eldest son (different issues, though tightly conjoined). The highly embellished conventual churches were one such justification—preemptive protests against any ready assumption that their daughters had been placed in convents merely to save family resources, as well as a public declaration by noble families that their progeny was well established, well cared for, and guided by spiritual and higher concerns, as Nicolò Giudice emphatically declared.

4

Living Like Ladies: Conventual Patronage

Inside Naples's grandest convents, nuns could live like ladies and behave like aristocratic barons. This chapter explores the social and economic arrangements that made this possible and shows how nuns used these resources to found convents and patronize art and architecture.

Conventual incomes varied enormously. Many were rich, and some were very rich indeed. Property owners in their own right, convents received income from land leases (*canoni*), government bonds (*luoghi di monte*), perpetual bequests (*legati perpetui*), tax farms (*arrendamenti*), indirect taxes (*gabelle*), rents, real and personal estate, and charges for boarders (*educande*). Moveable property was their most important source of income. In 1642 it represented 79.5 percent of the income of S. Giuseppe delle Eremitane, 66.7 percent of that of S. Maria Donnaregina, 63.1 percent of S. Giovanni Battista's income, and 61.4 percent of the Consolazione.[1] Most convents owned substantial property within the city and beyond, including vineyards and mills. Real estate provided 53.9 percent of the total income of S. Andrea and 48.3 percent of that of S. Gregorio Armeno in 1642.[2] Most convents rented out shops and houses in the city, often clustered around the convent itself, as at SS. Marcellino e Festo and the Consolazione.[3] Rents, or property appropriated because of rent failure, constituted important financial resources. Significant income came, too, from bequests, especially frequent from nuns and their families.[4] When Marco Antonio Ulcano died in 1612, three-quarters of his entire estate came to the Consolazione through his daughters, Bernardina and Lucretia, who were nuns there, and the rest went to the convent of S. Maria Maddalena through Vittoria Ulcano, professed nun there.[5] Sister Caterina Cecca, once a professed nun at the Consolazione, left it all her property in 1600.[6] And although Vittoria de Mauro Capobianco had to wait forty years for her promotion to professed nun at the Consolazione, she and her Sister Giulia, also a nun there, both bequeathed it property, including an annual rent worth 175 ducats from houses situated next to S. Pietro Martire, which the Consolazione promptly sold to S. Pietro.[7] Thus even a modest bequest could significantly advantage a convent in the intensely competitive urban market.

Had convents and their inmates been required to adhere to institutional and personal poverty, these sources of income would have sufficed. Conventual dowries, alongside these other sources of income, however, ensured that convents could be richly adorned and nuns could live in comfort, even stylish luxury.

CONVENT DOWRIES

Antonino Mongitore tells the story of Serafina Onorata, an impecunious *educanda* at S. Vincenzo Ferreri in Carini, who had always longed to take the religious habit but lacked the necessary dowry. Through the prayers of the remarkable Rosaria Caterina di Gesù, a nun at the same convent, "God inspired Donna Antonia Fazio, a rich *educanda* there, "to [make] of some of her income a free gift to be used as a dowry by Donna Serafina, who, as a result, before the year was over, had taken the religious habit."[8] This story indicates the crucial role dowries played in convent life socially, economically, and imaginatively.[9] Short of a miracle, there was little an aspirant but impecunious nun could hope for. Conventual dowries were not so much modes of oiling creaking conventual finances, as versatile instruments of social exclusion.

Poorer women were, on the whole, excluded from convents by the dowry demands and, at best, could opt to be tertiaries (religious laywomen loosely affiliated to monastic orders) or enter a conservatory, a cheaper alternative which shared with convents the physical rigors of enclosure.[10] Since conservatories were cheaper than convents, they were also of lower social class. It is wrong to assume that these institutions were filled with women burning with religious zeal. A crippling absence of vocation was regarded as no more of a barrier for lower-class women than it was for their more fortunate counterparts. Poorer women could also become *bizocche*, of which there were as many as 750 in Naples in 1579.[11] These women, known as "house nuns" or *pinzochere*, lived in their own homes and wore religious habit. They had to be at least forty years old, live with relations of first or second degree, be acceptable to the Ordinary, and be able to support themselves.[12] In short, the dedication of a woman's life to God, even in its institutionally humblest form, almost always required economic support from her family. When Trent emphatically raised the status of enclosed convents above all other forms of religious institution, it effectively made female dedication to a religious life not only stricter but more economically and socially exclusive.

Conventual dowries were often substantial. Among the aristocratic convents, dowries of several thousand ducats were not unusual in Naples and elsewhere. Don Martino de Leyva gave more than 6,000 ducats to the Benedictine convent of S. Margherita in Monza for his daughter Mariannina (the famous "Monaca di Monza").[13] In Naples no convent expected such towering riches, but the count of Piacento, Ottavio Ursino, paid 3,000 ducats in dowry for Sister Maria Giovanna at the grand and expensive convent of S. Maria della Sapienza in 1603. Dowries at S. Giuseppe dei Ruffo varied from Scolastica Muscettola's specially negotiated dowry of 1,000 ducats in 1605 to 2,000 ducats paid regularly by nuns entering between about 1607 and 1621.[14] At the Trinità, which accepted only noble girls, nuns from Naples paid the usual dowry, but girls from the Kingdom had to find 3,000 ducats (usually reduced to 2,000). At S. Geronimo (Franciscan), Divino Amore (Dominican), S. Maria Donnalbina (Benedictine), the Consolazione (Franciscan), S. Croce di Lucca (Carmelite), and S. Maria Egiziaca (Augustinian), dowries were 1,000 ducats; at S. Maria Donnaregina (Franciscan), S. Marcellino (Benedictine), S. Gregorio Armeno (Benedictine), S. Potito (Benedictine), SS. Trinità (Franciscan), the Sapienza (Dominican), and S. Francesco delle Cappuccine (Capuchin), dowries were established at 1,500 ducats.[15]

The Council of Trent attempted to balance the wealth of a convent with its population by limiting conventual intake. Convents were often eager to expand more rapidly than the religious authorities permitted. For example, at the Sapienza in Naples the maximum population was established in 1558 as 70 nuns, 50 choir nuns, and 20 lay sisters. When the nuns requested permission in 1661 to accept 20 more choir nuns and 10 more lay sisters, the Sacra Congregazione permitted them only 10 more choir nuns and 4 more lay sisters.[16] Trent also regulated the balance between lay sisters and nuns to one to three, though in practice the number of lay sisters (including the sick and infirm) was usually higher.

In addition to the conventual dowry, a *vitalizio* of 40 ducats a year or 500 ducats (*una tantum*) was required. During the novitiate, therefore, the nun's family paid a certain rate for her upkeep (about 70 ducats a year). The Council of Trent established that the novitiate should last only one year and that thereafter the nun should either make her profession or leave the convent. The practice of prolonging the novitiate much longer than one year, by which religious houses enjoyed the benefits of the dowry at no extra cost, was denounced.[17]

Attempts to systematize and moderate the conventual dowry system were never wholly successful. On 16 November 1629 the Sacra Congregazione in Rome addressed some of the most controversial aspects of the conventual dowry system, including the spiraling costs of conventual dowries and the exorbitant expenses associated with the rituals of monacation. It established a maximum of 1,500 ducats in normal circumstances and 2,500 for supernumeraries.[18] The revenue from such a sum, the letter acidly remarked, abundantly sufficed to maintain a nun. To avoid dowries being treated as simple payments guaranteeing entry to convents, it insisted that dowries should not be paid when a girl first entered a convent; rather, the monies should be deposited in cash, before entry, either in the Monte di Pietà or in a suitable public bank. Only after a nun's profession and with the license of the Vicario could a nun's dowry be used by her convent, and only then could it be inventoried in its entirety as real estate. Spending dowries on conventual needs, including building, required the Vicario's permission, and even then the dowries of supernumerary nuns could not be so used.[19] A similar measure was designed to stop office holders, such as the *portiere* or *refettoriere,* from having to meet the costs of their office (thereby effectively buying undue influence within their institution). Having forbidden this practice, the Sacra Congregazione coyly suggests instead that the official may "do something for the Church, or for the good of the monastery."[20]

These rulings did serve, by and large, to regularize conventual dowries, but policing each and every dowry was beyond the political will and bureaucratic capacity of the Church. Since it was in convents' own interests to receive higher sums and to accept girls from wealthy backgrounds, it was unrealistic to expect them to exercise restraint in this respect. The exception was the rule, and higher dowries were frequently paid. Just as dowries of "supernumerary" nuns were higher, so, too, were those of the third or fourth nun from the same family (as opposed to clan—in relation to which no formal limit on the number of nuns in any one convent existed). When widows took the veil, which they did not infrequently, they paid dowries slightly higher (about 300 ducats in cash) than usual. Archbishop Filomarino opposed this practice, arguing that it provoked "disturbance and disquiet." When Cardinal Panciroli asked him to allow the widow Antonia Serriana, daughter of the count of Casaduni, to enter the convent of S. Croce di Lucca, Filomarino replied that he would do so, but that this would be to allow what he had already denied to other women.[21] Families sometimes paid more to ensure acceptance of their daughters at particularly favored institutions. Instead of the customary 1,000 ducats, Giovanna d'Aquino paid 1,500 ducats at S. Maria Donnalbina in 1644, and Virginia Caposcacco paid the same at S. Geronimo in 1658; at the Divino Amore, Maddalena Montoya de Cardona paid 1,500 ducats in 1642, while Anna Brancaccio paid 2,000 in 1643, as did Ottavia Villani in 1646.[22]

The relationship between the conventual dowry and a convent's social and urbanistic ambitions was close. Convents routinely used dowries to cover the costs of food and debts, pay for repair work and new buildings, and buy income-bearing property. In theory, a dowry was dedicated to the needs of the individual nun to whom it belonged; in practice, convents regarded dowries as useful sources of loans, and even when a woman left the convent, her dowry did not entirely revert to her family.[23] Convents were advantaged in the dowry system in that when a nun died, the convent retained the capital and fruits of her dowry, whereas when a wife died in a marriage, her dowry was returned to its source.

In these circumstances, conventual dowries were of stark significance to convents. They not only safeguarded the standard of living of well-to-do women within their walls, but were a vital source of income for the convent as a whole. Raising dowries was an established mechanism for improving conventual finances. An important impetus behind transforming a conservatory into a convent was the chance to charge higher dowries, as well as the concomitant higher social status of those attracted. When the conservatory of S. Monica became enclosed in 1646, for example, its dowry was raised first from 600 to 800 and then to 1,000 ducats.[24] In the 1730s that modest Augustinian convent received about 1,600 ducats annually from the founder's legacy and about the same sum from properties and rents.[25] Annual expenditure was a little over 854 ducats, leaving 525 for food (paid for by *educande* and *passeggianti*), and a surplus of about 1,270 ducats. But when S. Monica lost money from the failure of its bank while spending thousands of ducats on building a new church and extensive reparations to convent buildings, it was able to meet the shortfall by raising dowries again to 1,200 in about 1741.[26] High dowries and the plentiful supply of daughters from rich families generally ensured that Neapolitan convents fared well.[27]

It has been suggested that the lavishness of Neapolitan conventual dowries served to compensate women for their loss of worldly pleasures.[28] That was certainly one of the effects of high dowries, but it was not their principal cause. There were many other ways in which families could ensure that daughters had access to the finer things of life (such as endowing them with a *vitalizio* or showering them with luxurious gifts). The single most important cause of high conventual dowries was to keep convents socially pure. For the grandest convents the imposition of a set dowry had the advantage of ensuring that their inmates came from among the richest and most powerful families of the kingdom. Good birth and rich girls enhanced a convent's prestige and attracted daughters from other distinguished families. But wealth, Francesco Vargas Macciucca argued, was even more important than blood: "If a girl wants to enter who is very noble but poor, and another rich but not at all of distinguished birth, it is not as impossible for the latter to see the doors open, that the former will find closed: because if it's a matter of a noble without a dowry, they will excuse their refusal, explaining it in terms of the poverty of the monastery. . . . Only what best suits the monastery has any weight."[29]

Conventual urbanistic ambitions were not simply the consequence of convents' housing women from richer families but actually came to determine their admissions practices. Financial packages were harnessed to potential nuns in order to persuade convents to accept them. One such accompanied Ippolita (later Dorotea) Capece Galeotta to the prestigious convent of S. Giuseppe dei Ruffi in 1611. The daughter of Ludovico Capece Galeotto and Olimpia Spana, and "heir and patron" of half of her father's property, Ippolita came to S. Giuseppe with an unusual dowry contract, bringing 2,000 ducats in dowry and a further 1,000 ducats "for building the convent."[30] This money was to remain in her name, to be made over to the monastery only after her profession. Tempting contingent clauses like this were hard for convents to resist. Sure enough, S. Giuseppe dei Ruffi bit the lure and accepted sister Dorotea as professed nun in 1613.[31]

Some convents were grander than others. Certain orders, especially the Dominicans and the Benedictines, gained a reputation for harboring noblewomen; others, such as the Franciscans, tended to be associated with the lower social classes. Reputations for particular social exclusivity were nurtured at S. Andrea, the Sapienza, Regina Coeli, S. Gregorio Armeno, S. Maria Donnaregina, S. Chiara, S. Marcellino, and S. Patrizia. Ranked slightly below them were the Croce di Lucca, S. Maria Donnalbina, S. Maria del Divino Amore, and S. Geronimo.[32] This ranking broadly corresponds to dowry rates, especially before their stricter regulation in 1629.

Just as aristocratic women were separated from their lower-class counterparts in the outside world, so they were within convents. A strict hierarchy obtained inside convents, so that aristocratic privileges were not demeaned by being shared with women from more plebeian backgrounds.[33] Dowries created a two-tiered system within convents, with sharp distinctions made between choir nuns (*coriste*) of upper social class and lay sisters (*converse*) of lower social class. Choir nuns played a key role in running the convent, occupying significant positions within it and voting on conventual policies and decisions. Lay sisters' pathways through conventual life were more circumscribed and less prestigious.

Spatial organization within convents reaffirmed hierarchical divisions. On entering a convent a girl received explicit and implicit spatial rules, according to her social class. Lay sisters were kept subordinate to choir nuns by conventual regulations. The constitutions of S. Andrea, for example, stipulate that literate girls would not readily be allowed in as lay sisters and, if they were accepted, they would not be permitted to sing Holy Office in the choir.[34] While lay sisters usually signed with a cross, professed nuns could nearly always write.[35] Choir nuns were even called "lady nuns," indicating that they lived like ladies and that their high social status was unblemished by taking the veil. Their cost of living was high, and dowries had to meet that cost.

Family influence was a double-edged sword. Just as rich families could assist conventual finances at crucial times, so family connections within convents could be useful to their families outside—to the cost of conventual finances. The presence of daughters in prestigious institutions was useful to aristocratic families. Blood relatives within a convent could help not only new young nuns entering that convent, but also the family outside. For instance, in 1672 at S. Chiara in Naples, notable damage occurred to conventual finances because of missed payments for some of the nuns. The abbess was compromised from denouncing the situation, because those nuns were related to governors of the Monti.[36] At such times, conventual finances suffered to the benefit of family fortunes because of the interrelated nature of the financial, economic, and familial concerns of the convent.

Convents were rendered materially and socially noble by the interdependence of conventual and ruling-class familial institutions. In addition to subsidizing the convent through their dowries and *vitalizi,* rich nuns and their families bore costs incurred by the *sacrestane, cellarare, refettoriere,* and other official postholders. Eleonora Zunica, for example, at S. Maria Donnalbina, received monies from her family to meet the costs of the offices of *sacristana* and *cellarara.*[37] Vargas Macciucca claimed that this system was unpopular: "The nuns moan about this with real feeling, and their honorable and generally poor families were distressed by it. The holy prelates and bishops, insofar as it was their responsibility, tried to find some solution, but in vain."[38] In fact, only a few of the less aristocratic convents, such as S. Monica, had a communal fund for the expenses of the *sacristana,* when she was unable to meet these herself.[39] The usual system allowed rich families to exercise power through dominating key positions within convents and was therefore intractable to reform.

The considerable wealth of convents and their inmates was tolerated as a convenient solution to several potential social problems. Whereas the tremendous wealth of male monastic houses provoked an outcry, that of their female counterparts, though criticized, was never the subject of serious reform.[40]

Nuns' dowries were a crucial source of income for conventual building and were regularly spent on buying property and land for conventual expansion. Typical is the record of the purchase of a chapel adjacent to its existing conventual buildings by S. Maria della Consolazione degli Afflitti in 1690 in exchange for nuns' dowry costs.[41] The same record explains why conventual dowries were essential to building:

> This convent having been founded under the said rule of the Seraphic St. Francis, which is principally bared on holy poverty, was sustained by charity with the assistance and help of the Reverend fathers of the same order, who, in about the year of our Lord 1600, were prohibited and forbidden from the protection and care of the convent by order of the Most Eminent Cardinal Gesualdo, then Archbishop of Naples, and in primitive times the monacands were enclosed there without paying any dowry, and so the convent for many years received no dowries whatsoever until the Pope temporarily considering that it was unable to meet the nuns' own needs, with general orders, prohibited the convent from doing this, and thereafter this convent began to receive monacands with their own dowries, or dotal alms, and the first dowries one reads in those times reached the sum of about 200 ducats.[42]

Some churchmen were disturbed by the traffic in dowries and nuns. In 1530 Gian Pietro Carafa wrote to his sister, Maria Carafa, abbess at the Sapienza, urging her to avoid the prevalent abuses:

> I order you on behalf of the omnipotent and strong zealous God, that you guard against receiving persons into the religion [religious life] through agreements, or promises, or hopes of money, of things, of favors, of support in victuals or buildings of the convent, or of whatsoever mundane thing: but you must accept only those whom God sends you: and these are those who with evidence of a good life, possess the fervor of spirit, and feel God's continuing inspiration, by which they are called to despise the world, and to mortification and denial of themselves: and particularly those who feel drawn to follow true poverty and humble condition, rather than to the reputation of rich convents.[43]

It was one thing for Carafa to exhort his sister to ensure that austerity prevailed at the Sapienza; it was quite another for Maria Carafa to enact this, faced with noblewomen who wished to enter the community without sacrificing their standard of living. Gian Pietro's impatient letter of September 1531 makes clear the relationship between laxity and ambition at the Sapienza and his refusal, as "spiritual father," to tolerate it:

> At your instance some letters have been written to me in which I saw little light of God, and little Christian truth . . . because all the letters were about nothing other than your poverty, and the necessity of building the

> convent, and of the need to receive daughters sufficient in number that they might bring money to spend on the building. . . . And I protest that if you search for something other than the Crucified Christ, I shall no longer want you as my sister. And if you want to make the convent large, and gather there the large number of young women in the way of today's world, I promise you, that within a short time, you'll regret it.[44]

Whether Maria Carafa came to regret it or not, her policies at the Sapienza paid off, as it was rapidly established as one of the premier convents of the city, noted both for its socially distinguished inhabitants and for its spiritual devotion.

The relative significance of dowries for conventual building emerges from the Sapienza's accounts. Building and decorating its church—including frescoes by Cesare Fracanzano and Baldassare Corenzio; paintings by Andrea Vaccaro, Carlo de Rosa, Giovanni Richa, Enrico Semer, and Spadaro; and marble inlay work by Giacomo Lazzari, Francesco Valentini, and Matteo and Pietro Pelliccia—cost a total of 19,767 ducats, 2 tarì, and 2 grani. Of this, most (14,166.2.17 ducats) was met from investments and interests, and dowries accounted for an additional 4,197.4.8 ducats, while ordinary income assigned to building came to only 232.3.6 ducats, with a further 1,170.1.11 from miscellaneous sources.[45] Dowries were, therefore, not the most important financial source for building, but a critical and necessary factor.

Sometimes convents plundered dowries for building with unseemly haste. At S. Giuseppe dei Ruffi, for instance, 2,000 ducats of the dowry of Antonia Boncompagni, who had taken her vows less than two weeks before, were spent on building work on 28 November 1672.[46] When the convent of S. Francesco dell'Osservanza ran out of funds in 1747 for the building campaign started the previous year, the providential dowry of sister Angela Mastellone provided 1,000 ducats of the necessary 1,500, allowing work to continue.[47] Indeed, Vargas Macciucca assumed that "if [convents] had been governed prudently, they would be very rich and paved with gold and precious stones."[48] His criticisms stung the author of the brief history of the Consolazione:

> Some wonder and say that this monastery should have a much richer patrimony than that which it currently holds, considering that since the time of its foundation until today as a result of so many dowries of dead nuns left behind in it, at the worst reading of one dowry each year would amount to 200 dowries, which calculated at the rate of 1,200 ducats each, would give a total dowry income of 240,000 ducats, plus the maturations, and inheritances acquired from the same, and of no small consideration: and consequently the walls of its enclosure should be of gold.[49]

The author retorts that it is from those very dowries the convent had to buy land and buildings to convert to institutional use, adding that between 1575 and the present 10,000 ducats from dowries had been spent in this way.[50]

Conventual dowries allowed for both sustained expansion and opportunistic purchase of property by convents. Rapid expansion at the recently established Augustinian convent of S. Monica in the 1680s was possible only because dowries were used systematically to buy up houses for this purpose.[51] And a similar picture appears at S. Francesco a Pontecorvo.[52] Elsewhere the encashment of a new dowry could allow a convent to make strategically driven purchases. Thus, in April 1632 S. Gregorio Armeno was able to buy houses belonging to the baron of Parascandolo, situated opposite the convent, for 5,000 ducats, part of which came from the dowry of Isabella di Somma's daughter.[53] This property was rapidly incorporated into the convent.

Institutional ambition guaranteed entry to convents for rich daughters. In 1749, when S. Francesco dell'Osservanza needed money for its new parlatory, Filippo Arcamone made special arrangements for his daughter's entry to that convent. Instead of paying the usual 1,500 ducats dowry for Lucia, he paid the same sum toward the new parlatory, with the agreement that, should his daughter not become a nun at the convent by the end of June 1751, the convent would repay Arcamone immediately.[54] It was the convent's desire to build that allowed Arcamone leeway to achieve his own ends.[55] Such arrangements inevitably compromised conventual religious ideals in favor of mundane pragmatics.

Not infrequently, special conditions were attached to dowry contracts to secure favorable terms. Strictly speaking, no more than two blood relations were allowed in any convent at any time to avoid the development of power blocs within convents, but in practice dowries were always negotiable.[56] This advantaged families with a grip over a convent; in turn, they were used to strengthen that hold still further. The value of financial support for the convent was calmly weighed by nuns and ecclesiastical authorities alike, as is shown by a document relating to the license issued by the Sacra Congregazione, giving permission to Vittoria Coppola to become a nun at S. Marcellino, where she already had two sisters: "Having drawn together the reports that they have of the excellent qualities of the *Oratrice* for which she is generally desired by the nuns, and the gifts and favors which the same monastery has received and continually receives from the Duke [Canzano], they had agreed to the requests of the nuns and of the girl soon to become a nun."[57]

Stowing daughters in convents strategically ensured a presence in circles which were often centers of considerable power and prestige. Aristocratic families built up power blocs within convents, deliberately concentrating their resources on fewer convents and ensuring the presence within them of family representatives spanning several generations to secure greatest influence in conventual affairs. Power blocs were common in Neapolitan and Sicilian convents but were often engineered as much, if not more, by the women themselves as by their fathers. The convent of the Sapienza, for example, founded by the Carafa, was dominated for generations by members of that clan. This phenomenon was strengthened by the determination of a number of Carafa women to take the veil, in spite of family plans for them to make prestigious marriages. Cornelia Carafa, daughter of Antonio Carafa, marquis of Monteballo, had been destined to marry the duke of Ferrara, but resisting this strenuously, she entered the Sapienza in 1553 and became prioress between 1596 and 1602. The Sisters Maria Carafa and Paola Carafa entered in 1562 and 1574, respectively. The former had been betrothed to the duke of Orleans and the latter to the only son of Ferrante Carafa, marquis of S. Lucido; but they rejected these socially distinguished marriages in favor of the convent. Again, their dedication to the convent was exceptional, with Maria Carafa serving as prioress for nine years.[58] In addition to the dowries and *vitalizi*, the Sapienza became the beneficiary of a handsome inheritance from Alfonso Carafa, count of Montorio, son of Diomede Carafa, and grandson of Giovanni Carafa, count of Montorio, including the *paraggio* for Sister Maria.[59] The convent was a handsome winner, gaining women of dedication, institutional astuteness, and determination while profiting financially, too. Thus, paradoxically, clan dominance sometimes favored the convent at the clan's expense. The Sapienza became so attractive to members of the Carafa clan that even those for whom the clan had other plans fought to go there, and it inherited substantial skills and monies as a result.

When a family or clan dominated a specific convent, the institutional world assumed strongly familial overtones. Fulvia Caracciolo was enrolled at the aristocratic Benedictine convent of S. Gregorio Armeno in 1541 at the age of two years.[60] Her mother, Ippolita, had also entered the convent as a child but left to get married and have children, returning to the convent once again at age sixty. Fulvia was the niece of Lucrezia, who was abbess for six years and sister of two other nuns, Anna and Elionora, who took vows when she did in 1579. In other words, in the convent Fulvia, like many other noblewomen in the grander female convents during this period, surrounded by members of her family and secure in the institution's status, was—almost literally—at home.

In the most ambitious undertaking of all, that of founding a new convent, three distinct models emerge in Naples in this period. As we shall see, all required strategic familial connections, both outside the conventual system and within it (the carefully established familial power blocks). Ambitious individual nuns could exploit familial connections within the Church, as Maria Carafa did to establish the Sapienza, or at court, as Maria Villani did in founding the Divino Amore. Or a family group could jointly found a convent, as was the case at S. Giuseppe dei Ruffi. Good connections were the most useful asset in the complicated game of establishing a new institution. Best of all were close affiliations, preferably blood links, with influential players in the ecclesiastical hierarchy.

Close ties to members of the upper echelons of the Church certainly assisted Maria Carafa in her foundation of the Sapienza convent (Figure 6). Her uncle was Cardinal Oliviero Carafa, archbishop of Naples, and her brother, Gian Pietro Carafa, to whom she was very close, later became Pope Paul IV (1555–59). In 1490 Maria fled her prestigious betrothal to Count Pandone and, with the help of Gian Pietro and the nuns of S. Sebastiano, entered that convent at the age of twenty-two.[61] During the French siege of 1528 when S. Sebastiano's inmates transferred to Donnaromita, Maria Carafa did not join them. Seeking a more rigorous religious life, she established in June that year the convent of the Sapienza, of which she remained prioress until her death in 1552 (Plate 8).[62]

The story of that establishment, its foundation, and its sustenance shows Maria Carafa's profound debt to influential members of her family. Her uncle, Cardinal Oliviero Carafa, had purchased a palace to establish an educational institution for poor students, but on his death in 1511, work ended. Lucrezia Dentice took over and established it instead as a convent for Franciscan nuns in 1519.[63] On her death Dentice urged her niece, Sister Sancia Carafa, a nun at S. Maria Donnaromita, to take on the project. Shrinking from such an enormous undertaking, Sancia managed to persuade Maria Carafa to shoulder the burden. With the support of the Theatine P. Bonifacio de' Colli, in Naples in the stead of Gian Pietro Carafa, Maria managed to gain papal support and transferred the convent to the Dominican order. Maria brought with her "only a woman for service, Sister Catarina and a breviary," and "she found there Sister Antonia Abate a novice and a lay sister, Lucrezia Abbate, without any possessions of her own, but only a bell, a handbell, and a few altar cloths."[64] A few other items also awaited Maria, mostly liturgical but including four books on the virtues, the sermons of Savonarola, and the Confessions of St. Augustine.[65] The establishment owed much to the support and guidance of the Theatines, just as Gian Pietro Carafa owed much to his sister.[66] It was Gian Pietro who managed to negotiate the Sapienza's independence from the Ordinary and direct subjection instead to the Holy See.[67] Where a nun lacked the exceptional close familial connections with zealous and powerful clergymen, such as those Maria Carafa enjoyed, she faced much greater obstacles in founding a convent and had to forge and shrewdly exploit a series of strategic alliances, weaving key players from church and state through the weft of the particular conventual ambitions at stake.

This approach is particularly apparent in one startling case in Naples, in which one woman, Sister Maria Villani (1584/5–1670), was not only involved in founding the convent of S. Giovanni Battista in 1610 but went on to establish the convent of the Divino Amore in 1638. Her complicated story sheds light on the interrelationships between familial ambitions and conventual institutions and on the ferocity with which convents protected their economic interests, and it provides a good example of how aristocratic nuns depended on their family connections both inside and outside convents and on familial influence in church and state to achieve their aims.[68] Conversely, it also demonstrates how convents could play multiple, sometimes contradictory roles within the fortunes of a family. In the space of three generations, close involvement with female convents allowed the Villani family to consolidate family property and provide for the spiritual glorification and institutional recognition of the family, but it also brought them protracted legal cases and bitter headaches. Families and convents could use and abuse each other.

Maria Villani, the daughter of Eleonora Costanza and Giovanni Villani, marquis of Polla and member of the Piazza of Montagna, was the youngest of twelve children and the dearest to her parents (a standard trope in this sort of quasi-hagiographical literature).[69] Marchese links together their nobility, wealth, and virtues: they were, he emphasizes, "of the noblest lineage and rich with the property of their patrimony, but more with excellent virtues, which in them shone brightly."[70] Beatrice's mother died when she was three, and from her earliest years she showed signs of occupying a special place in God's affections and of bearing a religious devotion out of the ordinary, evinced in physical suffering, even self-inflicted wounds.[71] Having heard, for instance, that a "Moor" in Naples had dedicated himself to the devil, Beatrice stabbed herself in the chest, almost as deep as the heart, wanting "to excavate her blood, with which she had to write the deed, that stipulated her dedication to God."[72]

Her familial connections within convents proved vital to Beatrice's construction of a holy career for herself. Her aunt, Sister Dorotea Villani, a nun in the aristocratic convent of the Sapienza in Naples, played a particularly crucial role. Dorotea's position at the Sapienza and the esteem in which she was held was linked to the Villani family's connections to the Carafa family by marriage.[73] In any case, Dorotea and two other well-connected nuns from the Sapienza were chosen to go and reform the monastery of S. Giovanni in Capua. In fact, Dorotea established at Capua a new Dominican convent, and it was to this pristine establishment that Beatrice and one of her sisters were sent as *educande*, under the tutelage of their aunt, and where Beatrice took the habit at age fourteen, and became the first professed nun in 1590.[74] Subsequently the family made a joint decision to found a convent in Naples. Although more prestigious than Capua, Naples posed greater problems: "The Marquis exhorted them to strict silence, in order to avoid those embarrassments that such foundations bring with them, either because of the interests of men, or the malevolence of demons, which always with all their strength, resist those undertakings which are in honor of God; above all when it is a matter of building, including a new enclosed convent."[75]

New foundations and buildings were particularly difficult enterprises, fraught with dangers from envious, rivalrous, or hostile parties. We can imagine the welter of jealousy, the sniping from rival Neapolitan families mingled with the skeptical voices of anticlericals, raised in critical chorus in fervent opposition to yet another religious institution. The marquis's worldly experience proved invaluable at preventing rumors from spreading too rapidly and scotching the entire project. It was he, too, who went to Naples to undertake the necessary negotiations to buy a suitable site: "The marquis returned to Naples, where with much intensity, and with no little prudence, he applied himself to settling this matter, and, in short, he arranged it: since, with the dowries of some young girls who wanted to become nuns, he sought, and after various careful inquiries, and changing sites, he bought a house, in the street which they call di Costantinopoli, opposite the convent of the Sapienza."[76] The choice of site is significant. The Sapienza was one of the most aristocratic convents, with an unblemished reputation for piety. The new convent would accrue advantages from being associated with the Sapienza topographically as well as genealogically—another Dominican convent born of that reforming impulse that sent Sister Dorotea from the Sapienza to Capua. Socially and topographically, therefore, the new foundation was deliberately entwined via Villani family connections with individual and institutional spiritual purity and institutional and aristocratic respectability.

But Sister Maria Villani was not content with her family's key role in the foundation of S. Giovanni Battista, having "simply helped" to found it, and harbored from 1612 a desire to found a new convent for herself, although she lacked the means to do so.[77] One day she heard the voice of God: "Come, my chosen one, and I shall place in thee my throne. I want you to build a house to my mother."[78] Thinking that this was a metaphorical request, Maria did nothing. It was not until 1625 that material progress was made toward the new foundation, when God made a third request to Maria to found a convent. That same day, her nephew, the marquis of Polla, while out hunting, experienced a vision of Christ bleeding profusely. He turned for advice to his aunt, who advised him to become a regular Theatine. Upon entering the order, Villani left 1,000 scudi and another 1,000 in jewels and cash to his aunt to be spent on the exposition of the sacrament. Shortly afterward, the duke of Salandra, former husband of one of Maria's nieces, also entered the Theatine order after discussing the matter with his aunt, leaving 1,000 ducats in her care for the same purpose.[79]

At this stage, Sister Maria Villani's confessor, Father Corcione S.J., suggested that since monies collected so far were insufficient for an enclosed convent, she should found instead a conservatory. Maria Villani's response to this is significant. She had interest in establishing only a convent of strict enclosure and had absolutely none in a conservatory, "because she was thinking of undertaking a project that as something belonging to God should be perfect throughout every part."[80] Although both institutions protected female virgins and functioned in the service of God, the higher social class of nuns in an enclosed convent ensured its greater "perfection" in Villani's eyes.

Even when she had raised enough money (about 15,000 scudi in capital and another 9,000 in goods and cash), Villani was barred from access to it, because the monies entrusted to her for the foundation of the new convent were registered in the name of the convent of S. Giovanni Battista.[81] She confided this predicament to a priest, only to find that things rapidly went from bad to worse. The priest kicked up a scandal, spreading the rumor that Sister Maria wanted to rob S. Giovanni Battista of its money, and he sought to distance himself from her by refusing to continue as her confessor.[82] Alarmed, the nuns of S. Giovanni Battista sequestered the convent's revenues, including all the money for Sister Maria's new foundation.[83] Villani's plans threatened them not only with loss of income and capital, but also with the loss of fifteen nuns and two lay sisters, which would have left only thirty choir nuns, sixteen lay sisters, and ten *educande* in their convent.[84]

In spite of this opposition, Maria Villani remained undeterred. Once again, close family networks within convents proved indispensable. Crucially, she received support from her cousin, Sister Candida Maria di Argenzio, who happened to be prioress of S. Giovanni Battista. Significant financial help and recognition also came from well-connected supporters outside the convent, who strategically involved Cardinal Francesco Buoncompagno. When Marcello Pignatelli and his wife, Camilla Sanfelice, donated 10,000 scudi on Christmas Eve 1636 for the new convent, they presented this in writing to Cardinal Buoncompagno, who was prompted to take a more decisive line by being involved so conspicuously in such a lavish donation. The matter was irrevocably clinched for him when the countess of Monterey, the vicereine herself, became involved in 1637.[85] Buoncompagno, encouraged by the vicereine, obtained a license for the new convent for twelve choir nuns and two lay sisters.

This high-level backing proved to be the turning point in the affair. Rapidly the purchase of a house—albeit rather a cramped one—went ahead. Marcello Pignatelli promised 5,400 ducats for this in 1637, and a further 700 scudi from the princess of Caserta allowed building to commence.[86] Even at this juncture, problems remained, but blood family members provided Maria Villani with indispensable allegiances within the conventual world and made possible the move to a new convent. A license was granted for the new convent to be built outside Porta Medina near S. Antonio, in the teeth of objections from the monks of S. Antonio, who claimed that the new convent would overshadow their church.[87] Nor was opposition from the nuns at S. Giovanni Battista over. They had recourse to the pope, promising to observe stricter rule in order to avoid scission.[88] On 17 April 1638 Monsignor Tamborelli accompanied the *Vicario Generale* to S. Giovanni and told Abbess Maria Felice Paolucci to allow Villani to leave, but granted permission for only one nun to accompany her.[89] Maria Villani chose her niece, Sister Maria Dorotea Villani, daughter of Fabrizio Villani and Feliciana Ruffo, as a reliable ally around which a conventual institution could be formed. The site was cramped, the air bad, and expansion difficult, but again family connections provided crucial solutions. In 1658 the convent of Divino Amore managed to purchase, for 18,000 scudi, the fifteenth-century palace where Maria Villani was born and which was then in the possession of her niece, the princess of Colobrano, tightly binding the fortunes of family and convent together, as Celano observed: "The church for the time being stands in the portico of the former palace of the Villani family, which one enters through the courtyard of the palace, which was very roomy and beautiful."[90] The social standing of the new convent seemed guaranteed when new building commenced in 1709 and no less a person than Cardinal d'Aragona, viceroy, laid the first stone and made a handsome donation for the convent's further expansion and decoration.[91]

Maria Villani's conventual foundation usefully delineates several important themes. The story is marked by Villani's implacable desire to found her own enclosed convent. One simply associated closely with her family would not do; she was searching for the maximum "purity" by starting from scratch at a pristine convent associated with her name, avoiding the corruption and contamination of institutional practices established elsewhere. Such determination to avoid anything defiled, her uninterest in founding anything other than an enclosed convent, indicates a considerable ambition. That ambition was also highly personal: it was with her own name, not that of her father, that Villani wished her convent to be associated. But notwithstanding her considerable personal ambition, Maria Villani was forced to be dependent on her family and on its strategic links, ranging from close connections with wealthy nobles, to timely alliances with significant figures within the church (such as Cardinal Buoncompagno) and state (the vicereine), to crucial ties within existing female religious institutions. Without these connections, Maria Villani's ambitions would have come to nothing. Since only noble families enjoyed such connections, the foundation and development of convents were inevitably intimately connected with noble politics.

Clan ambition spurred the foundation of S. Giuseppe dei Ruffi, which was, as its name indicates, in the hands of the Ruffo family from its foundation (Figures 7, 11). The convent was founded in 1604 by a group of five nuns, four of whom had Ruffo connections. The influential Neapolitan families of Tomacelli, Spinelli (both related by marriage to the Ruffo), and Caracciolo were also involved in its establishment, ensuring its financial stability and respectability. Chiara (Catarina) Tomacelli, daughter of Girolamo Tomacelli and Ippolita Ruffo, provided 10,000 ducats in March 1604 for the foundation and building and was twice elected prioress (July 1609 and July 1621);[92] and Catarina Ruffo, daughter and heir of Ottavio Ruffo and Isabella Sanchez, gave 20,000 ducats in March 1604 toward building the monastery, and was, not unrelatedly, elected prioress in July 1612.[93] Ippolita Ruffo, daughter of Paolo Ruffo, count of Sinopoli, and of Catarina Spinelli, widow of Geronimo Tomacelli, "banked many thousands of ducats" for the convent and was elected mother superior in March 1624.[94] The mighty Caracciolo family also played a crucial part. Maria Caracciolo, daughter of Baldassare Caracciolo and Giulia Monadoi, described as *fondatrice* in the conventual records, pledged an income of 200 ducats annually in March 1604 and was elected prioress in July 1615.[95] Thus the selection of prioress drew on a combination of wealth and signal dedication to the convent, thereby consolidating economic and personal assets to become powerful political forces on the convent's behalf.

Plans to establish S. Giuseppe were cemented through strategic links with ecclesiastical hierarchies. Two significant acts of architectural patronage undertaken for the Girolamini, the Oratorians' church in Naples, by Catarina Ruffo and Anna Colonna Barberini, secured the Oratorians' support in turn for the foundation of S. Giuseppe dei Ruffi. In 1600 Caterina Ruffo paid for the building and decoration of the marble-lined chapel on the right of the main altar, where the mortal remains of her father, Ottavio, were to be buried, and where burial rights were also granted (for 7,000 ducats) to the descendants of her cousin Vincenzo, prince of Scilla.[96] Meanwhile Anna Colonna Barberini patronized the chapel of S. Alessio (first on the right), securing Pietro da Cortona for the main altar painting and Cristoforo Roncalli for paintings elsewhere in the Girolamini.[97] Undoubtedly the Oratorians and these devout women had much in common, but that each lacked what the other had (money, political clout) was also important in creating alliances between them. Those bonds were articulated and cemented through architectural patronage and foundation. Celano records:

> These ladies [Ippolita and Caterina Ruffo, and Caterina Tomacelli], as beautiful as they were rich, having for their spiritual father one of the Congregation of the Oratorians, resolved to leave the world, and to lead an enclosed life; for which reason they purchased in the Seggio of Capuano the palace formerly belonging to the Arcella family, already extinct in that Seggio; and they erected there a small church dedicated to

the glorious St. Joseph, and [when the palace had been] converted from residence to conventual use, in the year 1604 with other companions on the 7 March they were enclosed there, leading there an exemplary life.[98]

The Ruffo family remained prominent at S. Giuseppe and continued to serve it financially and in terms of leadership. Male members of the Ruffo family also got involved. Fabrizio Ruffo paid for the small chapel dedicated to S. Rufo, inscribing it with a record of his patronage and his naval victories against the Turks (for which he was indebted to S. Rufo and which supplied the booty for his patronage).[99] Ecclesiastical recognition of (and perhaps ambivalence about) the Ruffo family's key contribution came with Cardinal Filomarino's involvement at the monacation of Ruffo girls at S. Giuseppe. In 1663 Filomarino attended the monacations of the twin daughters of Ugo Compagni, duke of Sola, and Maria Ruffo, and said he would have officiated but for poor health.[100]

In exceptional circumstances a family could become expert in managing the delicate political negotiations of establishing convents, gradually accumulating knowledge and expertise on this difficult issue. This was true of the Colonna family, one of the most powerful families in Italy. Sister Ippolita Maria Colonna, daughter of Filippo Colonna, grand Conestabile of Naples, and of Lucrezia Tomacelli, princess of Sonnino, is recorded as one of the founders of S. Giuseppe dei Ruffi.[101] In addition to the usual dowry, she gave the convent 8,000 ducats in April 1626, and she and her sister received extraordinary dispensations in return.[102] She and her sister, Anna Colonna (1601–58), joined the convent aged eight and three years old, respectively, and Anna spent most of the following years in Rome. Special treatment began when Anna arrived from Rome, on 7 January 1623, together with her sister, Vittoria, and two servants:[103] "D. Anna Colonna and Signora D. Vittoria Colonna her sister with two of their servants came from Rome and alighted from their carriage directly in front of the convent door. Then, having prayed a little in the church, and received the visits of some ladies who had gathered for such avail, they entered the convent with the title of *educande*."[104] After living at S. Giuseppe dei Ruffi for four years and eight months in secular dress as *educanda*, Anna Colonna left for Rome on 20 September 1627 to make her splendid society marriage to Taddeo Barberini, which elevated her to wife of the secular head of the Barberini family and niece of the pope.[105] The convent catalog includes the adulatory observation that Anna Colonna "adorned our convent no less with the nobility of her habits and virtues than with the luminosity of her blood, and always provided a singular example of modesty."[106] Although this statement adopts the familiar language of praising both noble blood and spiritual virtue, it may be more than a conventional paean to a powerful woman. Drawing on her husband's connections and on her family's Neapolitan experience, Anna Colonna established the Discalced Carmelite convent of S. Maria Regina Coeli in Rome, an undertaking requiring political skill and determination.[107] The Colonna story remains unusual, spanning as it does two cities, Rome and Naples, with their disparate politico-ecclesiastical structures. Much more usual was a pattern of patronage within one city by daughters of families prominent within that same city.

From founding convents and buying land for conventual building to paying for particularly conspicuous aspects of church decoration, such as magnificent marble altars, dramatic frescoes, and virtuoso oil paintings, patronage by individual or small groups of nuns embraced a spectrum of activities. Nuns' direct personal involvement extended to the supervision of specific artworks for their churches and was most often not instigated by the abbess.[108] Nuns paid for this work from their independent annuities, known as *vitalizi*, which most aristocratic nuns received from their families.[109] During the sixteenth and seventeenth centuries *vitalizi* became standard practice in southern Italy, intended to sustain younger siblings—male and female—in a system which depended on primogeniture.[110] *Vitalizi* were, Vargas Macciucca claimed, as high as possible and depended on the nuns' renunciation to any claim to family property.[111] They varied considerably. In the 1660s, while sister Anna Maria at the convent of S. Giuseppe received 12 ducats, sister Paola at S. Antonio received 40, sister Maria Antonia Carafa at the Sapienza received a handsome 99.4.19.[112] Some of the richest Neapolitan convents expected the family to continue to pay the *vitalizio* for two years after a nun's death.

Vitalizi were quite common, and in some convents they were even made (abusively) obligatory.[113] The Sacra Congregazione dei Regolari struggled to limit such abuses, instructing the Vicario of Naples in 1629 to ensure that:

> the annual subsidies that are assigned to particular nuns for their religious necessities be voluntary from the start, and the nuns then be obliged to keep the fruits for religious necessities only, and that the rest be employed for the common uses of the Monastery. However, may it please Your Most Illustrious Sir to ensure that of these subsidies they have promises which are well guaranteed by relations, procuring, if possible, that by those guarantees they are assigned in a few particular incomes, secured and collectible.[114]

Although *vitalizi* were officially earmarked for the individual nun's religious necessities and kept separate from institutional finances, in practice this distinction was frequently blurred. *Vitalizi* comprised one of the Consolazione's principal sources of income.[115] And at the relatively poor convent of S. Monica the sacristy had, in about 1741, a capital of 400 ducats "existing through its fund of cash donations from some individual nuns from the advance of *vitalizi*."[116] At the Augustinian convent of S. Giuseppe dei Ruffi, nuns used their *vitalizi* to pay for the inlaid main altar (1674–89; Plate 6) and the gilt copper pyx (1668), both fashioned by Dionisio Lazzari.[117] Sometimes nuns lent monies from their *vitalizi* to the convent, as Ippolita Ruffo did in May 1679, so that the convent could buy Diego Santolini's house, the site for the first two lateral chapels of its church.[118] A list of monies received from individual nuns for building works in the same church between 9 June 1674 and 18 November 1688 is dominated by the contributions of three nuns—Sister Maria Geronima Boncompagni (eleven payments totaling 1,759 ducats 8 carlini and 6 grani), Sister Ippolita Caterina Ruffo (five payments totaling 532.4.17 ducats, including one payment of 100 ducats (which was made together with Sister Maria Giacinta Ristaldo), and Sister Chiara Maria Ruffo (six smaller payments totaling 443.2.28). Not every entry refers to the purpose on which the money was spent, but Sister Maria Boncompagni's money was spent on "works of marble" and "the gratings for the communicatory and the confessionals," while the Ruffo sisters' money was focused on the altar.[119]

It was in convents' interests to harbor nuns from rich families, because they could be depended upon to meet special expenses, such as building, church decoration, and festivals. Patronage by individual nuns went far deeper than this and could be independent of their families. A few nuns enjoyed exceptionally large fortunes and could almost singlehandedly transform a convent's appearance (Figure 8). Sister Vittoria Felice Cottone, a professed nun at the Dominican convent of S. Caterina in Palermo, who came from a rich and distinguished old feudal aristocratic Sicilian family, is revealed in her will of 1704 as having property worth 3,890 scudi 14.10 tari, a very considerable sum.[120] The richly colored and costly marble decoration of the large church of S. Caterina advanced piecemeal until Cottone left substantial monies in her will with the instructions to spend part of it on decorating the church.[121] This decisive turn in fortunes for the convent was provided not by an abbess, but by a regular professed nun. Nevertheless, Gieronima Felice Cottone, Vittoria's sister, was responsible for the enactment of the will and was a key player as prioress of S. Caterina.[122] In fact, Vittoria Cottone's will was much more precise in relation to relatively small sums than in stipulating how the larger sum was to be spent decorating the church, but she and her sister had presumably discussed the matter in some detail.[123]

Considerable resolution and vigor were expressed in both the choice of designers and in the prompt start to the work, which must be attributed to the prioress's energetic involvement. Decoration of the chancel began promptly in 1705, to the design of Giacomo Amato and Antonino Grano, the most accomplished architects available in Palermo (Figure 8). Enclosure did not impede Vittoria from making bequests on both sides of the convent walls. She left her silver and gold objects to Geronima Felice for her personal use,[124] but bestowed a gold chain on her nephew, Carlo Cottone, prince of Castelnovo.[125] Her will stipulates that from the 3,890.14.10 of her estate, 1,400 scudi should be spent on 1,400 masses in her name to be celebrated in S. Caterina and on a special requiem mass according to her wishes ("ad intentionem Vittoriae").[126] Of what remained, half was for charity, the needy poor, those who were unable to beg for reasons of pride or rank, and prisoners.[127] These monies were to be distributed by the Congregation of the Immaculate Conception recently founded at the Jesuits' Casa Professa in Palermo.[128] The remaining half was for the convent, for whatever cropped up as necessary.[129] In addition, a separate income provided 145 scudi, which Vittoria Cottone earmarked for the following uses: 54 scudi was to be divided between three specific priests (18 scudi each) for daily masses; 18 scudi was to go to another priest, to be chosen by Geronima or, if she were dead, by the then prioress, for celebrating another daily mass.[130] An income of 73 scudi was for Geronima for annual expenditures communicated by Vittoria to Hieronyma orally and in confession, following the format of Scipio Cottone's will. Out of that 73 scudi, an annual income of 18 scudi was to be assigned to the provost, head of the Jesuit church, for religious celebration at S. Caterina itself, and for a daily mass at the Casa Professa for Vittoria Cottone, and 6 scudi was to be spent each year on Trinity Sunday for music, candles, and other necessities.[131]

Interventions on this scale were extremely rare, requiring not only access to huge financial sums but also powerful and sympathetic family members on both sides of the convent walls who would ensure the execution of the will. In return, family connections on both sides of convent walls were honored in Cottone's will. Indeed, this will provides a sort of map tracing familial and institutional connections important to Cottone, weaving complex connections between blood family and convent, between religious devotion and ecclesiastical institutions (including the Jesuits). The convent church itself, for the embellishment of which she left by far the largest sum, was the physical site which best expressed these complex interrelationships of family, convent, religious devotion, and institutional obligations that made up Vittoria Cottone's life—or at least how she chose to represent that life when contemplating her death.

Familial identities and lineages continued to be articulated and reinscribed through artworks inside convents. The extent to which blood families made their mark on conventual life is demonstrated in the familial coats-of-arms—which, more directly than any other sign or intervention, represent the blood family and its lineage—adorning conventual churches in Palermo, such as the prominent coats-of-arms of the Amato and Bruno families in the nave of the Dominican church of S. Caterina (Figure 8). Here the presence of the family is baldly represented, no longer transmuted in terms of patronage of an object of everyday conventual life. The Aragona family's massive coats-of-arms, on both sides of the chancel in the Benedictine convent church of the Immacolata Concezione in Palermo, overwhelm that most sacred area with the claims of dynasty.[132] These Palermitan examples have no equivalents in Naples, where the relationship was played out more subtly institutionally.

There are, of course, many dangers in presupposing an isomorphic reflection between the representations of dynastic lineage and those existing in family affairs.[133] The strong visual dynastic identifications made in convent churches indicate not only that families were eager to have their name connected with centers of spiritual and social prestige, but also that heads of patrician families feared the independence of their daughters inside those institutions and consequently chose to affirm the claims of lineage precisely where they faced their sharpest challenge, even obliteration. Competition between convents to attract members from the richest and best-connected families was intensified by the fact that patrician men and women were inclined to direct money toward those convents where they had kin.[134] The wealth and energy of the splendid new churches, richly adorned with marbles and paintings, was partly generated by a combination of familial vulnerability and pride represented by daughters in convents and competition between convents to attract rich recruits. The rise of lay institutions looking after young girls also prompted convents to more overtly showcase their aristocratic presence.[135]

Families sometimes made a gift of a devotional object to a convent while negotiating their daughter's conventual dowry or monacation. When she entered the convent of S. Giuseppe dei Ruffi in 1620, Maria Giovanna was promised by her father, in addition to her dowry of 2,000 ducats, a hand basin and large drinking vessel of silver for conventual use. She also received 200 ducats from her mother, which she spent on having six small jars made for the main altar in the church and on other things for the convent.[136] Maria Giovanna's focus on objects associated with Communion, to strengthen her relationship with the Host, was paralleled by nuns throughout Naples.

Promises of gifts could sweeten a daughter's application to join a convent. At the Benedictine convent of S. Maria del Cancelliere in Palermo, for example, Giuseppe Raineri promised to pay for the gilding of the pyx on the main altar, hoping to prompt the nuns to accept his daughter, Anna. Anna's involvement with the gilding of the pyx was unusually intense, and it was while she was gilding the figure of St. Benedict himself that she received the news of her acceptance to the convent.[137] This tale traces the relationship between convent and familial patronage through the daughter, connecting her closely to the object of patronage—itself associated with the convent's order and with the Eucharist, the most intense and intimate aspects of religious devotion. It is through the gilt touch of the nun-to-be that the circle is traced to completion. Thus the tangible draws and connects the corporeal to the noncorporeal, blood to flesh, the familial to the spiritual. The father's gift, transformed by his daughter, binds the convent to the family, even as his daughter is bound to the convent.

More usually, payment for specific work took more prosaic form, such as those underpinned by the Miroballo family and Beatrice Miroballo, a professed nun, at Donnalbina in the 1730s. They undertook substantial costs involved in structural and decorative work in the convent choir, including flooring, inlay and stuccowork, papier-mâché decoration of its cornice, chestnut wood architraves around the windows, and the "door to the *loggetta* of the choir in chestnut decorated inside and outside," and they also paid for a statue of St. Benedict with an inlaid base, and an inlaid lectern.[138] By 1741 the costs had reached 3,383 ducats and 74.5 carlinos, met by Beatrice.[139] Nevertheless, blood families did not have a free hand in inscribing their views on convent walls. An undated note indicates that Beatrice's aunt, Lucrezia Muscettola, also a nun at Donnalbina, was heavily involved. Her intervention went far beyond footing bills to playing one workman off against another and highlights the degree of autonomy art patronage could afford to nuns:

> Don Francesco, curiosity allows no delay, I am letting you know that this morning there came to me D. Liborio who wished to speak with you, but I, not wishing to cause inconvenience by making him descend, took it upon myself to write to you. In any case, he brought by word of mouth the opinion of Signore Don Antonio Carnavale, who did not want to commit it to paper so as not to cause jealousy, especially because our chap had come to find him and told him that he had been at the convent, but did not know what he had to do, he said however that you should settle the debt amicably as you have begun to do and it could be extended to 1,400 ducats; if the debt cannot be settled, then I will discuss the matter with him in another manner tomorrow, God willing, after holy mass, I will speak with him, even though it has been made clear to me [that] there is no other discrepancy in the debt other than that I support 30 carlini and not 20 together with as much wood provided for the inlay as he said. Otherwise everything was all right. And may your sense of justice last one hundred years, and your attention to this holy place, God will repay you, since I am not capable of thanking you as much as I should. . . . I said 1,400 because it seemed to me that you were thinking of asking 1,340, which he wants you to advance according to our calculation.[140]

Paradoxically, their cloistering granted nuns unusual freedoms in articulating artistic programs that helped define both themselves and their familial identities. Their interventions can be seen as ways of negotiating the paradoxes of their privileged circumscription, ways of changing received theological and familial discourses, even while not directly challenging them.

Enclosed nuns—as individuals or in groups—acted as patrons on a remarkable scale. Individual nuns most frequently undertook to pay for part of their conventual building or its decoration, rather than to commission and pay for a specific artwork. This pattern of patronage defies the stereotypical art historical model of a single patron commissioning a more or less autonomous artwork from a specific artist. Yet it represents a form of patronage vital to conventual institutions and their inmates, and it expressed the ideal that the communal worship of God and institutional grandeur and beauty are of greater significance than the celebration of the individual nun who met the cost.

Thus nuns did not necessarily adopt one readily identifiable part of a convent for their patronage, but sometimes paid for the completion of the decoration of a number of different chapels or parts of their conventual church. For instance, sister Maria Costanza Gesualdo gave 30,000 ducats to her convent of the Sapienza in 1630 on the condition that 28,000 ducats should be spent on "the building and decoration of the church" and 2,000 should be spent on the acquisition of a suitable *apparato* for the church.[141] At the same church Sister Giacinta Spinelli paid for work in several chapels. She paid more than 367 ducats to complete the Chapel of the Nativity in 1667, including frescoes by Giacinto de Popoli (on the vault, the lunette, medallions on the pendentives, and decorations flanking the altarpiece), the paintings of St. Anne and the Virgin, the stuccowork framing the paintings on the side walls, including some work by Marco di Notarnicola, and the paintings' frames.[142] She also paid for oil and fresco paintings by de Popoli (just over 325 ducats) in the Chapel of the Immaculate Conception and, for the Chapel of SS. Gaetano and Andrew a large painting by Giuseppe Marullo (costing 150 ducats) and gave 30 ducats "for the painting on the side wall of Blessed Gaetano . . . and the cleaning of the old painting of Blessed Andrew by the same man."[143]

Sometimes monies were earmarked for specific projects from nuns' private incomes; at other times contributions were made more generically. Patronage ranged from the fundamentals of buying land and paying for building to the adornment of pyxes and *coretti*. No contribution seems to have been too small for convents to accept. Even at a convent like S. Giuseppe dei Ruffi, whose foundation was dominated politically and financially by generous support from nuns from the Ruffo clan, individual nuns from the same clan also contributed relatively small sums of money toward the vast costs of buying a building plot and erecting a new church. Thus the cost of purchasing houses and building the new church between the spring of 1669 and December 1674 was partly met by individual nuns from the convent.[144] In June 1671, for example, sister Chiara Maria Ruffo gave 100 ducats toward building costs.

Besides contributing to the purchase of land and building costs, individual nuns spent their *vitalizi* on specific—usually conspicuous—furnishings for their churches. The Caracciolo nuns, comfortably established at S. Gregorio Armeno and socially and politically dominant there, chose to make their mark on the church in physical terms, too. Tommasa Caracciolo helped to pay for the epitaphs in the church atrium and for the main altar and marble crosses placed in the church in 1681;[145] Anna Caracciolo paid for marble work undertaken by Dionisio Lazzari on the main altar in 1687 (Plate 4);[146] and Luisa Caracciolo paid for the brass grating of the window through which nuns received Communion between June 1692 and January 1693 (Plate 5).[147]

Similarly, at S. Giuseppe dei Ruffi the Ruffo clan continued to shape the destiny of the church. Individual nuns from that clan paid for a range of objects and furnishings, mostly with eucharistic connotations. Dionisio Lazzari's majestic and lavishly inlaid main altar (Plate 6) was paid for in installments between 1674 and 1688 by nuns Chiara Maria Ruffo, Ippolita Caterina Ruffo, and Maria Geronima La Grua.[148] Sister Ippolita eventually spent over 2,000 ducats in many installments on this new altar, from her *vitalizio* of 300 ducats.[149] The gilt copper pyx (*custodia*), also designed by Lazzari, for the same church was paid for at least in part by sister Chiara Maria Ruffo in 1668.[150] These interventions, however, are not marked visually in dynastic terms. This contrasts with patronage by Fabrizio Ruffo, coming from outside the convent, whose patronage of the chapel dedicated to S. Rufo at S. Giuseppe was dynastically identified by clear inscriptions recording his name and family coat-of-arms.

The choice of objects patronized by individual nuns often indicates a particular concern with their status as virginal lady nuns, with their separation, elevation, or enclosure. This is the case at S. Giuseppe dei Ruffi, where Maria Giacinta Ristaldo, the prioress, paid for the *gratings* of the church and Sister Maria Geronima Boncompagni gave money for the gratings though which communion was taken (*communicatorio*) and for those of the confessionals.[151] Significantly, nuns tended to opt for objects associated with the mass, such as the main altar and communion grating which the Caracciolo nuns paid for at S. Gregorio. Not only were these nuns ensuring a gracious, even impressive, setting for the Host in their church but, given the central significance of the Eucharist, not just to Catholicism generally after Trent, but especially to members of religious orders and particularly to female virgins, they were also celebrating and cementing their personal relationships to the Eucharist through such patronage.

Despite their vows of poverty, nuns often lived in comfort, if not luxury, within their convents. Gossip outside convent walls told of fabulous riches. But no exaggeration was needed to reveal the palatial riches of S. Chiara (Plate 2), which in 1560 had 380 inhabitants and an annual income of 7,000 ducats: "there one sees the vastest dormitories furnished with every commodity for their seemly recreation."[152] Bulifon records the outstanding riches of the convent of the Trinità, with its fabulous church and remarkable pyx:

> On 11 June [1608] the nuns of the Trinity, who used to live near the gate known as Costantinopli, moved to their new convent at the foot of S. Martino, which, not only through its amenable and peaceful site, but also through the size of its building, on which were spent 150,000 scudi and more, has emerged as the most beautiful and prized in Naples, not including the very beautiful church, whose pyx alone, studded with jewels, with columns of lapis lazuli, with many delicately worked silver statuettes, exceeds the value of 40,000 ducats.[153]

The unabashed worldliness of it all embarrassed ecclesiastical authorities into calling for moderation and provoked antagonistic reaction from some, like Francesco Peccerillo in 1719: "One cannot enter without a holy disgust and, as it were, with a holy horror: there where gold, and precious marbles of the altar arouse magnificent ideas of mundane vanity, rather than the mortification due to the Sacred Mysteries."[154] The richness of convents' decoration was equaled —at least occasionally—by the splendor of refreshments and entertainments within those walls. Parties inside convents, known as *ricreationi* were frequent and sometimes exorbitantly expensive.[155] At S. Maria Egiziaca a Pizzofalcone, they were held regularly for two days every month. Splendid parties celebrated the visits of dignitaries, and dinners to celebrate liturgical feasts could assume the lavishness of secular banquets.[156] A special party for Maria of Austria, wife of King Ferdinand of Hungary, was prepared by the nuns of SS. Trinità in their convent and garden.[157] In 1646 the vicereine obtained a papal license to visit female monasteries together with twenty-four ladies, and in S. Chiara they were offered a "most sumptuous repast of sugary things."[158] Fuidoro's commentary on Filomarino's attempts at reform indicates the scale of the practice: "He prohibited there the creation during the solemn feasts for dedications of monasteries the gatherings of ladies and gentlemen which create in the church more of a profane abuse of a nuptial feast than of devotion, with [the practice of] bringing in *acqua concia*, cups of sweet things and almond paste: it was more of an uproar than an ecclesiastical feast."[159]

Nuns could bring property to their convents or inherit it while they were inmates. In 1658 Lucrezia Rocco arranged for her possessions to "be disposed of as agreed orally" by sister Maria Egiziaca Rocco, professed nun at the Consolazione. This included real estate, jewelry, and a dowry of 1,300 ducats. After Lucretia's death in February 1666 Maria Egiziaca accordingly arranged for sister Teresa to receive a small staff of emeralds and one of rubies.[160]

In some convents nuns had their own private rooms, furnished to their taste. Indeed, the buying and selling of cells and small rooms occurred on a free-market basis. Among the possessions of Sister Nicoletta de Rossi, who died on 7 June 1779 at the Regina Coeli in Naples, were two cells, each of which were sold for 30 ducats, and *due camerini* which sold for 20 ducats each.[161] Nuns represented themselves as aristocrats, as well as virginal nuns in the design of their surroundings. The allure of rich materials, comfortable furniture, soft bed linens, and beautifully decorated cells is apparent not only from the inventories of individual cells, which record the rich furnishings, but also from conventual regulations, which try to instill a respect for austerity and denial of the body. For example, in seven diocesan synods held by Archbishop Filomarino in 1642, 1644, 1646, 1649, 1652, 1658, and 1662, there were thirty-eight decrees regulating the behavior of nuns, including stipulations that they should refrain from keeping ornaments, paintings, carpets, and other such objects in their cells. Likewise the Constitutions of the convent of S. Giuseppe delle Eremitane called for nuns' cells to be furnished with no more than a bed, a chair, a wardrobe, images of the Crucifixion and the Madonna, and one other image depending on the nun's devotion, and a holy water stoup.[162] Despite such regulations, nuns' bodies could be wrapped in and surrounded by clothes and furnishings of beauty and comfort. After her death in 1675 the two cells of Sister Maria Giacinta Tomacelli, a nun at S. Maria Regina Coeli, contained two mattresses, four pillows, four new rochets, two spreads or bed hangings (*sprovieri,* one of new *rosciato,* one of *tela,* or linen) a crucifix of gilt copper, a reliquary, a relic of Pius V, the Office of the Virgin, a diurnal, two ebony writing desks (one large and one small), an ebony sideboard, thirteen boards of peach, thirteen new chairs, a washbasin with a green bowl, sixteen small faience plates, two large bowls, one old bed hanging of *rosciato,* and a *canna* of chambray cloth. She also owned thirty-five paintings of religious subjects, which had been housed in the choir and in the sacristy, and twenty-three small *conette* for the choir altar.[163] The possessions of Teresa Capano at the same convent included a silver watch and a crown; and Elisabetta del Tufo, who died probably in the 1640s, left possessions including books, a coffee mill, crystal objects and china, twelve paintings, and a clock.[164] Against the prescriptions of austerity and unworldliness, these objects insist upon comforting and stimulating the body and soul, satisfying appetites, and affording human contact.

Nuns' wills and lists of their possessions in cells convey a picture of comfort, sometimes even of splendor, in spite of the ecclesiastical authorities' intermittent attempts to prevent this. Papers pertaining to the convent of the Regina Coeli in Naples listing nuns' possessions in their cells after their funeral expenses, for the period c. 1643 to c. 1679, include paintings, gilt reliquaries, and crucifixes—as one might expect—but extended to ebony writing desks, silk clothes, crystals, and faience plates (the Abbess Maria Giacinta Tomacelli, who died on 7 March 1675, owned sixteen such plates).[165] Nuns' possessions at this convent generally amounted to about 300 ducats in value, although Nicoletta de Rossi, who died on 7 June 1779, left property amounting to as much as 539.64 ducats.[166] Sister Maria Villani (1584/5–1670), the future founder of the convent of Divino Amore, arranged that her cell at S. Giovanni Battista should be "very well decorated, with chairs, paintings, desks, and other curious inessentials, and in particular that there was introduced there a rich and precious clock."[167] She later saw the error of her ways, of course, and undertook an austere and selfless life, but at this stage, that she was surrounded by luxury goods in her cell did not damage her growing reputation as an unusually devout nun. Some nuns adorned their cells lavishly. Giulia Caracciolo, a nun at the convent of S. Arcangelo a Bajano in Naples, relished an impressive range of fine objects in her cell, revealed in the report of a scandalous visitation made in 1577 to that convent by the *Vicario Generale* of Naples. In her cell, sister Giulia enjoyed paintings representing the distinctly unbiblical subjects of Aurora, Cephalus, Diana, and Endymion; furnishings of ebony and ivory; carvings; marble busts in black and white; crystal vases with real and artificial flowers; a beautiful Persian carpet; the finest quality bed linen; and a large mirror that reflected its objects at twice life size. In her small oratory, a small statue of the Virgin stood on a marble prie-dieu; a guitar hung on one side, on the other stood a silver vase for holy water, a masterpiece of carving. When the visitor pointed out the inappropriateness of these fine objects for a nun, sister Giulia, without a hint of embarrassment, countered, "Upon my faith, His Excellency would need time to waste to spend it on my furnishings." And when the *Vicario Generale* ordered her to be silent, she burst forth:

> So it does not satisfy your capriciousness that I burn myself up here in cruel solitude? I, born of the noblest blood on earth, deprived of my freedom and of my rights, am not able even to enjoy these innocent objects? So it's a crime to adorn my prison when my relatives make ill use of my worldly belongings? You, minister of Heaven, you come here to commit cruelties beyond my family's savagery, you who preach charity come here to take away from a wretched woman a last and frivolous illusion and to remind us of a cruel and harsh fact: that age in which [because] we had no

capacity to know worldly things, they tricked us into renouncing our life![168]

Here we see clearly articulated how the politics of monacation exacerbated tensions within the Church over obedience to the vow of poverty in a convent inhabited by women with a pronounced sense of entitlement, quick to resent any curbs to their privileges.

Nuns enjoyed the services of individual servants (for whom they usually provided a dowry after several years service), allowing them some of the privileges of social class that, in theory, they had eschewed. In her account of S. Gregorio Armeno, written in 1577, Fulvia Caracciolo explained that when she entered that convent in 1542, before standardized enclosure was forced on it, there were about fifty nuns, each of whom had servants, rooms, withdrawing rooms, kitchens, and cellars.[169] Even in enclosed convents this practice continued. For instance, in October 1681 Eleonora Carafa completed payment of 50 ducats for the entry of Diana Del Chiano, her personal servant, to S. Gregorio Armeno.[170] Special permission from Rome, obtained by her mother, Eleonora Gaetano, daughter of the prince of Caserta, allowed Teodora Costanza Caracciolo to have her childhood nurse with her in her convent in Martina.[171] The ecclesiastical authorities tried to rein in this practice, particularly with regard to servants from outside. For them it was an embarrassment, the source of scandal: "[Ministers and servants from outside] should be common to all, and as many as are necessary and no more, for otherwise, as is notorious, scandals and very serious improprieties follow."[172] However, structural relationships between convents and rich families undermined ecclesiastical regulation.

Nuns continued to be daughters even after taking vows. Despite the nuns' apparently breaking with blood ties and social demands through their vows, those bonds often remained a lively and important aspect of their conventual lives. Likewise, families did not give up daughters who became nuns; instead the convent became another space to be inscribed by those families. The expensive architecture and fantastic decoration, which publicly declared the religious devotion of a particular family and allowed it to secure acceptance or influence within the conventual system, also allowed convents to demonstrate the high social class of their inmates, their wealth and standing. In turn, a convent could exploit this display to compete with its counterparts in order to persuade the wealthiest and most powerful aristocratic families to lodge their daughters there rather than in a rival institution. Thus it is that prestigious convents were able to retain their preeminence for decades, even centuries.

Within the conventual complex, it was the convent church which was the site of the most intense familial and monachal patronage. This was the most public space, the liminal space where convent and city intersected, and where an intervention—whether visual or oral, an inlaid marble altar or a sung mass—would reach both audiences. Dynastically marked patronage was focused almost exclusively on the conventual church. When nuns chose to pay for specific aspects of building or decoration, they tended to stipulate the church rather than other parts of the conventual complex. Inside the church nuns lavished patronage most conspicuously on objects related to the eucharist and those drawing attention to their exclusive or cloistered status. Thus they used their patronage to mark themselves in the public eye as virginal lady nuns rather than as members of a particular blood family.

Conventual patronage operated at several levels and from several different starting points simultaneously. Nuns' families intervened in various ways in the foundation, expansion, and decoration of convents and their churches, usually to consolidate a daughter's position either on entry to a convent or in its organizational structure. Inside the convent nuns drew on familial wealth to extend and decorate their institution.

Payments by individual enclosed nuns depart from the standard forms of patronage celebrated by art historians, where an individual patron, artwork, and artist can be tidily lined up in explanatory terms. As we have noted, individual nuns frequently made payments which were nonspecific, such as toward buying land for conventual expansion or toward the cost of a particularly expensive item, without marking that work to show this (such as with a coat-of-arms or inscription). Their gestures, known to us only from conventual records, were not extroverted in the conventional terms in which patronage is usually understood. Although these interventions were made to affect the world beyond the institution by glorifying the convent and its church, they were not made to enhance the nun's name *outside* the convent. Much of this patronage remained anonymous to outsiders' eyes, relatively small financial contributions swallowed up in protracted and expensive interventions, contributing toward institutional ends rather than the acquisition of a specific object earmarked by a patron. But the visual and external anonymity of this patronage should not lead us to become insensitive to the significance of its introverted nature. Their interventions served to enhance the standing of patron nuns within their convents, their involvement recognized as being for the good of the institution as a whole, a sign of their devotion, their self-effacement, and institutional subordination. It was, therefore, their individual reputation within the convent as well as their institutional reputation outside that nuns safeguarded and enhanced by acts of such patronage. For while they were anonymous to the world outside, these acts were, as the nuns involved fully knew, carefully recorded in the records within their own institutions. It is a mistake to assume that contributions that were invisible to outsiders were so to insiders, for this is to assume that all power and influence were located outside the convent walls.

5

Convents and Conflict: Conventual Urbanism in Naples

Convents were never far from conflict. A conspicuous presence in the city, the crucible of power relations, was vital for religious orders and aristocratic families. Rivalries spiraled as convents competed to crown the city skyline, dominate prominent sites, and occupy prestigious road frontages (Plate 7). Convents fought for power urbanistically, not only through aggrandizement in spatial terms, but also through architectural design. In Rome power struggles were fought urbanistically at a local level, as families struggled to make their palace jut farther out at a critical corner than the palace next door, command a view, or dominate a vista through densely packed streets.[1] In Naples similar struggles occurred between female convents, determined to occupy impressive street frontages, or to dominate a prominent part of the city, or its skyline. Conspicuousness within the urban fabric consolidated political power. Disputes between convents often focused on optical power, what could be seen, and who could overlook whom and from where. These struggles to assume dominance in terms of sight were constant within early modern Italian cities and were not restricted to convents. But because enclosed religious orders enjoyed few other avenues for expression and exploration, the right to determine what inmates could see and who could see them became particularly significant.

Clustered tightly together inside Naples's city walls, convents engaged in ceaseless emulation, born of rivalry over the limited resources of rich daughters and space in the fiercely competitive "vertical city." This chapter examines the forms conventual rivalries assumed urbanistically, and the means by which convents pursued their ends, legally through suits at law, legalistically through bureaucratic maneuverings, or illegally by violent occupation and trespass. It considers disputes between rival female convents, between male and female institutions, as well as between convents and layfolk; and it examines the terms in which disputes were framed and settled and the conditions which helped achieve success.

While the walls of convents remained generally modest, their skylines were a riot of energy and display, of proud exclamation and ambitious aspiration. Bell towers and belvederes were the principal subjects of opposition through the courts because dominance of the skyline and of the sight-lines across and through and over the city were highly prized visible signs of precedence (Plate 7 and Figures 9, 11, 12, 13 and 42). Seeing was as important as being seen; seeing over ensured that nuns could not be overseen.

This was true in almost all cities in Italy at this time, but competition for verticality was particularly marked in Naples, as institutions strove to counter the effects of the city's topography, steeply slanted toward the sea "in the form of a most noble theater."[2] Thus a tower built by a convent below could project impertinently into the air space of its neighbor higher up the hill. Such familiarity bred contempt.

Command of the city was epitomized vertically. Convents competed with each other to dominate vistas, to enjoy open views to the sea or the mountains, and to tower over surrounding buildings. In a cramped city where buildings were tall and space was at a premium, access to a roof terrace or belvedere or merely a good view from corridor windows had a high value (Figures 11, 12 and 42). Again, convents adopted aristocratic practices. As aristocrats jostled for better views, more salubrious air, and symbolic advantage in their palaces, towers, which were public signs of dominance, proliferated from baronial palaces (Figure 9).[3] Vertical preeminence was all the more significant to enclosed nuns, whose lack of freedom elsewhere might be compensated for by the eye's freedom to range far and wide over the city whose streets they could know only optically. It is for this reason that convents placed great emphasis on their command of good views and height, and why most interconventual disputes focus on bell towers, belvederes, or the height of new walls for dormitories.

Convents usually enjoyed the benefits of several belvederes. S. Maria Donnaregina had as many as five by 1706. Belvederes afforded access not only to good views and air, but also to the enjoyment of city processions and therefore symbolized the nuns' involvement in city events. For particularly important occasions, convents erected temporary belvederes, such as that of wood granted to Donnaregina so that the nuns could enjoy the Entry of King

Philip V.[4] In his 1689 account of the convent of Donnalbina, Bonifacio de Sanzio enthusiastically describes how from the belvedere "from each angle you can see mountains, the sea, and a large part of the city."[5] Likewise, Chiarini points out the glories of the views to be had from the prestigious convent of S. Chiara: "Up until the middle of the last century [i.e., the eighteenth century] there was built facing the eastern part of the convent a large loggia, for use as belvedere for the lady nuns, 300 *palmi* long and 40 *palmi* wide; and above it was raised another room whence one enjoys the view of the entire new mole and its surroundings, no less than the enchanting prospect of the Parthenopean gulf."[6]

Strikingly, in discussing the assets of the convent of SS. Trinità in via Costantinopoli, Celano praises the views from each of the rooms where the nuns slept, which were otherwise marked by their "very clean poverty": "each room has its views both of the sea and of the countryside and of almost the whole city."[7] Thus a grand view could signify nobility while not undercutting the notion of nuns' poverty. For this reason open views were particularly prized by aristocratic convents. Height also brought health, as Celano indicates in praising the convent of Divino Amore as "among the [most] delightful that exist, both for the good view that it has of the sea and of all the marshes and of the mountain of S. Martino, as for the quantity of water that one sees in it; while the royal aqueduct passes through this convent: and to achieve this, many commodious and beautiful palaces in this street were demolished."[8] Celano values the view not only aesthetically but as an asset to health, and as a sign of relative urban power.

Few accounts directly describe nuns using belvederes. Despite convents' evident determination to build high and safeguard their vertical dominance, there is a rhetoric of self-effacement with regard to individual nuns actually using these spaces of pleasure. Thus Sister Maria Aurelia Cecilia scolded a sister nun at the convent of S. Giuseppe in Martina for going up to the belvedere as was customary during Carnival to watch the people in masks, behavior she thought unseemly for a nun. Such a reproof urges the refocusing of eyes currently trained on the rest of the world from on high to turn inward to humble examination of the self.[9] An incident involving Sister Celestina Raineri at the Benedictine convent of S. Maria di Cancelliere in Palermo is particularly resonant in this regard. During the *festino* devoted to St. Rosalia, the entire city poured into a magnificent procession down via Toledo, where the Cancelliere convent stood.[10] Ordered by her Superior to go up to the belvedere to watch the procession, Celestina resisted the temptation of the sight, indeed of sight itself: "She obeyed the command, but to avoid the possibility of alienating her Spirit with the sight of so great a throng, and of such various things, and to mortify the curiosity of sight, she kept her eyes closed during that time so as not to gaze at them."[11] The subversiveness of Celestina's actions only becomes fully apparent the following day:

> It was customary in those days to solemnize the following day with a very sumptuous cavalcade of nobles, who in very showy dress rode through the city on high-spirited horses, richly adorned. The Mother Superior ordered Celestina to take herself to see the cavalcade. The servant of God obeyed the blind woman, and to satisfy her Superior's wish, she kept her eyes open and saw it. But throughout the function, she did nothing but laugh, in such a manner that made the nuns wonder, not knowing the reason.[12]

Interrogated by the priest, Celestina explained that she laughed because what she saw was a cavalcade of animals: "I saw that on the horses there were various animals of diverse species, such as monkeys and others."[13] Her priest interpreted this as a grace from her jealous heavenly Spouse, anxious that her mind should not be cluttered by the sight of the worldly gentlemen.[14] The nun's refusal to enjoy a privileged vantage point transforms hers into a superior view, no longer based on worldly pleasure but able to disdain and rise above the mundane. Sight and height become metaphors for spiritual superiority rather than worldly advantages enjoyed by the nuns within.

While vertical dominance was most often the subject of legal dispute, convents expanded horizontally, too. Purchasing houses and gardens for conventual expansion was the order of the day. Often convents, hungry for space, simply enclosed regular and irregular blocks (as we noted in chapter 1). But on occasion, ambitions to command a city presence were such that convents were willing to forego the advantages of extra space for building and sought instead to open up a square in front of their institution to create a pause in the unceasing clamor for attention of crowded buildings, and to announce their presence, paradoxically, by an absence. Thus S. Maria del Gesù purchased a large house standing between it at the public street running around S. Maria della Consolazione, in order to create a gracious square directly in front of the main entrance facade of the church of S. Maria del Gesù (Figure 10).

Most sought after of all was a grand symmetrical facade overlooking a square. This was achieved at S. Maria Donnaregina by moving the main entrance of the church to take advantage of the square between it and the archiepiscopal palace opposite. That square had been opened by Archbishop Filomarino in 1647 to replace a narrow street and to lend dignity to the palace and room for visitors' carriages.[15] The desirability of building a new bell tower to create a symmetrical facade for the church and allow full exploitation of the advantages of the open square is articulated clearly in a document of 1682: "as is the case in other churches, bell towers provide unity and symmetry to church facades, and far more so at the Church of Donnaregina, through its having a square, and very large space before it, together with the prospect to the Archiepiscopal Palace, in such a way that in the plan made in past years the said space was left empty so that it could be used for the bell tower."[16] Thus the church of S. Maria Donnaregina was turned, like a sunflower toward the sun, to bask in the reflected grandeur of the ecclesiastical palace mirrored in the elegant square.

In Naples lawsuits between the tightly clustered convents were the order of the day. Freedom to enjoy a good view and access to clean air and light were paralleled by claims to freedom from being overlooked by neighboring buildings. Ironically, despite convents' frequent reluctance to institute enclosure as advocated by the Council of Trent, they were quick to advance the principles of enclosure in attacking their rivals, frequently resorting to the argument that a new building would overlook their convent and violate their enclosure. Such arguments are haunted by the conception of a convent as an independent institution necessarily expressed architecturally as a freestanding mass. Thus the Council of Trent's emphasis on separation as the means to guarantee virginity received a new dimension as an urbanistic metaphor.

The Augustinian nuns at S. Giuseppe dei Ruffi were typical in this regard. They were at loggerheads in 1678 with the neighboring convent, S. Maria del Gesù, which, while taking down the upper doors of its bell tower (Figures 11, 12), had seized the chance secretly to erect a belvedere with windows overlooking S. Giuseppe.[17] The Augustinians appealed to the archiepiscopal court, requesting that the belvedere's apertures be closed up.[18] As if quarreling with one neighboring institution were not enough, S. Giuseppe took issue with "the Basilians" at S. Maria Donnaregina over their wish to build a second campanile and to raise the height of a dormitory wall, a struggle that lasted from c.1678 to 1706.[19] The new bell tower was prohibited on the grounds that it was too close to the choir of S. Giuseppe, which would cause "the utmost inconvenience" to nuns during recitation of the holy offices, and also because it was not necessary but "purely voluntary, for show."[20] That prohibition did not, however, settle the matter once and for all. Donnaregina's ambition to build a second bell tower soon resurfaced, this time as a bid to raise the height of the wall of their enclosure. But the nuns of S. Giuseppe were quick to challenge this ruse:

> [Donna Regina claimed the] need to raise the wall of the enclosure, including that opposite the convent of S. Giuseppe, on the apparent pretext of creating a loggia, and other necessary offices inside their convent, in order to gain a building license, but their real plan was to raise another really large belvedere, [something] attempted many times with other superiors and always refused, because of the unsuitability of the site, and because of the damage to the convent of S. Giuseppe.[21]

Donnaregina responded by hiring an architect to declare that not only would the new campanile be no problem to S. Giuseppe, but that if it were seen as a problem even at that distance, then all the other bell towers of the city should be removed, too.[22] This time Monsignor Parisi, Vicario Generale, capitulated on condition that the wall be built no higher than the old one and that the buildings be made "equal to the older walls" of the enclosure.[23] However, S. Giuseppe continued to be aggrieved because Donnaregina, it claimed in September 1706, was building up to the maximum height for rivalry alone:

> For pure emulation, and certainly, since to make the said workshops, dormitories, and so on, far from needing to raise the wall of enclosure as high as the old one, they need to lower it; but they want the freedom to be able to raise it as high as permitted, and to do to the convent of San Giuseppe a huge damage without achieving anything useful to them, but harm, since building higher than the old [walls], they obscure not only one quite small belvedere belonging to the convent of S. Giuseppe, but what matters more and is more displeasing to the convent of S. Giuseppe, the large choir window, in such a way, that even on the brightest day they will have to recite Holy Offices by candlelight.[24]

As the proposed site for Donnaregina's new bell tower was several stone's throws from S. Giuseppe, the Augustinians could not rely on the usual arguments. Instead, they claimed that the proposed bell tower would block sunlight and divert salubrious winds from their convent—a claim which was hard to support given the easterly position of Donnaregina. The absence of convincing practical arguments prompted S. Giuseppe to resort to the dubious high ground of self-righteous indignation. Donnaregina, it claimed, was undertaking something "unnecessary, but purely voluntary, for show, for magnificence" and "for sheer emulation."[25] One senses here the indignant frustration of a convent whose own splendid facade and urban prominence were threatened by a neighboring institution with similar ambitions, and the fervid competition for urban glamour, where a bell tower signified local supremacy and a belvedere social consequence.

Squabbles between rival convents could last for decades, often even longer, and they frequently became complex and bitter, as the rivalry between S. Chiara and S. Maria Donnalbina shows (Figures 13, 14). For over two hundred years they disputed the land purchased in 1574 by Donnalbina from the duke of Gravina, on which that convent built a dormitory. The nuns of S. Chiara claimed that Gravina had sold the land on condition that it should not be built on. In 1581 the Sacro Regio Concilio determined by deed that the new building should be closed, without apertures, either toward Gravina's garden or toward the convent of S. Chiara, so that S. Chiara would not be overlooked at all. The building that was completed in 1582, with two belvederes, accorded with this ruling. But a few years later Donnalbina began to pierce its new building with windows facing S. Chiara. The Sacra Congregazione responded in 1628 by requesting that all such doors and windows should be walled over and all other interventions removed. According to the nuns of S. Chiara, this "failed to dam the attempts by Donnalbina, while from time to time they attempted other innovations."[26] By 1678 back in court, on account of some egregious apertures and the belvederes's parapets, the Sacra Congregazione reaffirmed its ruling of 1628. For some time there was a truce, but in 1701 the quarrel reignited and again lasted for years. The Sacra Congregazione, with a shade of exasperation, attempted to settle the matter once and for all in 1715 by ordering Donnalbina not to create new windows, nor to undertake the slightest alteration to the entire convent which could infringe upon that of S. Chiara, imposing perpetual silence on both parties, and ordering that a stone inscribed to this effect should be set in the wall. But even inscribed stones proved ineffective, and in 1726 a new ruling was forced more or less to repeat that of almost one hundred years earlier. Although one issue had finally been laid to rest, resentments festered, rancor swelled, and a new conflict erupted in 1770, this time over Donnalbina's heightening the eastern belvedere. An attempt was made to patch things up informally at first, but suspicions ran so high on both sides that it was doomed to fail. Once again the Sacra Congregazione was called on to sort things out, and, once again, its ruling fell largely in favor of S. Chiara.[27]

To ensure that quarrels were settled in their favor, convents needed the protection of a powerful patron. The significance of such a patron emerges clearly in the settlement of a particularly acrid dispute, which broke out during the late 1630s between the Sapienza and the Croce di Lucca, both ambitious convents engaged in programs of rapid expansion. The proximity of these two convents and their relationship with the garden of the Palazzo Conca is best seen on a map prepared for a later and unrelated lawsuit (Figure 3).The Sapienza protested at the Croce di Lucca's proud new buildings, whose height threatened not only "the view of the sea, but also to cut off the air and sun, and to cause numerous disadvantages."[28] Building works were halted, and both parties had recourse to Rome. The Curia suggested that each convent should choose a representative to negotiate a reasonable agreement. The more aristocratic Sapienza chose the prince of Bisignano, while the up-and-coming Croce di Lucca opted for their patron, the prince of Cellamare, Nicolò Giudice.[29] The resulting compromise favored the Sapienza. In 1646 it was agreed that the dormitory that touched the wall between the two convents should rise no higher than one apartment above the Croce di Lucca's loggia's arcades; and the Croce di Lucca had to move its other wing, which reached back to the Palazzo Conca, to a distance of 50 *palmi* from the wall of the Sapienza's infirmary and its large window.[30] The height of this wing was also restricted to a maximum of two apartments above the level of the loggia. In return, the Sapienza sold to the Croce di Lucca for 8,500 ducats some houses which it had bought in 1596 from various laypeople for a total of 5,000 ducats.[31] The combined weight of the more aristocratic convent and grander representative advantaged the Sapienza more than the niceties of its case in relation to its opponent.

The contested expansion of S. Francesco delle Cappuccinelle gave rise for the first time the claim that on their own property nuns could do as they wished, regardless of the consequences for their neighbors—a reckless claim to make in a overcrowded city. The convent originated as a small church and conservatory or college for virgin girls, established by Eleonora Scarpato and her husband, the notary Giovanni Luca Giglio, who agreed to dissolve their marriage ties and to undertake a life of religious observance in their house, as thanksgiving for Eleonora's recovery from a grave illness.[32] Dressed in coarse Franciscan garments, they gathered girls from throughout the city to wear the habit and follow the hours for mass and prayer in imitation of the Capuchins.[33] Signs of ambition followed soon after. By 1604 they had obtained permission to house the Host in the church, and by 1613 Giglio purchased for 4,000 ducats a large house with a garden and three small adjoining houses, next to their church.[34] In 1621 the convent was enclosed under the rule of St. Clare. As was usual at such a juncture, professed nuns from existing convents, sister Maria de Cordua from the Consolazione, as abbess, and sister Silvia Ricci, a professed nun from S. Antonio, as mistress of novices, were called in to help in the establishment of S. Francesco as an enclosed convent.[35] Now that the convent was properly established, it could exact dowry charges from newcomers, a change in status and income which prompted the purchase of considerable property for expansion in the ensuing years.[36] The convent also benefited from a sizable donation made by Mother Teresa dello Spirito Santo, formerly duchess of Montalto and now a Discalced Carmelite, in 1628.[37] Thus status and benefactors came hand in hand in the expansion of S. Francesco.

S. Francesco delle Cappuccinelle's new church, begun in 1712 to plans by Michelangelo Nauclerio, provoked opposition from the Conservatory of the Maddalena, situated on the other side of the main street (Figure 15). The nuns of the Maddalena objected that its cupola "would deprive them of the benefit of the sun as much as of the winds," thereby emphasizing the necessarily shared nature of city space.[38] Against this claim, the Cappuccinelle boldly declared that "everybody on their own land can well erect buildings up to the stars." But they undercut this individualistic conception of the city with their arguments that "the aforementioned Conservatory [the Maddalena] and convent [of S. Francesco] were divided by the Royal street. And . . . as a result of the large distance that there was between one place and the other, it was not possible to create shadow damaging to the Conservatory."[39] The Cappuccinelle went on to point out that their convent's site was lower than that of the conservatory, thereby reducing any height advantage; and also that the Maddalena, engaged in the same politics of height, was the pot calling the kettle black, since it already had two belvederes, which were even higher than the proposed new church.[40] Nevertheless the claim to freedom to build as high as they wished on their own land should not be underestimated. Here the notion of a city as anything more than the sum of its parts collapses, as the convent acknowledged the rights and might of property alone. But such a view found little favor at this date and the Cappuccinelle did not get their way. In 1713 both parties agreed that the roof of the new church of S. Francesco would be thirty-four *palmi* high (three *palmi* lower than proposed) and that the bell tower would be built on the monastery instead of the church.[41] So the buildings went ahead, but not on the terms envisaged by the Cappuccinelle. The Maddalena successfully defended their air space and right to light and freedom from being overlooked.

In the politics of urban building, relative superiority was all. Convents purchased land and property not only so that they could expand but also to hinder their rivals' plans. During the late 1680s S. Maria della Consolazione of the Reformed Franciscans began to investigate the possibility of buying a large house belonging to S. Maria Donnalbina for the purposes of expansion but, after the initial inquiries and valuation, took no action. To their consternation, in December 1689 they heard that the house was to be sold instead to the nuns of S. Maria del Gesù and quickly appealed to Archbishop Pignatelli to protect their interests. "The convent of S. Maria del Gesù," they claimed, "had made the purchase not because it was useful to it, or necessary, but only for the sake of [making a] lawsuit, because its site being near this convent, [the convent of S. Maria del Gesù] could claim on this pretext that it needed some accommodations in relation to the height of the building that [S. Maria della Consolazione] was having built."[42] Unfortunately, we do not know the other side of the argument, but the Consolazione won the day with Pignatelli's pronouncement that Donnalbina should sell the house to it, dissolving the agreement with the Gesù. The archbishop, however, paid heed to the rival claims of the Gesù by insisting that the Franciscans' proposed expansion should be no higher than their existing enclosure.[43]

Over and above the urban rivalries themselves, the arguments advanced in self-defense or heated attack are revealing. The claim to inviolate enclosure was a commonplace. Sunlight and clean air were also frequently cited. By the early eighteenth century there surfaces more frequently an interesting tension between the defense of conventual autonomy, an institution's freedom to build as high as it wished, and recognition of the city as more than the sum of its parts, extending to a concern for the public realm.

A particularly acrimonious dispute which demonstrates these tensions arose between the Benedictine nuns of SS. Marcellino e Festo and the Jesuits —not by chance between a male and a female institution. The area around the female Benedictine convent of SS. Marcellino e Festo (itself a composite of S. Marcellino, S. Festo, and S. Donato) and, just opposite it, the male Benedictine monastery, S. Severino was something of a Benedictine enclave, with a formidable presence of both monks and nuns of that order (Figure 16).[44] Trouble started when the Jesuits, whose College and Gesù Vecchio stood just across the Strada Nuova and Strada del Gesù Vecchio (present-day via Paladino) from the rich and expansionist SS. Marcellino e Festo, began to advance their own position in the area (Figures 17 and 18 show their relationship). Simmering distrust erupted into open dispute in 1557 when the Jesuits proposed to extend their building with the regularization (*l'inquadramento*) of their college toward SS. Marcellino e Festo. First they increased the height of the college's wall, with the result that the nuns were unable to use one of their corridors until recourse to the Court of Rome resulted in the walling up of several windows "to rid themselves from the dangers of other controversies, in which with them [the Jesuits] at other times they had found themselves."[45] The Benedictines claimed that the planned extension was against their interests because it would obstruct their view, block healthy winds, restrict the movement of air, and overlook their enclosure, but the Jesuits continued to amplify their plans for systematization and improvement, shifting their attention in the first two decades of the seventeenth century from buildings to control of communications, to streets.

The Jesuits were well aware that urban dominance was achieved not simply by out-building one's immediate neighbors in height, but by achieving greater urban command through street layout. To the south of the Jesuit College, the land falls sharply in a kestrel's swoop down to the Porto district, making communication at this point between the two parts of town difficult. The Jesuits, perched on the edge of the high town, decided to build a road to link the street running in front of their college with that quarter down below. (Compare Figures 19, 20, 21, and 22, and see below.) Meanwhile, in 1708 the nuns of SS. Marcellino e Festo, wishing to expand their convent, applied to the Tribunal of Fortification for the concession of some streets running from the strada di Nido down to the strada di S. Angelillo to the church of S. Agnello de' Grassi.[46]

The Jesuits took issue with that *censuazione*, as it flew in the face of plans, dependent on concessions granted to them as early as 1614 and 1620, on precisely the same rooms and streets.[47] In the Jesuits' case the agreement included their undertaking to make a street, wide enough for carriages, on a straight line connecting their church to the lower quarters of the city (Figures 18, 20, 21).[48] In 1713 they appealed to the Tribunal of Fortification, producing the old concessions and asking to execute their street. Along the same lines as arguments advanced in May 1620, they argued that the new street would "be of the greatest convenience to the public, and to traffic, allowing by means of the aforementioned street the exchange of goods from the quarter of the Marina del Vino with that above, since there is not another that gives this convenience, apart from the street of Mezzocanone, and the street of the Ferri Vecchi."[49] And in another document, they emphasize the "great convenience, beauty and embellishment of the city" that it represents.[50] Thus in 1713, over and above advantage to individual institutions, it is the usefulness to the city as a whole and the public at large that is emphasized.

The nuns replied that there already existed many convenient streets by which one could reach the Seggio of Porto. The Jesuits, claimed the nuns, "mask themselves and make a shield of feigned zeal for the public weal."[51] Then, in a striking display of concern for the commonweal, the nuns themselves suggested that while the new street would attract villains, the bleak walls of convent and college would provide no help for their victims.[52] Far from enhancing the city, the new street would damage it: "Far, however, is the new street remote from being of public benefit, instead it would be damaging to the common good, because incorporating the houses in the College, would make the city ever more restricted, and those inhabitants would have to find for themselves lodgings farther from their workplace."[53] By this date, then, arguments about building still include enclosure, salubrious winds, air, and sunlight, but now the public good is the salient issue. This represents a striking shift in the discourse from the interests of individual religious institutions to issues of the general good and the city as a whole, from an introverted discourse of enclosure and the protection of virginity to an extroverted one of the commonweal. The Jesuits most skillfully adopted the new tactics of urban warfare, embracing the shift in emphasis from religious issues to secular issues, from a discourse focused on individual institutions to a direct evocation of urban consciousness.

The enclosed Benedictine nuns were wrong-footed by this. Unable to dress their case up in terms of the city's street systems without betraying their enclosure, they were forced to resort to their only legitimate claim to civic authority, reminding the Tribunal in a veiled threat: "In the convent of S. Marcellino live women of the first rank of this city, who to serve God and the public good, having chosen to spend their lives in perpetual claustration, placed in disregard to the pleasures of the world, and the comfort of their own homes, are deserving of all the greater justice, and attention, so that they do not change their minds about their condition, and in future do not cease to profess it."[54] Their social distinction, self-denial, and service of both God and the public good are all wielded to persuade the courts to allow them to retain an upper hand vis-à-vis the Jesuits. There are, of course, some parallels with the terms in which the Jesuits argued for building the new road. But references to their noble birth and their threat of withdrawal from religious service, with the concomitant damage to the public realm, find no parallel in the Jesuits' arguments and even at this date sound old-fashioned, revealing the desperation of the outmaneuvered aristocratic female convent.

In August 1713 the city Tribunal found in favor of the Jesuits on condition that they make their street suitable for carriages.[55] Thus streets, representing improvements in urban communications, won out against God and the self-sacrifice of nobility. The following year, in 1714, the royal engineer Giuseppe Lucchese and the architect Antonino di Notarnicola decided that it was practicable for the Jesuits to build their street, but that the new buildings planned by the Jesuits should not exceed forty-three palmi (as opposed to the forty-nine palmi on which they had set their sights), and that a portion of some of their buildings which were of no use either to the new construction or to the new street, could be taken over by the convent "to give it greater roominess."[56] The Tribunal also stipulated the conditions under which the Jesuits could go ahead and extend their college. The Jesuits were to sell to the Benedictines that part of the Palmieri's grand house which was not required for building the road; the new buildings (next to the library) were not to overlook SS. Marcellino e Festo; and the Jesuits' carriage gateway was not to face that of the nuns.[57] Thus many of the nuns' specific complaints were addressed, while allowing the Jesuits to go ahead with their more ambitious schemes.

The Jesuits planned a switchback street of three ramps zigzagging down the steep hill behind the college, most clearly recorded in a drawing made Antonio di Notarnicola and Giuseppe Lucchese (Figure 22). The arrangement of streets in this area before this new cut is shown in a drawing surviving in the Archivio di Stato in Naples (Figure 19). This drawing shows that the route from outside the Jesuits' church to the Porto area was circuitous, requiring a traveler to make three sides of a square; it was the fourth side of that square that the new street would cut through (albeit with steep ramps). An irregular alley running up beside the church of S. Agnello from the south meant that, in effect, the lowest of the three ramps was already in place, as is shown in two drawings. The clearer of the two drawings is dated 1 October 1717 and is by Lucchese and his colleague Antonino di Notarnicola (Figure 22); it shows the entire site of the new road, together with the extension to the Jesuit College and the new enclosure to SS. Marcellino e Festo (with the earlier streets shown in dotted lines); the second dated 28 October 1716, is a multi-flap drawing produced by the architect Notarnicola and the royal engineer Lucchese (Figure 18); it shows the Palmieri house, its relationship to the streets in the lower Porto quarter of the city (below nos. 6 and 8 on the drawing), and the proposed new road penciled in over the house (between H and 9). These drawings together with contemporary documents show that the Jesuits had to buy up the Falcone's house along with other houses belonging to the convent of SS. Marcellino and Festo, and the houses of the Palmieri (Figure 21).[58] The Palmieri's "palatial house" occupied a crucial part of the site intended for the new road (Figure 18). It was built on three levels, bridged the steep hill between the level of the church of S. Agnello de' Grassi and the upper level of the Jesuit College, and it hugged the southern walls of SS. Marcellino e Festo running west to the southeasternmost corner of the Jesuit College, divided from it by the street leading to S. Angelo de' Cardamoni. The completion of the new street was eventually marked with a plaque in 1733.[59]

Even after the Jesuits had begun to build the new road and to extend their buildings, troubles erupted anew in 1720. Instead of five new windows, as agreed, the Jesuits had opened nine, which boasted parapets three *palmi* high overlooking the convent. The Tribunal of Fortification duly ordered that the windows be reduced in height.[60] A couple of decades later in 1744 the Jesuits once again exceeded their brief by extending the building permitted next to their library to the adjacent loggia.[61] In response to a barrage of complaints from the nuns that these initiatives disrupted their views, blocked salutiferous winds, exceeded the height specified in the agreement, and meant that the Jesuits overlooked their convent, the Jesuits abandoned the enterprise.[62]

Despite their apparent concern about the effect on the city of the Jesuits' proposed interventions, the nuns of SS. Marcellino e Festo advanced their own plans to suck more of the city into their own enclosure. On 19 December 1718, they applied for a license to demolish certain houses and to embrace others inside the enclosure wall they were building, indicating that "they want to finish those houses that remain outside the aforementioned enclosure."[63] Clearly the Benedictines' opposition to the Jesuits was born as much from rival ambition as from any lofty motive. But the whole episode shows that, perhaps increasingly, male religious institutions had an advantage over their female counterparts, because they could be more extroverted in both planning and justifying urban interventions. While female convents relied on introversion and a rhetoric of enclosure, godliness, and self-sacrifice, the Jesuits were able to harness their ambitions to those of the city more broadly.

While, as we have seen, recourse to law was by far the most usual mode by which disputes were settled, desire to expand urbanistically could become so desperate that some convents resorted to violence to achieve their ends.[64] In one striking case, on 4 November 1728 about 300 nuns of the Santa Casa degl'Incurabili, furious at the restrictive space of their hospital, in which they slept in beds arranged "like books in a library," took action to remedy the situation by forcing the Pisan fathers next door at S. Maria delle Grazie a Caponapoli to surrender some of their garden for the expansion of the hospital.

During the night, holding aloft a cross, the nuns destroyed the garden wall, breaking through in procession to the adjoining male monastery, singing sacred hymns. Other people, dressed as if insane, came to help the nuns, some with arms and, beating the fathers, drove them from their monastery, making way for the nuns. Twelve days went by and even an angry excommunication from Cardinal Francesco Pignatelli and an enraged letter from the pope to the archbishop failed to dislodge the nuns from their occupation of S. Maria delle Grazie. But on 16 November 500 infantry and cavalry soldiers were squadroned in the square before the monastery. At 12 o'clock the order rang out to open the doors, and a maniple of soldiers occupied the building in the presence of civil and religious authorities. The hospital governor and the fiscals of the archiepiscopal Curia begged the nuns to withdraw, but the nuns, on their knees, declared that they would rather die as martyrs. However, when the soldiers produced short sticks hidden under their clothes and began to strike at the nuns, the sisters quickly fled the way they had entered. Nevertheless, after peace was reestablished, news came from Vienna that the city had leased the plot in question for 10 ducats a year, and on 30 August 1729 the first stone for the new wing of the hospital was laid.[65] The nuns had won. Such drastic action could only be resorted to in exceptional circumstances, however; shock tactics and popular support could not be relied on as a matter of course.

Powerful religious institutions were almost alone in being able to resist the encroachment of their counterparts. Between lay folk and convents there were fewer long-lasting and acrimonious cases over the right to build. The cards were stacked in favor of religious institutions, and laypeople without strong political protectors were vulnerable to losing property to the voracious jaws of expanding religious institutions. Typical is a perfunctory record in the archive of the Franciscan convent of S. Francesco delle Cappuccinelle to the effect that in 1706 the monastery prevented Nicola and Geronimo Magliuoli from increasing the height of their house opposite the convent.[66] The expansion of this convent illustrates the ease with which convents swallowed up dwellings of lay folk. In 1633 S. Francesco delle Cappuccinelle bought a large house with shops and garden from Cesare Maria Candia for 2,950 ducats. By 1647 a further purchase of a large house belonging to the estate of Paolo Macario was planned, "since the two palaces purchased by the said convent . . . were not large enough [to provide] comfortable residence for its religious, whose number, as a result of the recent enclosure, was continuing to increase."[67] Macario's widow and heir opposed the convent's plans, but she was defeated and the completion payment for her house was made in 1647.[68]

Good connections were all; and even minor nobility could be dangerously exposed to the conventual maw. A case between the Benedictine nuns at SS. Marcellino e Festo and a member of the minor nobility, the prince of Supino, is instructive in this regard. In December 1737, the courts ordered that a window in the duke of Andria's palace, where lived the prince of Supino, Giuseppe Maria della Leonessa, should be blocked, since it provided a view into the convent.[69] The prince retorted in May 1738 that the window did not look directly at the convent, but only obliquely through a corridor.[70] Then, with impeccable logic, he maintained that it was the nuns who overlooked the palace. After the palace was built, they had put up a belvedere equivalent in height, whence they could look straight into his palace.[71] The prince also pointed out that the palace window antedated the nuns' corridor and that from that room a view of the sea had "always been enjoyed."[72] Again the nuns insisted that the window in question provided views into a corridor, the choir, and two cells in the same corridor.[73] The nuns' persistence paid off. In August 1739 the Sacro Regio Consiglio formally required the offending window to be altered so that it granted no views into the convent.[74] Despite the prince's arguments that his palace had chronological precedence, the female convent triumphed.

The Dominican convent of S. Maria della Sapienza provides a telling example of the process by which by hook or by crook female convents managed to insert themselves prominently in the city, even in the teeth of resistance. An analysis of its facade affords an opportunity to see the ways in which particular expansionist histories could be hidden or suppressed by specific architectural forms, as well as ways in which tensions between enclosure and public space are organized architecturally (Plate 8).

The convent of S. Maria della Sapienza was begun in 1507, when Cardinal Oliviero Carafa acquired a building site in the vico Sole e Luna to establish an institution, based on the Roman model and known as the Sapienza, devoted to helping indigent students continue their studies.[75] The building, incomplete in 1511 when Oliviero Carafa died, was sold by his heirs to Giampiero and Marino Stendardo, who founded in 1519 a convent of the Clarissan order (Poor Clares) under the name S. Maria della Sapienza.[76] There Stendardo's aunt, Lucrezia Dentice, transferred from the convent of S. Maria del Gesù with two other nuns.[77] Under the leadership of its first abbess, Maria Carafa, who transferred to the Sapienza from the convent of SS. Pietro e Sebastiano in 1530, the community moved to the Dominican order and was afterward placed under the spiritual leadership of the Theatines: "Within a short time Sister Maria made the place perfectly happy. . . and immediately began building and restoration work of [that convent] which was quite tumbledown, and to expand [it], rendering it into a comfortable dwelling place, buying up other houses, and adjacent sites."[78] The convent's expansion continued steadily after Maria Carafa's death in 1552, requiring the acquisition of more property, including houses and land belonging to Giovanni Andrea delle Castelle, purchased for 1,200 ducats in June 1572, and another building "with a garden inside" belonging to the brothers Annibale and Scipione Caracciolo and others in via S. Pietro a Maiella to the west.[79] The Dominican nuns continued to buy up property throughout the 1570s and 1580s.[80] Significantly, they wanted the boundary between their convent and the adjoining one of Croce di Lucca to be an impressive (and readily policed) straight line and managed to acquire some of the property of the Croce di Lucca to allow this.[81] Building work was under way by 1598, when Caserta stone was purchased "for the monastery building."[82] The first decade of the seventeenth century saw construction surge ahead, with over 635 ducats spent on building in 1605 alone.[83] Once the monastic buildings had been taken care of, attention shifted in 1614 to the church, which was to be "considerably more magnificent and spacious than the old one."[84]

More property and land was bought up for the convent's expansion, a process that had to bypass an order of the Sacro Regio Consiglio, which had prohibited the sale of houses to religious institutions, because the number of monasteries in the street already rendered it uninhabited by laypeople.[85] The Dominicans resorted to subterfuge. To avoid the prohibition, the nuns bought the palace of Ottavio Messanello, baron of Teana, in the strada di S. Maria Costantinopoli, in the name of Andrea Cangiano. The following year, when the prohibition lapsed, Cangiano ceded the property to the convent, declaring that he had bought it independently from the convent.[86] Once this was accomplished, nothing stood in their way. More properties were purchased, the palace was demolished, and a new street was opened in part of the site; further land was prepared for the new church and the rest for the extension to the convent adjacent to the church.[87] The proud entrance added by Cosimo Fanzago in 1638 successfully masks these illegal shenanigans behind a respectable facade (Plate 8). Indeed, this facade strikes a deliberately secular note, closely resembling an aristocratic palace recalling the tradition of the grand urban loggia.[88] No one would think on passing that this was a church, and the inscription, "SAPIENTIA EDIFICAVIT SIBI DOMUM" (Wisdom has built herself a house), proclaims unequivocally that it is a house. It consists of a single-storied portico, in which the central three arcaded bays are articulated by coupled Ionic columns. The end bays, articulated by Corinthian pilasters, frame narrow rectangular entrances. Above these, set in roundels, are two busts in relief sculpted in stone and covered in stucco, representing Pope Paul IV (1555–59) and his sister Maria Carafa, announcing to the city the distinguished blood and institutional power of the founding family.[89] Two flights of steps lead at right angles to the facade, through the tall rectangular openings; landings link them to two more flights parallel to the facade, which lead to the central main entrance (Plate 8; Figure 23). Today the facade supports a terrace which leads back to the unarticulated wall, which closes the nave of the church.[90] Anthony Blunt sees the arrangement as expressing on the surface "exactly what is taking place behind the facade: the triple-arcade covers the enclosed central flights of steps, and the pairs of pilasters define the limits of the side steps."[91] The logic of the facade for Gaetano Cantone springs from the resolution between the convent church wall and the via di Costantinopoli, recently widened in 1634–35. The portico carries the church facade to the edge of the street, allowing for a discreet side elevation incorporating flights of stairs.[92] However, because the entrance staircase is incorporated into the facade itself rather than being set in front of it to mediate between it and the street, the facade is better interpreted as deliberately playing with an ambiguity between access and exclusion, entrance and boundary, and indeed purposefully making complex the relationships between access, visual penetration, and orientation in a mode that is suitable for a conventual church.[93] At the extreme edges of the facade, their narrowness emphasized by their height, the entrances are hardly welcoming. Indeed, they seem to expel the stairs, which appear to spill out onto the public space in front of the church as if released from their constricted passage between the narrow rectangular openings. There is no direct access to the central door, discernible from the street only as a dark shadow. Nor is any access visible: although one can see through the arcade, the high base on which it stands bars the visitor physically from the church, while from the street there is no indication that there is another staircase concealed behind the base. Blunt observed that, since the base corresponds to the height of the second flight of steps, "vertically the arches and pilasters represent the vestibule itself as distinct from the steps."[94] Although this is broadly true, it would be more precise to say that the base corresponds to the *top* of the central flight of steps, so that the match between volumes of space and pierced opening is not one of correspondence. Rather, the coherence of the facade as a whole is emphasized by a subtle play with the Serliana motif across it—a motif which can be read both in the arcade itself, with very short, architraved intervals between columns and arches, and across the whole facade, very loosely running from the two lateral passages.[95] The play of the Serliana motif emphasizes the surface of the facade as screen. It also deliberately relates the new facade to the existing nave decoration, which is structured through a repeated Serliana. This careful attempt to connect the facade visually with the interior suggests that the play on access and exclusion at the east-end interior was deliberately echoed by the architect in the facade. This is particularly clear if one contrasts the Sapienza with Fanzago's facade at S. Maria degli Angeli alle Croci, or his treatment of another church with a double facade, S. Giuseppe delle Scalze a Pontecorvo (Figure 24), where the staircase is completely swallowed up in the vestibule and the relationship between interior and exterior is unambiguous.

While a portico was recommended by Carlo Borromeo in his *Instructiones* for restricted sites, generally, porticoed entrances were preferred for churches located outside cities, offering pilgrims shade and protection, while not having to face the urban problem of a sheltered space encouraging vendors and dealers.[96] Fanzago's loggia offered shelter and protection for church users but did not afford a ready welcome to ruffians and vendors. That deliberate screening of the central staircase and access to the church from the viewer in the street is what sets the facade apart from a pedigree of church facades, dominated by female convents, which consists of porticoes below a palace-like story.[97]

This chapter has shown how the process by which female convents grew in number and influence within the city of Naples was complex and intricately connected with other developments, including viceregal strategies within the city, the ambitions and anxieties of both feudal and nonfeudal aristocracy through the structure of the Seggi, and a continuous series of compromises between ecclesiastical and secular powers. No simple picture emerges. Female religious institutions were powerful and became a conspicuous urban presence, but they could not get their way at will, even in small matters. They were often swept along in tides more powerful than themselves, such as when they were dragged in the slipstream of the Seggi. But they did sometimes triumph over distinct aristocratic interests and over male religious institutions. The interplay between gender and social rank within the city was too complex to allow a simple formulaic hierarchy to emerge in their regard.

I started this chapter by comparing Neapolitan conventual urbanism to that of Roman patricians, but Neapolitan female religious institutions concentrated far more than Roman princes on closely determining what they could see and who could see them. Whereas the issues at stake for the Roman patriciate frequently focused on "engineered prominence," whereby their palaces became visually significant within the city's circulatory systems, for convents contestation focused on what their inhabitants were able to see from within the convent or from high up on its terraces. Of course, convents, too, claimed their place aggressively in the urban environment, but their energies tended to be more focused on vistas outward. That a new building would overlook their convent and violate their enclosure was a commonly advanced argument. Convents' aggressive struggle over the optics of power sheds light on how new urban spatial relationships were forged and on the nature of conventual power itself. When he was rebuilding the Palazzo Muti-Bussi in Rome, mostly in 1642 and 1660–62, Giovanni Antonio De Rossi, renowned for his ability to aggrandize, cut a sight line through the very heart of the palace.[98] It is not simply that convents refused to be transparent in this way; their very claim to power was fought out in opposite terms urbanistically. The conventual model of the city is more static than that of the male patrician city. The site of conventual rivalry tended to be focused higher up spatially—on the sky and skylines, whereas the male patrician city was focused on the street, on routes of circulation through the city, and on visual relationships between buildings at ground level. One is concerned with the optics of power in a moving body through the city; the other from privileged but fixed positions within the city. In this regard, male religious institutions such as the Jesuits enjoyed a potential advantage over their female counterparts because they were able to draw on both discourses simultaneously—the male, extrovert rhetoric of ground level and improved communications for the city, as well as that of dignity and grandeur for their own institution's architecture. By contrast, female religious institutions had to rely on a more introverted discourse of their own well-being. The most they could contribute to the discussion of the commonweal was to flex their muscles by threatening to damage it spiritually if their own civic significance was not fully recognized. Even by the early eighteenth century the limitations of that discourse were apparent.

6

Conventual Optics of Power

Who enters to become a nun there, can be said to be truly leaving the world, because they have no grilles, not even in the Church, through which they can see men.
— CARLO CELANO *on the Augustinian Convent of S. Andrea, Notizie del Bello 1692*

We have seen how convents competed, often fiercely, to dominate vistas and to ensure that their inmates, while remaining invisible, were yet forcefully represented architecturally and urbanistically in relation to the city. Now we address the politics of sight within convents. How were power optics organized inside convents and particularly within their churches, the most porous and the most symbolically and liturgically charged places in the conventual complex?

The optics of power functioned externally, toward the city, and internally, within the conventual complex, but especially at the critical junctures and liminal spaces between the external and internal worlds. Parlatories and sacristies afforded heightened opportunity for contact between nuns and lay folk, but the risk of unseemly contact, including eye contact, was expressed with especial intensity with regard to conventual churches. To these risks, the ecclesiastical authorities were alive, persistently seeking to control the opening and closing of churches.[1] Much of the regulating of contact during services, however, was left to architecture. This chapter explores the architectural marshaling and control of the bodies of both nuns and outsiders, and the architectural organization of seeing and being seen inside convents and their churches.

Enclosed nuns were kept physically separate from other people, in clearly demarcated and separate spaces. This is apparent in the instructions issued before Trent, such as the *Consilium delectorum cardinalium de emendanda ecclesia* of 1537, which recommended attention to apertures and sight: "to lock and to place gratings in the parlatories . . . and to block up the windows of laity over the streets from which the nuns can be seen . . . to block the windows of the garden and to furnish the same with bars; to raise the walls opposite buildings."[2] Elaborate separate systems for the control of bodies were therefore devised. Spatial distinction between seculars and regulars was characterized by rules against the intrusion of unauthorized people (passive cloister) and regulations against nuns leaving the cloister (active cloister). Most of the convent was accessible to nuns only. Thus walls functioned to divide and contain; particularly sensitive spaces, such as dormitories or cells, were located on the first floor, up readily policed staircases. In two areas of conventual complexes, however, the bodies of nuns and visitors were brought close together. The parlatory allowed nuns to communicate with the outside world, an activity riven with suspicion, for which architectural safeguards were essential. Here the architecture allowed verbal exchange, while holding the interlocutors' bodies carefully apart in a relation of symmetry. Nuns and outsiders also shared the convent church. But here symmetry was dissolved; nuns were held loftily high above the congregation, and here their gaze triumphed over the space and people below.

Parlatories were focal points of anxiety, since here men and women could come face to face with enclosed nuns, and nuns' voices could thread their way through grilles and grates to forge contact with bodies from the outside world.[3] Located, like the conventual church, on the edge of the conventual enclosure, parlatories consisted of two separate spaces—an inner space (for nuns) and an outer one (for visitors), separated by a double-grated window. This interface, fetishized by Church officials, was carefully policed by chaperones when in use.[4]

A drawing of c. 1689 showing the parlatories at the Benedictine convent of S. Maria Donnalbina (Figure 25) indicates the elaborate systems of separation which obtained there before 1694. Visitors were divided not only from the nuns but by gender from each other.[5] Thus conventual authority impressed itself not only on inmates, but was ramified and amplified to all and through all who came into contact with the institution. On the left of the street entrance leading to the church was a "stanza del nuovo parlatorio dell'Uomini," a new parlatory for men. This consisted of a small, irregularly shaped room lined on one side with grates through which conversation with the nuns was possible. On the nuns' side, three small cubicles with separate entrances faced the "tamburro per parlare le signore Monache," or "drum," through which the nuns could speak.[6] At this point a thick, heavily grated wall separated male visitors from nuns. A little farther down the street, the principal entrance to the convent, with a carriage gateway, led to the convent's principal courtyard. This route opened first onto an atrium, off which to left and right were the older parlatories, for men and for women, respectively. At this date, therefore, there were two parlatories for male visitors, though it is not clear what distinction existed between them, both on the periphery of the convent and clearly separated from the single parlatory for female visitors. In 1689, with plans to create a grander atrium between the street and the church, the new parlatory for men was demolished (Figure 43). The new location of the parlatories clearly associated them with the conventual complex, rather than with the church, and created a transitional area between street and church that made a grand statement urbanistically while acting as a zone of evident respectability, devoid of any hint of fraternization with the nuns. These changes can, therefore, be read as emphasizing the purity of the church space, now markedly separate from contact with the nuns. Parlatories, mediating between public and enclosed, the spoken and the silent, were brought sharply under the convent's zealous wing.

A similar emphasis on the purity of the conventual church and on the separation of visitors from conventual inhabitants is evident in almost all convents after Trent. Consider the convent of S. Maria della Consolazione, shown in an early-eighteenth-century plan drawn up by Gennaro dell'Aquila (Figure 4). Founded in 1524, the conventual complex was transformed and enlarged in 1641 by the architect Arcangelo Guglielmelli.[7] It is an *isola,* separated from the city by its border of streets. Broadly rectangular, the convent fills the entire site available, resulting in motley-shaped rooms and spaces throughout, including an irregular-shaped interior courtyard. A cloister runs around part of one long and one short side, interrupted on the short side by the church and on the long side by a broad space behind the main carriage entrance. While the upper story is dedicated to the nuns' rooms, the ground floor is largely a working affair (kitchen, bakery) apart from the church and the L-shaped cloister. The staircases are tucked away: neither the principal staircase in the northwest corner nor the smaller stair in the little room next to the old kitchen are readily accessible to visitors to the church or to the parlatories. This arrangement signals the degree to which the upper floor and the church were vulnerable points, always a threat to enclosure through the potential contact it afforded between nuns and outsiders.

In accordance with the decrees of the Council of Trent, the church was entered through an atrium (*D* on the plan) directly off the street, obviating the need to pass through any buildings associated with the nuns' domestic arrangements. The parlatories ("inner" and "outer," marked *H* and *I* on the plan) were to the left of the atrium, between it and the staircase granting access to the nuns' cells on the first floor, again mediating between public space and enclosed space. At *G* was the doorkeeper, who guarded the convent and prevented anyone from entering or leaving without special consent. She could also keep an eye on the parlatories. Further efforts to keep visitors separate from the nuns are apparent in the location of the new kitchens (*R*), close to the *porta carrese* (*L*) through which produce could be delivered, now in a more peripheral location than the old kitchens (*P*).[8]

Conventual ground-floor plans, therefore, demonstrate an increasing determination to articulate the demands of enclosure. The significance given to the policing of parlatories tells us not that the greatest obstacle to spiritual progress was a nun's continued emotional attachment to her family, but that parlor visits remained vital both to enclosed nuns and to their religious institutions. Nuns were not denied all contact with the outside world—which would have been possible, at least in theory—but were permitted to participate in networks of influence to benefit their communities. More significantly still, the advertisement of strict enclosure, the careful and separate marshaling of inmates and visitors, and the sense of being watched at all times were crucial to maintaining conventual authority internally and externally. Authority was exercised on and through the body, especially at those points which were not only those of greatest vulnerability but, more crucially, of greatest visibility, the points, quite literally, of most flagrant publicity.

In spite of the rhetoric of enclosure, few convents denied their inmates all contact through parlatories with the outside world. One that did, singled out by Celano for special comment, was the Franciscan convent of S. Maria di Gerusalemme: "They can truly be called dead to the world, because having entered this holy place, they do not see a human face, apart from that of the priest at the altar and who communicates them."[9] Even when a nun was seriously ill, architecture made possible only minimal necessary contact, precluding any further sight or touch:

> There enter into the convent no doctors, or blood-letters, except in case of extreme necessity: but by these they are served and treated in this way. There is a large room, but longer than it is wide, where an altar stands, on which each morning Holy Mass is celebrated: from the inner part are the small cells of the infirmary: and each little cell has a small low window, which corresponds to the aforementioned room, through which the sick nun from her bed can listen to the mass, and be seen by the doctor. To be bled then there is a place, arranged so that the blood-letter can see only the [nun's] foot, where he has to prick the vein, and her arm.[10]

Important though the enclosure of conventual houses was, it was the convent church that was the subject of greatest anxiety. Two groups of worshipers—lay and nuns—had to be kept separate from each other while participating in a shared mass. Convent churches were riven with sight lines and abounded in opportunities for inappropriate visual encounters. At the least, the architectural design of convent churches had to prevent lay folk from seeing the nuns, while not preventing the nuns from seeing the mass. But seventeenth-century developments in Neapolitan convent church design went far beyond this.

To some extent convents simply carried to an extreme degree the separation of men and women that already occurred, at least in theory, during sermons, prayers, and all forms of religious worship available to secular people.[11] The ideal of sexual division within sacred space was firmly rooted in theological writings and was articulated concretely through permanent screening devices within churches.[12] Visual representations of church services show the sexes as separated within ecclesiastical space, sometimes by a curtain, men on one side of the church nave, women on the other. These representations have too often been interpreted literally, as evidence for the organization of the sexes during church service, leading to assertions that women sat on the left (north) and men on the right.[13] Concern to separate the sexes may have been particularly acute in relation to the mendicant orders, whose members more than those of enclosed orders were vulnerable to the "heat of flesh."[14]

Officially marked as chaste spaces in which men and women were separated physically and visually, nevertheless churches occupied an important position in nonecclesiastical discourses as the site for amatory encounters.[15] In other words, because ecclesiastical space was public and open to women, it became a strategic site for the marriage market. Its respectability meant that women accrued standing by being there; but women's public presence also eroticized that space. The amorous gaze cutting through sacred space was a well-known *topos* in Italian vernacular literature. Dante's description of his secret, public looking at Beatrice depicts an eroticized space where love's sight lines, if not love, are made visible:

> It happened one day that this most gracious of ladies was sitting in a place where words about the Queen of Glory were being spoken, and I was where I could behold my bliss. Halfway between her and me, in a direct line of vision, sat a gentlewoman of a very pleasing appearance, who glanced at me frequently as if bewildered by my gaze which seemed to be directed at her. And many began to notice her glances in my direction and paid close attention to them, and, as I left this place, I heard someone near me say: "see what a devastating effect that lady has had on that man." And, when her name was mentioned, I realized that the lady referred to was the one whose place had been halfway along the direct line which extended from the most gracious Beatrice, ending in my eyes. Then I was greatly relieved, feeling sure that my glances had not revealed my secret to others that day.[16]

The clandestinity of those snatched glances heightened their erotic impact, and churches became a standard setting for the self-consciously passionate, voyeuristic gaze: S. Chiara in Avignon is the setting for Petrarch's sight of Laura, and it was in S. Lorenzo in Naples where Maria d'Aquino was espied by Boccaccio. Writers made a staple of the "ecclesio-amorous encounter" in which sacred space added spice to the surveying and judging of women.[17] Generally, however, responsibility was shifted onto women. Conduct literature urged women to behave in such a way as to shun all erotic encounters or exchange. In 1568 Francesco Bonavventura Gonzaga da Reggio, instructing nuns on the correct behavior for the observance of religious life, urged: "Never be so sure of not being seen that you do not proceed to look with prudence, to touch with chastity and to do all other things with modesty and discipline as though the whole world were observing your actions. Remember that the holy angels are always with us and can see all our works. . . . God himself, our Lord and Judge, also sees us. Equally our own conscience observes us."[18] Here, in true Foucauldian fashion, the disciplined body is achieved. The act of looking constitutes the principal metaphor for defining disciplined behavior: not only does the expression of the eyes concern discipline, but the eye of God enters into the disciplinary process as a controlling factor. And conventual architecture and conventual discourses emphasize the necessity for women to remain modestly concealed, quiet, not attracting attention to themselves.

Architectural developments indicate that after enclosure nuns became observers, and even though the monastery church was no longer considered to be the province primarily of the nuns themselves, it was arranged to privilege them as invisible, elevated observers. Nuns' churches did not arrange sinners equally under God's roof. They set nuns apart, as consecrated virgins, elevated and closer to God than the community gathered below them. While medieval convent churches were usually aisleless rectangles without side chapels, early modern southern Italian nuns' churches, also aisleless rectangles, frequently had side chapels (Figures 8, 10, 23, 26).[19] After Trent, the Eucharist had become markedly more important, especially to women. The accommodation of lateral altars, allowing the performance of many masses throughout the day, and even simultaneously, is crucial in this regard. But after Trent, nuns were not allowed inside convent churches; they were relegated to the clerestory level of the church, from where they could look down through grilled openings (*gelosie*) at the performance of the mass down below (Figures 27, 28, 29). Nuns' bodily presence in conventual churches was greatly diminished after Trent; they became observers, participating in the services from within their own restricted spaces, suspended on high.[20] The absence of aisles in post-Tridentine churches was, therefore, determined less by lack of demand for separate masses than by the importance to nuns of watching the mass from up above, unimpeded by columns and aisles. This emphasis on "visual cleanliness" extended to the eradication of places that might accommodate scandalous assignations. In short, as nuns were transformed into observers, the politics of sight became correspondingly more important.

Within their convents nuns could see but not be seen. Conventual architecture granted the power of the gaze asymmetrically, affording nuns pleasures denied to laity. Grilles shielded nuns from scrutiny, rendered them anonymous and unidentifiable, and made snatched glimpses of a veil, a face, or a hand all the more tantalizing (Figures 28, 29, 30; Plate 5). A member of the congregation could only get a better view of the nuns if he stood very close to the grille and squinted through its gaps—that is, only by conspicuously and deliberately peering into the nuns' spaces, an advertency which could not be private or hidden from others. Indeed, at S. Chiara spikes on the grilles between the nave and the nuns' choir make such prying particularly perilous (Figure 31). Nuns had liturgical encouragement to look into the church, but the congregation had no good reason to look at them. Mystery added aura to the institution of convents and to their inhabitants.

Conventual churches functioned like an inverse version of Foucault's famous panopticon.[21] Those who could see without being seen (like Bentham's supervisor) were the nuns, elevated and hidden behind screens (Plate 9). They were closer to God, closer to the officiating priest, and had privileged access to hidden spaces, denied to lesser mortals. But those whom they could see—the congregation, who could not see them, and who were barred from the convent's interior—enjoyed freedoms denied to the nuns. Unlike Foucault's model, which allies the gaze to forces of control and surveillance, where the gaze is identified with power, conventual visual economies depended on a notion of the gaze as debasing to their most valuable currency. What was at issue was protecting the virginal nun *from* the impure and potentially defiling gaze—both from her own (inappropriate) looking and especially from the looking of others. In both systems visibility is a trap, and the fear of that trap can be exploited. In both systems invisibility is the guarantee of order. In both systems being seen without seeing, or seeing without being seen, ensures that the subjects of the architecture are the objects of information, not subjects in communication.

The significance of seeing was particularly important in this virginal context. Since the thirteenth century, the idea that virginity could be lost as a result of sight, of a man looking at a woman or a woman looking at a man, gained currency over the Thomasian emphasis on touch as the principal sense of intemperance.[22] Conduct books for secular women emphasized the importance of keeping their gaze lowered and modest, as did conventual regulations for nuns.[23] In convent churches, however, we find an explosion in the seeing of enclosed nuns, even as their being seen was increasingly limited.

The question of what nuns should be allowed to see was hotly discussed and contested both before and after Trent.[24] Carlo Borromeo's *Instructiones* (1577) sought to codify and formalize the relationship between the nuns in their choir and the performance of the mass.[25] Borromeo prescribed that an opening or grille as long as the altar should be set into the wall above the altar, so that the nuns in the inner church could see and hear mass, but he insisted that the opening should not provide views of anything else, such as glimpses of the street when the entrance door was open.[26] Control of sight was organized in terms not only of the building but of the nuns' bodies themselves. Thus two systems—body and building—functioned in parallel.

Rules governing convent nuns' sight lines in conventual churches were more restrictive than practice, at least in southern Italian convents. These rules relegated nuns to spaces in the back of the church or upper corridors behind grated and curtained openings, which deprived them of a clear view of the church or even the mass celebrated in it.[27] Ecclesiastical authorities sought to obviate the unimpeded free gaze of nuns across the church and into the congregation, as corrupting both to nuns and members of the congregation. Priests were ordered not to look into the faces of the women they confessed, because of the fear of a woman's eyes. The danger of the female gaze helps to explain the lavish attention given to the grilles that screened enclosed women, making their eyes invisible (Plates 5, 9; Figures 28, 29, 33, 35). These devices did not, of course, prevent the women from looking. In fact, the screened *gelosie* and the raised choirs of baroque churches elevated the female gaze to unprecedented heights. Nor was the sacred space of the church deeroticized by the grilles. The invisible presence of the nuns, who could be glimpsed indistinctly as they moved about and heard as they sang, was tantalizingly erotic; but the fact that they could not be clearly discerned and that their eyes could not be seen meant that the eroticization became generalized, impersonal, even architecturalized, as if emanating from the conventual church itself, rather than from a nun. Their "sacred charisma," the one form of authority enjoyed by nuns, was simultaneously strengthened and undermined by these sexualized optics of visual dominance.[28]

Nuns' deep-held concern with what they could see (and who could see them) emerges sharply in their lawsuits defending and expanding their urbanistic visual dominance, as we have seen. A similar determination to achieve dominance in terms of seeing within their churches emerges, too. In their letter asking Cardinal Buoncompagno's permission to make certain changes at their convent of S. Francesco dell'Osservanza in 1629, the abbess and nuns made clear that they wanted enhanced viewing into their church. They requested that the six chapels of the church be made as deep as the walls of the church, that they should be decorated, and that above them *gelosie* should be distributed in such a way that from the corridor it should be possible to see the mass from all around the church.[29] The Franciscan nuns hereby sought architecturally to enhance their visual command both of the church in general and of the mass in particular wherever it was performed. At the same time they petitioned to create two new rooms where they could store those objects used every day in the church and sacristy, thus avoiding disruption to peace in both inner and outer churches, whenever such objects were needed.[30] In other words, the nuns made a concerted effort to reduce bodily presence within the main church while opening it up instead to greater visual access. Such changes emphasize the conception and presentation of the church as a theater for the performance of the mass, and of the nuns as the most important audience of that performance.

As we have seen, clerestory *gelosie* were crucial in defining both men's presence and absence and in channeling nuns' looking. It was, however, above all in the nuns' choir that the issues of nuns' looking, their visibility, and their visual control of the space of the church were most signally explored. The nuns' choir was that part of the church which signified spatially the special position of professed nuns, a place of privilege and honor (Figure 32). It represented the nuns architecturally in relation to the public space of the church. It was here that choir nuns participated in church services, here where they gathered en masse, recited the Divine Office and rosary, and engaged in meditative prayer. Here, too, in most cases, they could be seen as a group, albeit indistinctly, from the public church. The nuns' choir was, therefore, a most important space liturgically and symbolically in the church, second only to the main altar. After Trent, nuns were prohibited to play music in their external church. Their choirs safeguarded both their musical creativity and their communal social position.[31]

Access to the choir was a privilege, open only to professed nuns, and it could be taken from them as punishment. The very name, *choriste*, which designated choir nuns (as opposed to lay sisters or nuns who had not yet taken their vows) refers explicitly to this architectural space, indicating the degree to which their privileged identity was spatially defined. Choir nuns were expected to display heightened religious devotion. They had to hear mass daily, recite Divine Office each morning and evening, and undertake one hour of mental prayer every day. That the choir was the focus of considerable architectural attention during this period suggests a heightened concern to emphasize the status of the choir nuns in relation not only to the congregation but also to other conventual inmates. This shift was part of an aristocratization of select female religious institutions.

Choirs were the special province of choir nuns during all church services, even those which touched the monastic community most closely. In her history of 1577 of S. Gregorio Armeno, the nun Fulvia Caracciolo describes how after the death of its abbess, her coffin was displayed in the church, while the nuns remained in the choir: "Four Deacons of the Chapter carried the bier and four knights accompanying it held their hands above the coffin as far as the church where it was set down for the funeral rites to be undertaken by the Reverend Canons, while the nuns remained in the church above in the choir."[32] Access to the choir was a mark of dedication to the nun's role. Fulvia Caracciolo describes the stages of progress for nuns, stages which are shaped in part in relation to access to the choir: "They received the veil from the Abbess. One day after Vespers, the nuns' hair was cut short, and after a few months, or years, depending on their age, they took the second rank which were certain [privileged positions] in the choir."[33] Entry to the choir was a privilege and it was marked visually on the nun's body by special clothes, given to her at the third stage of monacation, when she was at least fifteen years old.

When Sister Maria Aurelia Cecilia of the Augustinian nuns of S. Giuseppe in Martina near Naples demonstrated her sense of her own unworthiness, she did so by sitting not in the choir with the other nuns, but on the ground; when invited to join them, she replied that she was "not worthy of sitting where sit the brides of Jesus Christ."[34] Presence in the choir was a sign of religious dedication in part because of the physical rigors it demanded. Ignazio Vittorelli emphasized the strict observance of that same convent in Martina by drawing special attention to their rough habit and their "very long attendance in the choir, and very early in the morning, whether in winter or summer."[35]

The privacy and peace of the choir were defended with particular determination in lawsuits foisted by one convent on another throughout the second half of the seventeenth and early eighteenth centuries in Naples. Even more than the east end of the church or the main altar, the choir received special attention to protect its integrity, light, and tranquillity. Although the convent of S. Francesco delle Cappuccinelle and that of the Periclitanti nearby in Olimpiano experienced frequent disputes following the latter's foundation in 1674, their most ferocious disagreement focused on the threat to the choir of S. Francesco posed by the building of a new bell tower for the Periclitanti.[36] The proposed tower was "in a direct line" with the choir of the Cappuchin nuns. This meant, they argued, that "because of the considerable sound of the bell, they would not be able to achieve divine contemplation."[37] Safeguarding the peace and devotion of the choir was vital liturgically, spiritually and socially.

Nuns' choirs were traditionally found at the west end of churches, above the entrance. Raised above the entrance loggia, they marked the transitional space of entry and allowed nuns a clear view of the main altar when mass was performed. Nuns faced strictly the same way as the rest of the congregation, making eye contact impossible during the service. The propriety and efficiency of the west-end choir renders curious a significant change that occurred in seventeenth-century Naples. In several interesting cases the Neapolitan nuns'

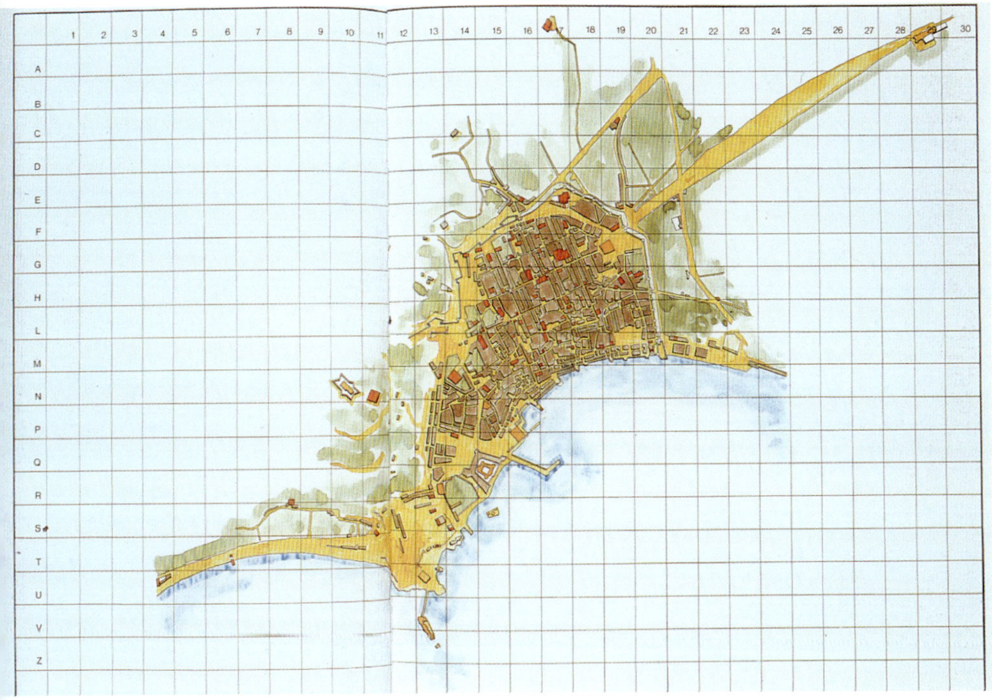

PLATE 1. Naples: Reconstruction, based on the view by Effige del Theti of 1560, with religious buildings in red, civic buildings in orange, and the Seggi in yellow. Map by Cesare de Seta, with his kind permission.

S. Andrea delle Dame, *G15*; S. Antonio Abate, *C19*; S. Chiara, *M15*; Croce di Lucca, *H15*; Le Covertite all'Incurabili, *G16*; Duomo, *G17*; S. Festo, *M17*; S. Gaudioso, *G15*; S. Geronimo, *M16*; Gesù delle Monache (S. Maria del Gesù), *F16*; S. Gregorio Armeno, *L16*; S. Lorenzo, *H17*; S. Marcellino, *M17*; S. Maria di Constantinopoli, *G14*; S. Maria Donnalbina, *M15*; S. Maria Donnaregina, *F17*; S. Maria Donnaromita, *L16*; S. Maria Regina Coeli, *G16*; S. Sebastiano, *L14*; Lo Spedale di S. Maria degli Incurabili, *F16*; Certosa di S. Martino, *N11*; S. Patrizia, *G16*; Castel Capuano, *G19*; Castel Nuovo, *R15*; Castel Sant'Elmo, *N10*; Palazzo Reale, *R14*; Seggio Capuano, *G17*; Seggio di Montagna, *H16*; Seggio di Nido, *L16*; Seggio di Porto, *N16*; Seggio di Porta Nuova, *M17*.

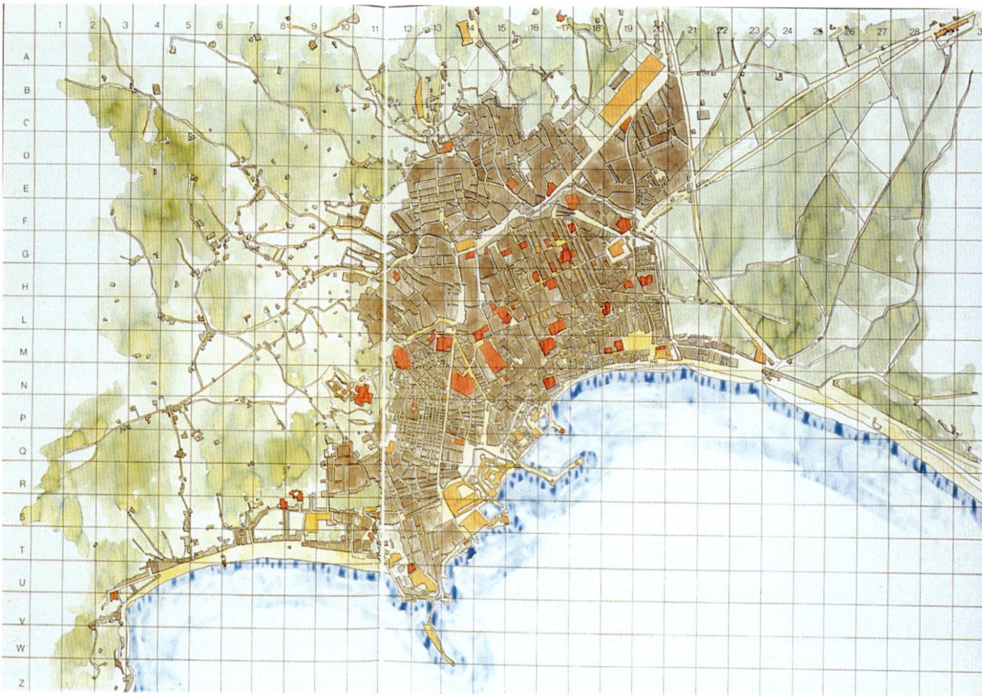

PLATE 2. Naples: reconstruction, based on the map of the Duke of Noja of 1775, with religious buildings in red, civic buildings in orange, and the Seggi in yellow. Via Toledo runs from *R13* to *M14*. Map by Cesare de Seta, with his kind permission.

S. Andrea delle Dame, *G15*; S. Antonio Abate, *C19*; S. Chiara, *M15*; Croce di Lucca, *H15*; Duomo, *G17*; S. Gaudioso, *G15*; Gesù e Maria, *H12*; Il Gesù Nuovo, *M15*; Gesù delle Monache (S. Maria del Gesù), *F16*; S. Giovanni Battista delle Monache, *H14*; S. Giuseppe dei Ruffi, *G17*; S. Gregorio Armeno, *L17*; S. Lorenzo, *H17*; SS. Marcellino e Festo, *M17*; S. Maria di Constantinopoli, *G14*; S. Maria Donnalbina, *M15*; S. Maria Donnaregina, *G17*; S. Maria Donnaromita, *L16*; S. Maria delle Grazie a Caponapoli, *G15*; Lo Spedale di S. Maria degli Incurabili, *F16*; S. Maria Regina Coeli, *G16*; S. Maria della Sapienza, *H15*; Certosa di S. Martino, *N11*; S. Patrizia, *G16*; SS. Trinità delle Monache, *M12*; Castel Capuano, *G19*; Il Castel Nuovo, *R15*; Castel Sant'Elmo, *N10*; Palazzo Cellamare, *S11*; Palazzo Reale, *S14*; Palazzo della Vicaria, *G19*; Seggio Capuano, *G18*; Seggio di Montagna, *H16*; Seggio di Nido, *L16*; Seggio di Porto, *N16*; Seggio di Porta Nuova, *M17*.

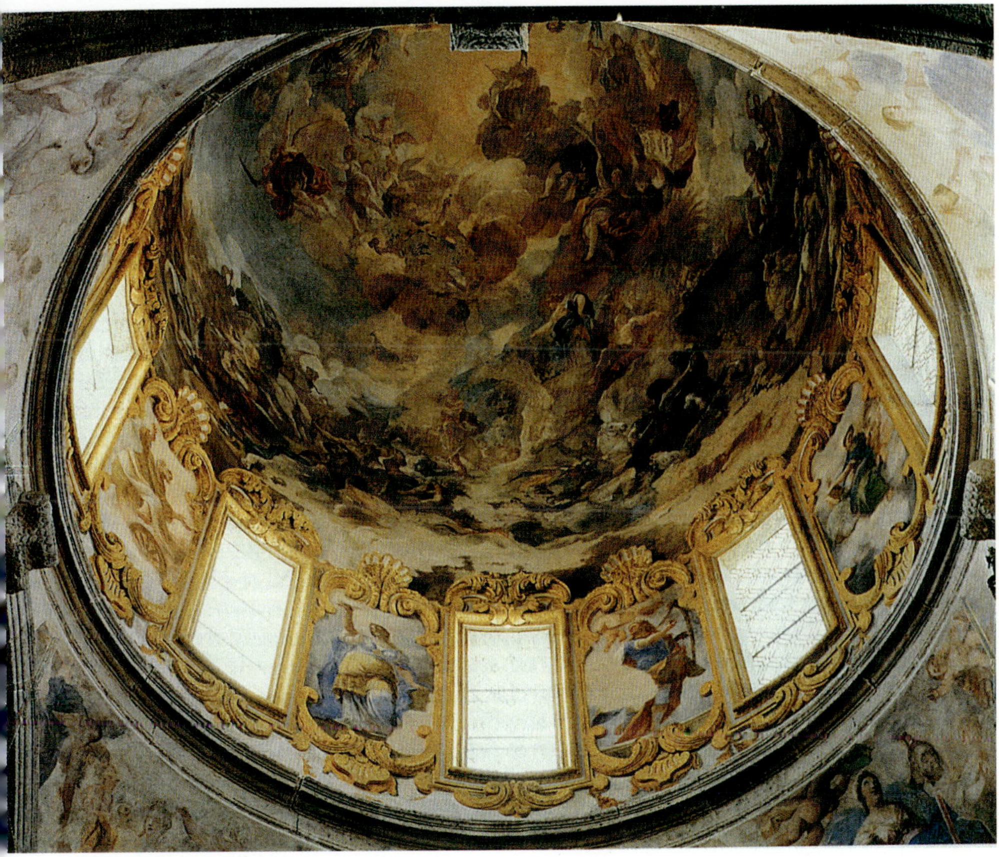

PLATE 3. Naples, S. Maria Donnaromita. Interior of dome with frescoes by Luca Giordano, *Crossing of the Red Sea*. Photo by the author.

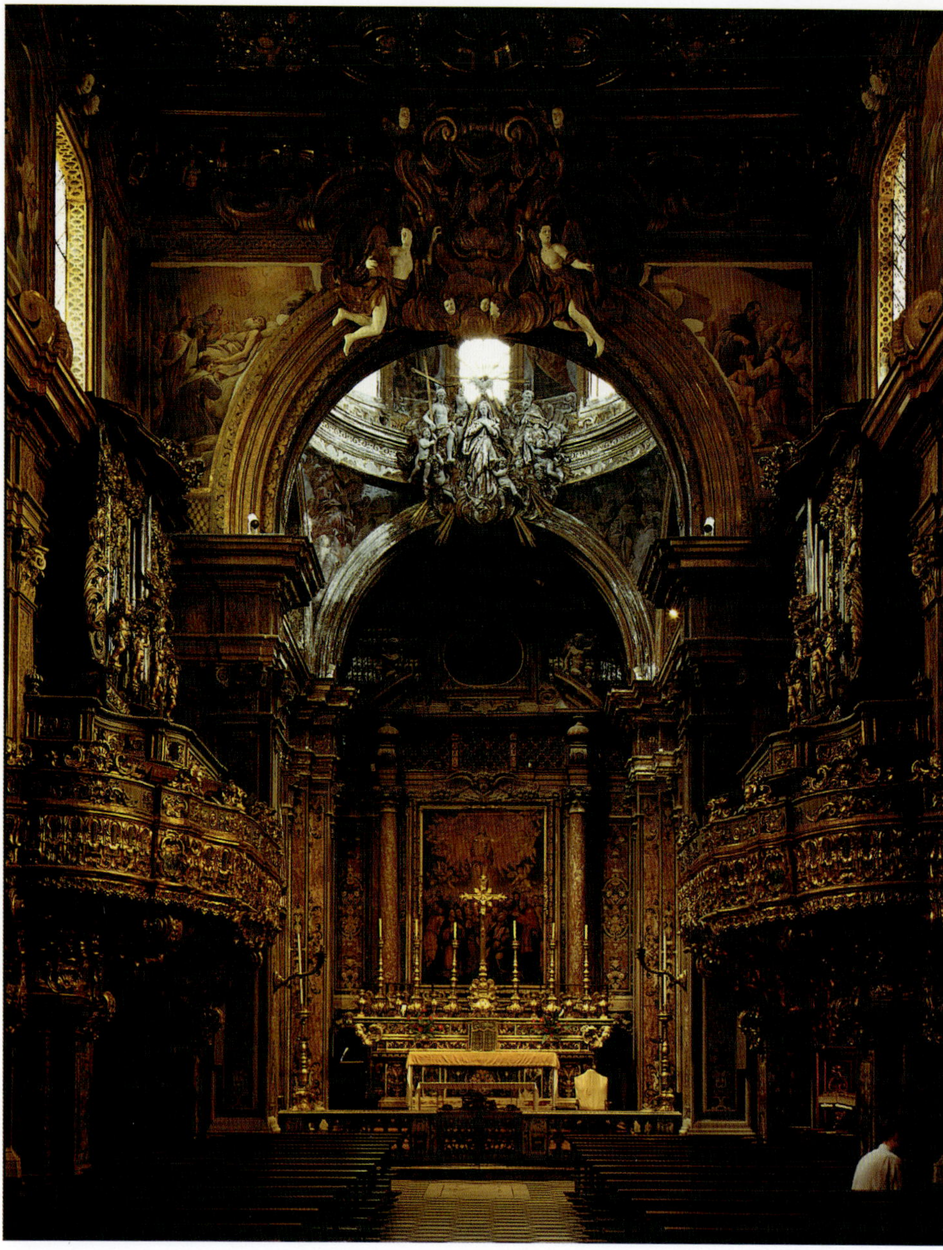

PLATE 4. Naples, S. Gregorio Armeno. East end with main altar by Dionisio Lazzari, 1687. Photo by Massimo Velo.

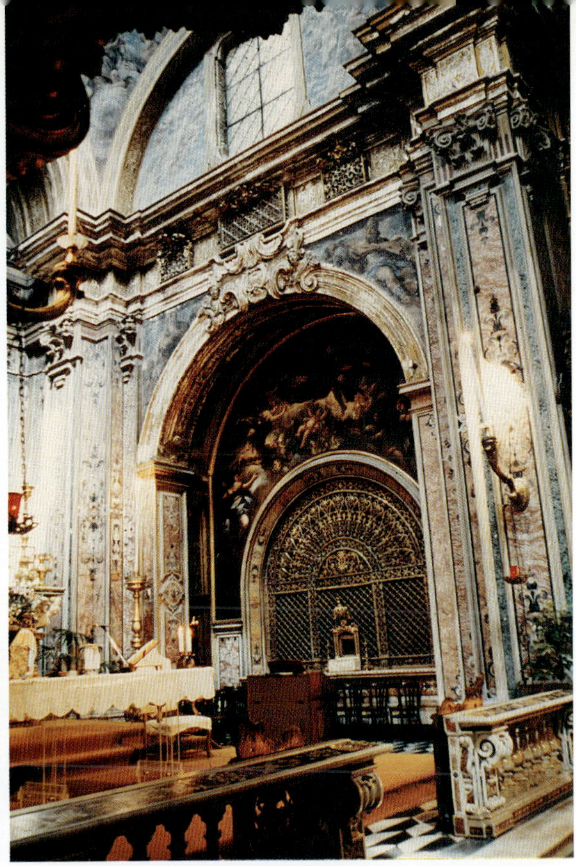

PLATE 5. Naples, S. Gregorio Armeno. South wall of the chancel of the convent church with the nuns' communion grille (1692). Photo by the author.

PLATE 6. Naples, S. Giuseppe dei Ruffi. Main altar by Dionisio Lazzari, 1688. Photo by Massimo Velo.

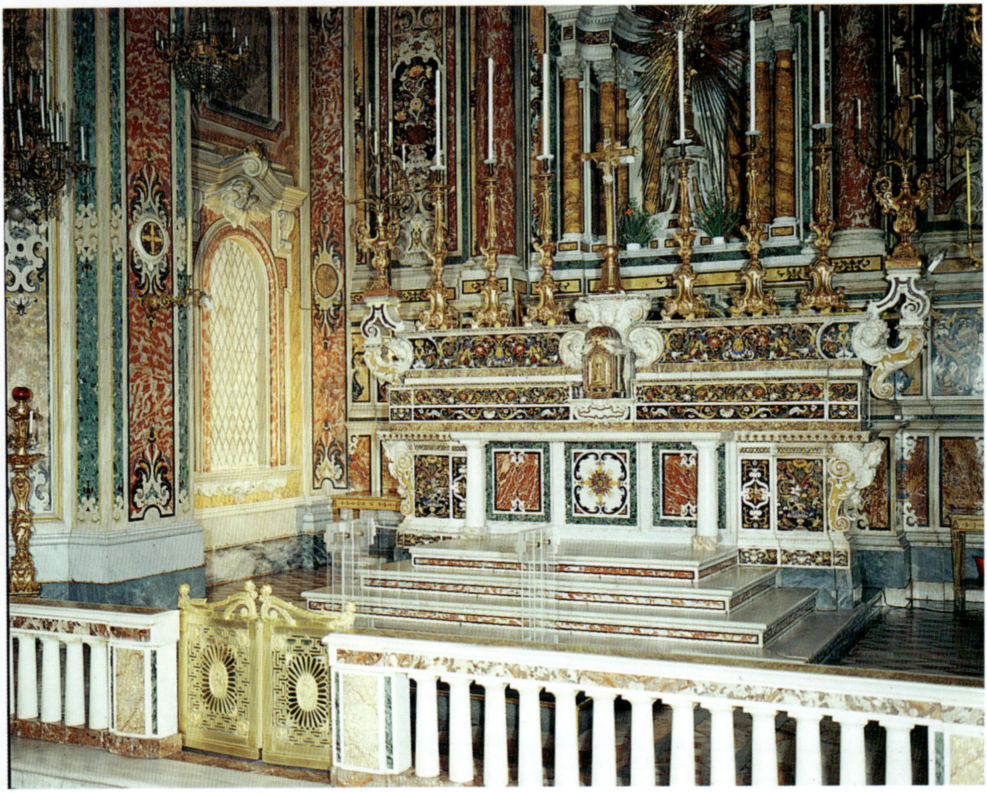

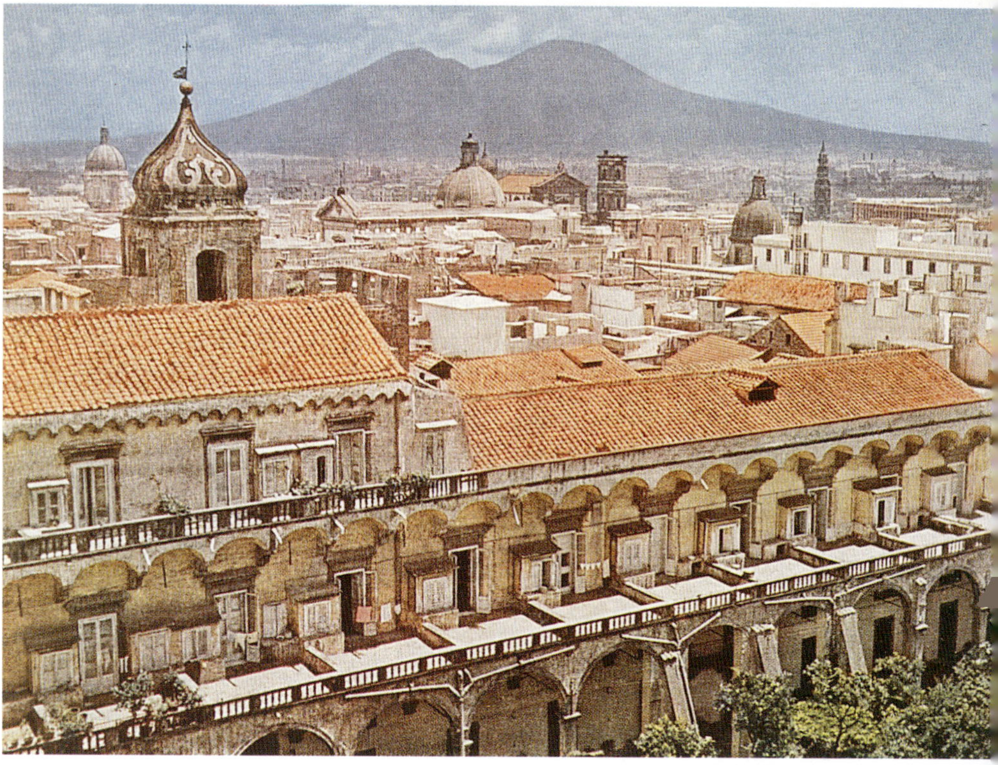

PLATE 7. Naples, S. Gregorio Armeno: the "vertical city." Photo by the author.

PLATE 8. Naples, S. Maria della Sapienza. Facade. Photo by the author.

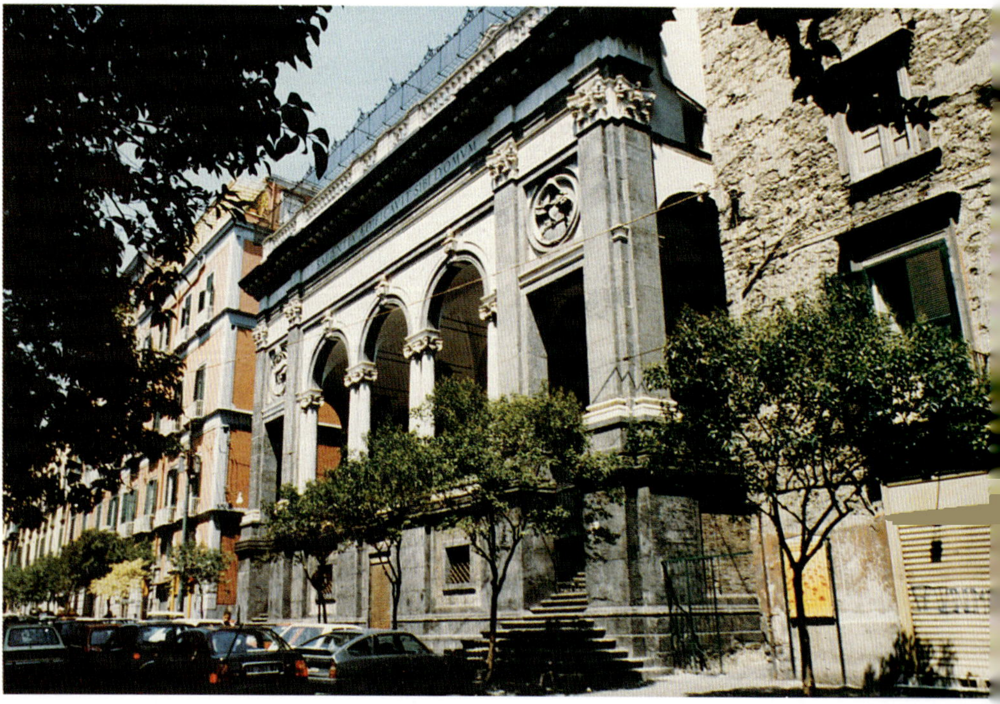

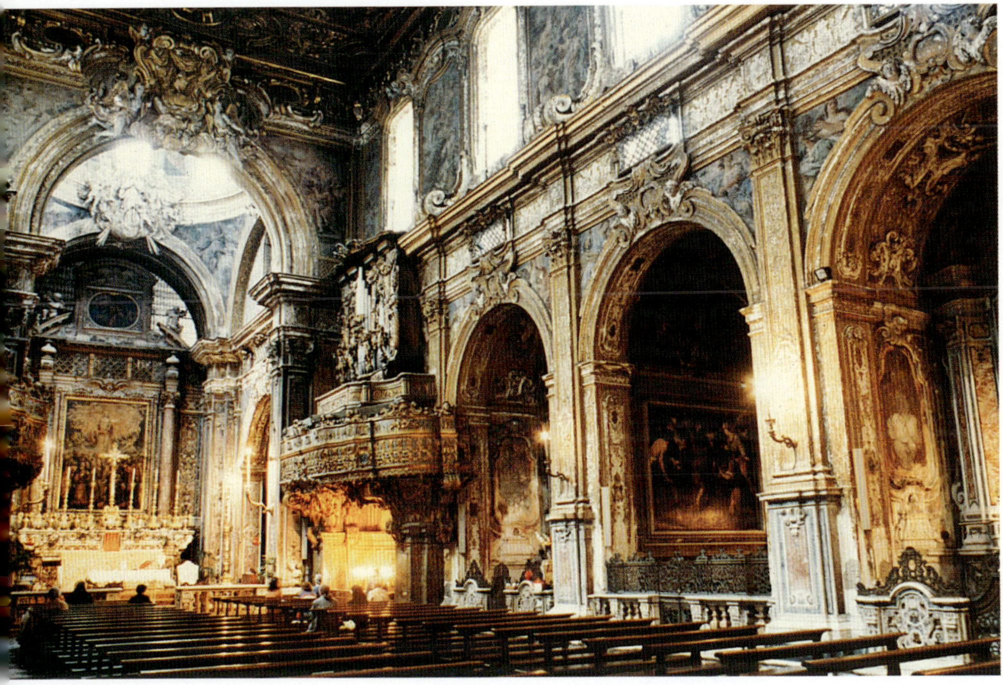

PLATE 9. Naples, S. Gregorio Armeno, interior looking southeast. Photo by the author.

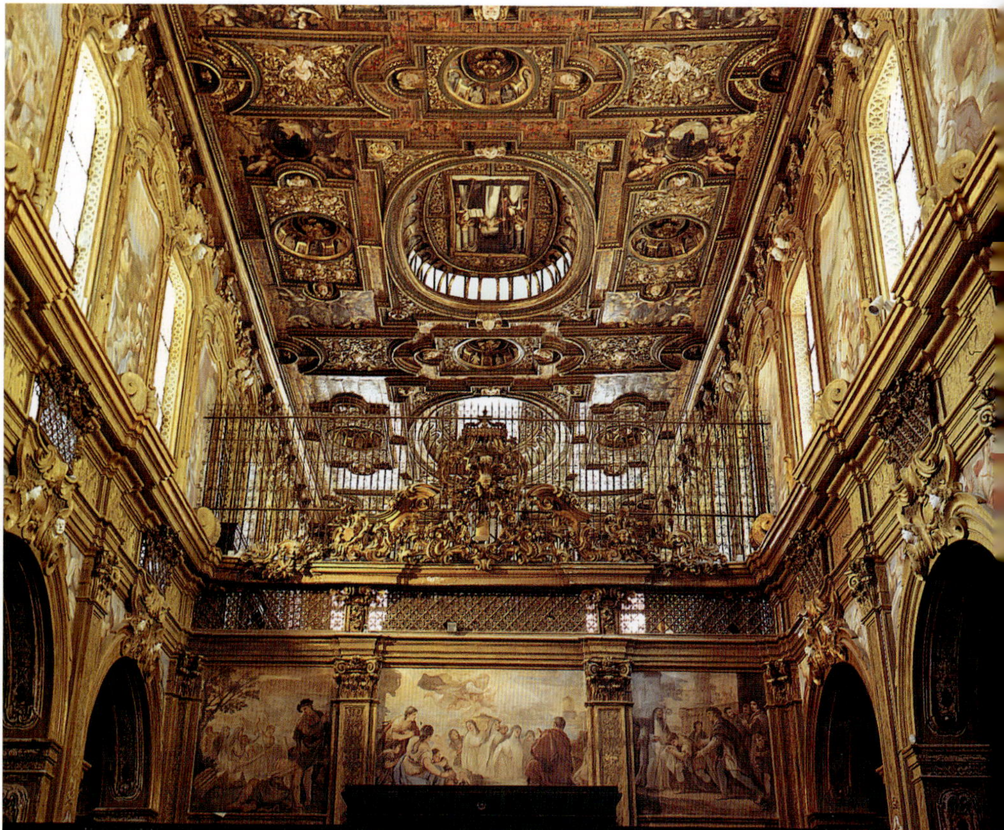

PLATE 10. Naples, S. Gregorio Armeno. West end of church looking up to the raised choir at clerestory level and, above that, through the special viewing window to the upper-level winter choir. Photo by Massimo Velo.

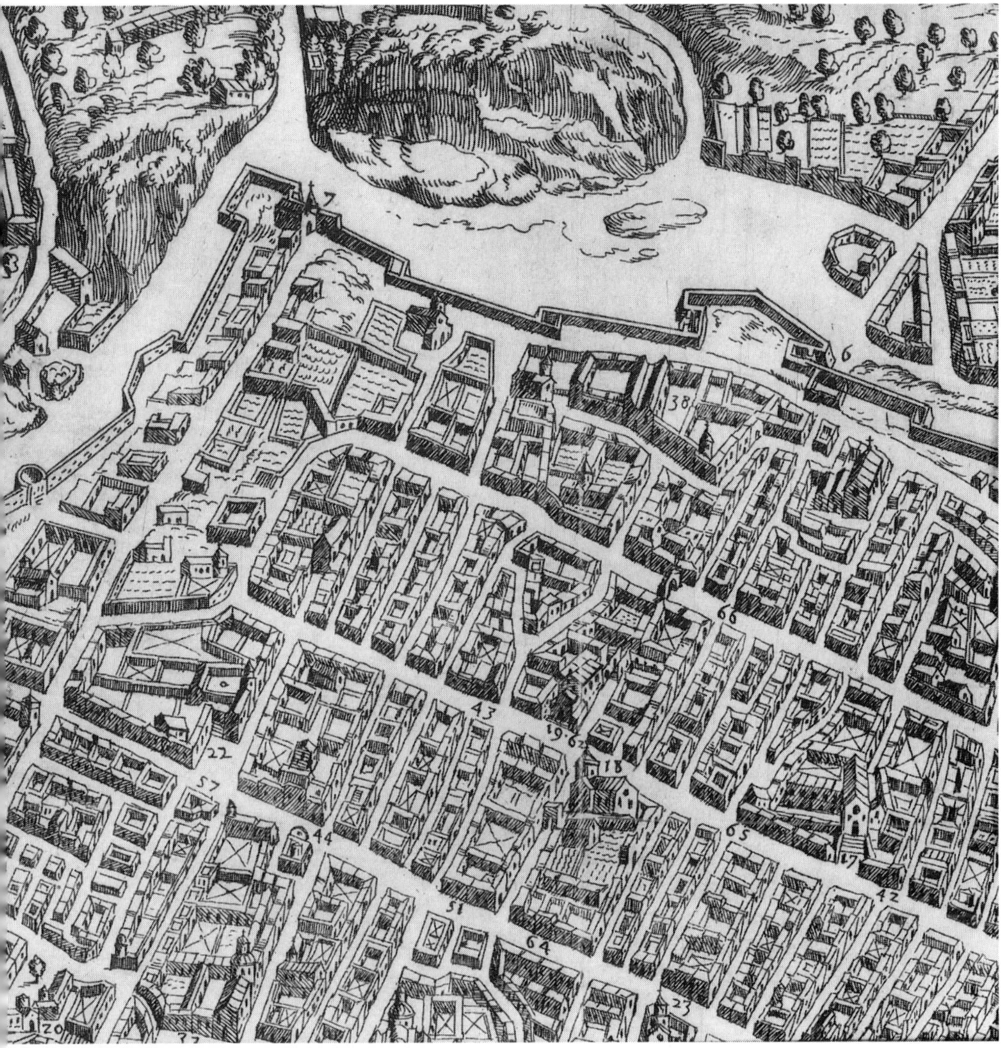

FIGURE 1. A. Lafréry, Quale e di quanta Importanza e bellezza sia la Nobile Cita di Napole in Italia, Map of Naples, 1566. Woodcut. Detail showing the northwest corner of the city. By permission of the British Library. BL Shelfmark: Maps C.7.e.2. (49).

7, Porta S. Maria di Costantinopoli; *22*, S. Agostino; *31*, S. Severino; *38*, Hospital of S. Maria degli Incurabili.

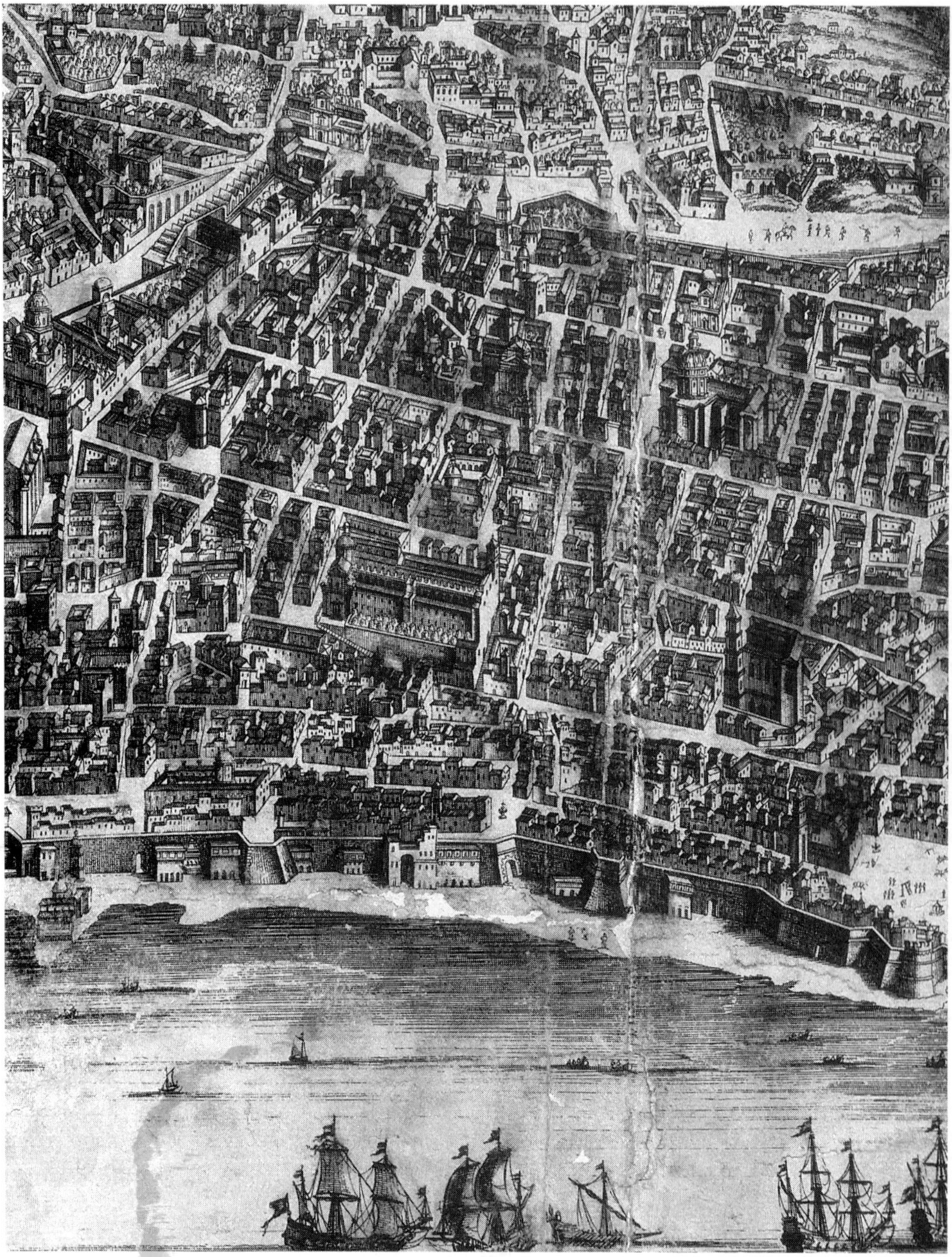

FIGURE 2. B. Stopendael, Map of Naples, 1653. Engraving on copper. Detail showing northwest corner of the city. Photo by Massimo Velo. By permission of the Ministero per i Beni e le Attività Culturali, Soprintendenza per il Patrimonio Artistico Storico e Demoetnoantropologico di Napoli.

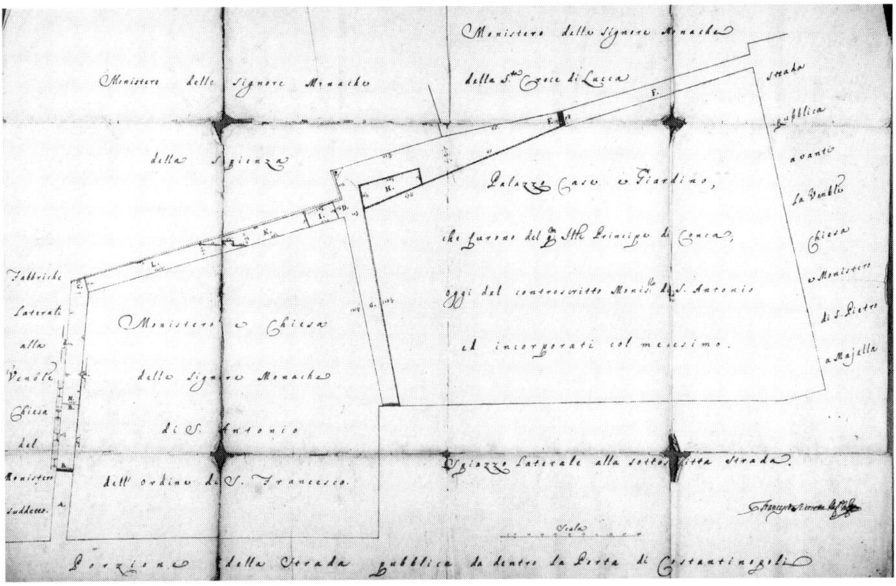

FIGURE 3. Drawing of the area within Porta di Costantinopoli, relating to a lawsuit and showing the close proximities of the religious houses of Sapienza, Croce di Lucca, S. Pietro a Maiella, and S. Antonio. The trapezoidal area represents the palace, houses, and gardens formerly owned by the Prince of Conca, purchased by the convent of S. Antonio. By permission of the Archivio di Stato, Naples.

FIGURE 4. Naples, S. Maria della Consolazione degli Afflitti. Plan of the convent, early eighteenth century, by Gennaro dell'Aquila. ASN, Mon. sop., 4672, f. 2 bis. By permission of the Archivio di Stato, Naples.

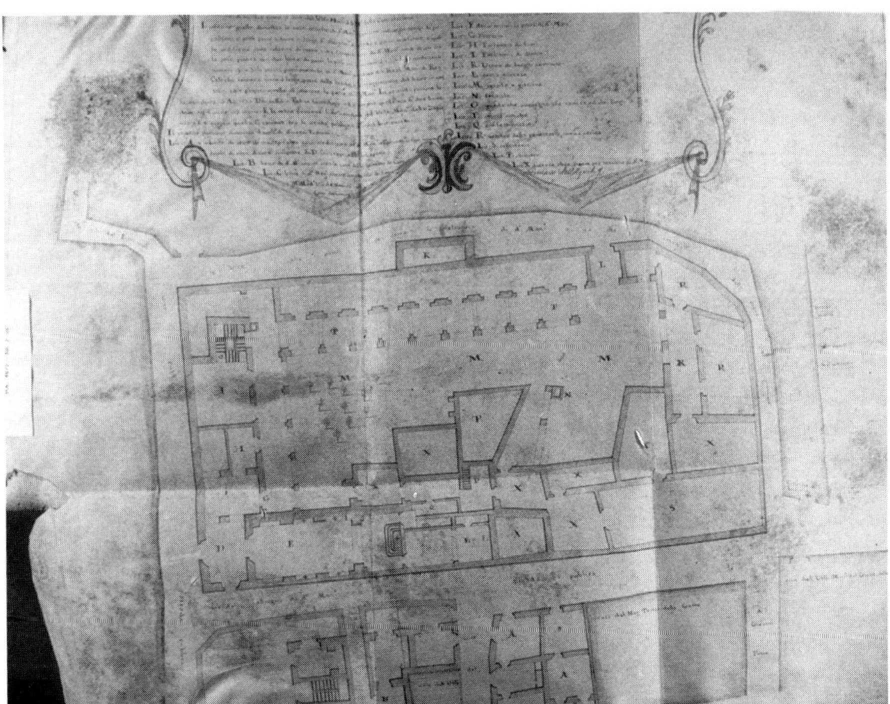

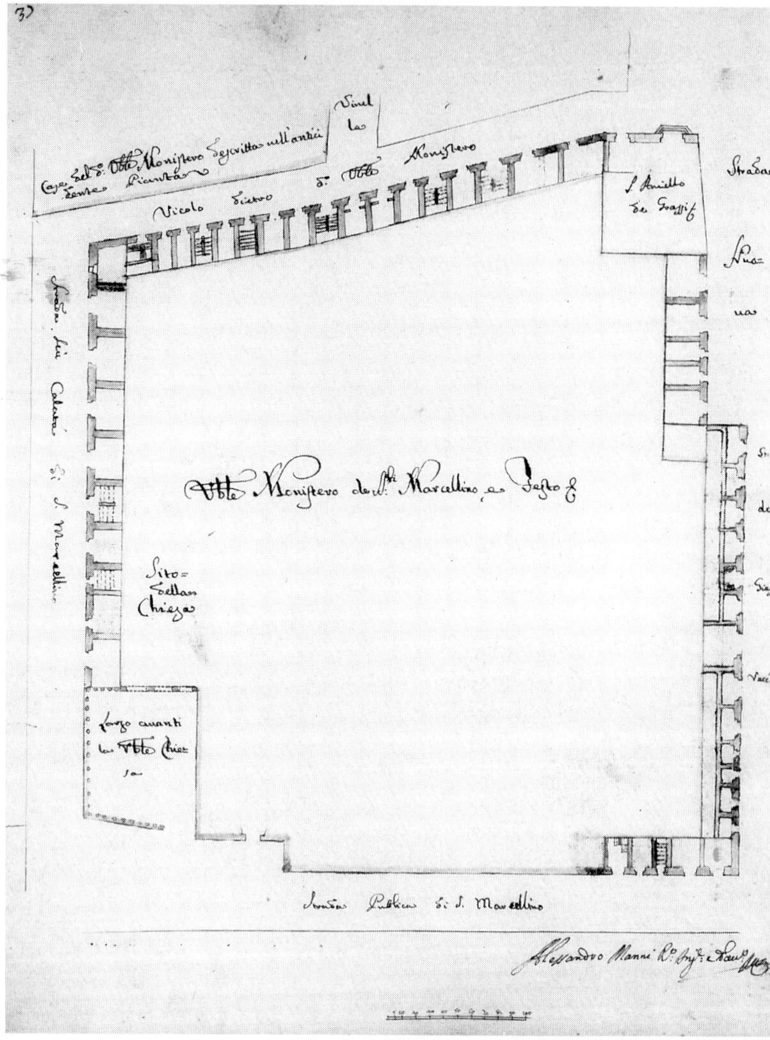

FIGURE 5. Naples: The *isola* or block of SS. Marcellino e Festo, 1732. Drawing by Alessandro Manni, Royal Engineer, relating to a lawsuit. ASN, Mon. sop., 2725, f. 37. By permission of the Archivio di Stato, Naples.

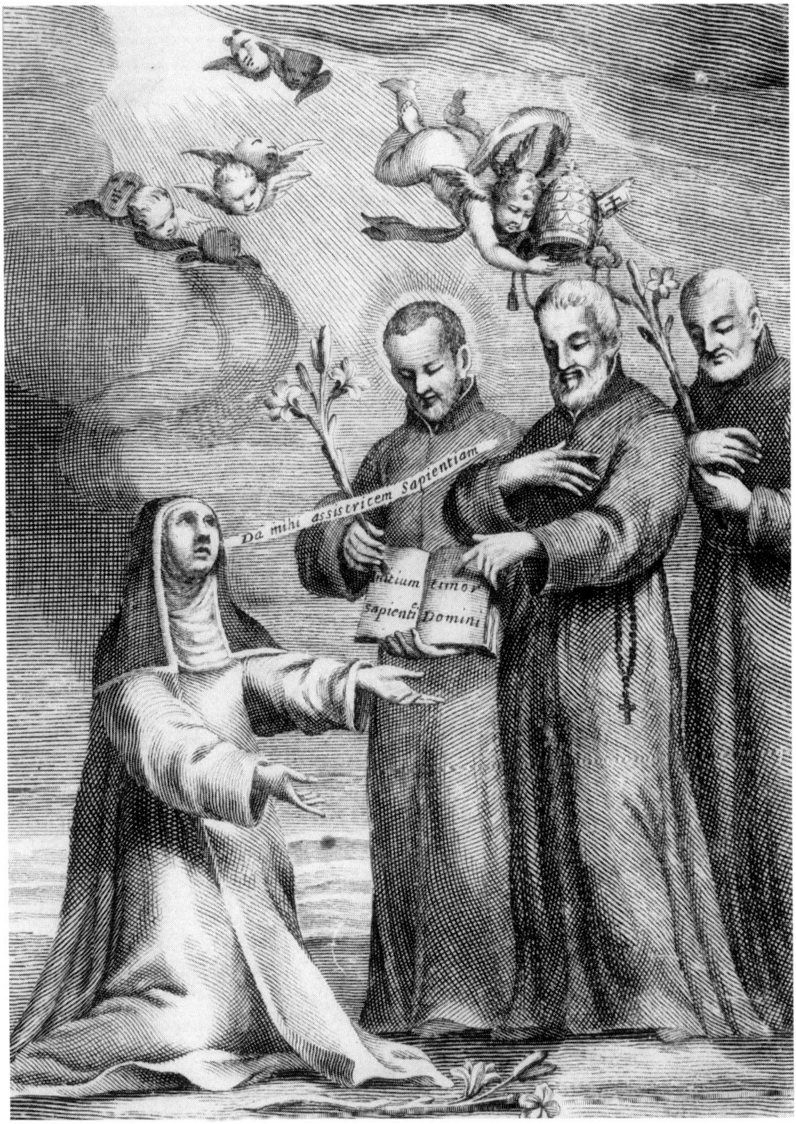

FIGURE 6. Maria Carafa, founder of the convent of S.M. della Sapienza, with Gaetano da Thiene, Gian Pietro Carafa, and Giovanni Marinoni. Frontispiece from F. M. Maggio, *Vita della Venerabile D. Maria Carafa Napoletana, sorella del Santiss. Pontefice Paolo IV e Fondatrice del Sacro Monistero di s. Maria della Sapienza di suore Domenicane,* Naples, 1670. Photo by Massimo Velo with permission of the Biblioteca della Società Napoletana di Storia Patria.

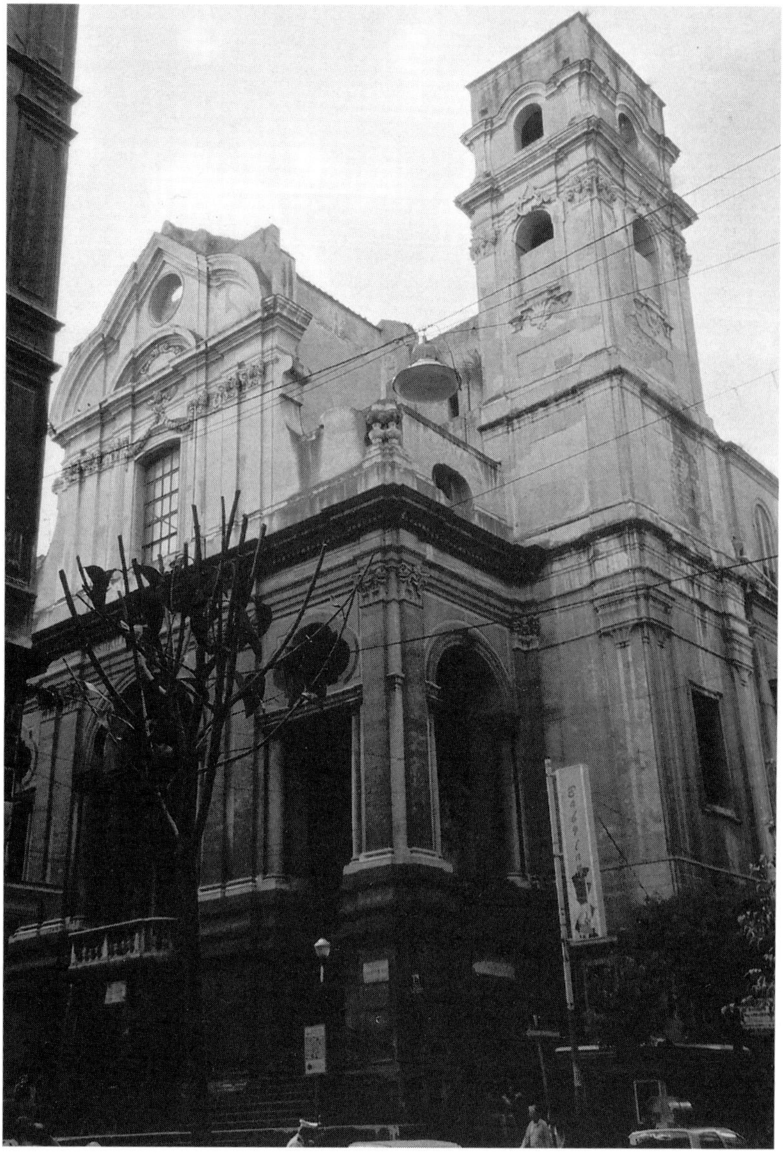

FIGURE 7. Naples, S. Giuseppe dei Ruffi, convent church. Facade and bell tower. Photo by the author.

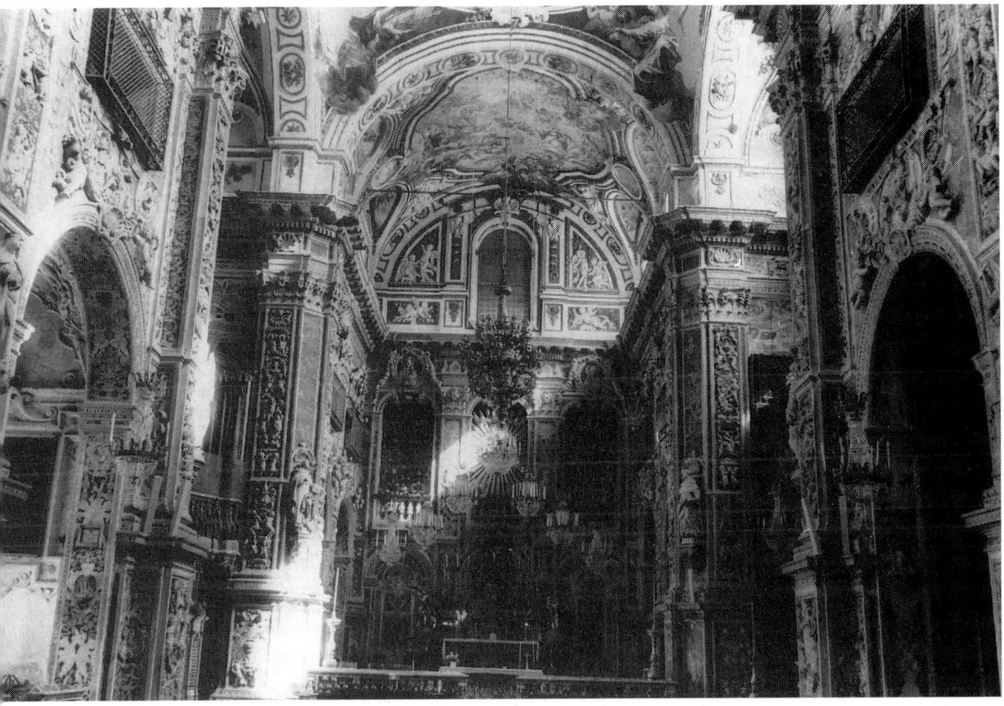

FIGURE 8. Palermo, S. Caterina. Convent church interior looking east. Photo by the author.

FIGURE 9. Alessandro Baratta, *Fidelissimae Urbis Neapolitanae,* Map of Naples, 1627. Detail of northern part of city, the Sanità Quarter. By permission of the British Library. BL Shelfmark: *Maps 24045. (2.)

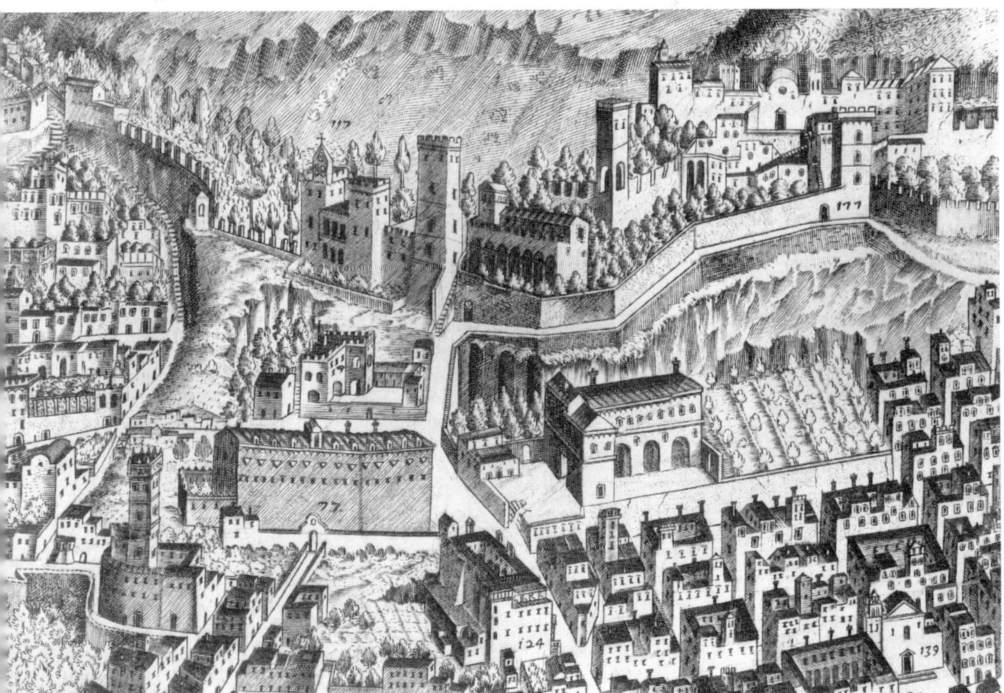

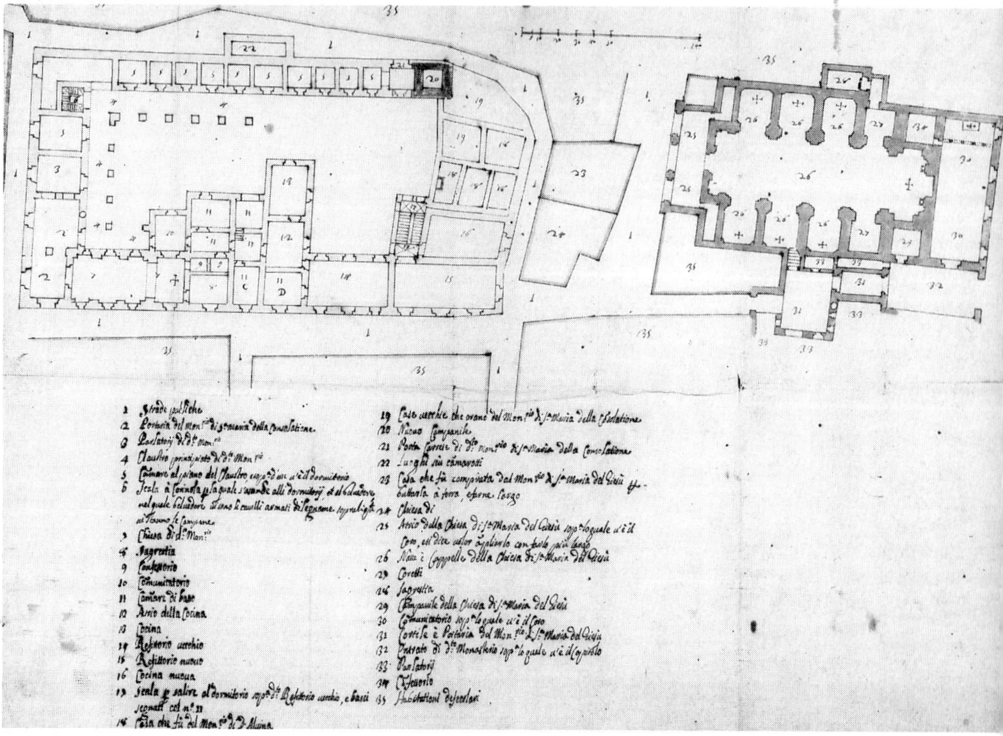

FIGURE 10. Naples. Drawing from a lawsuit showing buildings (23) bought by S. Maria del Gesù to create a square in front of its church (26). ASN, Mon. sop., 3168, pta. 3. By permission of the Archivio di Stato, Naples.

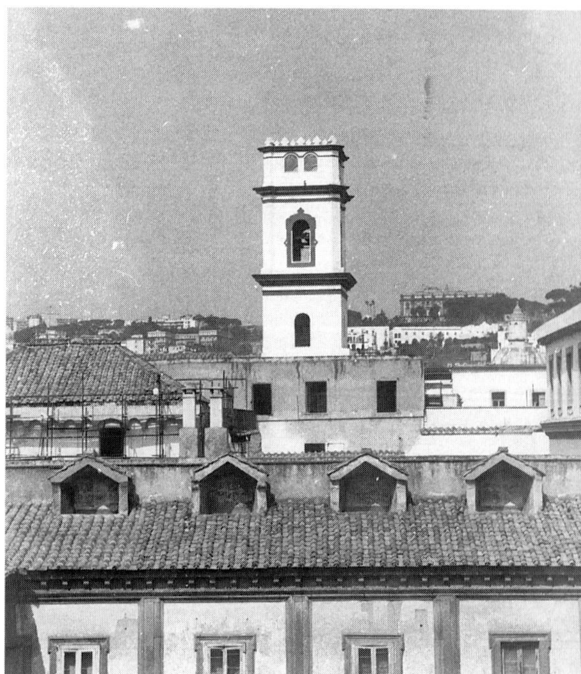

FIGURE 11. Naples, S. Giuseppe dei Ruffi. Cells in the north wing of the large cloister with the bell tower of the church of S. Maria del Gesù delle Monache in the background. Photo by C. Pasinetti, with kind permission.

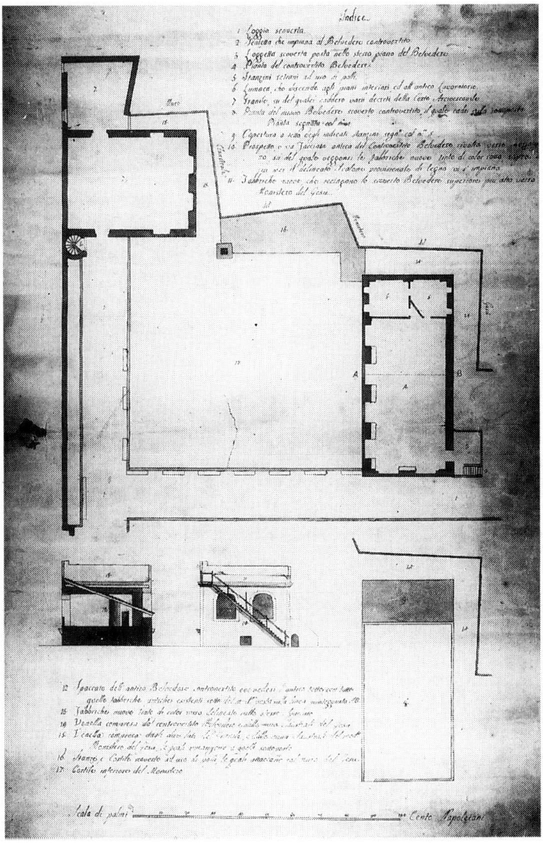

FIGURE 12. Naples. The disputed belvedere of S.M. di Gesù delle Monache. ASN, Mon. sop., 3168, pta. 1. By permission of the Archivio di Stato, Naples.

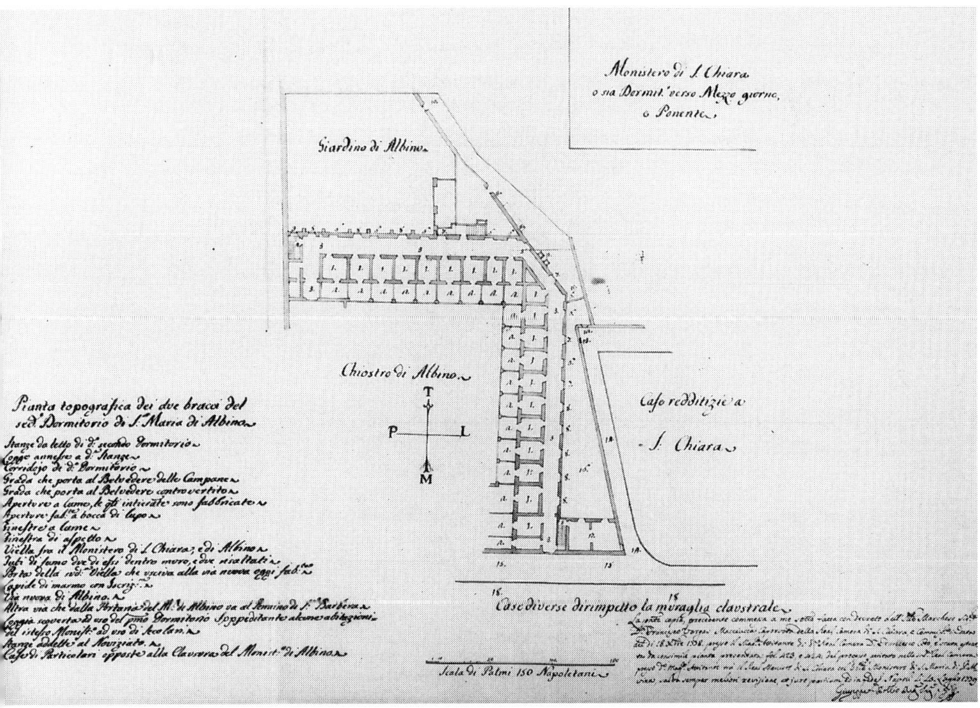

FIGURE 13. Naples, S. Maria Donnalbina. Plan of dormitory wings and disputed belvedere. ASN, Mon. sop., 3323, f. 402. By permission of the Archivio di Stato, Naples.

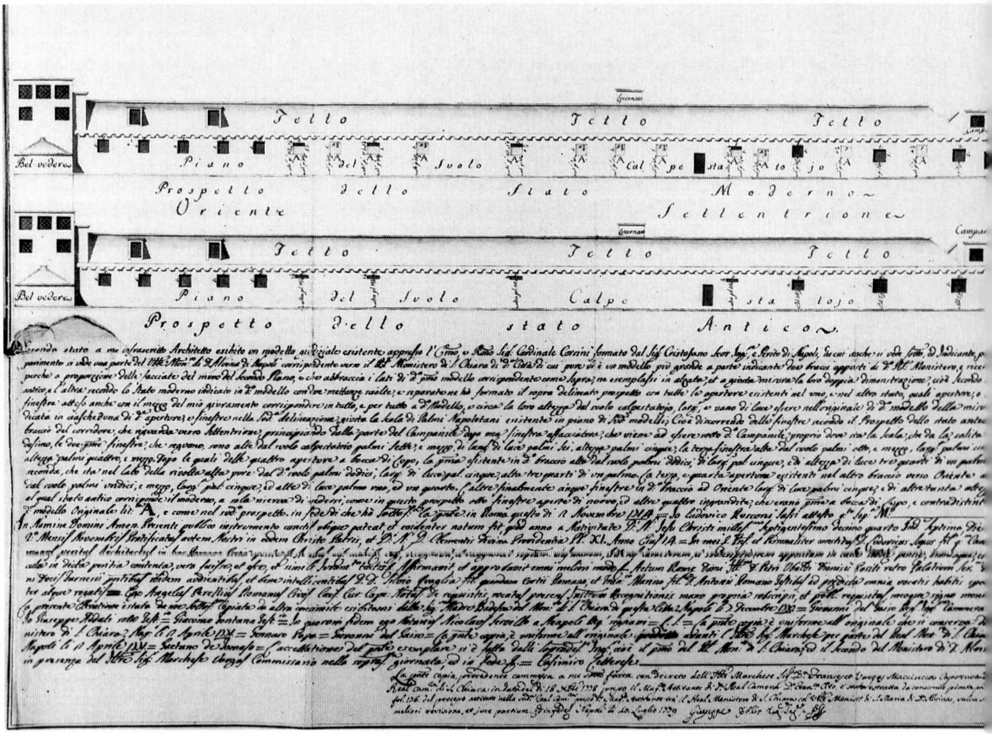

FIGURE 14. Naples. Drawing of 1778, a copy of a drawing of 1770, which, in turn, was a copy of one of 1711. It shows the old and new disputed walls between S. Chiara and S. Maria Donnalbina. ASN, Mon. sop., 3323, pta. 1, f. 171. By permission of the Archivio di Stato, Naples.

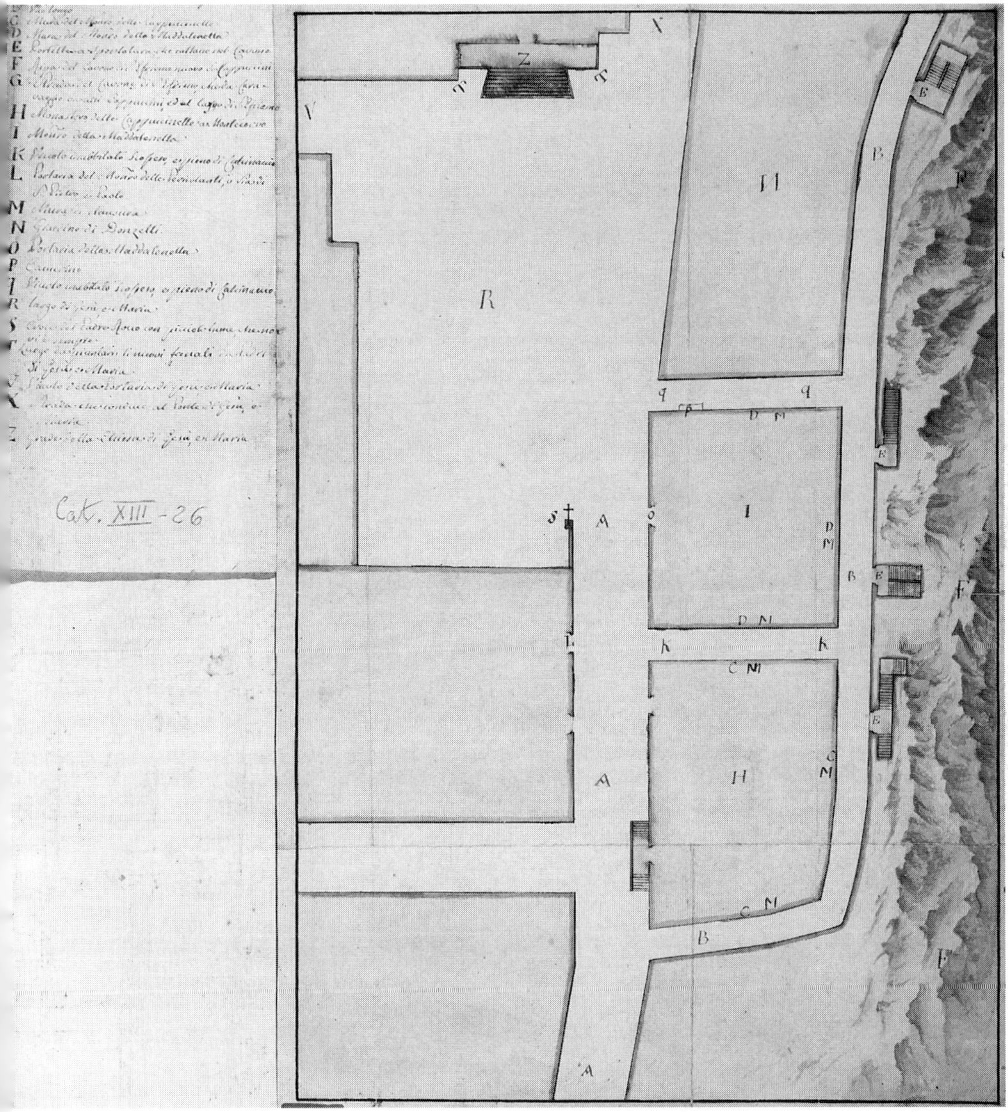

FIGURE 15. Naples. Drawing from a lawsuit. The square (*R*) in front of the church of Gesù e Maria (behind the steps at *Z*) showing the relationship between the convent of S. Francesco delle Cappuccinelle (*H*) and Maria Maddalena (*I*). BNSP 6.G.1.9–12371. By permission of the Biblioteca della Società Napoletana di Storia Patria.

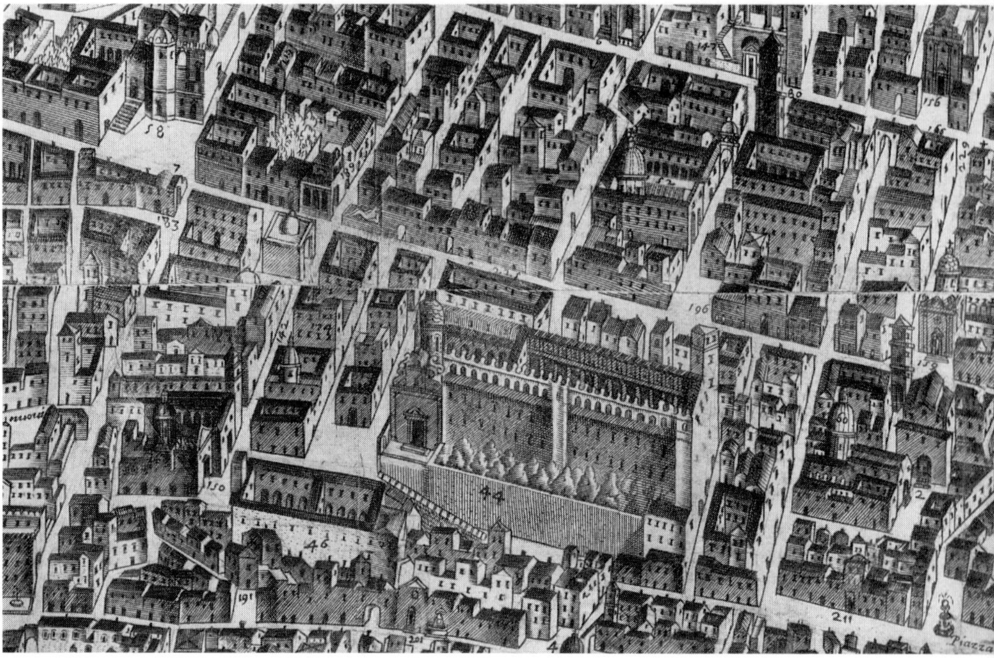

FIGURE 16. Alessandro Baratta, *Fidelissimae Urbis Neapolitanae,* Map of Naples, 1627. Detail showing SS. Marcellino e Festo and SS. Severio e Sossio. By permission of the British Library. BL Shelfmark: *Maps 24045. (2).

4, S. Maria a Porta Nuova;
44, SS. Severio e Sossio;
46, SS. Marcellino e Festo;
52, S. Gregorio Armeno;
58, S. Domenico;
189, S. Andrea a Seggio di Nido; *191,* S. Angelo delli Grassi; *201,* S. Caterina.

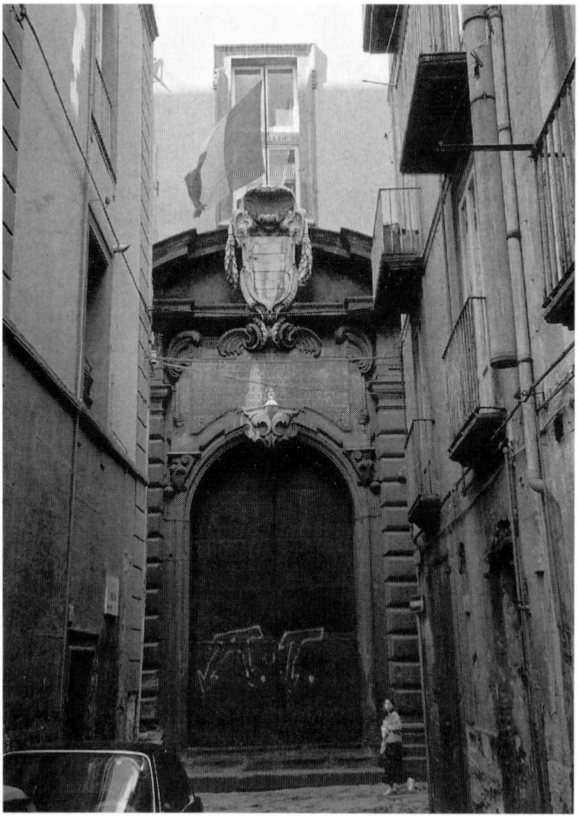

FIGURE 17. Naples. Entrance to the Jesuit College on via Paladino. Photo by the author.

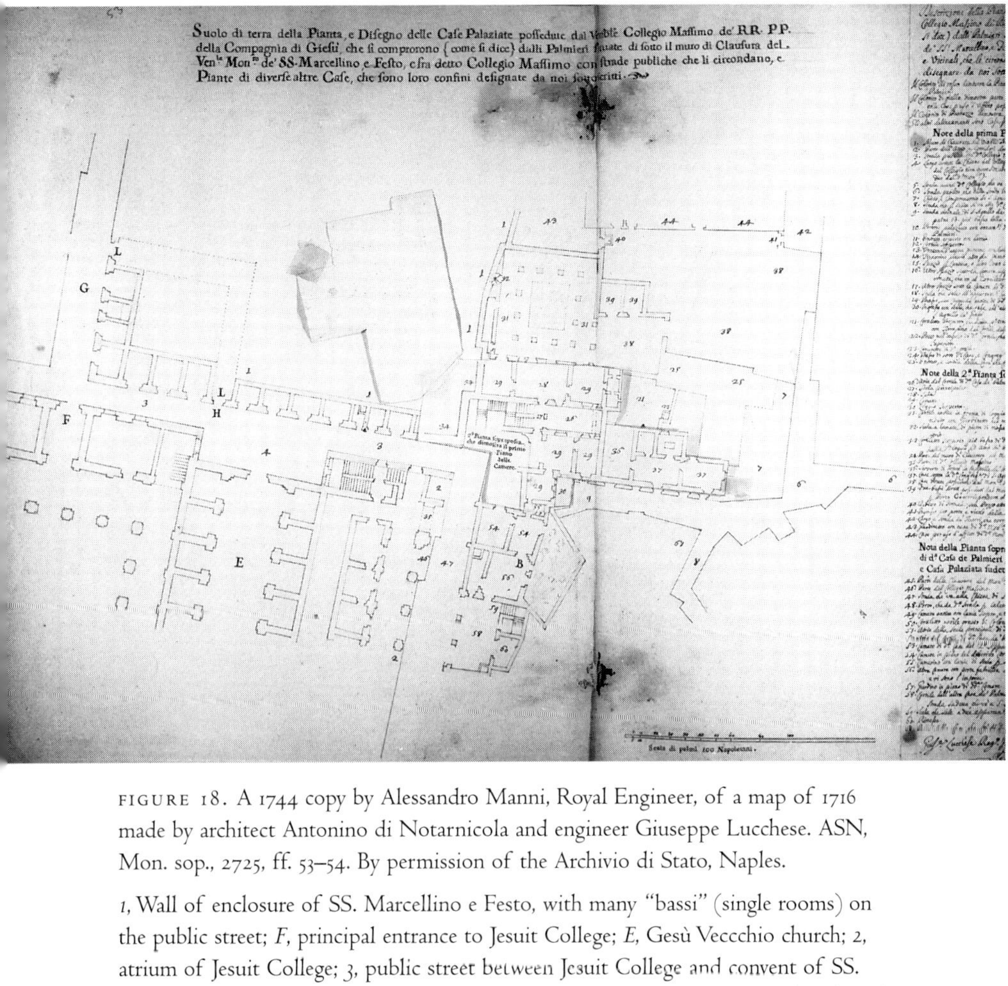

FIGURE 18. A 1744 copy by Alessandro Manni, Royal Engineer, of a map of 1716 made by architect Antonino di Notarnicola and engineer Giuseppe Lucchese. ASN, Mon. sop., 2725, ff. 53–54. By permission of the Archivio di Stato, Naples.

1, Wall of enclosure of SS. Marcellino e Festo, with many "bassi" (single rooms) on the public street; *F*, principal entrance to Jesuit College; *E*, Gesù Veccchio church; *2*, atrium of Jesuit College; *3*, public street between Jesuit College and convent of SS. Marcellino e Festo; *4*, square in front of Gesù Vecchio; *6*, public street; *7*, church and area owned by S. Agnello de' Grassi; *8*, street leading up to the church of S. Angelo de Cardamoni; *26–33*, the Palmieri house (first floor); *38*, *43*, *44*, property of the convent of SS. Marcellino e Festo.

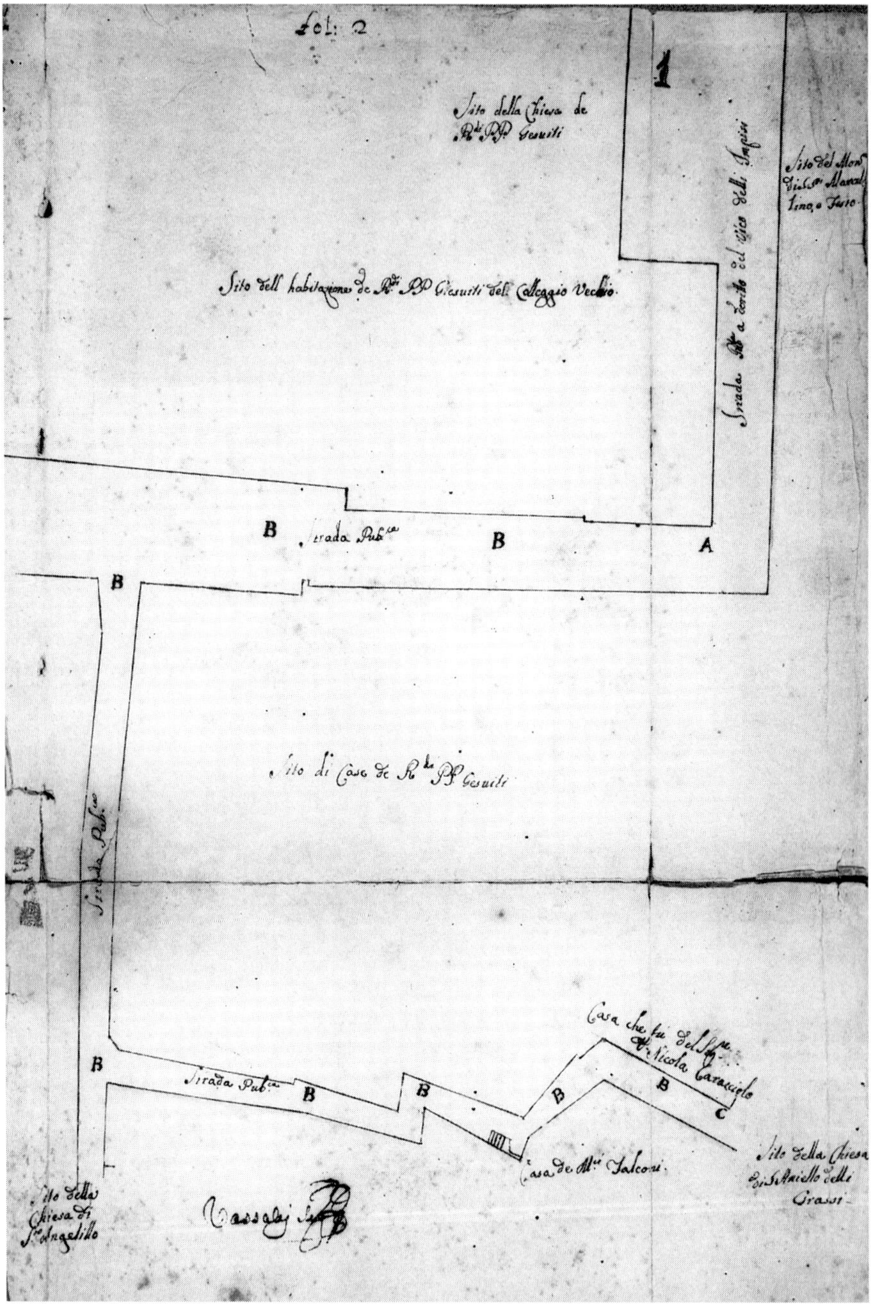

FIGURE 19. Naples. Undated drawing of street arrangement before the cutting of the Jesuits' new road (loosely indicated in pencil on the right). ASN, Mon. sop., 2879, pta. n. 3. By permission of the Archivio di Stato, Naples.

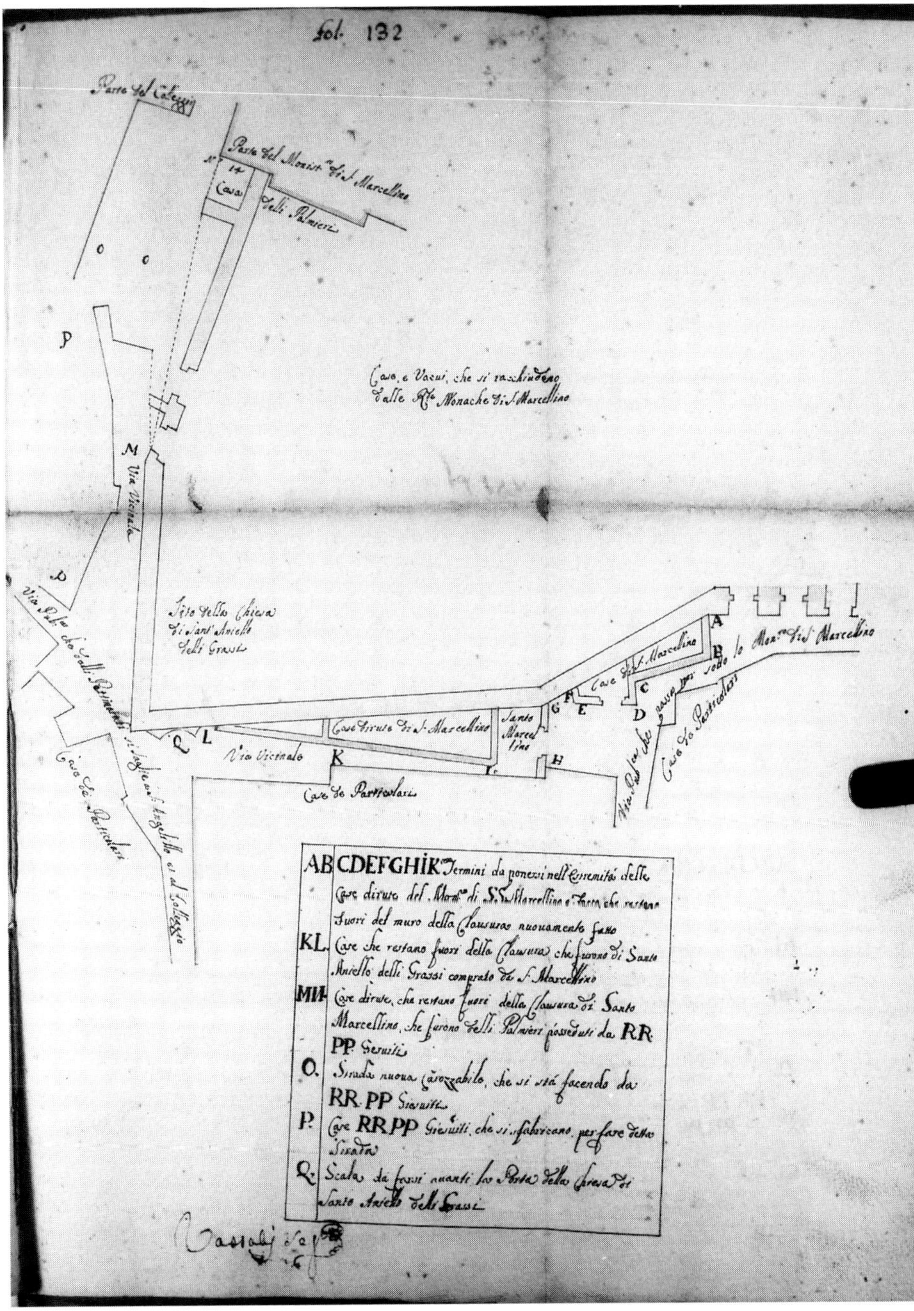

FIGURE 20. Drawing (ASN, Mon. sop., 2812, f. 420) showing Jesuits' intended cut through the erstwhile Palmieri property at *M* to create their new road. By permission of the Archivio di Stato, Naples.

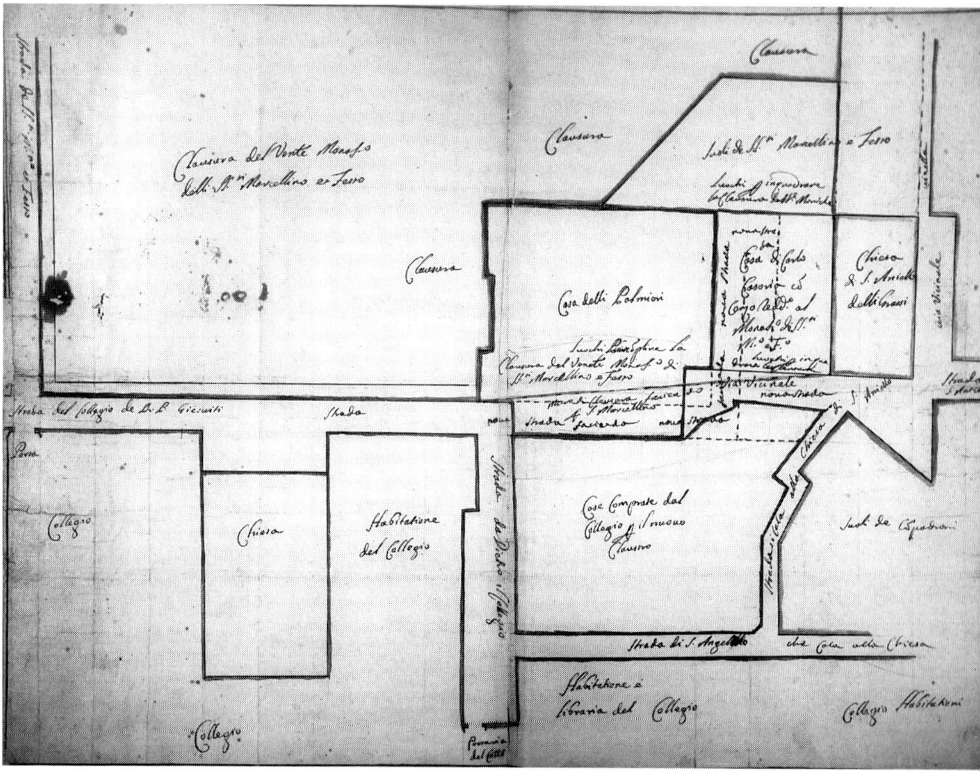

FIGURE 21. Drawing showing the Palmieri property with the new road projected. ASN, Mon. sop., 2725, ff. 77–78. By permission of the Archivio di Stato, Naples.

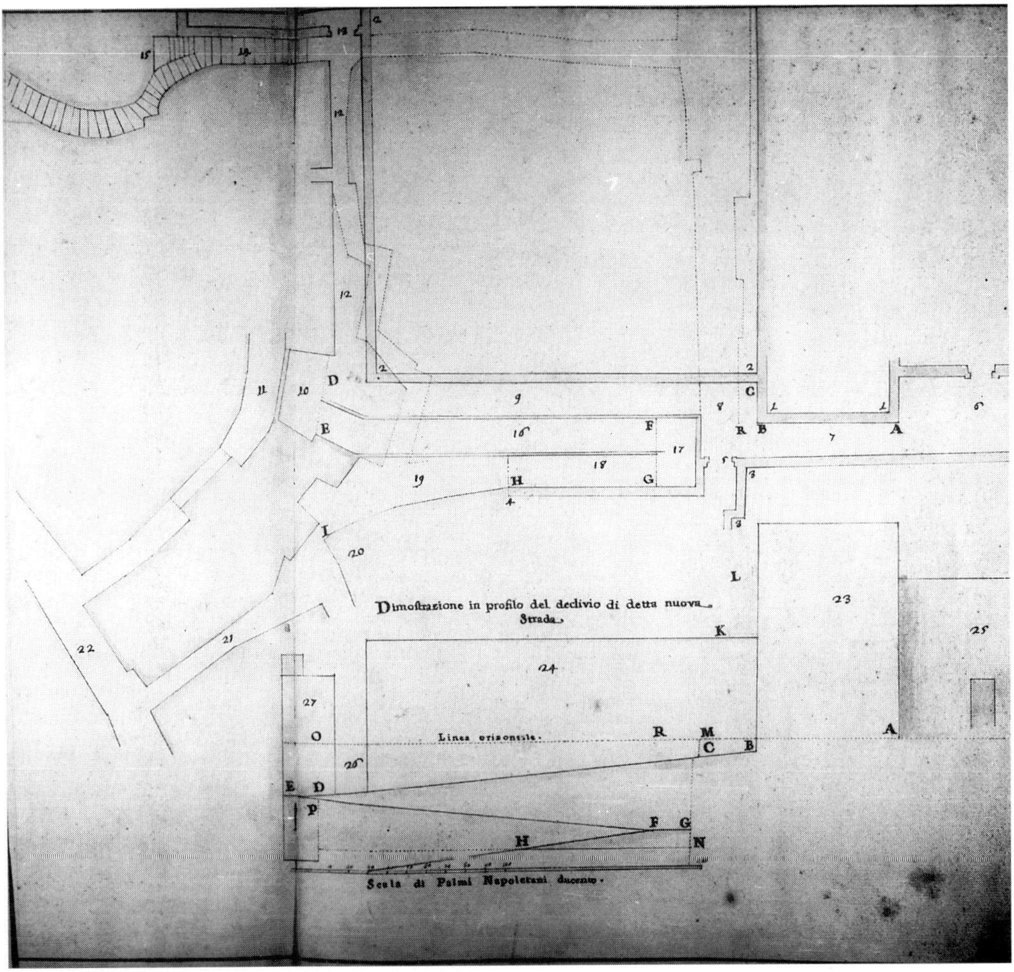

FIGURE 22. Drawing by Giuseppe Lucchese, Royal Engineer, and Antonio di Notaricola showing the proposed new road, 1717. ASN, Mon. sop., 2725, ff. 57–58. By permission of the Archivio di Stato, Naples.

1, part of the old wall of the Jesuit college with rooms and corridors above; *2,* new college wall; *3,* old wall of enclosure of SS. Marcellino e Festo; *4,* new wall of enclosure for SS. Marcellino e Festo; *5,* carriage entrance for SS. Marcellino e Festo; *7,* old street, between Jesuit College and SS. Marcellino convent, to be lowered; *8, 9, 10, 16, 17, 18* (near Congregation of S. Agnello de' Grassi), *19,* ramps and "landings" of proposed new street; *12,* new street for carriages linking carriage entrance of the College and S. Angelillo; *14,* old stepped street, leading down to the church of S. Angelillo and the Porto Seggio; *15,* church of S. Angelillo.

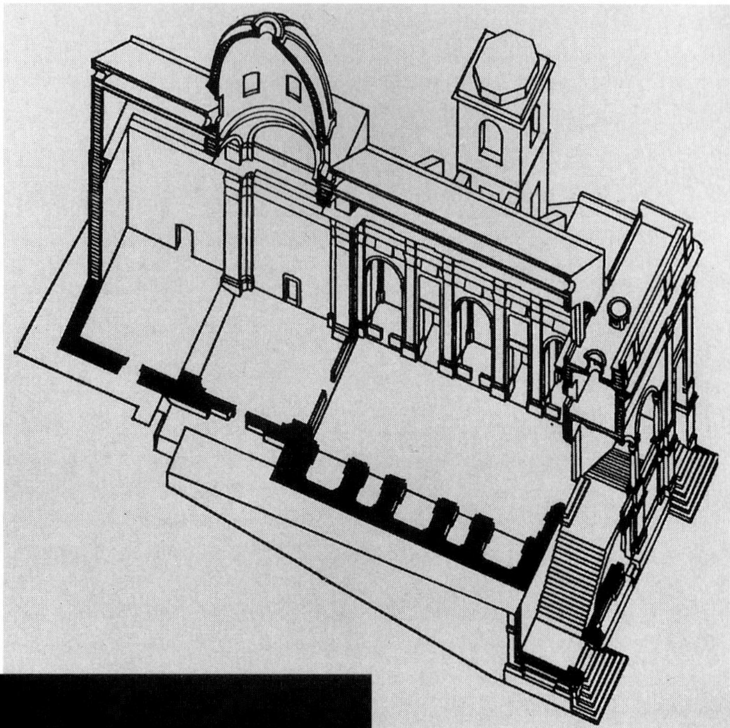

FIGURE 23. Naples, S. Maria della Sapienza. Axonometric section.

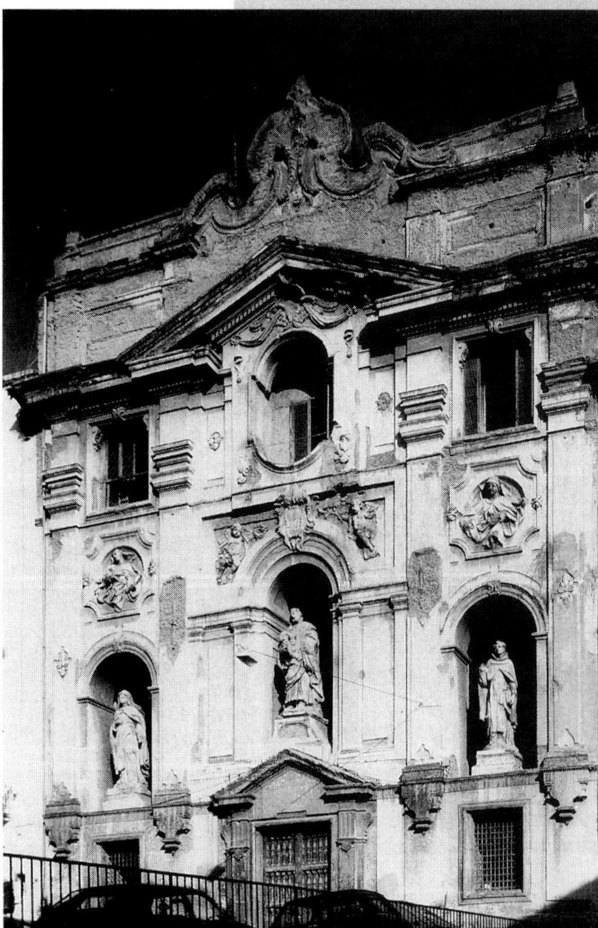

FIGURE 24. Naples, S. Giuseppe a Pontecorvo. Facade. Photo by the author.

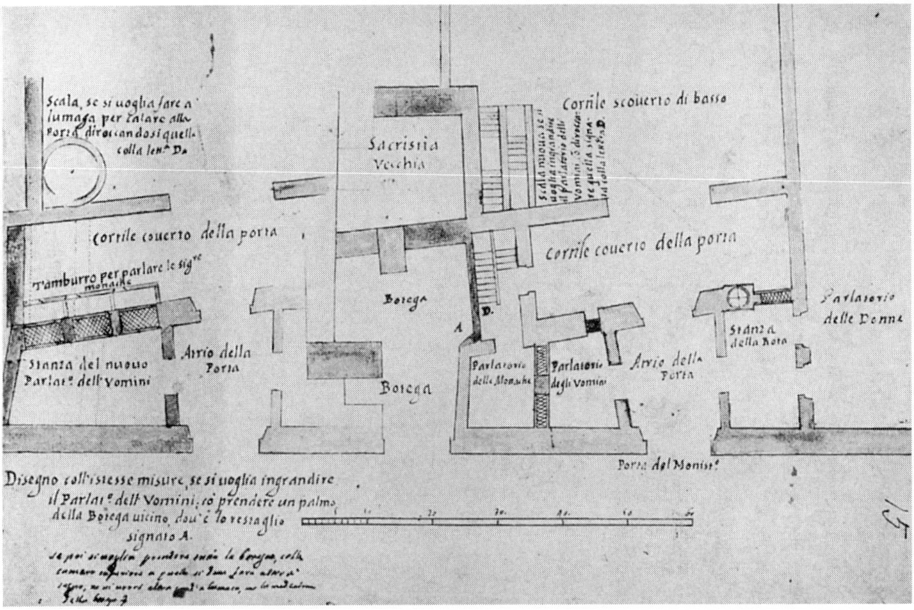

FIGURE 25. Naples, S. Maria Donnalbina. Drawing showing the arrangement of parlatories, relating to a project for the expansion of the parlatory for men in c. 1689. ASN, Mon. sop., S. Maria Donnalbina, 2426, f. 7. By permission of the Archivio di Stato, Naples.

FIGURE 26. Naples, S. Giuseppe dei Ruffi. Plan, drawn at the time of cutting of via Duomo. ASN. Photo by Giuseppe Russi. By permission of Gaetana Cantone.

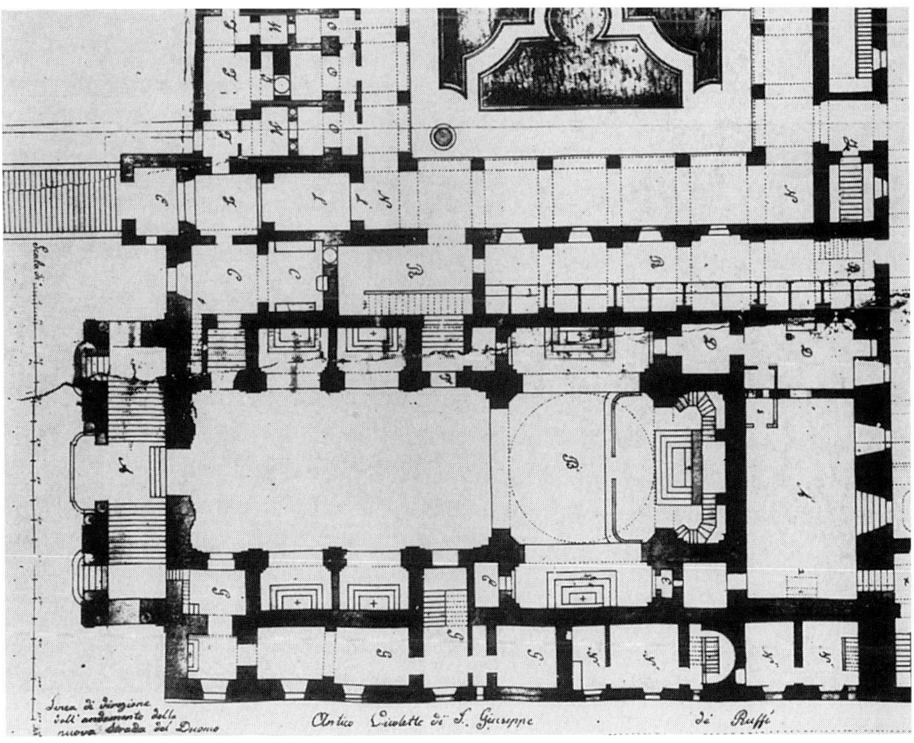

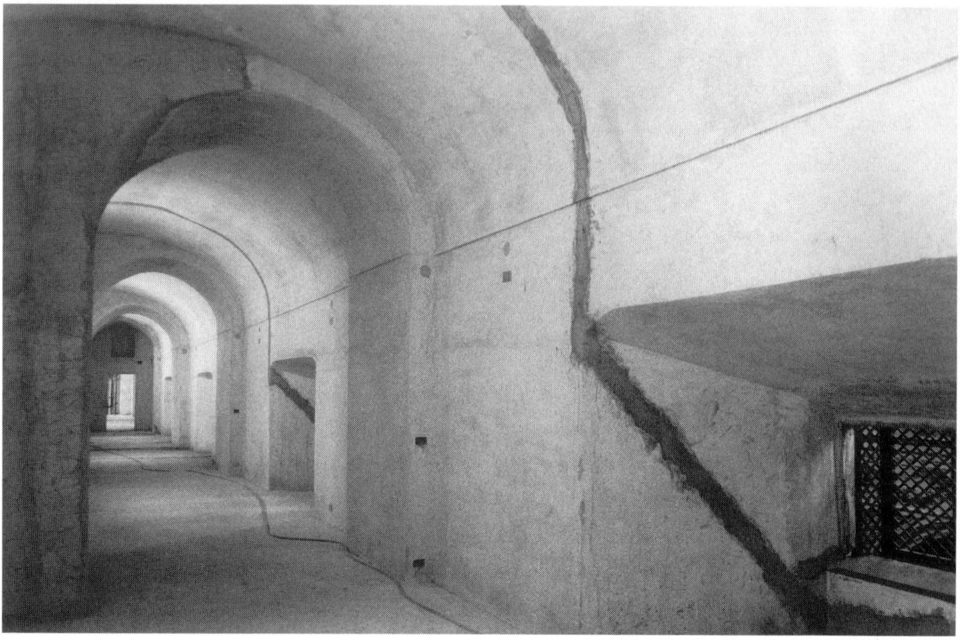

FIGURE 27. Naples, S. Maria Donnaregina. Nuns' corridor at clerestory level on the south side of the church, with gelosie to look down into the convent church. Photo by the author.

FIGURE 28. Naples, S. Maria Donnaregina. View from gelosia at clerestory level on the south side of the convent church looking down to a lateral chapel in the north side below. Photo by the author.

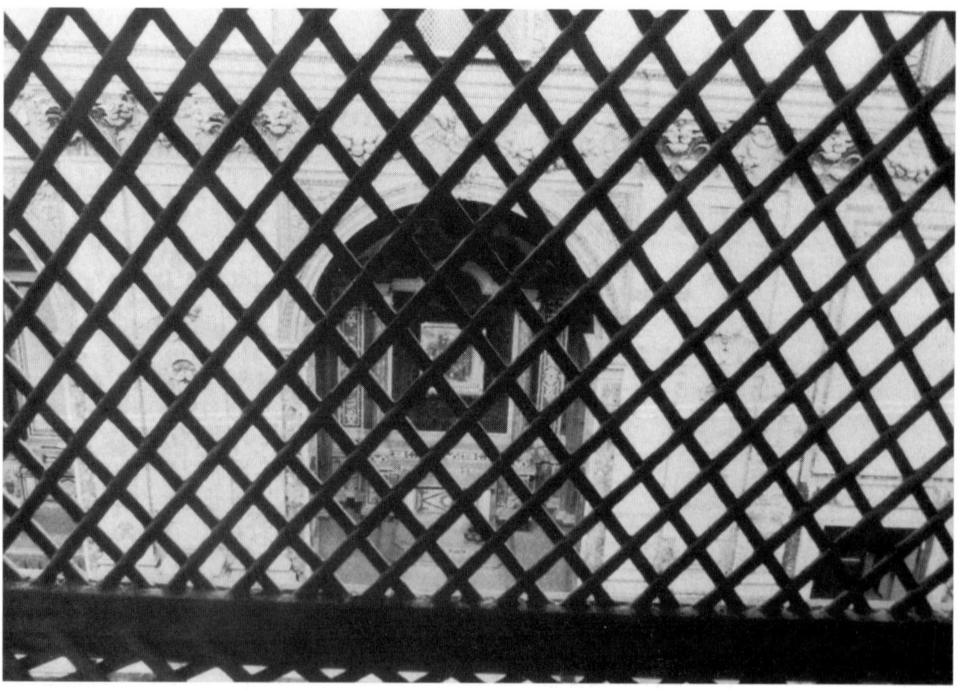

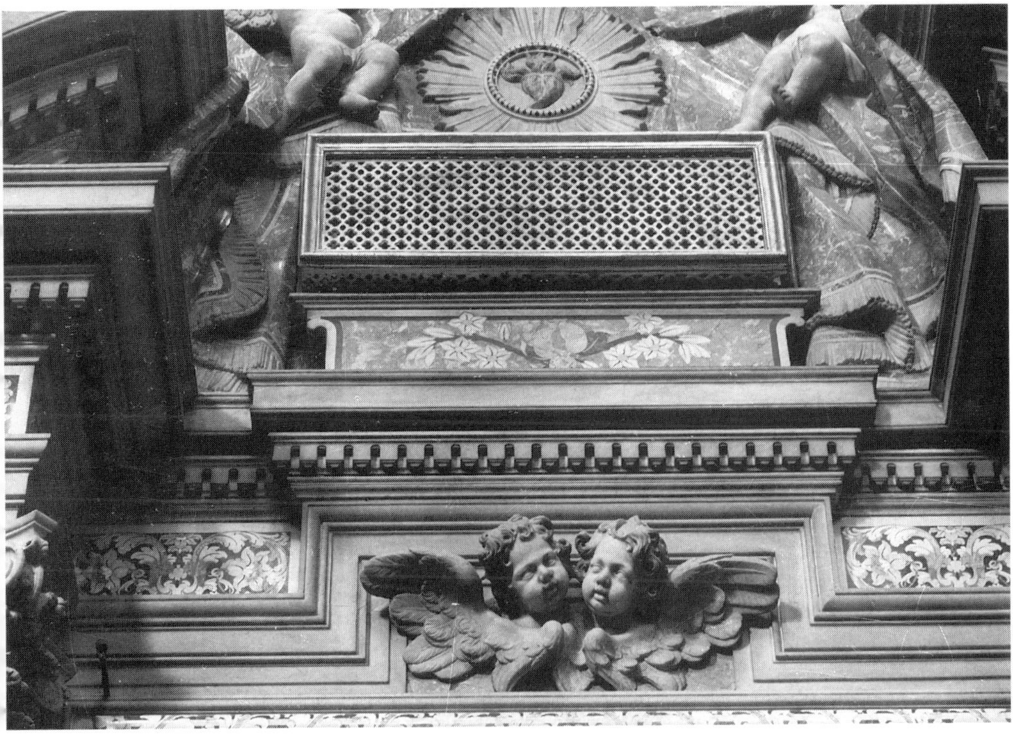

FIGURE 29. Naples, S. Giuseppe dei Ruffi. Detail of transept chapel of S. Agostino with gelosia. Photo by the author.

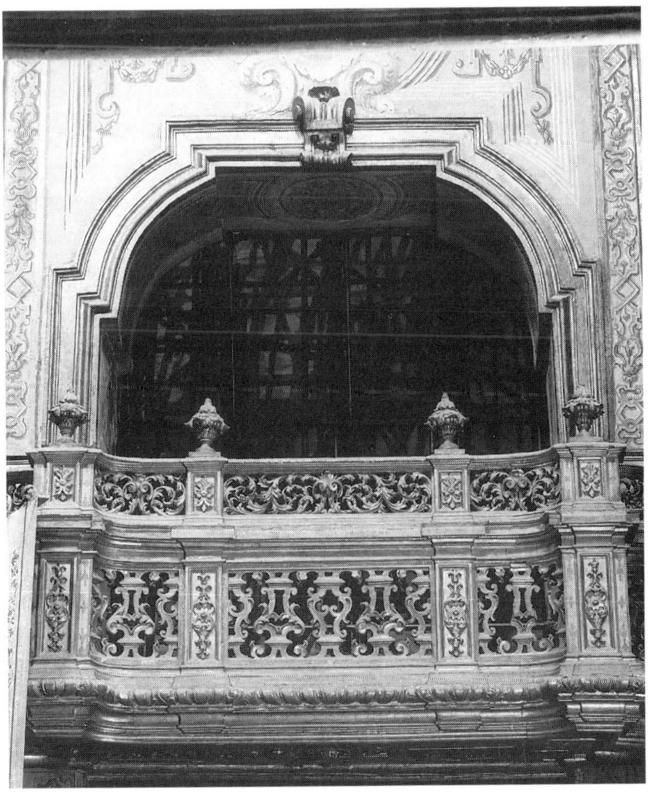

FIGURE 30. Naples, Gesù delle Monache. Cantoria. By kind permission of the Soprintendenza per i Beni Artistici e Storici di Napoli.

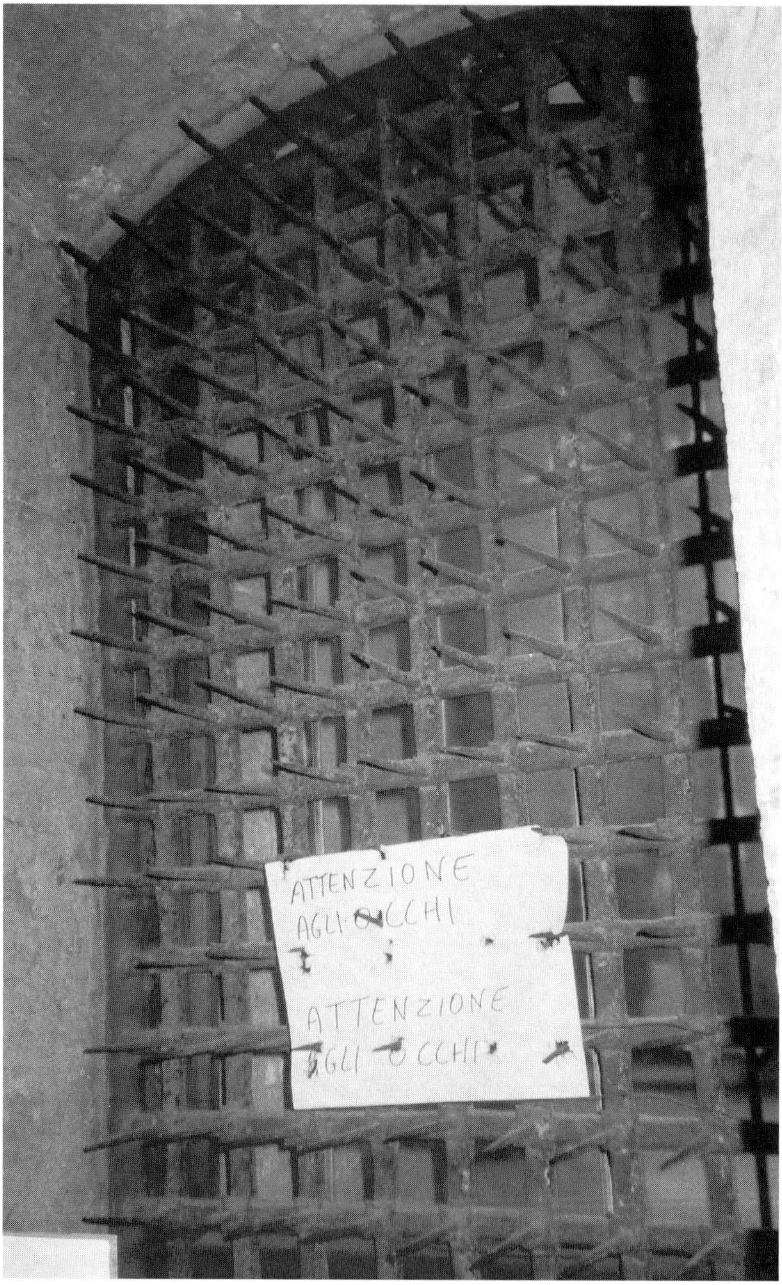

FIGURE 31. Naples, S. Chiara. Spiked grilles dividing the nuns' choir from the church nave. Photo by the author.

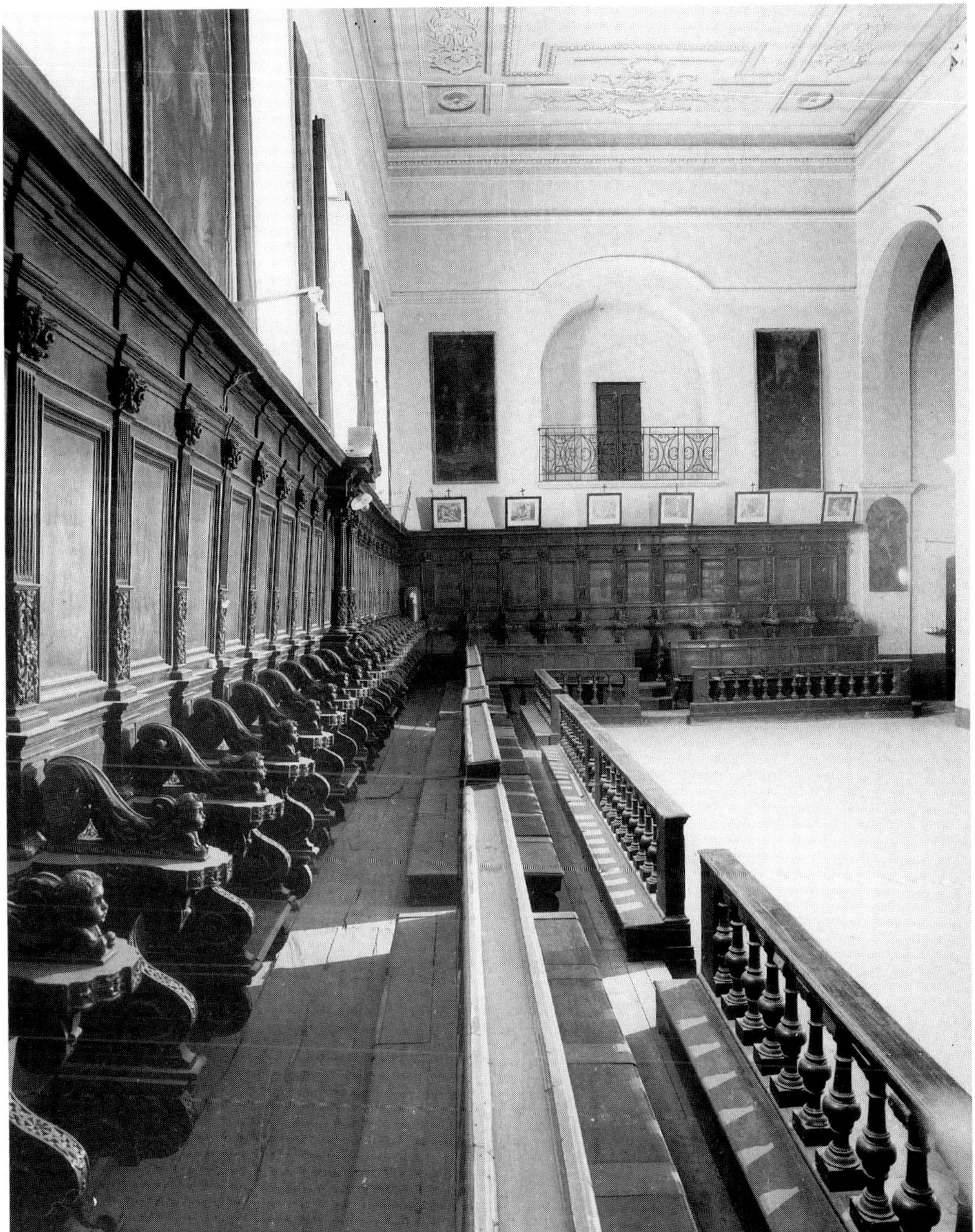

FIGURE 32. Naples, S. Giuseppe dei Ruffi. Nuns' choir. By kind permission of the Soprintendenza per i Beni Artistici e Storici di Napoli.

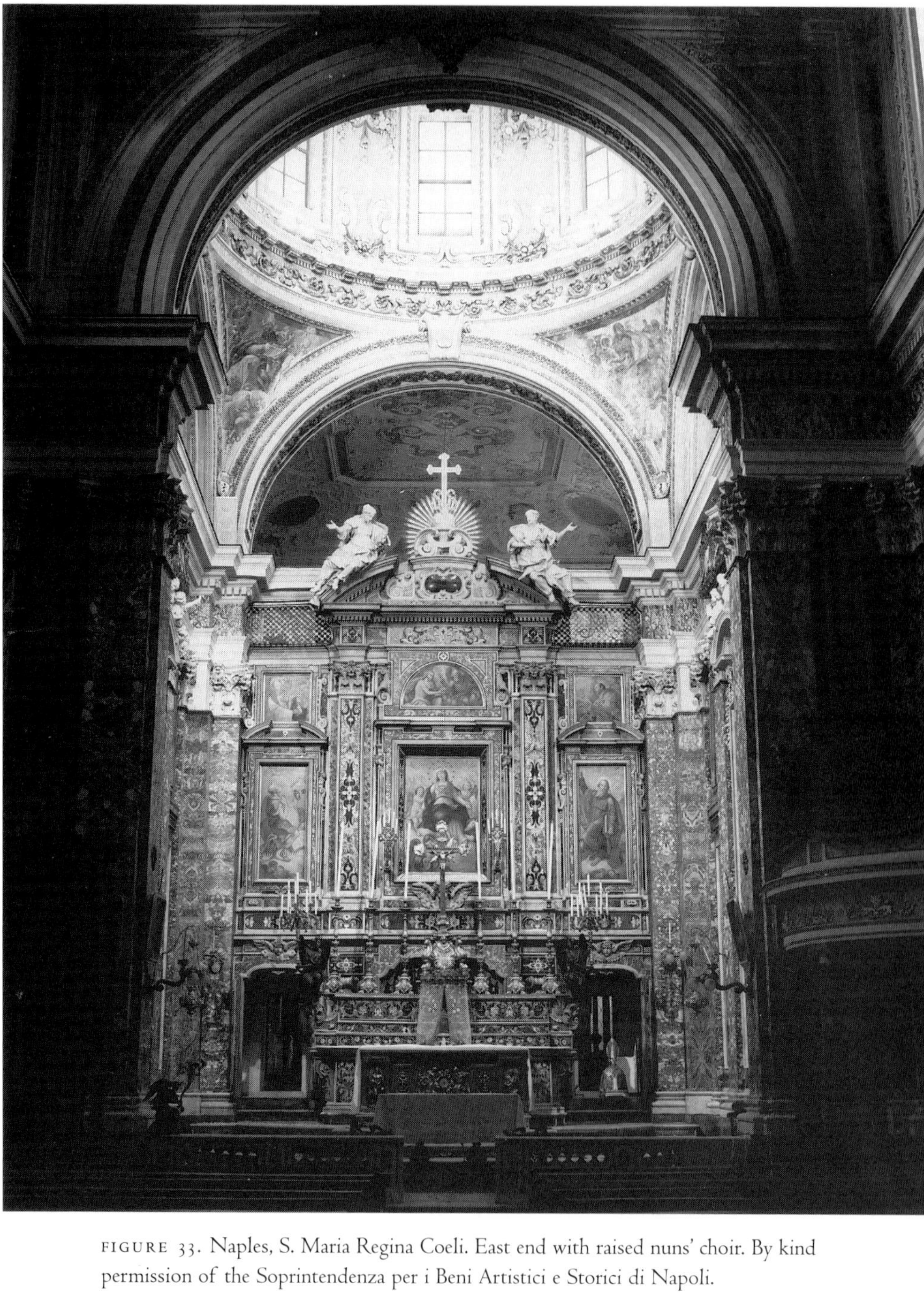

FIGURE 33. Naples, S. Maria Regina Coeli. East end with raised nuns' choir. By kind permission of the Soprintendenza per i Beni Artistici e Storici di Napoli.

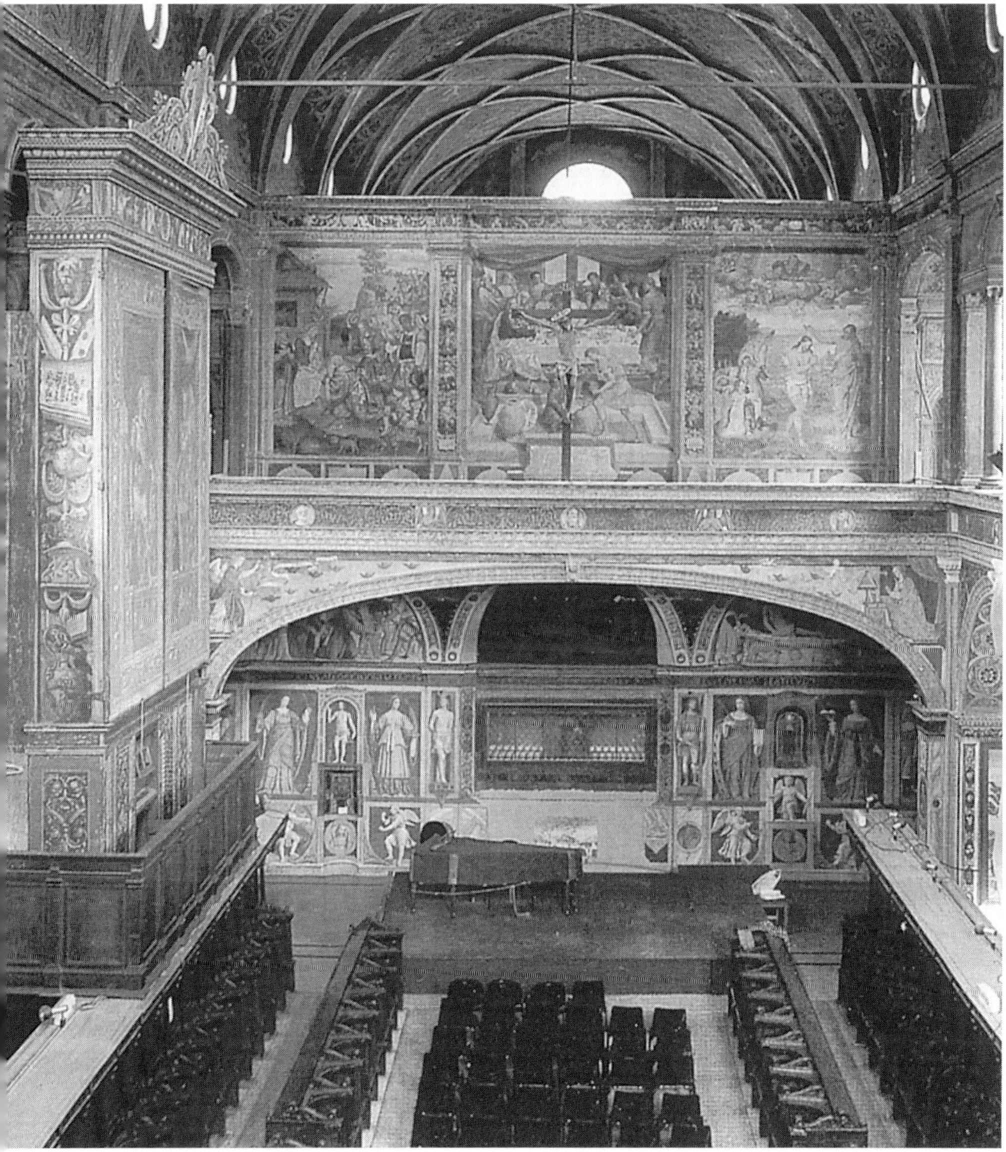

FIGURE 34. Milan, S. Maurizio. Nuns' choir looking west toward the main church, with dividing wall and raised walkway. Photo by the author.

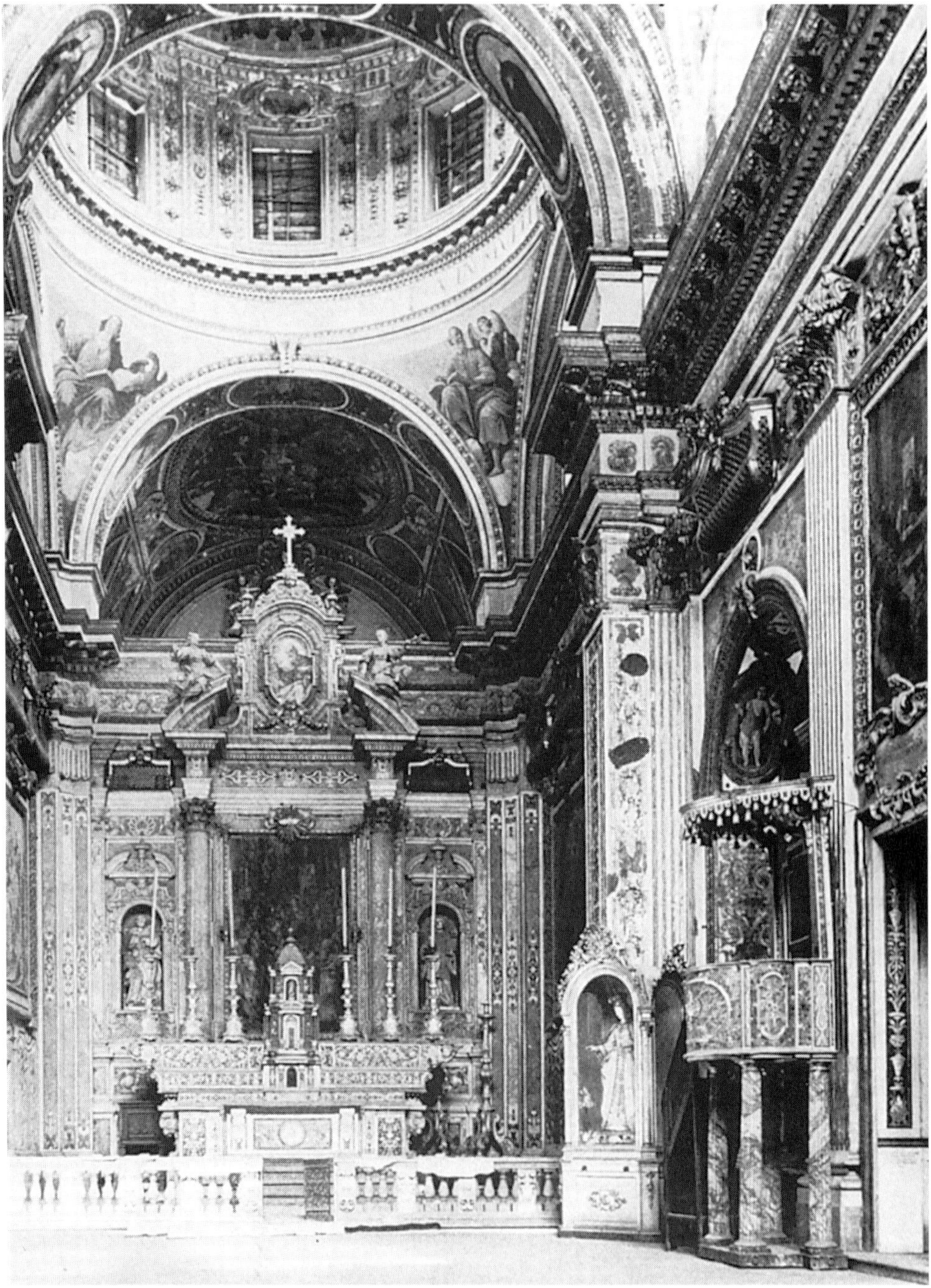

FIGURE 35. Naples, S. Maria della Sapienza. Interior looking east. Photo by Massimo Velo.

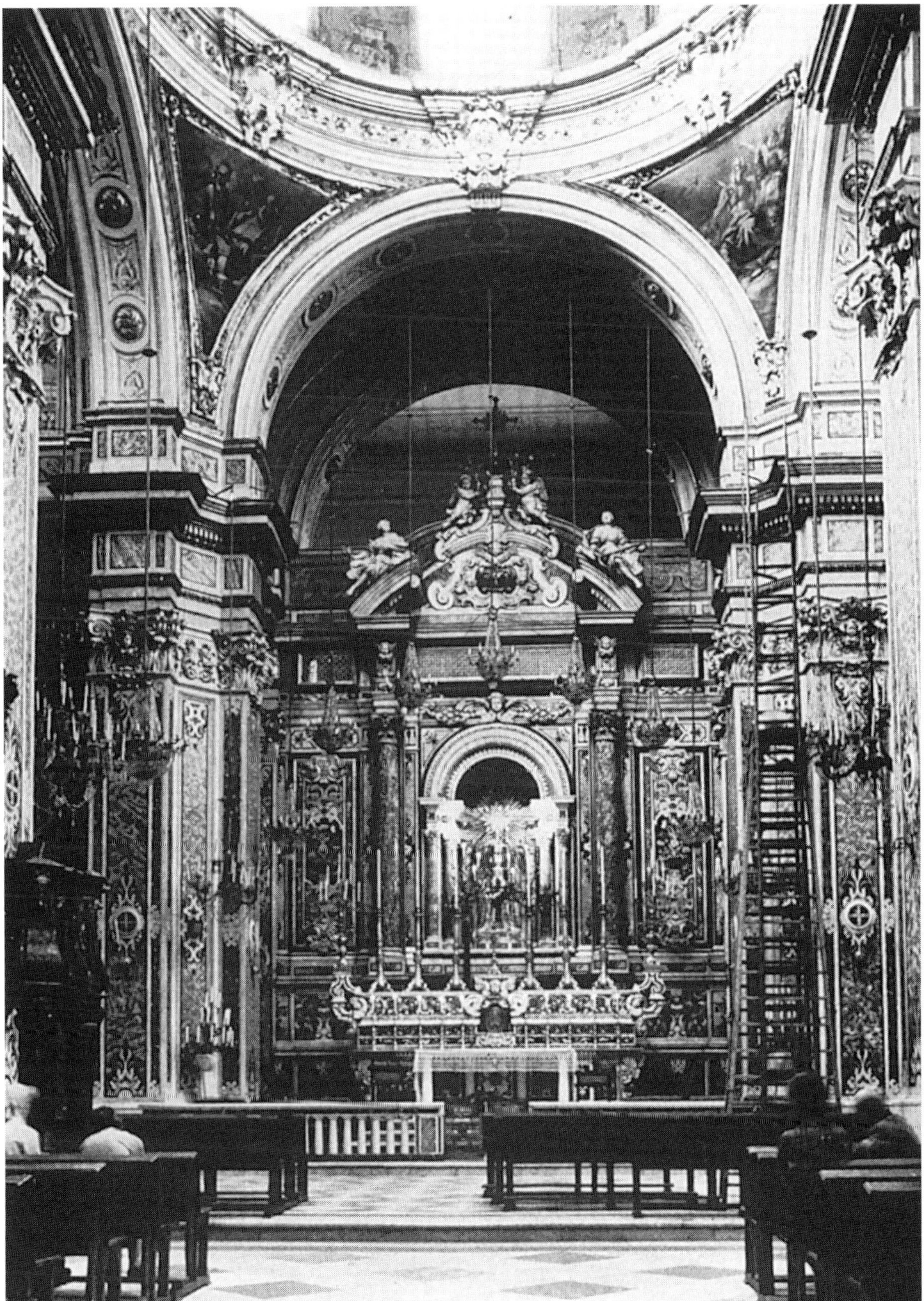

FIGURE 36. Naples, S. Giuseppe dei Ruffi. Convent church looking east. Choir added 1681–1682. Photo by the author.

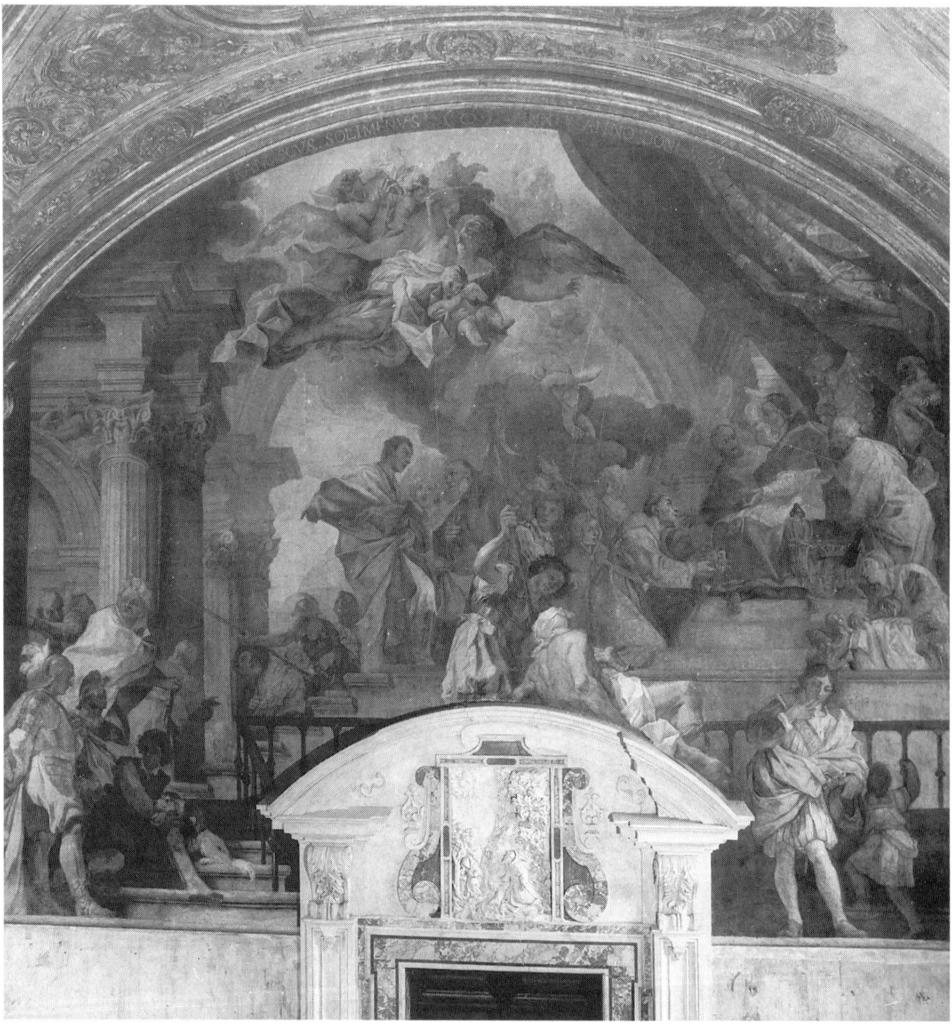

FIGURE 37. Naples, S. Maria Donnaregina Nuova. Raised nuns' choir, east wall. Photo by the author.

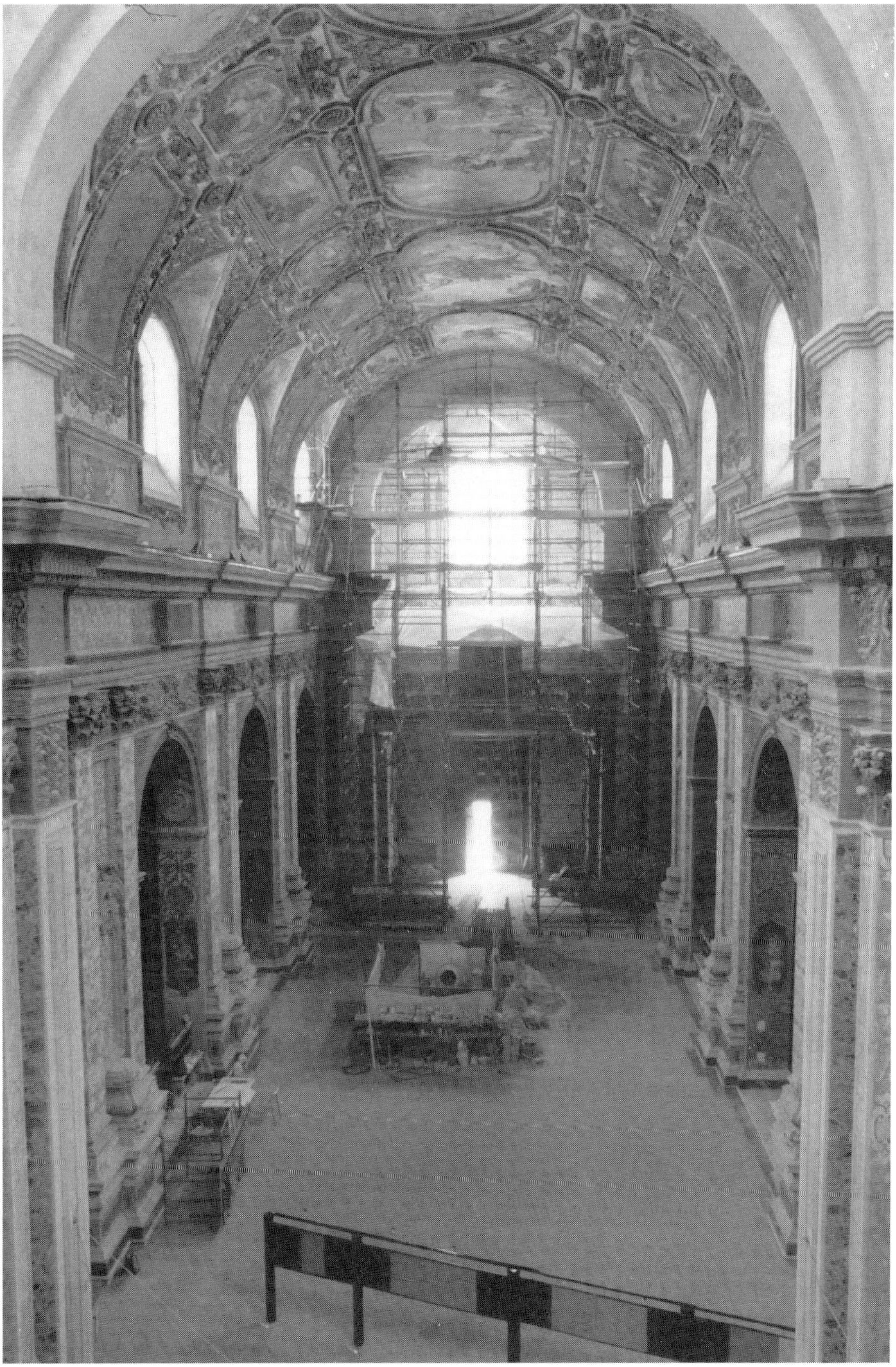

FIGURE 38. Naples, S. Maria Donnaregina Nuova. View from raised east-end nuns' choir looking west. Photo by the author.

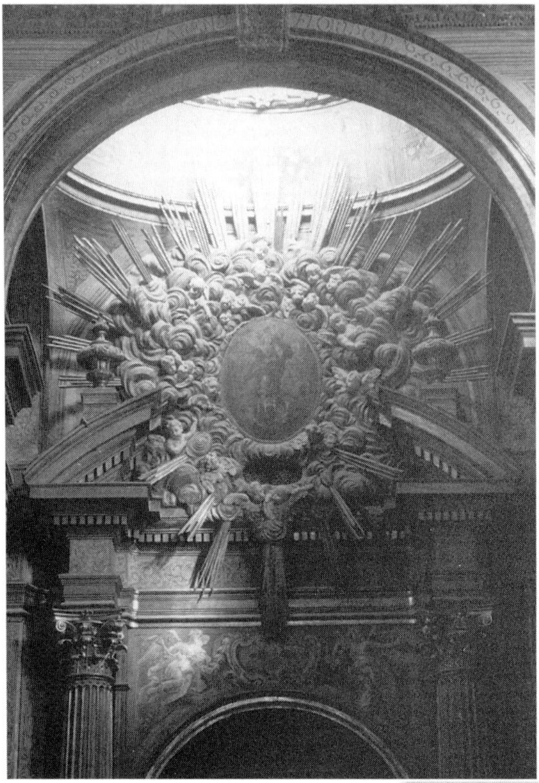

FIGURE 39. Naples, S. Maria del Gesù delle Monache. Nuns' choir and glory. Photo by the author.

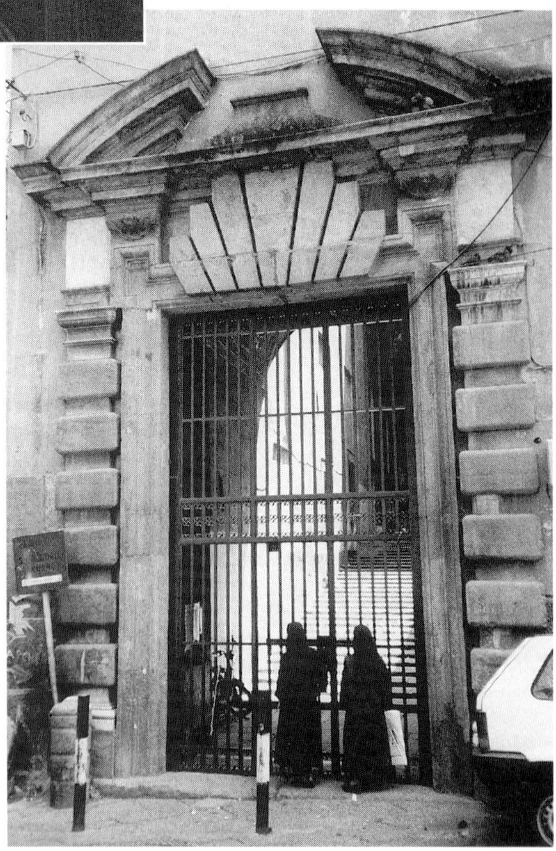

FIGURE 40. Naples, S. Gregorio Armeno. Rusticated entrance to the conventual complex. Photo by the author.

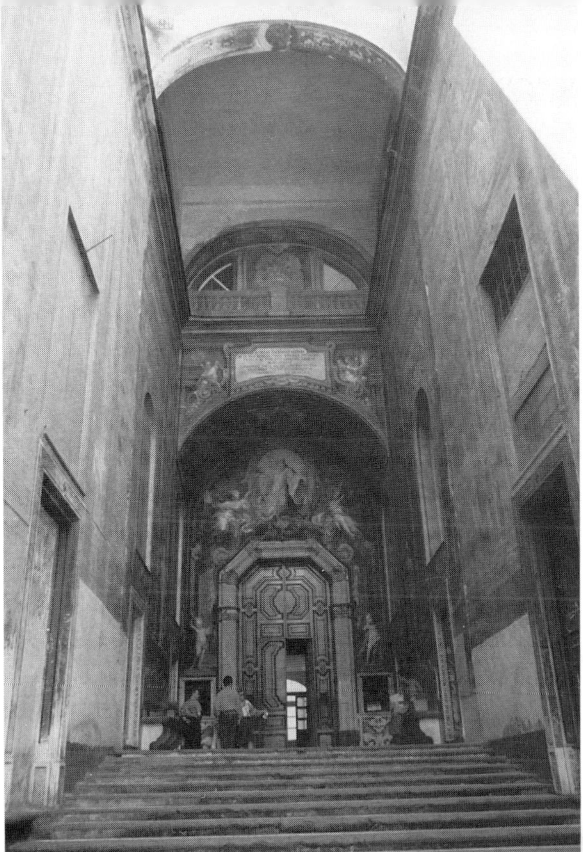

FIGURE 41. Naples, S. Gregorio Armeno. Entrance staircase to the convent, with goods wheels. Photo by the author.

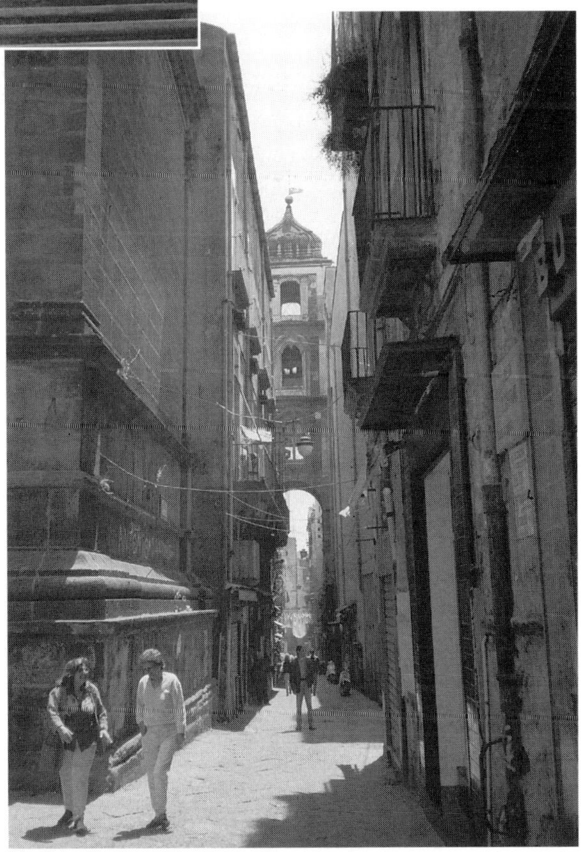

FIGURE 42. Naples. Covered bridge forming part of the convent of S. Gregorio Armeno over via S. Gregorio Armeno. Photo by the author.

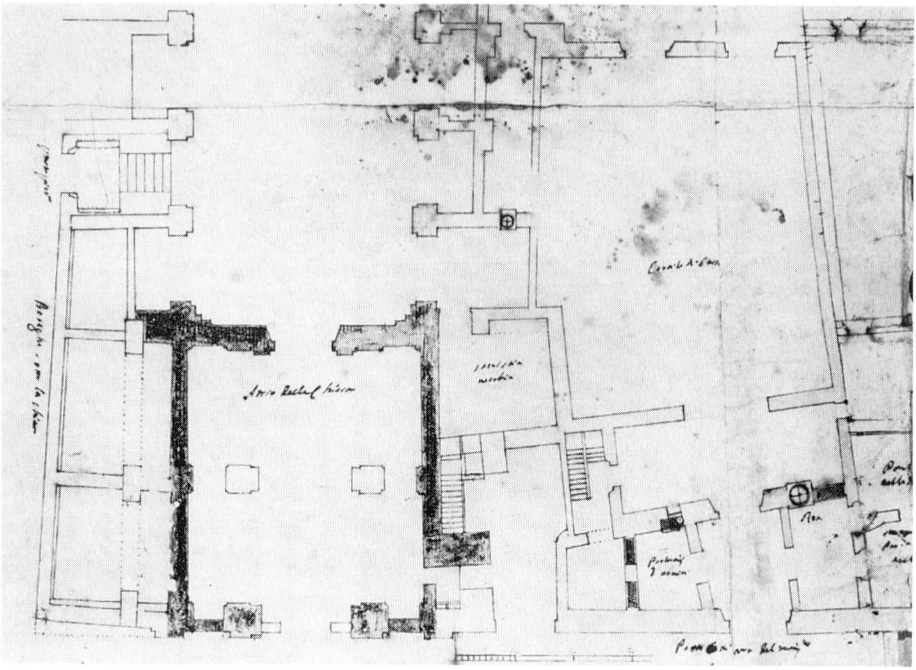

FIGURE 43. Naples, S. Maria Donnalbina. Project for atrium in front of the church, 1689. ASN, Mon. sop., 3324. Photograph by Massimo Velo. By permission of the Archivio di Stato, Naples.

FIGURE 44. Naples, S. Gregorio Armeno. Seventeenth-century golden reliquaries. By kind permission of the Soprintendenza per i Beni Artistici e Storici di Napoli.

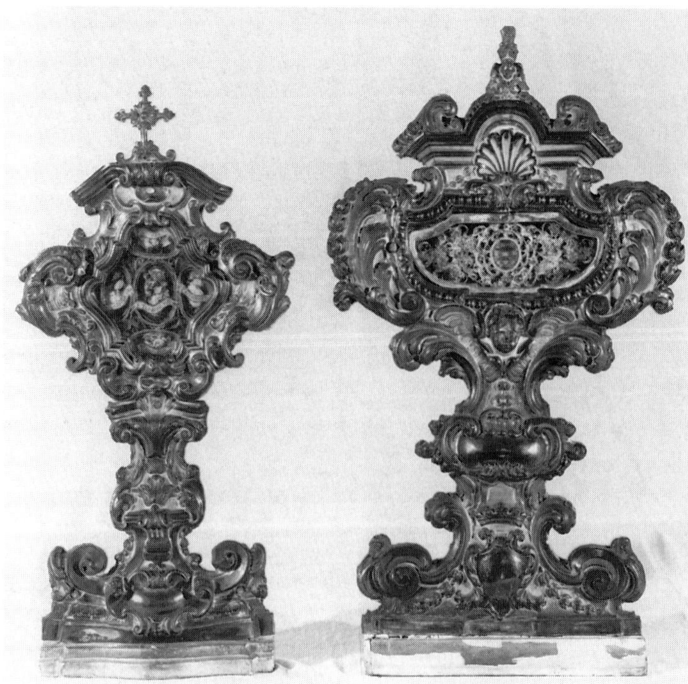

choir was built not at the west end but at the east. It was placed high up behind the altar, and the arch over the altar was opened so that the congregants could see right through into the space beyond (Plate 9, Figures 33, 35, 36, 37, 39).[38] To understand this phenomenon it helps to consider the nature of conventual churches and their choirs more broadly.

Female convents usually contained two churches, an inner one accessible only to nuns and an outer one accessible to the laity (Figure 23). During this period in Naples a significant number of convent churches built a second nuns' choir, raised at the east end, which functioned as an inner church (Figure 33, 35, 36, 37, and 39). In other words, the nuns' choir and the inner church were fused in significant ways at this date. In Naples, however, the space occupied during the mass was smaller, was raised to the upper order of the church, and is more appropriately termed a choir.

In spite of the commonplace that female convents adopted double churches as a result of post-Tridentine prescription, they stem in fact from a form used by medieval orders of strict enclosure. The practice of building them dates back to Benedictine practice during the tenth and eleventh centuries.[39] Medieval churches following this building type also have gratings, wheels, peepholes, and windows.[40] This model was taken up and adapted in many Cistercian convents well before the sixteenth century and by the Mendicant "Second" orders in Italy, including the Franciscans, Dominicans, and Augustinians.[41] Double churches existed in over forty fifteenth- and sixteenth-century Italian convents.[42]

Although prescriptions regarding the organization of space within the church did not number among the radical reforms for monastic practices established by Leo X at the Lateran Council in 1513, or among the measures issued by the Holy See in the *Consilium delectorum cardinalium de emendenda ecclesia* (1537), the diocese of Milan boasted numerous examples of this type antedating Trent.[43] As early as 1300, the archbishop of Milan requested the Benedictine nuns at S. Margherita to adapt their church to meet with the requirements of strict enclosure detailed in Boniface VIII's bull *Periculoso ac detestabili* of 1293, which, in effect, included creating a double church.

It was in Milan, home of the early double churches, that double churches of high architectural quality emerged in the sixteenth century. The splendid new double church at the Benedictine convent of S. Maurizio al Monastero Maggiore, in particular, is worth examining in some detail, especially for its treatment of the nuns' choir probably carried out during the first decade of the sixteenth century (Figure 34).[44] There are two separate churches at S. Maurizio: a larger inner church for nuns, and a smaller outer one for laity. The division between the two churches consists of a screen with the arch open above, as in the Neapolitan examples, but in this case the nuns' church is at ground level.

A grille, as wide as and immediately above the altar, provides the visual link between the nuns and the outer church. An open walkway or choir platform at first-floor level on the nuns' side of the dividing wall also allows nuns access to a higher level. The similarity with the east-end choirs of the Neapolitan churches ends here, however, because at S. Maurizio the platform is screened from the main church by the solid transverse wall dividing the churches. Both outer and inner churches have lateral chapels, and in both the bays of the upper order are defined by serlian arches. But the nuns' church is two bays larger than the outer church, firmly indicating that the center of gravity is on the nuns' side of the dividing wall. This represents S. Maurizio's distinguished clientele, the daughters of the city's most prominent aristocratic families.[45]

The churches of S. Vittore a Meda (1515–20), S. Vincenzino (an ancient Benedictine convent whose nuns' church was built in the first decade of the sixteenth century and whose outer church was added in the second half of the century), and S. Paolo Converso (begun in 1549) also in Milan follow the organization of S. Maurizio closely, with separate nuns' churches at ground level, although these last two, unlike S. Maurizio, do not have a choir platform.[46]

Carlo Borromeo, who came to Milan as archbishop in 1565, would have known S. Maurizio and the other double churches there. His visitations included frequent instructions to alter the relationship between nuns' churches and that of the laity in conformity with this type.[47] The appeal of this type of church in the years after Trent can be readily understood from the remarks of Alessandro de' Medici, archbishop of Florence. In his *Trattato sopra il governo de' monasteri,* written in 1601, he declares that choirs are "rather high, most of them made at great expense and with *disegno,* for which reason they require a lot of space, but they occupy half or a third of the church, which does not happen in those that are made behind the altar with the grate above, as some are and which all the same I prefer. And if, in my time, some new ones were to be made or ones that are already built were to be restored, it would be good to arrange them in this way, so that the nuns cannot see laypeople, and have no occasion to let their minds wander from the excitement of the Divine Praises."[48]

It is important to emphasize that although the arrangement of these churches generally corresponds to that advocated by Borromeo in his *Instructiones Fabricae,* their organization was not necessarily created in response either to criticisms of laxity within convents or to desire for reform. Indeed, the differences between the sixteenth-century Milanese examples and the models Carlo Borromeo advocates indicate that the Milanese nuns were driven, at least in part, by a growing sense of their own social and spiritual significance. S. Maurizio's nuns' church boasts lateral chapels, while Borromeo's *Instructiones* insist that there should be no chapels (and therefore no need for priestly presence) in this part of the institution. These early sixteenth-century Milanese developments indicate not so much early signs of a reforming impulse as nuns' growing ambition, emphatic manifestations of their desire for separate churches to grant them architectural splendor, dignity, and liturgical privilege.[49]

Nonetheless, Borromeo had a marked impact on conventual church design. After his elevation to the archbishopric of Milan in 1565 and the publication of the *Instructiones* in 1577, several Milanese convents followed his prescriptions, apparently to the letter, in building new double churches, including S. Caterina alla Chiusa (an Augustinian convent, founded in 1570), S. Vincenzino, and S. Barbara (an Augustinian convent built from around 1580).[50] After Borromeo's death, the distinctions between the outer and inner churches became more marked. Rather than a continuous volume divided by a cross wall, the two churches were handled very differently (the outer church was given round, elliptical, oval, octagonal, or cruciform plans, while the inner one was treated severely), and nuns focused expenditure on the public rather than the private church.[51] This development is marked by the use of the term *coro delle monache* (nuns' choir) to designate this space, rather than the term "inner church," most usually adopted when churches were conceived as double.[52] In Milan, as nuns' choirs shrank and became more austere, they remained on ground-floor level. In Naples, by contrast, nuns' choirs were emphatically elevated and the continuous space between outer church and inner nuns' choir was made visible.

The earliest instance of a nuns' choir being raised to clerestory level at the east end behind the altar occurred in Naples at the Dominican (former Clarissan) convent church of La Sapienza (Figure 35), begun in 1613 and opened and blessed in May 1641;[53] but it was followed in a spate of other Neapolitan female convent churches, such as S. Gregorio Armeno and S. Maria Regina Coeli (Plate 9; Figures 33, 36). It was probably the Theatine architect G. B. Grimaldi who established this pattern at the Sapienza.[54] Plans were prepared shortly before Grimaldi's death in 1613, but building probably did not begin until after 1621 and continued into the 1630s.[55]

The basic design of S. Maria della Sapienza is straightforward, with a single nave leading to a domed choir (Figures 23, 35). Behind the main altar is an oratory (frescoed in the eighteenth century) where the present-day nuns, from the Order of the Piccole Ancelle del Sacro Cuore, continue to celebrate religious functions. The effect of spacious coherence is enhanced by allowing the nuns' choir to dominate the whole church. This is achieved partly because Grimaldi (or the architect who replaced him) resisted superimposing pilasters and breaking the entablature, thus creating an open and resonant clear space.[56] The use of a domed choir, derived from Neapolitan sixteenth-century models, such as S. Giacomo degli Spagnoli by F. Manlio and S. Gregorio Armeno by

G. B. Cavagna (Plate 9), rather than the more usual solution of a domed transept, further enhances the nuns' choir, rendering it, even more than the main altar itself, the spiritual center of the church.[57]

The aristocratic nun Sister Eufrosina da Silva, cofounder of the Franciscan convent of SS. Trinità in via di Costantinopoli, may have prompted the building of the raised east-end choir.[58] She first requested that the church, as God's house, should be "much more beautiful, more commodious, and richer" than the nuns' quarters. It is significant that this ambitious aristocratic woman selected the Theatine Francesco Grimaldi as architect and instructed him to make "the most beautiful and most delightful" church design he had ever produced.[59] Celano records: "The good Father promised them to do as much as he could; so that in 1620 to the design of the aforementioned Father the building of this church was begun; and because Sister Eufrosina wanted the main altar to remain at the east end . . . , it was practical that the entrance or door should be situated at the west, and that the nuns' choir should be sited above the chancel from the side of the Evangelist."[60] Here Celano presents the east-end choir as an inevitable result of accommodating certain liturgical requirements. But Eufrosina's insistence on creating a church of outstanding beauty, combined with Theatine sympathy to female aristocratic devotion, points to a deliberate decision by Grimaldi to make the church exceptionally graceful by elevating the particularly devout and aristocratic nuns themselves in their choir above the main altar.

Whatever its origins, this daring approach was pushed still further at the Sapienza by the decision to pierce, or leave open, the wall above the choir. This has paradoxical effect. On the one hand, being able to see into the space of the nuns' choir draws that space into that of the rest of the church; on the other, the limitations of this sight line emphasize the separation of the nuns' area from that of the rest of the church. This paradox is enhanced further by the separate decoration afforded this space. Cesare Fracanzano frescoed the choir, while the rest of the church was frescoed by Corenzio and hung with oil paintings.[61] Thus the architecture and its decoration emphasizes the ambiguity inherent in the nuns' situation of being part of but separate from the rest of the world.

The practice of opening up the wall between the nuns' choir and the exterior church recalls Palladio's S. Giorgio for Benedictine monks in Venice, where a screen of Corinthian columns marks a caesura between the presbytery and the monks' choir, which is raised, though only slightly, above the presbytery; and where above the screen, the arch is open.[62] While the architect at S. Giorgio directs attention to the Benedictine monks, the open and raised choirs of the convent churches in Naples not only celebrate their female aristocratic occupants but deliberately flirt with the affirmation and deaffirmation of their separation.

That the nuns' choir was the focus of considerable architectural attention throughout the seventeenth and early eighteenth centuries in Naples indicates a heightened concern to emphasize the status of the choir nuns. Given the large number of new commissions for convents, convent churches, and alterations to earlier buildings, unusual opportunities arose for architects to develop expertise in this field and to experiment in design. By the 1680s at S. Giuseppe dei Ruffi (founded in 1669, with the addition of the choir in 1681–82), the architect Dionisio Lazzari followed Grimaldi in opening the arch, but he elegantly fused the grilles with the architectural order by setting them in place of the frieze in the entablature at the east end (Figure 36).[63] This architectural refinement at S. Giuseppe and at Regina Coeli (Figure 33) represents the culmination of decades of concern and experiment with the unorthodox position of the choir.

While in some churches, such as S. Gregorio Armeno, the east-end raised nuns' choir was relatively shallow, the new church of the convent of S. Maria Donnaregina, by Giovanni Guarini, a Theatine and pupil of Grimaldi, built between 1620 and 1649 for the nuns who abandoned their Gothic church, boasts an unusually deep nuns' choir (Figure 37). Here a substantial room is opened above the altar, which runs back to a wall decorated with one of Solimena's earliest frescoes.[64] It overlooks a broad and spacious aisleless nave, flanked by deep chapels separated by piers, each of which is articulated by two Corinthian pilasters flanking a statue in a shallow niche (Figure 38).

In Naples a nuns' choir was first placed directly behind the altar in a retrochoir to the east at S. Chiara, the Clarissan convent founded by Sancia of Mallorca, Blessed Clare Morì, in 1311.[65] The seventeenth-century architects may have been deliberately referring to this queen of Neapolitan convents. At S. Chiara three large grated openings, flanged on the nuns' sides and spiked on the side of the church nave to dissuade Peeping Toms, connect the nuns' choir to the main church (Figure 31). Two separate groups, therefore, one in the nuns' choir and one in the main church, face but cannot see each other, while sharing the same service and making the Eucharist on the main altar "the hinge" between the nuns' choir and the nave to the west.[66] Caroline Bruzelius suggests that this important change occurred at S. Chiara, because of the special dedication to the Eucharist of its powerful patron, Queen Sancia.[67] While at S. Chiara the nuns enjoyed a vast ground-floor space behind the main altar which was their private church, the seventeenth-century churches afforded the nuns far less space for their choirs, but elevated them, as if in compensation for this loss of space.

It has been suggested that nuns' choirs were built at the east end simply to satisfy the requirements of enclosure.[68] This fails to explain why this pattern was not adopted universally by female convents after Trent. In the few instances where conventual documents refer to the east-end choirs, they justify them in purely practical terms. Yet practical arguments are insufficient to account for this development and certainly do not explain its success, which depends on representing the relationship between nuns and priest, and nuns and congregation.

Let us consider three examples: two Franciscan convents, S. Francesco dell'Osservanza and S. Francesco delle Cappuccinelle a Pontecorvo; and the Benedictine S. Gregorio Armeno. In 1629 the abbess and nuns of S. Francesco dell'Osservanza requested permission from the archbishop of Naples to make a number of changes to their convent, including repainting and embellishing the church, enlarging their choir above the entrance to the church, and opening a grating, or *gelosia,* between the east-end choir and the public church: "to demolish the vaults of the exterior church as well as those of the interior one, and raise there wooden vaults, like bowls, stuccoed in white, so as to lighten [the load] on those churches' walls"[69] and above the main altar "to make there a *gelosia* for the inner choir for the night office, and for the convenience of the infirm nuns."[70] Alterations to the choir at the east end of the church are justified in the name of affording greater comfort to sick nuns and for night-time offices. These were not inconsiderable motives for nuns: a choir on the upper story of their convents precluded nocturnal treks down to the cold ground-floor church, but elsewhere the long nocturnal trek is noted as a sign of nuns' religious dedication.[71] It is vital to remember for whose eyes these justifications are being made and to read them in relation to other architectural changes being requested and executed in convents at this time. Particularly pertinent is the increased puncturing of church walls in the same church to grant nuns visual access to the church nave below, which also allowed their presence to be felt more clearly by the congregation assembled below. In other words, these changes combined to elevate nuns in more ways than one.

Sometimes aesthetic considerations are mentioned with regard to having two choirs. The conventual account of the new church for S. Francesco delle Cappuccinelle a Pontecorvo begun in 1712 emphasizes the symmetry afforded by having two choirs, one at each end of the church. The choir at the west end is described as being above the main door, with carved and gilt *gelosie*[72] and the eastern choir was designed to balance it.[73] But more was at stake here than aesthetic improvements. That choirs were not built at the east end for practical or liturgical reasons alone is demonstrated by a document of 1757 written to justify the building of a "winter choir," at the west end of the church above the old choir, at S. Gregorio Armeno in Naples. At this point S. Gregorio already had a ground-level choir at the west end and an elevated eastern choir (Plate 9), which had proved to be very impractical:

> Because this [old choir] had its entrance at the level of the cloister which, due to the topography of our city, works out as the ground floor of the

monastery, during the winter nuns wanting to make use of it for matins and other hours in the night, suffered discomfort, as did elderly nuns. This was the reason why some time ago, wanting to set this right, a small grilled tribune was made at the east end at the level of the first dormitory. This, although oblong, because of its narrowness anyway bothered the ladies in reciting the Holy Offices, due to the confusion of their voices, and the heat, which the space accumulated in the summer, which sent the nuns' heads spinning, there being no more space between one lady opposite the next than six *palmi*. Furthermore, to the inconvenience described above, was added the fact that the aforesaid recital of divine offices could not be made in front of the sacrament in accord with the pontifical statutes. And this also had the effect that if a nun who was ill wanted to frequent the sacrament, she could not do so, as she could not go down to that space.[74]

The east-end choir is found inadequate on two principal grounds: it is incommodiously small, and its position meant that offices could not be said in front of the Eucharist. The solution in this case was to build a very large elevated choir at the west end, producing a total of three choirs: one at clerestory level at each end of the church, which face each other above the space of the ordinary congregation, and an additional choir, elevated still higher at the west end (Plate 10). Thus this petition resulted in the creation of further space designated exclusively for choir nuns. The new choir guaranteed them elevated space all around and above the church, above the lay congregation, and separate from nonchoir nuns.

It is surely significant that the new nuns' choir was added at S. Gregorio at the time when, with enclosure, nuns lost privileges they had enjoyed elsewhere. The pre-Tridentine church was surrounded by irregularly grouped habitations of nuns, built over successive periods and independent from each other: "At that time there were about fifty nuns in the convent and each possessed servants, rooms, passages, kitchens, cellars, and other conveniences. They held many female servants for their services; each nun bore the weight after some years of their servitude, to dower them and to settle them honorably, not as servants, but with much tender affection."[75] With the new requirements for enclosure, the old structures were demolished and replaced with uniform conventual buildings (1572–77).[76] Forty new rooms were built, the nuns' rooms with loggias looking out on a courtyard, corresponding to strict enclosure.[77] Thus as the nuns' lives closely resembling those of secular aristocratic women were reduced to institutional conformity in their dwelling spaces at S. Gregorio, so the convent church assumed greater relative significance in affording them almost the only space in which they could articulate their relative prestige and status. In short, the nuns' choirs were part of an aristocratization of enclosed conventual space.

Not only were Neapolitan nuns' choirs often proudly elevated at the east end, but they were usually distinctively decorated. Their plans were uninventive (rectangular and generally small), but they were decorated with considerable care, designed to enhance the status of the choir nuns through the adornment of their designated space.

The remarkable thing about moving nuns' choirs from above the entrance door at the west of the church to a position east of the main altar is that it changes directly the relationship of the nuns to the Eucharist during mass. At the east not only are they much closer to the sacred Host, but they see the mass performed from the side opposite to that of the lay population in the church. Therefore, the actions of the clergy during the administration of the sacrament become accessible perhaps as never before. At the Sapienza and the other seventeenth-century churches in Naples where the nuns' choirs were raised above the main altar, their relationship to the Host was, if anything, intensified beyond anything achieved at S. Chiara or in the Milanese double churches. Not only did the nuns face the Eucharist directly, but when the priest elevated the chalice, he did so in their direction (in conformity with San Carlo Borromeo's *Instructiones*).[78] Borromeo's insistence that the nuns' grille should not provide views of anything other than the mass, such as glimpses of the street when the entrance door is open was flagrantly disregarded in Naples.[79] In the convent churches in Naples, the nuns' view down through the entire church toward the west end was opened up magnificently as a result of raising their east-end choir. They not only towered above the altar itself, but from their new crow's nests they commanded views of the church, congregation, and even out into the street when the entrance doors were open (Figure 38). Their position, therefore, was enormously enhanced both physically and symbolically by the decision to raise their choir above the principal altar.

Crucially, the nuns enjoyed a privileged view of the Host at the moment of its elevation, when the officiating priest would turn towards the altar, his back towards the congregation in the nave. Therefore, at the very moment of the consecration of the Host, the greatest difference emerges between the two audiences; or, to put it another way, the relationships between the nuns and the Host, and the congregation and the Host are deliberately marked as different at the climax of the service.

The remarkable physical and symbolic elevation of the nuns above the main altar at the east end of their churches was promoted and made possible by increased veneration not just of the Eucharist, but of virginity and virgins also. Arguably it resulted from an intensification in the identification of those two terms after Trent. The transubstantative nature of the Eucharist had, of course, been reaffirmed at Trent.[80] The belief that God was present in the Eucharist more literally than in any other sacrament enhanced the importance of attending mass and the cult of the eucharistic Host gained renewed vigor.[81] Moreover, women's veneration of the Eucharist was more pronounced than men's.[82] Christ was their Bridegroom; with the mass their bodies became as one, a sweet foretaste of the ecstasies of heavenly union. Late medieval saints, especially women, frequently received from confessors, or from the pope, the privilege of daily communion as an almost official recognition of their reputations for sanctity.[83] That star of Neapolitan female devotion, Sister Orsola Benincasa (1547–1618), "was swept into ecstasy each time that she received the bread of life."[84]

The practice of removing the Eucharist in order to punish nuns for noncompliance with the decrees of Trent and the terror that this removal typically provoked vividly illustrate both the nuns' intense devotion to the sacrament and the Church hierarchy's exploitation of that devotion. When the convent of S. Gregorio Armeno in Naples was deprived of its eucharistic Host in March 1565 as punishment for not obeying archiepiscopal instructions, Fulvia Caracciolo, a nun in the convent, described the church as "like a widowed house" (*una casa vedovata*) and the nuns as "lost sheep, without a place where they could rest."[85] The nuns wandered bereft, abandoned and aimless, while the convent church itself was deprived of union with the heavenly Spouse.

Virginity and the Eucharist were bound more tightly together in late-sixteenth- and seventeenth-century thought.[86] This notion was repeated in devotional works, such as Alfonso Rodriguez's *Ejercitio de perfeccion y virtudes christianas* of 1614 (a book urged on enclosed nuns in early modern Naples by their confessors),[87] which devotes a chapter to the proposition that "the frequentation of Holy Communion is a great remedy against all temptations, and particularly for the preservation of chastity."[88] The sacrament "quietens the movements of the flesh, mitigates concupiscence, that fuel of sin, and appeases the ardor and appetite of sensuality as water extinguishes fire."[89] Rodriguez discusses the need to approach the sacrament with "cleanliness and purity, not only from mortal sins, but also from venial sins and imperfections."[90] The Council of Trent emphasized the necessity of confession to receive grace in the sacrament, and Rodriguez follows, underlining that Holy Communion requires careful preparation, "since the greater the excellence of the sacraments, the greater the preparation and purity needed to receive them . . . For, though venial sins do not extinguish charity, they deaden fervor and diminish that devotion which is the most proper disposition required for this Divine Sacrament."[91]

Most significantly, *integritas* meant resistance to concupiscence. Therefore, perfect chastity became the infallible sign of divine grace in the soul. In contemporary exegetical literature, such as that of the Jesuit Cornelis à Lapide, chastity is described as "the principal, regal, and divine virtue," the sign of the integration of mind, will, and passion.[92] Therefore, as chastity became more tightly connected to sainthood, so communion had to be taken more frequently, because it alone could provide the grace necessary for chastity: "The special virtue and effect of this food is to engender virgins. Bodily nourishment, when it is good, engenders good blood and good humors; so this divine food engenders in us chastity and purity of affections."[93] Just as frequent communion and reverence for the Eucharist bound the celebrants to God, so communion prompted greater self-control, or *integritas,* the right order within humanity which had been lost at the Fall.[94] Most significantly, *integritas* meant resistance to concupiscence. Therefore, perfect chastity became the infallible sign of divine grace in the soul. The *Catechism of the Council of Trent* articulated anew the traditional link between the Eucharist and chastity: "The Eucharist restrains and represses the lust of the flesh; for whilst it inflames souls more with the fire of charity, it of necessity extinguishes the ardour of concupiscence."[95] Referring in support to the writings of Saints Thomas and Jerome, which promoted the Eucharist as prophylactic against concupiscence, it was argued that as chastity became more tightly connected to sainthood, it was necessary to take communion more frequently, because it alone could provide the grace necessary for chastity. In turn, personal integrity was seen as closely allied to social and political order.[96] Virginity, celebrated for its basis in renunciation, detachment, and mortification of the senses, allowed the upward movement of the contemplative soul. This disdain for worldliness allowed the formation of an elite within the Church—and this, in turn, was attractive to the aristocratic elite outside the Church as an appropriate harbor for their privileged daughters. Thus the scene was set for a celebration of female virginity in the architectural environment which helped safeguard it. Virginity, already associated with "perfect" or "angelic" chastity, came to be regarded as the most complete expression of integrity, wrought with the aid of communion.[97] The development of the lofty nuns' choirs in Naples is best understood in this context.

The nuns' position, therefore, was enormously enhanced both physically and symbolically by the decision to raise their choir above the principal altar, resonating as this move did with theological, ecclesiastical, and social currents. Indeed, nuns in their choirs were regarded as something superhuman, heavenly, even angelic. Describing the exacting religious observance of the convent of S. Maria di Gerusalemme, Celano says, "In short they can be said to be so many Seraphim, and their life more angelic than human."[98] Illuminating here is Anton Blok's suggestion that the emphasis on virginity actually serves to muddy the sharp distinction between men and women: virgins are neither men nor women, but are rather liminal between the two categories, and therefore can mediate between these groups.[99] Precisely because of their intermediate position between men and women, virgins may assume a variety of roles of mediation between social groups, and in the religious sphere between the human and the divine.[100]

The architectural innovations in Naples allowed the virginal nuns to occupy such a place, posed above men and women, and hovering between mortals and the divine.

It is notable in relation to the nuns' angelic choir that a painting of the Immaculate Conception in glory among a choir of angels and seraphs by Francesco De Mura was deemed a suitable gift to the Villani family at the time of the foundation of the church of Divino Amore and was sent to them from Rome.[101] Similarly, in the church of S. Gregorio Armeno in Naples a large painting, *Choir of Angels* by Giuseppe Simonelli (1699), has pride of place above the ornate communion grating which occupies most of the south wall of the chancel (Plate 5). The grate in question separated the chancel of the church (and, therefore, the priest and congregation) from the nuns who were able to receive communion through a specially crafted opening in the grating. The nuns gathered for communion on their side of the grating in a small room, also known as a *comunichino*, where there was the famous wooden *scala santa*. On each Friday in March the nuns, including the abbess, were obliged to climb this staircase on their knees, reciting prayers to gain indulgences. The link between resistance and temptation, self-abnegation, purity, Holy Communion, and chastity is thus declared and celebrated through architecture and practice.

But nowhere is the dramatic positioning of nuns in their choir exploited to greater effect than at S. Maria del Gesù delle Monache, undertaken by the architect Arcangelo Guglielmelli in 1677 (Figure 39). Here the east-end raised nuns' choir is located behind a segmental pediment through which erupts a gloria, dramatically top-lit from the cupola and lantern above. A host of cherubim, fashioned from papier-mâché and gilded wood, swarm around a painted medallion of God the Father, immediately below which nuns in their choir can look out through an opening into the church below. Thus the nuns in their choir perform part of the glory, and are figured here as angels and seraphim. The grand *apparato* is animated by sunlight streaming down from above and by living nuns at its heart to evoke and make real the Heavenly Paradise on Earth.

The significance attached to the female gaze makes all the more striking the elevation of enclosed women and the granting to them such dominant vistas in their churches, allowing them to survey the laity with ease. Ornament and gilding were used to draw attention to the grilles and *gelosie* within churches and sometimes to bind them to the choirs which they screened. *Gelosie* were emphasized and adorned materially, with highly wrought metal, gilded to draw the light. Many choirs were also treated in this way, as well as *coretti* looking into the church (Plates 5, 9; Figures 29, 30).[102] Thus the choir for the new church at S. Francesco delle Cappuccinelle, begun in 1712, was gilded: "Above the said door is the above-mentioned choir for officiation with its *gelosia*, carved and covered in gold. . . . Beneath the cornice of the said church are six little *coretti* with their gilt grilles."[103] Thus conventual architectural decoration deliberately draws attention both to the invisibility of nuns' bodies and to their imperceptible looking.

What we see here, then, is a paradox: women, marginalized because of their gender, exploit the advantages of their religious enclosure and economic privilege to articulate a new and bold identity for themselves. Virgins could straddle the principal opposition in Mediterranean cultures, the distinction between men and women, and could thereby assume a variety of roles of mediation between social classes and between the human and the divine.[104] The noble-born assured aristocratic choir nuns proudly assumed this role.

Conventual architecture marshaled and separated. Lay were kept separate from nuns, and male visitors separate from female visitors. It is an architecture particularly articulate in the arts of hierarchy and separation, a quality which extended to organizing the divisions within the monachical body also. We have seen how choir nuns enjoyed greater status through greater elevation (and more space) architecturally within their churches, even as they were losing autonomy within their conventual lodgings. And we have seen that they gained visual command of their churches, even as they were barred from entering them physically, thereby shifting the emphasis within convent churches from performance to visuality, from acting to seeing and being seen. In other words, religiosity is marked ever less by specific actions than by specific positions, bodies of privilege in places of privilege.

Perhaps emboldened by their newfound cultural centrality, seventeenth-century Neapolitan nuns discovered that they could contest theological and familial discourses about chastity, virginity, honor, and shame through specific forms of conventual architecture. The placement of the nuns' choir at the east above the main altar, rather than in its traditional place at the west above the entrance, can best be understood as a means by which these privileged aristocratic nuns negotiated their role and position in relation to the patriarchal familial and theological discourses of virginity without directly challenging them. As more aristocratic women found themselves living in enclosed convents to meet the economic needs of their families, so the conventual space itself became increasingly aristocratized, even while subject to the demands of Trent. The tension between nuns as part and parcel of this world and symbols of the angelic order is manifest in the architectural organization of conventual churches.

CONCLUSION

Conventual Architecture as Metaphor for the Body

This book has traced a path which avoids the prevalent dichotomy between a heroic and a passive view of religious women and architecture and has shown that the nun's body, conventual architecture and institutional politics, the social body, the city's built fabric, and the dynamics of aristocratic familial politics of survival are intimately interconnected. The bifurcation which persists in much scholarship between attention to nuns' social identities and religious practices and studies of the architecture which housed them cannot be amended by simply appending considerations of conventual architecture to existing interpretations of social organization within convents. Space does not merely provide the locus for social relations; it is primary to the construction of gendered and social identity. If we think of architecture as a material metaphor for the bodies it houses—that is, specifically the architecture of aristocratic female convents as metaphor for the body of the aristocratic female virgin nun—we avoid some of the dichotomies which inevitably result from splitting architecture from the nonarchitectural "social."[1] In other words, the advantage of conceiving of architecture as metaphor (or at least metonymy) for the aristocratic female body is that it necessarily avoids the split (from which the existing literature suffers) between studies of the architecture and studies of the bodies it houses. In this model, the architecture stands in metonymically for the female body in the city, allowing an analysis of architecture as the site of a permanent battle, of deliberate and inevitable ambiguity, while avoiding the temptation to displace the investigation from the "text" to the context. It is our means of effecting instantaneous fusion of two separated realms of experience into one illuminating, iconic, encapsulating image.[2]

Of course, the built environment cannot be simply collapsed into metaphor. This risks too smoothly sliding behind a linguistic structure all the rough edges of material architecture and its production, from iconology to the division of labor in the building trades. Such an approach cannot provide an account of the architecture. But considering conventual architecture as material metaphor allows us to step beyond a conception of it as a "shell" or "stage" for the performance of specific social relationships, to considering it as embodying those relationships, representing those aristocratic virginal bodies. This approach cuts through architecture's apparent self-assured, self-contained detachment to expose its anxieties and uncertainties. Crucial here is the relationship between flesh and stone, the connections between the clothing of bodies and the layered cloaks applied to the walls that housed them, their unclothing, and the fears of their nakedness.[3]

Monastic architecture was central to the social construction of difference between religious men and women, between lay men and women, and between noble and non-noble religious women. Religious identities, sexual purity, and social exclusivity were maintained through separated spaces, thick walls, policed boundaries, barred windows, towering choirs and domineering belvederes, and rich architectural adornment. Architecture constructed the habitus which connected common interest groups. After Trent, convents were aristocratized, just as noble families were "conventualized." The second half of the sixteenth century saw important changes in the structure of aristocratic families, the organization of inheritance, increased limits on numbers of sons and daughters allowed to marry, and a concomitant increase in the numbers of daughters advanced for monacation. The increase in the practice of primogeniture occurred alongside the shift from a system in which feudal property and marriage were shared among children to a system which increasingly concentrated this wealth on the firstborn son and imposed celibacy on cadets and daughters. Convents were not so much a means by which families could save money, as some historians have assumed, but somewhere secure and respectable to place daughters without surrendering land with feudal privileges attached. And families could also gain from the religious and social benefits intrinsic to aristocratic convent life. Convents were connected to the aristocracy through their material culture, to particular families through sites and donations, but above all they were connected to the habitus of aristocratic women.

In early modern Italy, architecture tended to work to render invisible the body of aristocratic women, whether nuns or not. In baronial palaces women's quarters were usually situated in segregated areas of the palace, looking toward the rear or inward to an enclosed court or garden.[4] Unlike their husbands or brothers, women rarely had direct access from their apartment to the city (men's apartments often had small, private stairways and exits); and women were hemmed in by a raft of female servants, whose rooms abutted their apartments, and had limited access to the rest of the palace.[5] The parental home, the marital home, and the convent were the three types of enclosure available to respectable women.[6]

If noblewomen's bodies were hidden in domestic palaces, inside convents they became even more secret. Unlike celibate priests who become asexual, nuns committed their virginity to the Church as brides of Christ. Whereas monks' bodies became more public, nuns' bodies became more private. Their inaccessibility was itself key because their sensuality, unlike that of their male counterparts, was not simply banished—but was redirected toward Christ. The distinctions between the spaces men and women occupied were marked by and on their bodies. Tonsure was a symbolic negation of male sexuality, following the taking of monastic vows. Celibacy, symbolized by the tonsure, created a public space within the body: celibate priests became accessible to others through the creation of public space in lieu of personal sexuality.[7] The reverse was true of nuns. When early modern women gave religious sanction to their virginity, their celibacy became private and secret. It was also aristocratized; nuns' chastity was governed by concepts shared with upper-class, particularly aristocratic, secular women.[8]

Not only did nuns' bodies become private spaces; they became individually hidden, invisible. But, simultaneously, their collective consecrated virginity assumed a public, urban significance. Consequently, the work of sustaining their presence within the city and within urban politics had to be carried by the architecture that hid them. In the case of virgin nuns, convent architecture does not simply provide a public representation of an idealized social body; it stands in metonymically for that body which is made publicly invisible through that very architecture. In other words, it reveals what it hides. In this way conventual architecture differs radically from, say, the architecture of a palace or a hospital, whose inmates remain visible to the outside world alongside their architecture. Part of the crucial significance of convents was that conventual communities were able to articulate a public recognizable presence in the city. Convents therefore represent the increasingly "noble" public face of a sanctioned female group. This female public presence was sanctioned by being both aristocratic and religious.[9]

Gabriele Zarri formulated the term *recinti sacri* or "sacred enclosures" to describe how convents represented sacred spaces that assumed a decidedly female character. For her this female character remained steadfastly social in nature. It is my contention that we should think of convents in physical and architectural terms as representing the virginal aristocratic body within urban space, a connection that became vital after the Council of Trent insisted on identifying women's chastity with the physical enclosure of convents.

The Council of Trent marked a turning point for female convents in terms of aristocratizing them. The process of disciplining beliefs and behavior began with Trent and found in relation to women one of its points of most intense expression. Trent resulted in unprecedented centralized control over female convents, the curtailment of liberties within them, and, above all, greater insistence on enclosure. Despite the haste and lack of attention to detail, its attempts to ensure that all female orders would henceforth be enclosed had far-reaching, and in some cases devastating, consequences for female monasticism in Catholic Europe.

Enclosure was deeply implicated in the process of aristocratization. Faced with the threat of enclosure, religious orders claimed that they needed more accommodation for an increased number of inhabitants. As expansion was never possible without adequate funds, the logic was one of setting high dowries and attracting rich women. In fact, only enclosed convents could charge dowries, which were, in turn, essential to pay for the expansion and new buildings justified in the name of enclosure. The enclosure of S. Francesco a Pontecorvo in 1621, for example, was followed in 1633 by the purchase for the purposes of expansion of a large house with shops and garden, costing nearly 3,000 ducats, paid for in part by nuns' dowries.[10] The purchase for 4,000 ducats in 1636 of another big property to provide for the convent's expansion was followed in 1647 by the acquisition of a further sizable building by compulsory purchase from the heirs of the deceased Paolo Macario, justified on the grounds that the convent needed more space as "the two palaces [already] bought . . . were not large enough to provide commodious residence for its nuns, who, on the occasion of the recent enclosure, were increasing in number."[11] Between 1681 and about 1711, twenty-two nuns' dowries were used to fund the expansion of this convent; and in the period 1712–23—during which eleven monacations occurred—no fewer than ten dowries were used in the same way.[12] Almost all these dowries were spent to their full 1,500 ducats' worth on expansion and building.

In fine, Trent caused Italian female convents to become more introverted.[13] The architectural and urbanistic consequences of this change were great and are particularly evident in the confined city of baroque Naples. Nuns invested in the splendor of *apparati* and of their churches and conventual buildings that energetic striving which once had been turned outward in the public life of the city.

This book has demonstrated the permeability of conventual enclosure in early modern Naples, the degree to which *claustrum* was not closure, but *apertura*, or the fear of openness in the female aristocratic body, and how this brought in turn architectural and urbanistic attempts to secure its impenetrability, or the appearance of such. Architecture was martialed to represent and to fortify virginity. Far more successful than the process of ironing out abuses and the strengthening of communal life encouraged by Trent were attempts to enforce strict enclosure—measures to isolate convents from the outside world with locks, bars, wheels, and high walls (Figures 40, 41). Architects steeped attention on elements which became symbolic of enclosure (Figure 42).

"Enclosure is the principal thing as far as the vow of chastity is concerned," declared Alessandro de' Medici, archbishop of Florence, in his *Trattato sopra il governo de' monasteri*, written in 1601.[14] Indeed, convent architecture above all represented control over sexuality.[15] Just as the decrees of the Council of Trent demanded sharp separation of the spheres, so the architecture of female monasteries responded with a rhetoric of fortification both in relation to its immediate urban context and the surrounding streets, and within the conventual churches which doubled as parish churches. That rhetoric was focused on those areas of the convent where contact between inmates and outsiders was most possible—doors and windows, the symbolic orifices. Paradoxically, then, apertures and points of access became the most conspicuous parts of the convent. A warning tale, recounted by Antonio Ardia, S.J., in 1713 links a would-be nun's access to windows to her loss of commitment to Christ and death:

> A damsel raised in very honored education, and attention, uprightness and virtue . . . having been called by God to be his spouse, and moved by his voice, she was already negotiating to enter a convent; but, in the meantime, somewhat forgetting withdrawal, she began to make room for a few amusements. She already relished a little gap in the windows, [which allowed her] to see with freedom, and began even not to feel torment in being seen . . . and little by little, sometimes by glances, sometimes by messages, and by letters, she committed herself so much to the love of a young man, that she reached the point of desiring him through merit, having already forgotten her heavenly Spouse.[16]

Architectural penetration, sexual temptation, and religious failure were intimately entwined—indeed, one is presented as leading inexorably to the other. Concern with maintaining the architecture of separation was not simply to privilege superficial form or mere appearance over practice; it was to regulate the conventual building itself. Architecture regulated nuns' bodies, rendered certain actions possible, others impossible. More than that, architecture represented behavior; behavior could be gauged and determined architecturally. Penetration of the architectural body signified penetration of the nun's body.

Mary Douglas reminds us that "we should expect the orifices of the body to symbolise its specially vulnerable points." The same holds true of architecture. "The mistake is to treat bodily margins in isolation from all other margins. There is no reason to assume any primacy for the individual's attitude to his [*sic*] own bodily and emotional experience, any more than for his cultural and social experience."[17] Pronounced rustication on portals, narrow entranceways reached through cast-iron gateways and up steep flights of stairs, heavy wooden doors flanked by wheels (*ruote*), which obviated the need for contact between human beings while allowing goods to pass to and from the convent, set up a clear sense of policed and controlled boundaries and apertures (Figures 40, 41). Inside, bars, grilles, screens, curtains, and choirs not only separated nuns from laity but served to draw attention to that separation. Nuns' choirs and windows inside their churches were often framed by elaborate gilt iron grilles that billowed out into the space above the entrance to the church, resembling the elaborate cages of exotic birds. Architectural attention focused on the elements symbolic of enclosure.

Separate circulation routes allowed nuns to move around their convents, to circulate in cloisters, corridors, sheltered walkways, to move between convent and church, and even, in the case of some convents, to cross busy public thoroughfares in the center of cities (Figure 27). The convent of S. Gregorio Armeno, for example, has a covered bridge forming part of the campanile tower, which allowed nuns to pass at *piano nobile* level from one part of the convent to another across the busy via S. Gregorio Armeno, without coming into contact with laity (Figure 42). Such walkways made individual nuns' bodies invisible to passersby in the street below, but reified or made permanently visible in the city the presence of the institutionalized nuns' body.

Desire to emphasize nuns' claustration was sharpened by the constant erosion of its distinction in practice and by the contradictions and ambiguities inherent in the nuns' position. Sometimes this resulted in the extension of gardens and courtyards, where in compensation for rigorous enclosure an image of the garden of Eden or of heavenly Jerusalem was created.[18] "The cloister should be a Paradise, safe and happy," insisted G. N. Chiesa.[19] This is not an architecture of modest enclosure, but of fabulously advertised confinement. What mattered was not simply that daughters were respectably cloistered, but that their separation from the world—the guarantee of their virginity—was made visible to all. With its carefully articulated concern for the physical enclosure of monastic space, the Tridentine decrees shift the anxiety of inviolability previously focused on nuns' virginity onto the separateness of their space.[20]

Virginity had long been conceived in spatial terms. The metaphors of *porta clausa, claustra, hortus conclusus,* and *fons signatus* used to describe virginity and its protection are themselves architectural, evoking a defended space, enclosed and sealed.[21] In 1427 Bernardino da Siena gave a sermon in which he imagined Madonna Clausura as the virgin's doorkeeper, one of the virgin Mary's twelve handmaidens.[22] Bernardino seizes upon the metaphor of the window as signaling an orifice, open and available, in his discussion of the Annunciation: "Let's talk of where the Angel found [the Virgin]. Where do you think she was? At the window or engaging in some other sort of vanity? O no! She was enclosed in a room, reading, to give an example to you, girls, so that you will never be tempted to stand either at the doorway or the window, but that you will remain inside the house, reciting Ave Marias and Our Fathers."[23] The rhetoric of fortification of chastity had a long and respectable lineage in architectural theory. Writing in the mid–fifteenth century, Leon Battista Alberti urged incarceration: "A military camp with its rampart and ditches need not be defended as strongly as this, fortified, as it should be, with a high, unbroken wall, not even pierced by a single aperture through which temptations of the eye or incitement of the tongue might enter to weaken resolve, let alone actual people with designs on their chastity."[24]

Italian Renaissance architectural theoretical literature tended to conceive prisons and monasteries together. The prison Alberti describes as suitable for those who have committed the most abominable of crimes shared important characteristics with convents: "Suffice it to make the walls, openings, and vaults of the work strong enough to make it difficult for any prisoner to escape; and, to achieve the necessary thickness, depth and height, it is vital to use large blocks of hard stone, held together with iron and brass. You may also use a lining of boards, lofty barred openings, and so on. . . . And to my mind they are quite right when they say that the only impregnable prison is the eye of the vigilant guard."[25] When Alberti discusses the external architecture of the prison and its relationship to the city, the parallels with convents emerge equally sharply: "Select a space of ground in a secure and not deserted part of the city, and surround it with a strong, high wall, pierced by no opening, and supply it with towers and galleries."[26] With the determination to ensure that convents resembled prisons more nearly than places of prayer, emphasis shifted from virginity conceived as a moral and mental condition (back) to a conception of virginity as overwhelmingly physical.[27] With their carefully articulated concern for the physical enclosure of monastic space, the Tridentine decrees redirected the anxiety of inviolability, previously focused on nuns' virginity, onto the separateness of their space.

Separation was crucial to female convents. Beyond the significant theological notion of symbolic separation from the world, it assumed further social and ideological significance in relation to gender and sexuality. Convents and their churches functioned to celebrate and represent God in the city, to house nuns in decorous comfort and style commensurate with their social rank, and to separate nuns from laity, clergy from nuns, virgins from their potential defilers. It is an architecture of definition through separation.

Conventual institutional and urban presence was defined principally through the architecture of convent buildings. Although convents were a massive physical presence within the city, lining streets from one end to the other, occupying entire blocks of the city centers, dominating prime squares, and towering over the city in height, nevertheless in terms of architectural treatment and handling they appeared deliberately to turn their backs on the city, presenting an appearance of indifference, even despite, toward it, with their small-eyed exterior walls, largely unadorned facades pierced by few grated windows (Figure 14). The often magnificent interior spaces of the churches themselves erupt unexpectedly from within those austere external shells. Where contact between nuns and public was physically closest, the greatest architectural orchestration was focused. Beyond the church, a system of screening, filtering, and separation prevented deeper penetration within the conventual complex except to a few carefully regulated visitors. Certain areas were foreclosed to all but the nuns (except in extraordinary circumstances, such as an official visitation), and sometimes only to an elite within them (such as the choir nuns who alone had access to the choir).

Grilled windows—*campanili* and *belvederi*—allowed nuns to look out into the city streets, over walls, into neighboring houses, courtyards, and cloisters; inside their churches, *gelosie* and choirs, again grilled, gave them visual access to the congregation below. They could see without being seen; they could see without having physical access to what they saw. Convent architecture represented those unseen seeing eyes and functioned at once as the effect and the support of such a gaze. Allowing nuns to see but not be seen meant enclosure functioned unequally; nuns could see more of the outside world than the outside world could see of them. Their architecture stood in for their bodies to represent them in the public eye. Power here was not wholly in the hands of one person or group (ecclesiastical authorities, the priest, senior nuns) to exercise over others; rather, it was a machine in which everyone was caught, those who exercised power just as much as those over whom it was exercised. Of course everyone did not occupy equal positions: architecture allowed certain positions, such as that of the priest or of the nuns in their raised choirs, to dominate, producing an effect of control. But ambiguities and uncertainties were embedded within conventual architectural organization and decoration and were themselves an important aspect of conventual technology of power.[28]

Conventual church interiors contrasted dramatically with their exteriors, just as by analogical extension nuns' external appearance concealed the rich treasures of their spiritual dedication and virginity. In convent churches the convent met the city; here men and women came to worship and were reminded of the presence of the nuns above them and around them, but separated from and invisible to them, in spaces that were contiguous but not continuous with theirs. Whereas conventual exteriors were de-adorned, austere, and shut off from public contact, the church interiors were frequently fabulously decorated, richly adorned, and open to the public (Plates 6, 8, 9). Ornament is crucial in this regard, not something to be perceived—as architectural historians tend to do—as something additional, extra, applied, but to be taken as seriously as structure because it is as revealing of social relations as spatial organization, style, or the tectonic. "Ornament," argues Gadamer, "is part of presentation. But presentation is an ontological event; it is representation."[29] The rich interiors of conventual churches can be read as representations of the trousseaux of the spouses of Christ.

The richness of the decoration of aristocratic convent churches publicly demonstrated the familial, worldly, and spiritual riches of the nuns. Paintings, gilt stucco, and colored marble revetment evoked not just the heavenly reward awaiting redeemed humanity, but physically separated the congregation from the nuns and became, as it were, a rich and splendid cloak for the nuns.[30] Architecture, rather than the female bodies it shielded, was adorned. The bodies of aristocratic young women were made austere and stripped of their rich finery. Conventual regulations inveighed against "precious clothes" or clothes that were elaborately fashioned, rings or earrings, or "other secular profanities."[31] That rich costume was transferred to convent church walls. Architecture assumed the place both of the clothes and of the women themselves, a substitute, working by metonymy, replacing the ascetic body of the invisible virgin with the richly adorned body of the church. Thus these virginal churches came to represent self-sacrifice, transformation, and redemption, not only for the virgin who had dedicated her life to God, but for the members of its congregation who worshipped there and for the city where they stood. They were monumental in Lefebvre's sense, offering each member of a society an image of that membership, an image of his or her social visage: "the element of repression in it and the element of exaltation could scarcely be disentangled; or perhaps it would be more accurate to say that the repressive element was metamorphosed into exaltation."[32]

Clothing was the outward sign that revealed the body's state to be virginal, privileged, in a state of contrition or transience. Dressing and undressing, concealing and revealing themselves, removing their signs of virginity, transforming themselves and their environments through draping themselves in strange clothing, erecting *apparati,* draping statuary, bringing the lifeless to life, nuns layered fabrics over their bodies and the architecture surrounding them to suggest, to signify, to celebrate, and to hide.

If the female gaze was dangerous, so too was the female body. Keeping it covered was an act of piety toward the heavenly Bridegroom, a form of self-protection for the nun. Sister Celestina Raineri's biographer and priest explained her pudeur in terms of chastity: "From the great love that this virgin harbored toward purity originated also her very jealous guardianship of her body, not allowing, in so far as possible, that any part of it should be uncovered to human eyes."[33] Nuns' bodies, sealed in chastity, had to be covered to protect them from corruption. Convent regulations also insisted on this: "And so that the internal chastity of the mind may shine in the exterior, in conversation, in the choir, in the parlatory, and in going about the convent, they should hold the hands in their sleeves, or at least under their scapulars."[34]

Just as the habit itself signified the dedication of the body to the heavenly Spouse, so within the convent specific clothing designated the distinctions between boarders, novitiates, and choir nuns. Certain clothing had to be donned to enter the choir on feast days, and this was what endowed nuns with the active and passive voice and granted them a share in conventual property.[35] In fact, the significance of the choir was always marked by appropriate clothing: "On ferial days mass was said in the choir with a black cloak, without which you could not say a single line in that place."[36] Thus clothing represented a privileged position within the hierarchy, which was itself conceived spatially in relation to the choir.

Dressing and undressing in nonconventual clothes exercised a strong attraction to the nuns, as seeing nuns dressed up fascinated others. Fra Cirillo da Varese, for instance, allowed the nuns of S. Chiara in Naples inside the church on 15 May 1650 to perform a play, a comedy with nine characters dressed in secular clothing, of which he and his brethren were spectators.[37] Such activities were liminal, drawing attention to the relationship between the body clothed and unclothed, the sacred and the profane (there is no such thing as profaneness in itself), the way in which the habit, the sign of virginity, could be removed and replaced by a sign of its absence. Thus the dressing and undressing can be seen as a way of turning virginity inside out, exploring its limits and its limitlessness. Did that secular sign threaten the virginal body, undermine it, or even strengthen it? If it strengthened the nuns, then it did so in a way unacceptable to the ecclesiastical authorities, who took a very dim view of such proceedings, concerned as usual to eliminate ambiguity and ambivalence. Two synods (1646 and

1649) forbade nuns from putting on plays, even if they were religious, in their churches and from dressing up in women's or men's clothing.[38]

But it was the veil, which both obscured the nun's sight as it hid her face from view and rendered the nun metonymically the altar of sacrifice, that was paramount. In their account published in 1670 of the life of sister Maria Carafa, founder of S. Maria della Sapienza, Francesco Maria Maggio and the prioress of the Sapienza, sister Angelica Caterina Carafa, dedicate considerable energy to the question of veiling the face. Maggio cites a number of biblical sources in support of veiling: the Song of Songs, when the Lord says to his Heavenly Wife, "I shall lead you in to solitude, and there shall I speak to your heart"; and Genesis 20 ("Ahimelech, King of Gerara, when he married Abraham and Sarah, he gave them many presents. To Abraham he gave sheep, cows, servants, and maids, but to Sarah he gave a veil to cover her face").[39] The *Hortus Conclusus* and *fons signatus* of Song of Songs were comparably covered, he claims. Maggio argues that Maria Carafa wanted nuns to veil their faces because of their role as altars of God, reminding his reader that St. Ignatius called nuns *Altare Dei*; St. Jerome in Letter 8, after having spoken of the altar of the temple, writing to a virgin, puts it like this: "Et de altari transiam ad Altare."[40] Maggio cites Giacomo Corono in *Clypeus Patientiae* to argue that just as altars are covered, so should nuns be.[41] The nun's body functions as metonym both for the altar and for the sacrifice.

Maria Carafa felt strongly about veiling, wanting the virgins at S. Maria della Sapienza to cover their faces "since it could avail them nothing to be seen by men."[42] She quoted a hermit saint fleeing from the sight of his relations: *Si homines video, Angelos videre non possum* (If I can see men, I cannot see angels).[43] She justified her order that all the nuns at the Sapienza should cover their faces in terms of carnal love. Their Heavenly Husband was jealous of them, she claimed.[44] Such a claim locates the nun's body—specifically her face—as the site of potential contest between spiritual and mundane bridegrooms. The veil therefore signaled that Christ was the nun's bridegroom, but it also became a sign in itself, an acknowledgment of the beauty and temptation of the nun's face beneath it. Thus, in truly Foucauldian fashion, the practice of veiling signified the sexual allure of the veiled enclosed nun.

Just as the nun's body was veiled when she was at risk of contact with others, as during communion, so conventual architecture was veiled at points of especial porosity. For instance, a Florentine synodal law of 1517 required convents to cover grates with a veil when professed nuns were speaking with a man unrelated to them.[45] Nuns dressed not only their own bodies, but also the statuary and architecture of the convent. During festivals they adorned statues of saints with rich clothes and jewels. This led to nuns borrowing furnishings and to attempts by the Church (for instance, by synodal decree in 1660 and 1662) to limit convents' spending on *apparati* and using anything that did not belong to them.[46] Again we see the fear of commerce and exchange as corrupting the conventual body (even as economic exchange was positively encouraged by ecclesiastical authorities eager to ensure that convents' finances broke even).

Like the nun's body, conventual architecture was dressed and specially adorned to mark feasts and transitions. Nowhere is the fascination with dress played out more clearly than during the rituals of monacation. Nuns' families frequently bore the cost of special festival celebrations in order to publicly associate the family with an exclusive and conspicuous form of religious patronage—a flamboyant announcement to the city's social and ecclesiastical hierarchies alike.[47] Consequently, when Viceroy Pietro d'Aragona introduced financial support for the Quarant'ore celebrations, the Collateral was relieved because it would end families' shouldering of excessive costs and help avert undue display.[48] The rituals of vestiture, profession, and consecration offered a nun's family plenty of opportunities to celebrate their social significance, piety, and institutional connections. Consequently, these occasions were lavishly celebrated with *apparati*, hangings, music, special sweets, and distinguished visitors from family and ecclesiastical authorities.

When a nun from an important Neapolitan family took the habit, the celebrations were carried on at city level, just as when daughters made social marriages.[49] Before taking her vows, a novice returned to her parents' home for a short period of reflection. Her physical removal from the convent at this stage emphasized her position between spiritual and familial affinities. On the day of her vestiture, the novice burst upon the scene, dressed like a princess, and was paraded through the streets to her conventual church. Vargas Macciucca comments acerbically on this practice of self-advertisement: "As the day in which she must take the religious habit draws near, she dresses like a queen if she can, rather than a bride, and so with all the greatest imaginable womanly luxury, she, magnificent, takes a turn around the city, almost so that there is no one left who does not know the great sacrifice that she is about to make."[50] Thus the liminal state preceding profession was full of energy, social life, movement, and visibility, before the end of those things in the state of being a nun. Self-denial, the mortification of the flesh, enclosure, and the deprivation of sensual stimulation were endowed with meaning only in relation to their opposites, publicly enacted by the novice at this stage.[51] The future nun was displayed in the city, advertising to people from all walks of life the wealth, beauty, and youth which convents possessed and which their blind outer walls screened. This rite of passage—in theory the last time the young woman was free to see and be seen out in the city streets—allowed her to symbolically bid her city farewell. But the flamboyance of the gesture, which drew attention to the girl's wealth and nubile status, also served to announce to the city the power of convents, storehouses of such resources, repositories for the inconspicuous consumption of youth, beauty and nobility, and able to determine a young woman's fate, underlining conventual power in the city and in aristocratic society more widely.

This process intensified up to the point of the first communion: "When finally the morning of the great deed comes, her body (persona) is adorned [even] more than before, the most splendidly that is possible, and her head is weighed down with a crown of the richest dazzling jewels, she is led about a little more, and then she is led to her convent's church."[52] After the public gesture in the city, the next ceremony of monacation occurred within the conventual church—a liminal space between city and convent. The conventual church was treated in parallel fashion to the body of the nun, and the ceremony filled with sensory delight: "[The church was] gorgeous with the most sumptuous tapestry hangings in which the city abounds, and to the pleasant sweet sound of harmonious instruments and the most excellent singing, between a group of *Cavalieri* and ladies, she is received and carried to the altar, where she then receives the most holy body of the Lord to whom she will be married."[53] A sensual feast to the eyes, ears, and mouth marked the beginning of their denial. The splendor of this stage contrasted with the austerity of the next, when the nun was carried into the monastery and her secular adornments replaced by monastic garb, the bejeweled crown by a garland of flowers, and her hair cut and covered with a veil.

The bill for brocade alone for the monacation party for Signora Ullone at Donnalbina in 1732 came to 22 ducats 2 tarì 10 grani.[54] Eight *canne* of white brocade with a green background, worked in silver, decorated the church facade to advertise to the city the special event taking place inside.[55] Its atrium was hung with blue brocade, four *canne* of *broccato camorcio* adorned its entablature, while festoons of pale blue brocade on a deep blue background embellished its interior. Lavish *apparati* on church facades advertised to the city the nun's rites of passage and declared the liminality of both the nun's body and the convent church.

Large numbers of participants were orchestrated to celebrate these heavenly matrimonies, which also represented institutional marriages of family to convent. As many as four choirs were brought in to sing at the monacations of Maria Geronima and Maria Cecilia, twin daughters of Ugo Boncompagni and Maria Ruffo, duke and duchess of Sora, which took place at S. Giuseppe dei Ruffi in 1663.[56] Cardinal Filomarino himself organized the music, which continued for eight hours.[57] For sister Arcangela (in secular Ippolita) Maria Ruffo, in 1673 the festivities befitted a daughter of Carlo Ruffo and Adriana Caracciolo, duke and duchess of Bagnara. At a great *festa*, "Archbishop Caracciolo not only brought with him his own music but invited other outsiders and conducted many solemnities for the function and the entire church, and square were adorned."[58]

Meanwhile, the liminality of the conventual church, perched between city and convent, and its permeability to familial influence rendered it a place of potential danger to those monacands who were at odds with their family. When Teodora Caracciolo took the habit of novice, against her father's wish, on 19 March 1738, she resisted her father's plan to hold the celebrations publicly in the church and insisted that they be held instead more modestly inside the convent: "The Duke her father wanted it to be held in the church, but she, afraid of seeing herself outside those Holy Walls, almost as if the most innocent dove was in fear of some sparrow-hawk, insisted it should be held inside the convent."[59] Usually, however, monacation celebrations went ahead with all the pomp necessary to render a spiritual and familial turning point into a civic event. The decorations temporarily transformed the church and its entrance into a celebratory space, connecting church to street with colorful and expensive cloth paid for by the monacand's family, making visible the link between the family outside and the convent inside.

Money for the music, the decoration of the church, food for all the nuns, and presents to the various people who played an important role in that event had to be found by the family. It is as if, Vargas Macciucca complained, they believed that the more money was spent, the more meritorious they were, "so much does one seek to surpass another in prodigality."[60] Families competed with each other so intensely that in 1629 the Sacra Congregazione dei Regolari of Rome issued nine new regulations to moderate expenditure on dowries and monacations, including allowing "only at entry an honest voluntary recreation, which does not exceed in total the sum of 5 carlinos for each nun."[61] In 1657 Alexander VII promulgated a bull banning fireworks and the offering of cakes and tarts on these occasions.[62] But rich aristocrats, determined to advertise their worth, defied mere ecclesiastical prescription.

The principal subject and object of conventual architecture was the body of the nun. Architecture framed and organized relationships between the nun's body and God's Body (the Eucharist), between it and the familial body and the body politic of the city, both inside and outside its walls. Convent buildings were a metaphor for the virginal upper-class female body. Even if outsiders were kept out, anxieties about unseemly physical contact lingered. Space inside the convent was subject to sharp hierarchical divisions.[63] Grilles and grates separated nuns' bodies from those of the congregation or priest, but not from each other. If communal conventual spaces were too confined it was feared that nuns' bodies might rub together. This was why the small grilled tribune at the east end of S. Gregorio Armeno in Naples was deemed unsuitable: "This, although oblong, because of its narrowness anyway bothered the ladies in reciting the

Holy Offices, due to the confusion of their voices, and the heat, which the space accumulated in the summer, which sent the nuns' heads spinning, there being no more space between one lady opposite the next than six palms."[64] Nuns' bodies were not to be at risk of touching each other or their heads would start to spin. Here is evident the fear of carnal pleasure sabotaging from within the whole precarious edifice of respectability, the fear of loss of control of mind and body that persistently and constantly threatened an institution dedicated to subduing them.

That so much depended on the apparent and advertised respectability, chastity, and virginity of the nuns' bodies provoked rampant anxieties resulting in regulations, visitations, and inspections. The collective virginal body had to be protected—and emphatically separated—from the bodies of potential violators, both sexual and social. Thus both laity and priests, servants and aristocrats were carefully regulated in terms of access to convents. The possibility of intimate bodily contact became the focus of surveillance, obstruction, and fantasy.

Architectural organization was supplemented by detailed regulations attempting to control access, to keep visitors separate from nuns and nuns separate from each other. A flotilla of rules and regulations sought to keep most people out of convents, allow in only a carefully chosen few, and to control where that select few might physically tread and what they might see. Spatial distinction between seculars and regulars was characterized by rules against the intrusion of unauthorized people (passive cloister) and regulations against nuns leaving the cloister (active cloister). In April 1658 Archbishop Rubio of Palermo issued an edict stipulating that abbesses should ensure that lay folk could not see the nuns while they were dining, whether from "the grates of the church, the parlors, the sacristy, or any other part."[65] Pius V's *Decori et honestati* decreed punishment by excommunication for those who broke enclosure and those who admitted outsiders into enclosed convents. Only fire, flood, plague, or invasion justified egress.

Silence, a precondition of a sealed body, was the ideal. Rules and regulations attempted to control when, where, and to whom nuns might speak.[66] The myth of chastity and purity within their walls was too important to all concerned to allow truth to spill out. What happened inside should not be seen; nor should it be heard. The constitutions of the Convertite degli Incurabili in Naples included a strict admonition in this regard: "The visitor . . . having visited, admonished, and corrected the sisters as he will have done, in their presence must extirpate the visit from his mind (*abrusciare la visita*), so that their transgressions do not reach the ears of laymen, to whom it is not fitting that they should understand the troubles of religious women."[67]

Silence was used to block rumor and scandal. Considered worse even than his "carnal commerce" with a laysister of S. Marcellino was the possibility that Luca Coppola might lay pen to paper in its regard.[68] Even Archbishop Filomarino was wary as to what he committed to paper about his conventual visitations in Naples during the 1650s. When he criticized the strictly observant convent of S. Maria in Gerusalemme, because the confessor's house stood between the convent and the church and sometimes nuns confessed before matins during the night, Filomarino added darkly, "I could add other things about which for respect of your Holiness and for not being able to trust the pen I shall be silent."[69] Likewise, when he interdicted the Neapolitan convent of Donnaregina, he dodged the law to avoid specifying the precise abuses so as not to make them known to laypeople.[70] The rule of silence formed an invisible wall between the nuns and the world outside; it acted as a barrier, preventing truth seeping from one world into the other, part of the policy of the male ecclesiastical hierarchy of making the world dead to nuns and nuns dead to the world, sealing them inside, obstructing real understanding among outsiders of the lives and doubts and difficulties with which conventual inmates struggled. Silence, however, tended to breed not respect, but suspicion and fantasy, producing in turn a cycle of scandal and rumor which necessitated ever more vigilant policing, deeper silences, darker shadows.

While conventual regulations focused on behavior, episcopal visitations investigated conventual architecture.[71] Small and dark corners inside convents were ferreted out by episcopal visitation. In 1648 Archbishop Filomarino ordered the nuns at S. Maria Regina Coeli to close up a room which had no apparent purpose. This they did just before his next visit in 1652. The threat of excommunication and interdict was essential to achieve his ends.[72] Visitations attempted to banish all kinds of abuses. Their language and preoccupation with routing out secrets and intimacy reveal as much about their executors as about the convents. Consider the following passage by the archbishop of Florence (1601): "I have also in visits had an eye to check that through the convent there are no holes, through which from the church or from outside it is possible to see into hidden places, these are often made, and they are very dangerous, even if they are very small, because with threads it is possible to receive and send notes."[73] Architecture could reveal probity or abuse. Convents had to be impermeable because gaps or holes, however small, posed temptation, specifically sexual temptation. Convent walls, like the body of the nun smothered in a habit, were to be sheathed from temptation, made impenetrable. Architecture and the body were conflated.

Convents could not, of course, be completely sealed off from the outside world, and architecture did a lot of the work of regulating separation. Indeed, the interior organization of Alberti's prisons bears striking similarities to that of convents: "There should be a hall, none too depressing, to serve as a vestibule for assembling those sent to be taught a discipline; beyond this the first entrances should be to the quarters of the armed guards, protected behind bars and a palisade; next there should be an open court, flanked by porticoes on either side, containing a large number of openings into several of the cells. Here the bankrupts and insolvent debtors should be kept, not all together, but in separate cells."[74] The plan of the Neapolitan convent of S. Maria della Consolazione degli Afflitti shows comparable assembly hall, entrances subject to easy protection, the exploitation of anterooms, and a cloister with openings to separate cells (Figure 4).

CHRIST'S BODY AND THE NUN'S BODY

Just as the relationship between city and convent was crucial to its external architecture, so was that between the nuns and the Body of Christ to convent interiors. At the center of the mass, protected in a pyx, was the most sacred body of all. Screened, securely placed in ornate boxes, the body of the nun and the Body of the Host receive parallel treatments in the conventual church. Although conventual regulations devote more attention to the bodies of nuns, liturgically the Body of Christ remained central. Indeed, celebration of that body was what made enclosure particularly vulnerable, bringing as it did into the midst of the nuns contact with the priest and the presence of the congregation. Anxiety about sexual relations between nuns and priests or confessors was constant, not only because of the close physical contact that religious functions made possible, indeed inevitable; but also because of the intimacy of the confessional relationship. Alexander VII's bull, published on 20 October 1664, was characteristic of the concern with maintaining boundaries and separation. Focused on when and how it was licit for regular superiors of nuns and confessors to enter convents or stay there, it stipulated that confessors, whether ordinary or extraordinary, should enter enclosed convents as little as possible, and should be accompanied by a brother of old age and good mores. The presence of a (supposedly) unsexual old man, functioning as a sort of prophylactic, was intended to guard against potential sexual contact.[75]

Just as the body of the nun was subject to tight control, so was the Body of Christ. All kinds of restrictions focused on the altar and position and visibility of the host. The *ostiola*, where the sacrament was ministered, was expected to conform to the dimensions established by the Sacra Congregazione; and if it were found to be smaller, it had to be enlarged.[76] The archbishop of Florence, Alessandro de' Medici, goes to some length to stipulate the requirements of a suitable grate for communion in his treatise on conventual government (1601): "Its opening should not exceed one palm, whether of thick stone cut so that the nun's face cannot reach the skin of the outside wall, but may remain in such a way inside, that the kneeling communicant nun cannot see the eyes or forehead of the priest."[77] Thus architecture and clothing functioned to fragment the body of the nun and the bodies she could see.

The communion window was usually emphatically gilded: "Behind the main altar the Communicatory is built, entirely of white marble with its little door of brass."[78] Again architectural requirements were reinforced by regulations governing the nuns' behavior and dress: "Having prepared to receive this most august Sacrament . . . , they will approach the little window two by two, with faces covered by the veil, in such a way however that the mouth is conveniently left uncovered, so that the priest can, with every ease, and without any danger of any inconvenience, administer the Sacrament."[79] The grilles emphasized the separation of the priest's body and the virgin's body as they drew together at the moment of greatest tension through the exchange of the Body of Christ (Plate 5).

Indulgence in eating must be seen in the context of the transubstantative mass and of the regular fastings that marked the conventual calendar. Sugary sweets, music, feasts, and display were among nuns' most pressing concerns in baroque Naples. Food occupied a central point in relation to female devotion in conventual life.[80] Fridays were a day of fasting in most convents. At S. Giuseppe delle Ermitane in Naples fasting also occurred during Advent and on the eve of Epiphany, Ascension, Corpus Domini, the Purification, the Birth of the Virgin, and the eve of S. Agostino.[81]

Saporific seductions of the body permeate conventual documents. References to drinking, eating, and temptations to the palate are quite common. And the convents were renowned for their rivalries in speciality sweet-making. Sweets not only stimulated sensory indulgence within the convent; they also effected commerce with the outside world. Sweet sticky cakes, manufactured by virgins, given as favors in return for favors, left sticky trails along orectic paths of passage in and out of convents, to the mouths of monks, nobles, and priests. The sealed and secretive convents oozed enticing luxury sweets, which served both to exoticize their internal secrets, including the nuns, and to bind their clients to them in this exotic and sticky exchange. While S. Chiara produced syrupy egriots or cherries (*marasche*), little pears in jars, *mostaccciuli* (a spiced cake laced with must), lasagne, and fritters known as *zeppole,* the nuns of S. Maria Maddalena turned their hands to marzipan *mattoni,* and those at S. Maria Egiziaca to *biscotti di galera*; the speciality of Regina Coeli was candied fruit, such as citron and peach.[82] The exchange of sweets and glances in the erotic economy of convents alarmed the archbishop of Palermo sufficiently to rule that during Good Friday celebrations "all conventual grates should be locked so that [nuns] may not be seen by people from outside and nobody may give things of sugar, or anything else for similar effect."[83]

Meanwhile, the sugar economy greatly strengthened convents financially. Discussing the problem of the sugar economy at the Sapienza in Naples, the Sacra Congregazione dei Regolari observed: "A large part of the aforementioned sweets go for the exactions of the entries of the convent, and they make notable presents to diverse persons for having the payment of the Court and City, of which the convent has 124,000 *scudi* in capital. Furthermore, a portion of the sweets is given for lawsuits and to other people who serve the convent, such as lawyers, procurators, clerks, officials, collectors, clergymen [*chierici*], servants of the convent, doctors, surgeons, sacristans, and other similar persons."[84] The quantities were considerable, indicating the level of penetration of convents. The same document reveals that no fewer than forty jars were given to the Theatine fathers for the nurse of S. Paolo, forty jars for the SS. Apostoli, and twenty for S. Maria dell'Angeli.[85] During the revolt of Masaniello, large gifts of sugar and sweets were made to lawyers, procurators and so on, to prevent attacks on convents.

NUNS AS LIVING RELICS

The gaze has been theorized in terms of the asymmetrical power relations it produces, "power through transparency" and subjection by illumination.[86] But what did it mean to be looked at by a nun? Or to have your looking rendered suspect and furtive? Was it at all comparable to being looked down on by the patron saints of the city, who usually line the skies of representations of cities of this period? As most saints came from religious orders, and given the notions surrounding virginity and the angelic choir, could it be that nuns, regarded as intercessors on behalf of the city, were thought of rather like saints, or as potential saints? Certainly convents themselves were seen as bulwarks, physically protecting the city from divine disgrace. An ecclesiastical treatise on the role of women by Agostino Valier, bishop of Verona, describes cloistered virgins as playing an important role in reconstituting the discipline of their city, by furnishing through their well-ordered, respected convents a bulwark (*baluardo*) against evil.[87] A city's safety could be strengthened by the intercessive prayers of religious, which in turn depended on the strength of its religious institutions. Nuns' bodies functioned like relics in that they enhanced the spiritual significance of the place where they were housed and functioned extrovertedly to benefit those in contact with them. Indeed, the gilded grilles behind which nuns sheltered inside their churches celebrated them in much the same way as the decorated pierced metal on a relic protected and celebrated its treasures (Plates 5, 10; Figures 29, 43).

In a description of the exhibition of the nuns' choir on feast days at S. Patrizia in Naples, Celano draws a suggestive parallel between nuns and relics, between the viewing of nuns' dedicated spaces during their absence and the worship of relics, which represented both the absence and presence of saints:

> And it is notable that this place has two churches. One is that which is seen every day and is called the outer church, where the nuns recite divine office. And in this on the main altar is to be seen a very beautiful painting, known as "all the saints" . . . The other is called the inner church, a most beautiful and magnificent structure. This one is not open to public visits, except twice a year, and that occurs from the first vespers until the morning of the day after the birthday feast of the saint, and on Ash Wednesday until the evening of Good Friday, and on that day all the holy relics, which are special and admirable, are displayed.[88]

In other words, when the nuns' choir was opened to public view, it displayed not the nuns' bodies directly, but the convents' precious relics, which represented them metonymically. Celano goes on to describe a special relic which was kept in the altar of the nuns' church: "In this altar there is a silver casket, seven *palmi* long, and gilded in many places, with very fine glass windows, where the body of the holy virgin Patricia is conserved, who, for the many graces received by Neapolitans is inscribed in the number of patron saints."[88] The message is clear. St. Patricia is marked as a special model for the nuns at the convent dedicated to her. Her body, her relics, are kept in particularly close, exclusive association with the nuns through the privileged space of their choir. Similarly, at S. Gregorio Armeno the first west-end choir was covered by a splendid wooden ceiling, created by Teodoro d'Errico and his collaborators (1580–82), and carved and inserted with paintings to celebrate the precious relics in the church's keeping. The nuns, gathered under this ceiling, thus come to occupy a position related to this celebration of relics (Plate 10). In a sense, nuns were living relics, their convent their gorgeous reliquary.

Conventual buildings represented nuns' bodies metaphorically and metonymically. The austerity of their outer walls paralleled the austerity of monastic habits, while the richly decorated interiors represented the precious balsam of virginity. Architecture and the body of the nun occupied mimetic fields, while the denial of the corporeal endlessly evoked it. The internal organization of conventual churches was particularly redolent of the optics of power and the temptation and fear of sight, its architecture emphasizing separation from the laity and ambiguously both consolidating and fragmenting the religious body. The coverings of walls, habits, pyx that revealed and concealed the bodies of Christ and of the nuns functioned metonymically and metaphorically in a system of mutual representation.

The fortress-like appearance of convents strengthened and urbanized discourses of chastity. Emphasis on enclosure and separation, both inside the conventual church and out, visibly forged segregation and exclusivity in relation to laypeople and implied—while simultaneously obscuring—the nuns' intimacy with the Divine. The promise of their presence was constantly suggested by angelic singing from the choir, sounds muffled behind screens, an indistinct glimpse snatched between grilles—but always obscurely, never directly; conventual architecture served to shatter and fragment, to tantalize and obscure, to disembody and to mystify. The spectacular richness of convent church decoration advertised not only the familial and institutional wealth (and influence) to which nuns had access, but celebrated their bodily presence, too, as virgins, quasi-angelic, a divine urban resource that could be tapped but never fully possessed.

Notes

INTRODUCTION

1. Hamburger, "Art, Enclosure, and the *Cura Monialium*," 126, called attention to this problem. For the extent of this problem, see Chiappa, "'De Monialibus,'" 643–715. Gabriella Zarri and other scholars have attended to the connections between rapidly developing Italian urban cultures and particular forms of religious devotion, but their work does not embrace architectural or urbanistic analysis (Zarri, "Il Monachesimo femminile"; "Monasteri femminili e città," 359–429; "Le Sante Vive," 371–445). This bifurcation tends to mar otherwise exemplary scholarship in Monson, *The Crannied Wall*, 2–7; Gilchrist, *Gender and Material Culture* (see esp. 17). The split between the analysis of devotion and practice and that of architectural space and form extends beyond the boundaries of conventual scholarship to recent theoretical work on gender and architecture, which too often treats buildings by way of plans or photographs, ignoring practice altogether. See Colomina, "The Split Wall," in *Sexuality and Space*, 73–130. Exceptions to this rule include: Boesch-Gajano and Scaraffia, *Luoghi sacri*; Bruzelius, "Hearing Is Believing," 83–91, and "Queen Sancia of Mallorca," 69–100; Bruzelius and Berman, "Monastic Architecture for Women"; Dunn, "Piety and Patronage," 644–663, and "Women as Convent Patrons," 154–188; Mann, "The Annunciation Chapel," 113–134; Miele, "Sisto V e la Riforma," 129; Wood, *Women, Art, and Spirituality*, esp. 32–35.

2. Hamburger, *Nuns as Artists*; Monson, "La Pratica della Musica"; Winkelmes, "Taking Part," 91–110.

3. Croce, *Storia del Regno di Napoli*; Galasso, *Il Mezzogiorno nella Storia d'Italia*, 1–14;

Barbagallo, *Mezzogiorno e questione meridionale.* For the representation of Naples and Neapolitans as unchanging "Other," see Villari, "Masaniello," 117–132.

4. Astarita, *Continuity of Feudal Power,* 19.

5. In Sicily the percentage of the population under feudal jurisdiction was 44 percent in 1583, 50 percent in 1652, and 59 percent in 1748. Ligresti, *Sicilia moderna,* 85.

6. These considerations are central to Novi Chavarria's exemplary *Monache e Gentildonne,* sadly available to me too late for inclusion in this study. See also Novi Chavarria, "Nobiltà di Seggio," 84–111; Visceglia, "Corpo e Sepoltura," 583–597; "Linee per uno studio unitario," 393–470; *Il Bisogno di Eternità*; *Signori, Patrizi, Cavalieri.* Broadly similar approaches emerged earlier in the excellent scholarship on female religious devotion in early modern France. See especially Chaunu, *L'église, culture et société,* 184, 401; Rapley, *The Dévotes,* 5; Brémond, *Histoire littéraire,* 2:36ff; Dagens, *Bérulle,* 105; Davis, *Society and Culture,* 85–87. See also note 1 above.

7. See especially Ozment, *The Reformation.* The debate assumes wider form in Kelly Gadol, "Did Women Have a Renaissance?," 19–50; Niccoli, *Rinascimento al Femminile*; Herlihy, "Did Women Have a Renaissance?," 1–22.

8. Norberg, "The Counter Reformation and Women," 133; Delumeau, *La Peur en Occident,* 422.

9. Zarri, "Le Sante Vive," 371–445.

10. Williams, "Music and Dancing," in Monson, *The Crannied Wall*; Greaves, *Triumph over Silence*; Norberg, "The Counter Reformation and Women," 133–135; Delumeau, *La Peur en Occident,* 405–421.

11. Putnam, *The Lady,* 71. For a judiciously balanced viewpoint, see Monson, *The Crannied Wall,* 2–7.

12. See, for example, Bruzelius, "Hearing Is Believing," 83–91, and "Queen Sancia of Mallorca," 69–100; Bruzelius and Berman, *Gesta,* 31.

13. See, for example, Schulte van Kessel, "Virgins and Mothers," 132–66. The absurdity of applying a measure as crude as "good" or "bad" to conventual realities is neatly exposed by C. Bologna's illuminating study of the etymology and uses of key concepts such as "claustrum," "space," "separation," and "interiority." Bologna, "L'Invenzione dell'interiorità," 243–66.

14. Bornstein, "Women and Religion," 4.

15. Ibid., 5.

16. Delooz, ; Sallman, "Sainteté mystique," 681–702; Sallman, *Naples et ses saints*; Weinstein and Bell, *Saints and Society.*

17. Enclosure, which Trent insisted upon, not only set religious women apart from laypeople but also, because it depended on architectural expression, demanded extra money—thereby justifying expensive entrance fees, in the shape of conventual dowries. Those dowries effectively restricted acceptance by certain convents to the daughters of the richest or best-connected families.

18. Canosa, *Il Velo e il Cappuccio*; Odorisio, *Donne e Società*; Medioli, "To Take or Not to Take the Veil," 122–131; "Le Monacazioni forzate," 431–454; Panizza, *Arcangela Tarabotti*; Tarabotti, "L'Inferno monacale"; Zanette, *Suor Arcangela.*

19. See especially De Giorgio and Klapisch-Zuber, *Storia del Matrimonio*; Klapisch-

Zuber, *Women, Family, and Ritual,* 117–131; Jordan, "Renaissance Women and the Question of Class," 90–106; Howell, "Marriage, Property, and Patriarchy," 203–224; Dean and Lowe, *Marriage in Italy*; Zarri, "Recinti," 203–250.

20. Issues demanding further investigation include the role of parents in arranging marriages, the frequency of childbirth, the determination of the newly married couple's residence, and remarriage for widows and widowers.

21. Jordan, "Renaissance Women and the Question of Class," 98; D'Amelia, "La Conquista di una dote."

22. From *Nicomachean Ethics,* quoted by Jordan, "Renaissance Women and the Question of Class," 94.

23. Wiesner, *Women and Gender,* 9–40.

24. *Il Merito,* 69, quoted by M. Rosenthal, "Venetian Women Writers," 128.

25. See Klapisch-Zuber, *Women, Family, and Ritual,* 120–121.

26. Cohen, "Asylums for Women," 166–188. That in Naples was founded in 1564.

27. For example, Church officials in 1646 ruled to prevent members of the Zitelle Disperse in Rome from contracting out as servants and from begging in the streets as alms-seekers. The Church preferred inmates to await benefactions passively inside the refuges and to give thanks in the form of religious rites when they were forthcoming. Cohen, "Asylums for Women," 176–178.

28. Bilinkoff, "Navigating the Waves"; Chaunu, *L'église, culture et société,* 184, 401; Schulte van Kessel, "Virgins and Mothers," esp. 138–148.

29. Zarri, "Le sante vive," 371–445; Sallmann, "La sainteté mystique féminine à Naples," esp. 698–701; Scaraffia and Zarri, *Donne e Fede,* esp. Matthews Grieco, "Modelli di santità femminile," 303–325; Boesch-Gajano and Sebastiani, *Culto dei Santi.*

30. Miele, "Sisto V e la Riforma"; Bolton, "Mulieres Sanctae," 141–158; Thompson, "The Problem of the Cistercian Nuns," 227–252.

31. Dunn cites examples of seventeenth-century Roman aristocratic women who protested that they would have preferred a religious life but were forced to adopt a secular one. Dunn, "Spiritual Philanthropists," 156.

32. Bornstein, "Women and Religion," 8–9.

33. See, for example, the discussion by Kate Lowe, "Nuns and Choice," 129–130. The stipulation in some conventual contracts that an artwork should be made like that in another convent or church is not necessarily a sign that they "may have considered it wise to play safe" (ibid., 130); such practices indicate emulation between convents, eager not to be outdone by their rivals, and evince enclosed nuns' knowledge of artwork commissioned elsewhere.

34. Dunn, "Spiritual Philanthropists," 155.

35. A criticism made by Lawrence, "Introduction," 2. But see Labrot, *Collections,* 4–18.

36. Monson, "Introduction," 6.

37. Novi Chavarria, "Nobiltà di Seggio," 84–111; Visceglia, "Corpo e Sepoltura," 583–614; "Linee per uno Studio," 393–470; *Il Bisogno di Eternità.*

38. Foucault, *Discipline and Punish,* 149–155.

CHAPTER 1

1. Giannone, *Istoria Civile*, 3:42.

2. Pietro Giannone (1676–1748) fled to the Austrian Habsburg Court from Naples after the publication of this adamantly anticlerical work. Penco, *Storia della Chiesa*, 2:115.

3. Giuseppe Sanfelice, under the patriotic pseudonym Filopatro, squarely countered Giannone's arguments. Filopatro, *Riflessioni Morali*, 1:88–89, 1:96.

4. Celano, *Notitie del Bello*, 5(i): 776.

5. Peccerillo, *I Ragioni*, 4.

6. Ibid., 5.

7. Noted in the hand of the copyist in Bulifon's diaries. Bulifon, *Giornali*, 98.

8. Burnet, *Voyage*, 15. For further comment by foreign visitors to Italy on the superabundance of ecclesiastical buildings, see Strazzullo, *Edilizia e Urbanistica*, 195–199.

9. Giannone, *Istoria Civile*, 8:103.

10. Russo, *Monasteri femminili*, 40; Rosa, "L'Onda che ritorna," 398. Strazzullo claims that in 1580–1585 there were twenty-two female monasteries with 1,774 inhabitants and seventy male monasteries with 1,997 inhabitants. Strazzullo, *Edilizia e Urbanistica*, 102.

11. Female convent churches established between 1600 and 1650 alone comprised SS. Trinità (1606), S. Giuseppe delle Scalze (1607), S. Giuseppe delle Eremitane (1607), S. Giovanni Battista (1610), S. Caterina da Siena (1613), S. Francesco delle Cappuccine (1616), S. Teresa del SS. Sacramento (1632), S. Maria Maddalena (1638), the Divino Amore (1638), and S. Maria Egiziaca al Pizzofalcone (1639). Russo, *Monasteri femminili*, 40.

12. Ibid., 40, 42.

13. While in 1610–11 there were 2,239 nuns, by 1629 their number had risen to 2,717. Rosa, "L'Onda che ritorna," 400–401.

14. The number of Franciscans rose from 875 in 1610–1611 to 1,051 by 1629, while Benedictines increased in the same period from 600 to 710, Dominicans from 262 to 310, Augustinian nuns from 174 to 246, and Carmelites from 126 to 140; Spanish nuns rose in number from 102 in 1610–1611 to 160 in 1629, although the population of Lateran nuns at Regina Coeli remained stable at about 100. The increase in population at the Sapienza was fairly typical, from 58 nuns in 1595, to 68 in 1598, and to 80 in the early years of the seventeenth century. Colombo, *Il Monastero*, 23.

15. From its foundation by Queen Sancia and King Robert, S. Chiara was intended to support 200 nuns. Celano, *Notitie del Bello*, 1:69. Chiarini notes that at S. Chiara in 1560, during the tenure of Abbess Beatrice Portogallo, the nuns numbered 380 and the convent enjoyed an annual income of 7,000 gold ducats. Chiarini, *Aggiunzioni* to Celano, *Notitie del Bello*, 3:425.

16. Beltrano, *Breve Descrittione*, 8–11.

17. Ibid.

18. Where laws on family property transmission were particularly strict, more women joined convents. Nuns comprised about 1 percent of the population in Naples in 1623, compared to 5.5 percent in Florence in 1622, 9.3 percent in Prato, and a

staggering 13 percent in Gubbio. Beloch, *Bevölkerungsgeschichte*, 23–24; Zarri et al., "*De Monialibus*," 676–677.

19. Celano, *Notitie del Bello*, 1:197.

20. Labrot, "Comportement collectif," 56–57.

21. Innocent X's brief stated that the new convent should accept no more than thirty-three sisters, including supranumeraries; and he established the dowries as 2,000 ducats for eleven nuns (numerary) and 1,500 for the supranumerary. Russo, *I Monasteri femminili*, 42.

22. Blunt, *Neapolitan Baroque Architecture*, 37; De Seta, *Napoli*, 137–138.

23. De Seta, *Napoli*, 138.

24. Ibid., 137–139; Colombo, *Il Monastero*, 15–17. The convent of S. Antonio di Padova was begun in 1565 under the auspices of sister Paola Cappella, a Neapolitan nun who had left the convent of S. Maria del Gesù. The grand and spacious Palazzo di Conca, adjacent to the convent, was incorporated into it and divided up for dwelling space. Celano, *Notitie del Bello*, 3:26–27.

25. For escalating prices, see Labrot, "Naissance et croissance," lxi–lxiv.

26. Russo, *Monasteri femminili*, 20.

27. Other convents in this area were S. Francesco, S. Geronimo, S.M. Egiziaca, and S.M. Maddalena della Penitenza. Celano describes S. Chiara as "una mezza Città." Celano, *Notitie del Bello*, 1:63.

28. This area also housed SS. Pietro e Sebastiano, S. Giovanni Battista, S. Antonio di Padova, the Conciliazione, S. Giuseppe delle Eremitane, S. Andrea, S.M. Regina Coeli, S. Gaudioso, S. Patrizia, the Incurabili, and S.M. in Gerusalemme.

29. Male orders dominated in the prosperous new Chiaia district.

30. Cantone, "I Conservatorii," 215. Cantone points out that the concentration of prostitutes was pushed to various places across the city, from the port area to the *quartieri* or Spanish quarters, from there to the Borgo of S. Antonio Abate, Porta Nolana, toward Capodichino. Ibid., 218 n. 82.

31. Ibid., 215.

32. "Diedero principio a farvi entrare alcune figliuole, chi andavano radunando per la Città, e sortandole à prende detto abito, ed assistere nell'ore determinate dicendosi l'officio, ed altre orazioni, ad imitazione de PP. Cappuccini." ASN, Mon. sop., S. Francesco delle Cappuccinelle a Pontecorvo, 4540, f. 2r.

33. Cantone, "I Conservatorii," 215.

34. Celano, *Notitie del Bello*, 4:799.

35. Cantone, "I Conservatorii," 215.

36. De Seta, *Napoli*, 137.

37. Battaglia, *Grande Dizionario*, 3:201, s.v.

38. For aristocratic palaces as fortresses, see Labrot, "Comportement collectif," 48–50.

39. Caracciolo, *Le Couvent de Baïano*, 6–7.

40. Peccerillo, *I Ragioni*, 9.

41. De Seta, *Napoli*, 138. For the aristocratic policy of block-taking, see Labrot, "Comportement collectif," 47–48.

42. "Facendosi detta spesa per l'ampliazione predetta questo Monastero sarebbe rimasto in Isola, ed a nessuno soggetto, arioso, e libero da ogni oscurità; anzi in esso per ricreazione delle Monache sarebbe rimasto Giardino lungo palmi 140 e largo palmi 76, e con la medesima spesa facendosi Botteghe con camere a lamia nel Circuito dell'isola da fuori la clausura, conforme si ricerca ne la Riforma, importarebbe d'utilità da c. 400 ducati che di piggione se ne potrebbe percepire ogn'Anno." ASN, Mon. sop., S. Maria della Consolazione, 4672, f. 12.

43. This approach was also adopted, although generally reluctantly, by some nobles who leased the outside ground floor of their palaces to shops. Labrot, "Comportement collectif," 50.

44. Celano, *Notitie del Bello*, 1:254.

45. Ibid., 1:262; Russo, *Monasteri femminili*, 18.

46. "Nè vi sarebbe speranza à i Cittadini d'alcun' ajuto, e soccorso da` i vicini, atteso essendovi da ambia i lati le mura del Collegio, e del Monastero." ASN, Mon. sop., Marcellino e Festo, 2882, undated published pamphlet, n.p.

47. Cantone, "I Conservatorii," 212.

48. De Seta, *Napoli*, 137; Strazzullo, *Edilizia e Urbanistica*, 204.

49. On 14 September 1642 Parliament petitioned the viceroy to spare Neapolitans the tax on lime. Strazzullo, *Edilizia e Urbanistica*, 204–5.

50. Giannone, *Istoria Civile*, 8:103.

51. "Che si levino parimente dell'intutte le spese delle Sacrestane, Cellerarie, Refettoriere, ed altre officiali, e particolarmente si tolga onninamente il prestito che fanno le Portinare, con questo però, che solamente possino l'officiale far qualche cosa per la Chiesa, ò per servizio del monasterio, ad arbitrio di V.S. Illustrissima, alla cui cura si lascia anche la moderazione delle spese delle fabbriche superbe, e sontuose." ASN, Mon. sop., S. Francesco delle Cappuccinelle a Pontecorvo, 4540, f. 4r.

52. Fuidoro, *Giornali*, 1:15.

53. Ibid., 1:35.

54. Ibid., 1:22–23.

55. Peccerillo, *I Ragioni*, 85.

56. ASN, Mon. sop., S. Monica, 4637, f. 7.

57. Peccerillo, *I Ragioni*, 17–18.

58. Giannone, *Istoria Civile*, 8:104.

59. Quoted by Evans, *Monastic Architecture*, 29.

60. Ibid.

61. Ibid.

62. De Seta, *Napoli*, 129. Pasquale Villani, who takes a dimmer view of the reliability of the hearths census figures, has suggested a population as high as 300,000 in 1595. In 1596 the census on hearths (which gives a false sense of precision) recorded 225,769 inhabitants, to which should be added the 17,615 members of the clergy, soldiers, and people in hospitals. Sposato, "Dati statistici," 156–160.

63. Capaccio, *Napoli descritta*, 534.

64. Galasso, *Napoli spagnola*, 1:xx, 2:747, n. 17.

65. De Seta, *Napoli*, 147. Ottavio Beltrano's figure is much higher. He calculated a pop-

ulation for Naples of 167,972 people in 1614, which he estimated had risen to 500,000 by 1640, a figure which did not include monasteries and churchmen. Beltrano, *Breve Descrittione,* 11. Beltrano's figure looks exaggeratedly high, but there is no doubt that during the seventeenth century the number of inhabitants of the city increased dramatically.

66. Celano, *Notitie del Bello,* 1:23, 4:316–317.

67. See Galasso, *Napoli spagnola,* 1:xxii–xxiii.

68. De Seta, *Napoli,* 130–132.

69. Capaccio, "Napoli descritta," 537.

70. Ibid., 535.

71. Labrot, "Naissance et croissance," xlvii–lxvi; Capasso, "La Vicaria vecchia," 690; Nicolini, "La murazione," 129–135, 156–815; Strazzullo, *Edilizia e Urbanistica,* 6–12. Rapid development in the Chiaia and on the Pizzofalcone and Mortelle hills led to the construction in 1636, under the direction of Viceroy Manuel de Guzman, count of Monterey, of the Chiaia bridge, also known as the Monterey bridge, to link those two areas previously sharply divided by the precipitous drop of the valley (present-day via Chiaia). De la Ville sur Yllon, "Il Ponte di Chiaia," 146; Savarese, *Palazzo Cellamare,* 10–11; for the exploitation of Pedro de Toledo's plans by the Monte Oliveto monastery, see Labrot, "Naissance et croissance," xlix.

72. Strazzullo, *Edilizia e Urbanistica,* 71–73; De Seta, *Napoli,* 136.

73. Palermo, "Narrazioni," 247.

74. Galasso, *Napoli spagnola,* 1:xx.

75. Bacco, *Naples,* 55–65.

76. The aristocracy maintained a migratory existence, moving between the city and their country seats, to which they retired during the hot summers.

77. Mantelli, *Il pubblico impiego,* 151–213.

78. Palermo, "Narrazioni," 247.

79. Lepre points out that agricultural revenue increased during the seventeenth century, particularly in the period 1600–1630. He suggests that this indicates a reality quite unlike that sketched by many economic historians of economic decline during the 1590s and may well have been a direct result of Naples' massive urban expansion. Lepre, "Rendite di monasteri," 846–847.

80. Labrot, "Comportement collectif," 46–51.

81. Labrot, *Collections,* 6.

82. See, for instance, Russo, *Monasteri femminili,* 40; Strazzullo, *Edilizia e Urbanistica,* 17; Rosa, "L'Onda che ritorna," 398, 403, 412–413.

83. Lepre, "Rendite di monasteri," 844–865, esp. 852.

84. Giannone, *Istoria Civile,* 8:103.

85. Ibid.

86. Ibid.

87. Ibid.

88. Ibid.

89. Penco, *Storia della Chiesa,* 2:22.

90. Giannone, *Istoria Civile,* 4:438, 4:439. See also Nappi, "I Viceré," 41–57.

91. Giannone, *Istoria Civile,* 8:102.

92. Ibid.; Nappi, "I Viceré," 53–55.

93. Giannone, *Istoria Civile,* 8:102–103.

94. Galasso, *Napoli spagnola,* 1:128.

95. Ibid., 1:103.

96. Ibid., 1:18–19, 58. See also Miele, "Sisto V e la Riforma," 123–204.

97. Astarita, *Continuity of Feudal Power,* 14, 159–160.

98. Ibid., 20.

99. Ibid., 9, 39–67, 159–201. The extension of feudal privileges was not pursued elsewhere in Europe, although the exploitation of primogeniture and entail was intensified. Cooper, "Patterns of Inheritance," 192–327. That feudalism was reinforced in southern Italy as it was being eroded elsewhere has contributed to the dominant model of the south as "backward." Aymard, "L'Europe Moderne," 426–435.

100. Astarita, *Continuity of Feudal Power,* 9, 11.

101. Ibid., 14.

102. Ibid., 26.

103. Novi Chavarria, "Nobiltà di Seggio," 93.

104. In the early years of the seventeenth century the system of municipal government was based on less than 100 noble families and about 20,000 families that were politically active in the Ottine (out of a population that reached a peak of at least three times that figure). Galasso, *Napoli spagnola,* 1:x–xiv.

105. Celano, *Notitie del Bello,* 3:629–635, 4:110–112, 4:133–134.

106. Attempts to open Seggi to aristocratic families who were not members were thwarted in the sixteenth century, and after 1599 all applications required preliminary approval from the king. Thereafter each case was treated individually. Astarita, *Continuity of Feudal Power,* 24.

107. Ibid.

108. Galasso, *Napoli spagnola,* 1:xiv.

109. Ibid.

110. Novi Chavarria, "Nobiltà di Seggio," 87–88.

111. Celano, *Notitie del Bello,* 3:140.

112. Novi Chavarria, "Nobiltà di Seggio," 86. See also Visceglia, "Corpo e sepoltura," 107–139.

113. ASN, Mon. sop., S. Gregorio Armeno, 3435, ff. 166r–167r; F. Caracciola, "Esemplare delle nobili," ASN, Mon. sop., S. Gregorio Armeno, 3435, ff. 156v–164r; Novi Chavarria, "Nobiltà di Seggio," 87.

114. Facchiano, *Monasteri femminili,* 55; Novi Chavarria, "Nobiltà di Seggio," 87.

115. Novi Chavarria, "Nobiltà di Seggio," 105; Boccadamo, "Una Riforma impossible?," 96–98.

116. Novi Chavarria, "Nobiltà di Seggio," 87, 104.

117. Ibid., 92.

118. Ibid., 87. For the Muscettola family, see Visceglia, *Bisogno di eternità,* 175–262.

119. Celano, *Notitie del Bello,* 3:80–81.

120. Novi Chavarria, "Nobiltà di Seggio," 89; Zarri, "Monasteri femminili e città,"

37. In Florence, Cosimo I issued the *reformatio monasteriorum* in 1545, which attempted to assert greater rigor in conventual behavior and insisted on correct administration of their goods. D'Addario, *Aspetti della Controriforma,* 132–144. The Council of Ten in Venice assumed analogous measures as early as the 1530s. Cecchetti, *La Repubblica di Venezia,* 1:197–201.

121. Visceglia, *Bisogno di eternità,* 35; Novi Chavarria, "Nobiltà di Seggio," 90.

122. Novi Chavarria, "Nobiltà di Seggio," 87; Sicola, "Cronaca," 506.

123. Sicola, *La Nobiltà gloriosa,* 506.

124. Ibid.

125. Ibid.

126. Ibid., 502.

127. Boccadamo, "Una Riforma impossibile?," 98, 105, 110–113; Miele, "Sisto V e la Riforma," 125–130.

128. Novi Chavarria, "Nobiltà di Seggio," 88.

129. The nuns failed, however, to pay their debt to Oliva, and further suits followed. Ibid., 88, 104 n. 23.

130. Ibid., 88.

131. Ibid., 80–81.

132. Strazzullo, "Il Monastero e la chiesa," 437.

133. Strazzullo, *Edilizia e Urbanistica,* 202; Russo, *Monasteri femminili,* 15; Miele, "Sisto V e la Riforma," 175–179.

134. Novi Chavarria, "Nobiltà di Seggio," 90.

135. The monasteries of S. Arcangelo a Baiano, S. Maria degli Angeli, and S. Antonio were closed by brief issued on 10 April 1577. Ibid., 105, n. 36.

136. Ibid., 87, 90–91.

137. Ibid., 91.

138. Novi Chavarria, "Pastorale e devozione," 390.

139. Novi Chavarria, "Nobiltà di Seggio," 91.

140. Ibid., 91.

141. A similar situation obtained in fifteenth-century Florence. Weddle, "Enclosing Le Murate," 55–57.

142. Alberti, *On the Art of Building,* 127.

143. Vittorelli, *Vita,* 82.

144. Ibid., 83.

145. "Che le sue delizie tutte le trovava in quel piccolo Monastero di Martina, e che questo solo le sembrava più grande della Città di Napoli." Ibid.

146. Ibid., 84.

147. Peter Brown has shown that monasticism in late antiquity not only destroyed the particularity of the city but threatened to weaken the city's hold on its notables at one of its most intimate points: it challenged the role of the public spaces of the city as the principal locus for the socialization of young males. Brown, *Making of Late Antiquity,* 292.

148. Novi Chavarria, "Nobiltà di Seggio," 91–92.

CHAPTER 2

1. Bugge, *Virginitas*, 6, 30–58.

2. Ibid., 5.

3. Ricoeur, *Symbolism of Evil*, 250–251.

4. See Bugge, *Virginitas*, 5–29.

5. Ibid., 17; Chrysostom, *On Virginity*, 19.

6. Bugge, *Virginitas*, 17–20.

7. Gregory of Nyssa, De *hominis opificio*, 16.7; Chrysostom, *On Virginity*, xiv, 20–22.

8. Chrysostom, *On Virginity*, 21, 22; Bugge, *Virginitas*, 20.

9. Bugge, *Virginitas*, 21–22.

10. Brown, *The Body and Society*, 405.

11. Ibid., 399–407.

12. Ibid., 408.

13. Bugge, *Virginitas*, 30.

14. Thus Luke 20:34–36; cf. Matthew 22:30, Mark 12:25.

15. Ambrose, *On Virginity*, 6.27, p. 18.

16. Methodius, *Symposium*, 57.

17. Bugge, *Virginitas*, 30, 32–33. All the monastic fathers make this claim.

18. Ibid., 23. This is not the case in St. Augustine's thought, in which virginity has no etiological significance.

19. Gregory of Nyssa, *De virginitate*, ii; Bugge, *Virginitas*, 13, 24–26.

20. Ambrose, *On Virginity*, 18.

21. Chrysostom, *On Virginity*, x–xi; Cyprian, *De bono patientiae*, vii, 4.855.

22. Ambrose, "Exhortatio virginitatis," cap. 14, in Ambrose, *Verginità e Vedovanza* (ed. F. Gori), 2:62–63.

23. Consolino, "Modelli di santità," 83–113; Schulenburg, "Heroics of Virginity," 11.

24. Schulenburg, "Heroics of Virginity," 32.

25. Bugge, *Virginitas*, 30–31.

26. Boureau, "L'Imene e l'ulivo," 791–792.

27. Knox, "Disciplina," 63–99; "Civility, Courtesy, and Women," 2–10.

28. Knox, "Civility, Courtesy, and Women," 5.

29. Ibid., 10.

30. Sissa, "Verginità materiale," 739–756; Boureau, "L'Imene e l'ulivo," 791–803.

31. Chrysostom, *On Virginity*, 2; Clark, "Introduction," x.

32. Chrysostom, *On Virginity*, 8, 14–15.

33. Ibid., 57.

34. Ibid., 14–15.

35. I Corinthians 7:1–9, 7:25–40.

36. I Corinthians 7:34. Cf. Ambrose, *On Virginity*, 19–21.

37. Leander of Seville, *Training of Nuns*, 191.

38. Jerome, *Select Letters*, 22.6; 19.25; 53.7–9; 45; 107; 108; 127.

39. Rice, *Saint Jerome*.

40. Augustine, *De bono coniugali*, 3, 18; Jerome, *Select Letters*, 107, 13, 338, 339.

41. Thomas Aquinas, *Summa theologica*, 168–169.

42. Ibid., 170–171.

43. Zarrabini, *Dello stato verginale,* 12r.

44. Jerome, *Letters,* 138.

45. Zarrabini, *Dello stato verginale,* 12r–12v.

46. Ibid., 12v.

47. Ibid., 14r.

48. Thomas Aquinas argued that the integrity of the bodily member could be miraculously restored by God. *Summa theologica,* 172.

49. Methodius, *The Symposium,* 281–282; Sissa, "La verginità materiale," 743.

50. Jerome devised a graduated system in which he regarded virgins as 100 percent, widows as 60 percent, and a chaste marriage as 30 percent. This idea was quoted by Augustine and Thomas Aquinas. Boureau, "L'Imene e l'ulivo," 792.

51. Valier, *La istituzione,* 3:17–38.

52. Ibid., 24.

53. Atkinson, "Precious Balsam," 139–140.

54. Camiz, "Virgo non-sterilis," 282, n. 80.

55. Ibid., 159.

56. Zarrabini, *Dello stato verginale,* 12v.

57. Ibid., 2v–3r, 13v.

58. Ibid., 14v.

59. Ibid.

60. Zarrabini goes on to dedicate an entire chapter to this subject. Ibid., 7v–11r.

61. Ibid., 17v–18r.

62. Liebowitz, "Virgins," 132–147; Davis, *Society and Culture,* 65–95; Schulte van Kessel, "Virgins and Mothers," 137; Papi, "'Velut in sepulchro,'" 365–455; Solfaroli Camillocci, "L'obbedienza femminile," 269–284; Terpstra, *Lay Confraternities.*

63. Schulte van Kessel, "Virgins and Mothers," 139–140.

64. Ibid., 146.

65. Creytens, "La Riforma," 51–52.

66. It was not until 1880 that the full sources were revealed. Jedin, *History of the Council,* 503; Morris, *The Lady Was a Bishop,* 151.

67. *Canons and Decrees,* sess. 25, cap. V, 240.

68. Ibid. On *Periculoso,* see Brundage and Makowski, "Enclosure," 143–155; Makowski, *Canon Law,* 3–15.

69. The council ruled that professed nuns, or *sanctimoniales* (itself an ambivalent term, since it was not clear whether it included tertiaries), not be allowed out of the convent except for a legitimate cause and with episcopal approval. The rulings were based on the mistaken assumption that nuns who took the three solemn vows necessarily abdicated their free will, even in those cases where the rule allowed nuns to leave the convent. In fact, this renunciation had not been demanded by the popes from Sixtus IV onward, when the solemn vows were changed to simple vows and regular tertiaries had been recognized as true professed nuns. In the event, Pope Pius V (1559–1565) interpreted the Fifth Canon of Trent much more rigidly than the way proposed by the Curia. Pius chose to return to Boniface VIII's legislation and to recognize one single

category of true convents, in which nuns took the three solemn vows and observed strict enclosure. This resulted in the abolition of all the open monasteries which had been officially recognized by the Church from the time of Sixtus IV. Pius V was strongly supported in this more radical and aggressive interpretation by cardinals of the Congregation of the Council, especially by Cardinal Carlo Borromeo, who claimed that reform of convents was impossible without a uniformity preventing jealousies between convents. Creytens, "La Riforma," 50–53, 60, 64, 65.

70. Ibid., 49. For earlier approaches along the same lines to the problem, see Patetta, "L'Età di Carlo," 171.

71. Pius V and Gregory XIII rigidified the rulings of Trent still further. Creytens, "La Riforma," 69–70.

72. Foucault, *Discipline and Punish*, 141.

73. Creytens, "Giurisprudenza," 251–285; Miele, "Riforma dei conventi," 89–113; Caiazza, "Nunziatura di Napoli," 39–41; Wright, "Religious Life," 252–274; Fiorani, "Monache e monasteri," 84–85, 85 n. 60.

74. Wright, "Venetian View," 96–97.

75. Zarri, "Recinti sacri," 381–386.

76. Creytens, "La Riforma," 73.

77. Wright, "Venetian View," 97–98.

78. Responding to the issue of strict enclosure and reform, one Udinese commentator emphasized the importance of avoiding episcopally enforced austerity and of refusing to allow nuns lacking a religious vocation to leave the convent to avoid strict discipline. Such action would threaten discipline in all the other convents of the state, and the social standing and economic well-being of the patriciate and provincial nobility would be shattered if unmarried and undowered daughters returned to their homes. Ibid., 97.

79. For Filomarino's visitations see Russo, *Monasteri femminili*. Filomarino undertook three series of visitations in 1642, then from 1648 to 1654, and finally after the plague, between 1657 and 1662, successively assisted by canons Germano Quaranta and Luigi de Urso, *Vicari delle monache*. Cardinal Filomarino has received much credit for bringing religious dignity to Neapolitan nuns. According to his reports to Rome, the worst damage done to monasteries by the revolt of 1647 and the plague of 1656 was not the deaths of many nuns, but the necessary alleviation of *clausura*. De Maio, *Religiosità a Napoli*, 109.

80. Ibid.

81. Zarri, "Monasteri femminili," 18.

82. Celano (ed. Chiarini), *Notizie del Bello*, 3:800.

83. Celano, *Notitie del Bello*, 1:249.

84. Caracciolo, "Esemplare," ASN, Mon. sop., S. Gregorio Armeno, 3435, ff. 133f–144r; Celano, *Notitie del Bello*, 1:250–251.

85. Zarri, "Christian Good Manners," 84–85. The renewal of observance of the rule in female convents and the imposition of enclosure became the main concern of Church authorities in the period after Trent, so that regulations became specialized differentiating them from the fifteenth-century spiritual rules directed indiscriminately at both clergy and laity.

86. Gonzaga, *Alcuni avvertimenti*, 36.

87. Ibid.

88. Ibid.

89. Zarri, "Monasteri femminili," 29.

90. Ibid.

91. Bologna, "L' "Invenzione" dell'interiorità," 243–266.

92. Augustine speaks of "eyes of the soul" and "ears of the soul." So body/soul, exterior/interior, and surface/depth become the expressive modes of a dialectic of knowledge and communication that claim to spread beyond the traditional confines of the inexpressible. Brown, *Augustine*.

93. *Regola o Costitutioni*, 33.

94. Liebowitz, "Virgins," esp. 134–136.

95. Zarrabini, *Dello stato verginale*, 22r.

96. Ibid., 2r.

97. Ibid., 22v.

98. Ibid., 29r.

99. Ibid., 23r–24r.

100. Borromeo, *Instructiones*, 87.

101. Zarri et al., *"De Monialibus,"* 657.

102. The monastic profession taken by a man differs from the *consecratio virginum* in not emphasizing the question of virginity beyond and above life in a community, obedience, and a rule. Ibid., 657–661.

103. Bugge, *Virginitas*, 59.

104. Chrysostom, *On Virginity*, 96.

105. Oulton, *Alexandrian Christianity*, 57–58; Ambrose interpreted the Song in several different ways, including as a conversation between Christ, the Word of God, and the Church, his bride. For his interpretations and his significance in this regard for Christianity in the West, see Bugge, *Virginitas*, 63.

106. Tertullian, *Treatises*, 2:9.

107. Bugge, *Virginitas*, 66–67.

108. Ibid.

109. Zarri, "Marriage of Virgins," 262–263.

110. Zarri et al., *"De Monialibus,"* 661–662.

111. Gill, "Open Monasteries," 15–47.

112. Leander of Seville, *The Training of Nuns*, 185–186.

113. Ibid., 186.

114. Ibid., 189.

115. An explanation of the readiness with which this slippage was embraced has still to be made.

116. For the shift from male to female (the maternal) in the metaphorical sexuality of Christ in twelfth- and thirteenth-century texts, see Bugge, *Virginitas*, 100–101.

117. Teresa of Jesus, *Complete Works*, 2:393.

118. Marchese, *Vita*, 15, 116, 205–229; Vittorelli, *Vita e virtù di suor Maria Aurelia Cecilia*, 86–87; Vittorelli, *Vita e virtù di suor Maria Rosa*, 43–48.

119. Vittorelli, *Lettere spirituali*, 5.

120. Although Marian cults have complex origins and are not simply an offshoot of the renewed concern with virginity, and although Marian theology is oriented toward the relationship between Mary and the divine and to her heavenly nature rather than toward the tribulations of her earthly life and her virginity as a woman, the growth of Marian cults during the sixteenth and seventeenth centuries are intimately linked to the issue of virginity and its practice.

121. Ambrosius et al., *De virginitate opuscula.*

122. McGinness, "Roma sancta," 99–116.

CHAPTER 3

1. For a bibliographical synopsis of the patrilineal orientation of ancien regime society, see Evangelisti, "Wives, Widows, and Brides," 236–237.

2. Stone, *Family, Sex, and Marriage*; 23–25; Harris, "Power, Profit, and Passion," 59–88; Klapisch-Zuber, *Women, Family, and Ritual*, 216.

3. Klapisch-Zuber, *Women, Family, and Ritual*, 215–218.

4. See in particular Hughes, "From Bridepiece to Dowry"; Klapisch-Zuber, *Women, Family, and Ritual*, 215–218; Goody, *Development of the Family*, 87; Goody, "Inheritance," 10–36.

5. The best general study of inheritance systems in relation to gender in the early modern period remains Goody et al., *Family and Inheritance*. For the feudal, military origins of the dowry system in Sicily and its gender implications, see Motta, *Strategie familiari*; see also Benigno, 1989, 165–194, esp. 189, n. 16.

6. For the freedom for maneuver of widows and regents, see Harris, "Women and Politics," 259–281; Tolley, "States of Independence," 236–257; d'Amelia, "Scatole cinesi."

7. Goddard, *Anthropology*, 190.

8. Monter, "Protestant Wives," 203–208.

9. De Luca, *La Dama e il cavaliere*, 501.

10. Astarita, *Continuity of Feudal Power*, 179, n. 43.

11. Confuorto, "Notizie" (ms., 1693), BNN, I-D-5, ff. 14–18.

12. Villari, *La rivolta antispagnola*, 124.

13. Visceglia, "Linee per uno studio," 446.

14. Frigo, "Dal caos all'ordine," 87.

15. There was nothing new in itself in this practice. In a sermon delivered at S. Maria Novella in Florence in the early fourteenth century, Fra Giordano da Rivalto suggested that convents were little more than dumping grounds for women who could not make it in marriage: "Which woman today enters the monastery, called by the spirit? No one. She enters there either through lack of beauty, because they are ugly, or through a defect of poverty so that they cannot have a husband." Quoted by Weddle, "Enclosing Le Murate," 49.

16. De Luca, *La Dama e il Cavaliere*, 502.

17. The eldest daughters were allowed to marry. Astarita, *Continuity of Feudal Power*, 176. The Caracciola Brienza clan was particularly disinclined to the convent solution.

18. Foucault exaggerated the differences between aristocratic (backward-looking)

and bourgeois (forward-looking) attitudes in this regard. Foucault, *History of Sexuality,* 1:123–124.

19. Despite persisting tendencies among historians to regard the "Mediterranean family" as something distinct and homogenous, the family in southern Italy during the early modern period is emerging from recent research as more richly varied than uniform and monolithic.

20. Giuseppe Galasso, Maria Visceglia, Tommaso Astarita, and other historians have shown that during the second half of the sixteenth century the Neapolitan aristocracy began to make important changes in hereditary transmission and in the provision of dowries for their daughters. Astarita, *Continuity of Feudal Power;* Visceglia, "Linee per uno studio," 393–470.

21. Visceglia, "Corpo e Sepoltura," 584. However, once the position of the firstborn son was secure, Neapolitan noblewomen frequently contributed to their daughter's dowry, sometimes with sums higher than those specified in their wills for their second-born sons. In other words, women tried, to some extent, to balance the distribution of their own property. Visceglia, "Linee per uno studio," 416–417.

22. The principal aim of the "Costitutioni di Melfi" was to establish the breadth of the feudal succession, forbidding the passage of goods to cousins and safeguarding royal control of feudal property in the kingdom. Visceglia, "Corpo e Sepoltura," 585, 608 n. 4.

23. Visceglia, "Linee per uno studio," 396.

24. Visceglia, *Bisogno di eternità,* 17.

25. Women were excluded from feudal inheritance under Frederick II, but they had to be dowered. Visceglia, "Linee per uno studio," 396–397.

26. Ibid. I am grateful to Rosalba Piazza for her help in clarifying this argument for me.

27. Diomede Carafa di Maddaloni married Portia Gaetani with a contract which restricted inheritance to male successors. That clause was later annulled, because it ran against the initial act of investiture: the Maddaloni's estate had been conceded by King Ferdinand to the first Diomede Carafa "for him and his heirs of both sexes." Ibid., 398.

28. Ibid., 398–399.

29. In his *Commentaria super primo (secundo, tertio) feudorum libro* (Venice, 3 vols., 1545–1547), M. d'Afflitto listed eight cases in which deviation from the principle of male prerogative in succession was permitted. Ibid., 399.

30. Ibid., 399–401. Second sons and daughters had rights to shares of revenues of fiefs, not the fief itself, nor to share of the capital value.

31. See ibid., 402.

32. Quoted by ibid., 403.

33. Ibid., 404.

34. Visceglia, *Bisogno di eternità,* 14–15.

35. The Sanseverino, like other Neapolitan feudal aristocratic families, chose between possible regulations according to their interests. Ibid., 464; Caridi, *La Spada,* 95–140, esp. 121–122. The Sanseverino began to bar women from inheritance formally

in 1473, although they had taken practical measures to disqualify female heirs since 1447. Visceglia, "Linee per uno studio," 405–406, 436.

36. Visceglia, "Linee per uno studio," 404–405.

37. In Sicily, the demographic, economic, and financial crises of the late sixteenth and early seventeenth centuries forced the aristocracy to rigidify its marriage patterns, and increasingly strict endogamy limited to one son and one daughter among the noble class became ever more the rule from the early seventeenth century, with a corresponding increase in the number of young women who became nuns. Aymard, "Une famille," 29–66; Delille and Ciuffreda, "Scambio dei ruoli," 507–525. In non-aristocratic families, primogeniture obtained more often in practice than in theory and nuclear family households predominated throughout the seventeenth and eighteenth centuries. Benigno, "The Southern Italian Family," 168–171; Benigno, *Una Casa*, 47–72.

38. Astarita, *Continuity of Feudal Power*, 14, 159–160.

39. Muto, "Come leggere il Mezzogiorno," 55–80.

40. Astarita, *Continuity of Feudal Power*, 9, 39–67, 159–201. Feudal aristocracies throughout Europe suffered from the rise of the bureaucrats, but their responses varied. The extension of feudal privileges was not pursued elsewhere in Europe, although the exploitation of primogeniture and entail was intensified. Stone, *Crisis*; Cooper, "Patterns of Inheritance," 192–327; Billaçois, "Crise de la noblesse," 258–277. The fact that feudalism was reinforced in southern Italy at a time when it was being eroded elsewhere has tended to contribute to the dominant model of the south as "backward." Aymard, "L'Europe Moderne," 426–435.

41. The foundation of the common dowry fund in 1585 evinces that greatest contingent priority went to the clan: if the replacement of extinct families with new members was called for, preference should be given to "noblemen of the same clans to which the extinct families [belonged]." Astarita, *Continuity of Feudal Power*, 162.

42. Ibid., 163.

43. Ibid., 162–163.

44. Ibid., 161, 163.

45. Ibid., 163.

46. The practice of primogeniture and the use of entail gained ground later and more slowly in the Kingdom of Naples than in Spain and Sicily. Monter, "Protestant Wives," 208; Astarita, *Continuity of Feudal Power*, 4; Visceglia, *Bisogno di eternità*, 15.

47. Visceglia, *Territorio, feudo e potere locale*, 223.

48. Benigno, 1989, 183. Marriage contracts increasingly stipulated that a new couple should live in the groom's family palace, thereby tightening the identification of the new family with that of the groom. Visceglia, "Linee per uno studio," 465.

49. Visceglia, "Linee per uno studio," 420. Likewise, the palace of the Caracciolo Brienza at San Giovanni a Carbonara was entailed in 1671. Astarita, *Continuity of Feudal Power*, 166.

50. For aristocratic privatization of city space, see Labrot, "Comportement collectif," 68–71.

51. Visceglia, "Linee per uno studio," 421.

52. Caridi, *La Spada*, 139.

53. Ibid.

54. Visceglia, "Linee per uno studio," 424. Extension of entail to feudal property occurred later in Sicily. Aymard, "Une famille," 29–66; Motta, *Strategie familiari*, 14–21.

55. Visceglia, "Linee per uno studio," 426.

56. Ibid., 412, 416–417.

57. Ibid., 412.

58. Ibid., 416.

59. Ibid., 448.

60. The Caracciolo clan established several such funds in the last quarter of the sixteenth century. Astarita, *Continuity of Feudal Power*, 162, 164; Caracciolo di Torchiarolo, "Monti di previdenza," 337–361.

61. Caridi, *La Spada*, 115, 121–122.

62. Visceglia, "Linee per uno studio," 436.

63. Ibid., 427.

64. Quoted in ibid., 406.

65. Astarita, *Continuity of Feudal Power*, 165.

66. Ibid., 32–33.

67. Caridi, *La Spada*, 147.

68. Visceglia, "Linee per uno studio," 450.

69. Without this money the Brienza patrimony would have been lost at Giovan Battista's death, as he had accrued terrible debts. Astarita, *Continuity of Feudal Power*, 171.

70. Caridi, *La Spada*, 172.

71. Astarita, *Continuity of Feudal Power*, 172.

72. Visceglia, "Linee per uno studio," 464–465.

73. Ibid., 450 and tables 8, 9.

74. Ibid., 467–468.

75. Ibid., 450, 454–455.

76. Astarita, *Continuity of Feudal Power*, 172 and n. 28.

77. Ibid., 172.

78. Ibid.

79. Ibid., 173.

80. Visceglia, "Linee per uno studio," 454–455.

81. Ibid., 414–415.

82. Ibid., 455.

83. Quoted in ibid.

84. Ibid., 456.

85. Caridi, *La Spada*, 115.

86. For example, the Ruffo di Scilla family raised their dowry level to 60,000 ducats, and the Sanseverino established their family dowry level at 50,000. Visceglia, "Linee per uno studio," 456.

87. "She renounces family inheritance whatsoever including for her successors and promises to ratify this undertaking as many times as it is requested of her under pain of the suspension of dowry payments."

88. Ibid., 458.

89. Ibid., 458–459.

90. Ibid., 469.

91. Quoted in ibid., 433. For the Sanseverino family entails, see ibid., 422–433.

92. Ibid., 468–469.

93. By the late eighteenth century, the Neapolitan, like other aristocracies, was shrugging itself free of some of the tight ligatures of entail and sought their dissolution through royal licence. Astarita, *Continuity of Feudal Power*, 166–167.

94. Titled barons occupied important positions within the Spanish armies; cadets were usually in the lower officer ranks. Army careers became less attractive to aristocratic sons by the mid–seventeenth century, due in part to the decline of the Spanish army, in part to the "relative domestication of the aristocracy through life in the capital and at court." Astarita, *Continuity of Feudal Power*, 168–169. For the enforced religious profession of men, see Zarri et al., "De Monialibus," 653–656.

95. In the Caracciolo Brienza family of Naples, no son married before the death of his father until 1792. Astarita, *Continuity of Feudal Power*, 171.

96. The 1298 bull of Boniface VIII, *Periculoso*, which the Tridentine decree on cloister (sess. 25, Decree on Regulars, 5) renewed, applied only to certain convents. In 1566 Pius V by his edict *Circa Pastoralis* applied it to all nuns and tertiaries. Creytens, "La Riforma." In practice, of course, lawsuits did occur for the return of conventual dowries.

97. Quoted by Visceglia, "Linee per uno studio," 411.

98. De la Ville sur Yllon, "Strada di S. Giovanni," 23.

99. In this they were successful, and the seminary was built and administered by the Somaschi fathers until the end of the eighteenth century. Boys were taught accomplishments useful to the *cavaliere,* such as fencing, horsemanship, and music. Only sons of the Caracciolo family were allowed, and at its largest numbers reached twenty-five. De la Ville sur Yllon, "Strada di S. Giovanni," 23; Caracciolo di Torchiarolo, "Monti di previdenza," 348–349.

100. Zanetti, *Demografia*, 85–87.

101. Burr Litchfield, "Demographic Characteristics," 197.

102. Astarita, *Continuity of Feudal Power*, 175.

103. Ibid., 175–176. Moreover, the Caracciolo Brienza were particularly disinclined to the convent solution.

104. Ibid., 176.

105. ASN, Mon. sop., S Gregorio Armeno, 3435.

106. ASN, Mon. sop., Donna Regina, 3501, ff. 15–18.

107. ASN, S.Maria della Sapienza, 3194, f. 37r.

108. Delille and Ciuffreda, "Scambio dei ruoli," 509, 511.

109. Anyone found to be forcing "any virgin, or widow, or any other woman whatsoever" to enter a convent, except in cases provided by law, was declared anathema. *Canons and Decrees of the Council of Trent* (sess. 25, cap. 18), 249. "If a girl, being more than twelve years of age, desire to take the religious habit, she shall not take that habit, neither shall she, nor any other, at a later period, make her profession, until the bishop,

or, if he be absent, . . . his vicar, or someone deputed thereunto by them, . . . has carefully examined into the inclination of the virgin, whether she has been compelled or enticed thereunto, or knows what she is doing." Ibid., 248. However, whereas previously aristocratic women had been able to choose open convents, now that Trent had, in effect, abolished them, they were compelled to live their lives under stricter regimes, despite not necessarily enjoying any religious vocation. In turn, this situation prompted a certain laxity in enforcing the rules in aristocratic convents. Thus political and social obstacles facing rigorous visitations and enforcement of vows gradually led to less rigorous application of the rules. Creytens, "La Riforma," 73.

110. Bossy, "Counter-Reformation," 55.

111. Russo, *Monasteri femminili,* 51.

112. Ibid., 50. Similarly, a relative of Porzia San Marco, an *educanda* at S. Maria Egiziaca a Pizzofalcone, complained that she had been coerced into taking the habit there by nuns determined to get their hands on her inheritance and that they had prevented her relations from talking to her. Ibid., 51.

113. "Alle quale due figlie mie con ogni affetto possibile lasso la mia paterna beneditione, et le prego a bene[di]re memoria dell'anima mia nelle loro orationi a le quali confido assai p[er] la santissima elettione che volontariamente han' fatto della loro vita." ASN, Mon. sop., Divino Amore, 3811, f. 1.

114. Fiorani, "Monache e monasteri," 73–74.

115. Sicola, *La Nobiltà gloriosa,* 125.

116. Ibid.

117. Ibid.

118. ASN, Mon. sop., S. Francesco delle Cappuccinelle a Pontecorvo, 4540, ff. 92r, 100r, and 108r.

119. ASN, Mon. sop., S. Giuseppe dei Ruffo, 4922, f. 18.

120. Ibid., f. 18.

121. ASN, Mon. sop., S. Gregorio Armeno, 3435, f. 170r.

122. "Sig[nore] Carlo Brancaccio Governatore di Monte eretto per la q[uonda]m Giulia Caracciola ha promesso pagare al mon[aster]io di S[an]to Ligorio docati 105 p.a. p[er] l'alimenti, di Donna Isabella Acquaviva. Di più ha promesso docati mille et cinquecento per la dote di d[ett]a D. Isabella, et altri d[uca]ti 800 cioè ducati quattrocenti p[er] le spese del monacato, et d[uca]ti quattrocento per le spese della professione, et d[uca]ti cinquanta l'anno durante sua vita ed altre promesse." ASN, Mon. sop., S. Gregorio Armeno, 3435, f. 176r.

123. ASN, Mon. sop., S. Francesco delle Cappuccinelle a Pontecorvo, 4540, f. 144r.

124. Bulifon, *Giornali,* 77.

125. Ibid.

126. For this group, see Galasso, *Napoli spagnola,* 23–54.

127. Novi Chavarria, "Nobiltà di Seggio," 94.

128. Ibid.

129. Galasso, *Napoli spagnola,* 1:278, 1:285, 1:318; Novi Chavarria, "Nobiltà di Seggio," 97.

130. Ibid., 95.

131. Celano, *Notitie del Bello*, 2:201.

132. D'Engenio Carracciolo, *Napoli sacra*, 72.

133. Ibid., 73.

134. In 1590 the daughter of the convent's doctor, Diana Pisano, took the veil there; in 1594 the daughter of Giovan Francesco De Ponte, formerly holder of the position of Reggente della Cancelleria, entered the convent as an *educanda*. There between 1599 and 1623 Beatrice and Vittoria de Stefano became nuns, and in 1616 Anna Maria De Ponte, daughter of Marco Antonio, Reggente del Collaterale, became a novice. Later both Giovan Francesco and Marco Antonio De Ponte were ennobled (*attraverso la toga*). Maria de Quiros, daughter of Francesco Bernando, a member of the Sacro Regio Consiglio of 1593, entered as *educanda* in 1623. Novi Chavarria, "Nobiltà di Seggi," 107, n. 61.

135. Ibid., 93–94. For Stefano's family see Musi "Il patriziato," 123–130.

136. ASN, Mon. sop., Croce di Lucca, 3110, Expenditure of Prince Nicolo Giudice. "Prefatus vero Inq. Eccellentissimo Princeps sopradetto cora[m] nobis in vulgari eloquio pro m[aio]ri facti intelligentia [for greater understanding of the fact] dixit qualmente nell'anno 1643 essendo stato dett'Ecc[ellentissi]mo P[rincip]e dall Em[inentissi]mo P. Card[ina]le Filamarino [sic] Arciv[escov]o di q[ue]sta Città di Nap[oli] com[m]andanto che haveste asservito et aggiutato le d[ett]e s[uo]re Moniche della costrutt[ion]e della Nova fabrica, che per d[ett]e s[uo]re moniche si voleva fare, per la reedificat[ion]e del mon[aste]rio p[rede]tto, Detto Coma[n]dam[en]to fù per dett'Ecc[ellentissi]mo S[ignor]e P[rincip]e eseguito con quella puntualità che si é visto. . . . Havendo non solam[en]te in essa assistito, ma con quello amore et accuratezza che ad esso S[igno]r[e] P[rincip]e si conveniva con suoi proprj denari d[ett]o Mon[aste]rio a fundamentis principiato, et quello mandatolo quasi a perfettione." Ibid., 3610, 16v.

137. Celano, *Notitie del Bello*, 1:202.

138. Ibid.

139. Quoted by Novi Chavarria, "Nobiltà di Seggio," 96.

140. ASN, Mon. sop., Croce di Lucca, 3610, ff. 20r, 25r, 153r–155v; Novi Chavarria, Nobiltà di Seggio," 96.

141. It is significant that Celano has no hesitation in recording the figure as "more than 120,000 scudi." Celano, *Notitie del Bello*, 3:278.

142. ASN, Mon. sop., Croce di Lucca, 3610, ff. 155r–v. The obligation of the four chaplains was still adhered to as late as 1754. Novi Chavarria, "Nobiltà di Seggio," 108, n. 76.

143. For aristocratic burial arrangements see Visceglia, *Bisogno di eternità*, 107–139; "Corpo e sepoltura," 595–602.

144. Novi Chavarria, "Nobiltà di Seggio," 96.

145. Ibid., 85.

146. Labrot, "Comportement collectif," 65.

147. Novi Chavarria, "Nobiltà di seggio," p. 94.

148. For Domenico's son, Antonio Giudice (b. 1657), prince of Cellamare and duke of Giovanazzo, who purchased the Palazzo Carafa di Stigliano (later Palazzo Cellamare) in 1696, see Savarese, *Palazzo Cellamare*, 37–42.

149. Novi Chavarria "Nobiltà di Seggio," 97, 109 n. 90.

150. Cornelia Giudice married the duke of Bisaccia, Carlo Pignatelli, and after Cornelia's death, Chiara Giudice took him as her husband. Ibid., 98, 109 n. 96.

151. Ibid., 109 n. 97.

152. Aurelia and Francesca Caracciolo entered Donnaromita; Ippolita and Zenobia Pignatelli were the daughters of the duke of Bisaccia. Ibid., 98, 110 nn. 98, 99.

153. Ibid., 110 n. 99.

154. Discussing elite families in seventeenth-century Rome, Ago used the term "team games" to emphasize the complementary aspect of family members' actions. Ago, *Carriera,* 45–71.

155. For the palace, see Savarese, *Palazzo Cellamare,* esp. 37–40.

156. Novi Chavarria, "Nobiltà di Seggio," 101.

157. Ibid., 101.

158. After his death the full terms of his bequest were recorded in the conventual records in February 1729. ASN, Mon. sop., S. Francesco delle Cappuccinelle a Pontecorvo, 4540, f. 7v.

159. Ibid., f. 164r–164v.

160. They were sister Paola dell'Incarnazione (formerly D. Emanuela Diez y Gomez), sister Maria Brigida del SS. Crocefisso (formerly D. Giuseppa), sister Maria Teresa del Giesù (formerly D. Antonia), and sister Maria Vittoria della Croce (formerly D. Maria), who became a nun on 6 March 1725. Ibid., ff. 103r, 104r, 111r.

161. Ibid., f. 92r.

162. Ibid., ff. 22r, 59r.

163. Ibid., ff. 59r, 144r.

164. This issue, which I shall take up elsewhere, extends beyond the relatively well worked territory of the relationship between sanctity and social class to more quotidian aspects of the practices of holiness, particularly its spatial practices.

CHAPTER 4

1. Russo, *Monasteri femminili,* 20–37; ASN, Mon. sop., S.Maria della Consolazione S. Maria della Consolazione, 4672, f. 175ff.

2. Russo, *Monasteri femminili,* 20.

3. ASN, Mon. sop., S. Maria Donnalbina, 3307, and S. Maria della Consolazione degli Afflitti, 4672, ff. 12–17. The Consolazione's history wryly observes that this income has diminished, because the convent's expansion prompted incorporation of this property.

4. For example, special bequests occupy over 300 pages of the conventual record of S. Francesco delle Cappuccinelle of 1734. ASN, Mon. sop., S. Francesco delle Cappuccinelle a Pontecorvo, 4540, ff. 22r–190v.

5. ASN, Mon. sop., S. Maria della Consolazione, 4672, f. 41.

6. Ibid., f. 37.

7. The bequests were made in 1619 and 1631. ASN, Mon. sop., S. Maria della Consolazione S. Maria della Consolazione, 4672, f. 51.

8. Mongitore, *Compendio della vita,* 87–88.

9. See also Weaver, "The Convent Wall," 73–86.

10. Tertiaries lived in convents, in communal households with other tertiaries, or with their families. See Creytens, "La Riforma," 1, 46–49.

11. Boccadamo, "Bizzoche," 361.

12. Ibid., 369; Russo, *Monasteri femminili*, 55–57.

13. Mazzucchelli, *Monaca di Monza*, 28.

14. The daughter of Giovanni Angelo Muscettola and Laura Caracciolo, Scolastica entered S. Giuseppe dei Ruffo at age fourteen, with a dowry of 1,000 ducats "to be paid after her mother's death." ASN, Mon. sop., S. Giuseppe dei Ruffo, 4922, ff. 15, 20–28.

15. Russo, *Monasteri femminili*, 54; ASN, Mon. sop., S. Gregorio Armeno, 3451, passim. Elsewhere in Italy, as in Naples, dowries varied, despite attempts to establish standard sums. See Zarri et al., "De Monialibus," 688.

16. Russo, *Monasteri femminili*, 58.

17. Ibid., 58, 58 n. 128.

18. ASN, Mon. sop., S. Francesco delle Cappuccinelle a Pontecorvo, 4540, f. 4r. Nevertheless, at the Sapienza dowries rose to 3,000 ducats by the 1630s.

19. Russo, *Monasteri femminili*, 58.

20. ASN, Mon. sop., S. Francesco delle Cappuccinelle a Pontecorvo, 4540, f. 4r.

21. Russo, *Monasteri femminili*, 54.

22. Ibid., 54, 54 n. 112.

23. When, for instance, sister Ippolita Sebastiano, daughter of Tommasina Candido and Giovan Francesco, the Razionale of the Reale Camera della Sommaria, decided in 1622 to leave the convent of S. Francesco delle Cappucinelle a Pontecorvo, where she and her sister had become nuns in September 1607, the convent repaid to her family only half of the annual income on her dowry. ASN, Mon. sop., S. Francesco delle Cappuccinelle a Pontecorvo, 4540, f. 22r.

24. ASN, Mon. sop., S. Monica, 4637, f. 13r.

25. Ibid., f. 11r.

26. Ibid., ff. 12v–13r.

27. Neapolitan convents perhaps did rather better than their counterparts in Rome. By the mid–seventeenth century, Roman convents frequently complained about the inadequacy of their means of subsistence, the decline in income, and the impossibility of increasing the number of nuns in order to obtain larger dowry income, all arising from regulations governing convents. Fiorani, "Monache e monasteri," 80.

28. Strazzullo, *Edilizia e Urbanistica*, 221.

29. Vargas Macciucca, *Dissertazione*, lxviii.

30. ASN, Mon. sop., S. Giuseppe dei Ruffo, 4922, f. 26.

31. Ibid.

32. Russo, *Monasteri femminili*, 69. See p. 92 above.

33. This practice extended throughout the peninsula and to France and Spain.

34. Russo, *Monasteri femminili*, 64.

35. Ibid., 60.

36. Ibid., 68.

37. She received 40 ducats as *vitalizio,* 100 for when she took the veil; 100 ducats for when she would be sacrestana; and a further 100 for when she took up the conventual post of *cellarara.* Ibid., 90.

38. Vargas Macciucca, *Dissertazione,* iii.

39. ASN, Mon. sop., S. Monica, 4637, f. 10r.

40. De Maio, *Società e vita religiosa,* 106–107. Greatest concern arose if a convent was financially unstable. Brett, "Humbert," 20–21.

41. ASN, Mon. sop., S. Maria della Consolazione, 4672, f. 8.

42. Ibid., f. 10.

43. Quoted by Monti, *Ricerche,* 193–194.

44. Ibid., 196–197.

45. Bonazzi, *Dei veri autori,* 3 n. 2.

46. ASN, Mon. sop., S. Giuseppe dei Ruffi, 4933, n.f.

47. Scarano, "La Chiesa e il monastero," 59.

48. Macciucca, *Dissertazione,* cxii–cxiii.

49. "Ammiransi alcuni e dicono, che questo monistero dovrebbe avere assai più pingue il Patrimonio di quello, che al presente egli tiene: considerando, che dal tempo de la fondazione sin oggi per tante doti di Defonte Monache in esso rimaste, a la peggior lettura di una ogn'Anno ascenderebbero al numero di doti duecento quali calculate a ragione de ducati mille duecento l'una avrebbero un pieno dotale à più di ducati duecento quaranta mila, con aggiongersi ancora l'escadenze, ed Eredità dal medesimo acquistate, e non di poca considerazione: e per conseguente dovrebbe tenere le mura d'oro de la propria clausura." ASN, Mon. sop., S. Maria della Consolazione, 4672, f. 6.

50. Ibid.

51. ASN, Mon. sop., S. Monica, 4637, ff. 10–11.

52. ASN, Mon. sop., S. Francesco delle Cappuccinelle a Pontecorvo, 4540, ff. 5v–6r.

53. ASN, Mon. sop., S. Gregorio Armeno, 3435, f. 192.

54. Scarano, "La Chiesa e il monastero," 59.

55. Similarly, the dowry of 2,000 ducats of the Reverend sister Margarita Arcamone was spent by the same convent in June 1751 on the new parlatory and adjacent buildings. Ibid., 60.

56. The Decrees of the Sacra Congregazione stipulated that lay sisters should not have blood sisters (and preferably not other relations either) in the same religious house. But having a relative inside the same convent was not seen as a problem for boarders (*educande*) and nuns (*monache*), except in the more extreme instances. When three or more sisters entered the same convent, the third had to pay a higher dowry and was deprived of active and passive voice until the death of a sister. Russo, *Monasteri femminili,* 65, n. 155.

57. Quoted by Russo, *Monasteri femminili,* 72.

58. Colombo, *Il Monastero,* 28, 28 n. 5.

59. Ibid., 28 n. 5.

60. Pane, *Monastero di S. Gregorio Armeno,* 48.

61. Monti, *Ricerche,* 181.

62. Ibid., 181, 202.

63. Ibid., 182.

64. "Solamente una donna per servitij chiamata sor Catarina et uno breviario . . . ritrovò la Sig. Antonia Abate novitia et una sorella secolare chiamata Lucrezia Abbate, senza però roba sua, ma solo una campana, uno campanello et alcuni panni d'altare." ASN, Mon. sop., Sapienza, 3170, 4.

65. The list of these items is published as document 1 in the appendix to Monti, *Ricerche*, 211, and is to be found in ASN, Mon. sop., S. Maria la Sapienza, 3190, f. 702A.

66. The spiritual directors of the Sapienza and the nuns' confessors were initially Gaetano da Tiene and Giovanni Marinono (see fig. 6). Up until 1538 Theatines were responsible for conducting mass at the Sapienza; after that date this duty fell to two chaplains of the clergy. Monti, *Ricerche*, 184–185. For the ensuing controversy, see BNN S. Martino, 99, ff. 35r–58r. For the spiritual and personal debt to his sister articulated in Gian Pietro Carafa's letters, see Monti, *Ricerche*, 212–339. See also BNN S. Martino 90, ff. 263r–255v.

67. Ibid., 201.

68. D. M. Marchese's *Vita della venerabile serva di Dio suor Maria Villani*, published in Naples in 1778, is the principal source for this story. Hagiographic and uncritical in tone, it is an invaluable source not only in terms of delineating the story, but also in its fine-tuning of the narrative, with telling inclusion of and emphasis on *topoi* of spirituality, family worth, and so on. This narrative is complemented by the records of protracted legal cases kept in the archive pertaining to the convent of Divino Amore.

69. Marchese, *Vita*, 1–3; Celano, *Notitie del Bello*, 1:263.

70. Marchese, *Vita*, 3.

71. Ibid., 5–7.

72. Ibid., 15.

73. Giovanni Villani's wife, Eleonora di Costanza, was the daughter of a Carafa. ASN, Mon. sop., Divino Amore, 3811, f. 78r.

74. Celano, *Notitie del Bello*, 1:264.

75. Marchese, *Vita*, 53.

76. Ibid.

77. Ibid., 116–124.

78. Ibid., 124.

79. Ibid., 126–129.

80. Ibid., 129.

81. Ibid., 130–134.

82. Ibid., 138.

83. Ibid., 135.

84. Ibid., 140–141.

85. Ibid., 138–140.

86. Ibid., 142–143.

87. Ibid., 143.

88. Russo, *Monasteri femminili*, 44.

89. Marchese describes sister Maria Dorotea Villani as Maria Villani's sister cousin

(*sorella cugina*). Marchese, *Vita*, 147. Celano states that fifteen nuns accompanied sister Maria from S. Giovanni Battista. Celano, *Notitie del Bello*, 1:264.

90. Celano, *Notitie del Bello*, 3:779.

91. Ibid., 3:776–779; Chiarini, *Aggiunzioni* to ibid., p. 780.

92. ASN, Mon. sop., S. Giuseppe dei Ruffo, 4922, f. 6.

93. Ibid., ff. 1, 8.

94. Ibid., f. 1.

95. Ibid., f. 4.

96. The chapel was founded by Caterina in execution of her father's will, in which he requested her to procure a worthy burial place if his brother Fabrizio failed to procure a place in S. Domenico Maggiore, where the most prestigious families of the Nido Seggio had their own chapels. The most prestigious of all these chapels had once belonged to the Ruffo di Montalto family, but they had sold it to the Carafa della Spina, princes of Stigliano. Caridi, *La Spada*, 151.

97. Celano, *Notitie del Bello*, 3:93, 3:98.

98. Ibid., 1:234–235.

99. The inscriptions read as follows: on the right, "D. Fabrizio Ruffo nato al 1619 de' Duchi di Bagnara eletto Gran Croce et Priore di Bagnara al 1641 et dopo Gran Priore di Capua occupato in molte cariche anco di Capitan Generale delle Galere di Malta nel 1660 prese tre saiche et la fortezza di s. Veneranda Calorno et Piazza di Lampicorno"; and on the left, "Et nel 1661 un ricchissimo vascella armato a guerra et a 27 agosto di s. Ruffo messe a fundo 7 galere turche et altre 4 dopo una fiera battaglia prese e condusse in Malta dove sono dipinte e registrate in cancelleria et in honore e lode di s. Ruffo a sue spese ha eretta questa cappella facendo ricco monte a beneficio de' Ruffi." Fabrizio Ruffo entered the order of Malta, was made captain general of the Knights of St. John of Jersualem, and received the titles of prior of Bagnara and grand prior of Capua. He was renowned for his naval victories against the Turks and for his effective administration of his patrimony, especially through the foundation of the Monte of the Grand Prior in 1691, which was of long-lasting and profound benefit to his family. See Caridi, *La Spada*, 146–147, 149–150, 189.

100. ASN, Mon. sop., S. Giuseppe dei Ruffo, 4922, ff. 161–162.

101. Ibid., ff. 1–16. Sonnino is in Lazio.

102. Ibid., f. 16.

103. Ibid., f. 17.

104. "Venne da Roma D. Anna Colonna and Sig. D. Vitt. Colonna sua sorella con due loro create e smontorno dritto alla porta del Mon[aster]io poi fatta un poco d'oratione alla Chiesa ricevute le visite d'alcune Sig[no]re che erano concorse p. tal effetto, entrorno con titolo d'educatione nel monasterio." Ibid., f. 17.

105. Ibid. For Anna Colonna Barberini, see Dunn, "Spiritual Philanthropists."

106. "Ill.rò questa sig.ra nostro mon.ro non meno con la nobiltà di costumi e virtù sue che con la chiarezza del sangue, diede sempre singolo esempio di modestia." Ibid., 4922, f. 17.

107. Dunn, "Piety and Patronage," 651–653.

108. Marilyn Dunn has shown that individual nuns played a vital role in the

patronage of building and artwork in convents in Seicento Rome. She has usefully faulted the too-ready assumption that abbesses were the principal instigators of art patronage, showing how individual nuns played a crucial role. Dunn, "Nuns as Art Patrons," 451–477. The picture in southern Italy is similar but is more marked by interventions driven by extraconventual family ambition.

109. See Kealy, *Dowry of Women Religious*, 29; Fiorani, "Monache e monasteri," 81–82; Dunn, "Nuns as Art Patrons," 451–452. Kate Lowe observes that in fifteenth-century Florentine patronage, "some projects—such as raising walls, building churches, refectories and dormitories—seem to have been more popular than other less status-driven works, such as roofing or routine maintenance." Lowe, "Nuns and Choice," 27.

110. See Visceglia, "Linee per uno studio," 413. *Vitalizi* are, therefore, one of the signs of the shift in noble conceptions of the family from the clan with all its branches to the linear nuclear family.

111. Vargas Macciucca, *Dissertazione*, vii.

112. Russo, *Monasteri femminili*, 56.

113. Ibid. In 1663 at S. Francesco delle Cappuccinelle, eleven out of thirty-three choir nuns enjoyed *vitalizi*.

114. "Che le sovvenzioni annue che s'assegnano alle monache particolari per le loro religiose necessità siano da principio volontarie, e le Monache poi siano obligate à tener j frutti di religiose necessità solamente, e ch'il residuo s'impieghi negl'usi communi del Monastero, compiacendosi però V.S. Ill.ma d'avertire, che di queste sovvenzioni si faccino fare promesse ben cautelate da Parenti, e procurando, se sarà possibile, che da medesimi s'assegnino in qualche entrada particolare, sicura, ed esigibile." Letter of 16 November from the Sacra Congregazione dei Regolari in Rome to the *Vicario* of Naples. ASN, Mon. sop., S. Francesco, S. Francesco delle Cappuccinelle a Pontecorvo, 4540, f. 4r.

115. ASN, Mon. sop., S. Maria della Consolazione degli Afflitti, 4672, f. 17.

116. "Esistente per suo fondo donatili contanti da alcune moniche particolari dall'avanzo de vitalizij." ASN, Mon. sop., S. Monica, 4637, f. 5r.

117. ASN, Mon. sop., S Giuseppe dei Ruffi, 4926, n.f.

118. Ibid., n.p.

119. Ibid., n.f.

120. The Cottone titles included that of marquis of Altamira, counts of Bavuso, and princes of Castronuovo and Villermate. Vittoria Cottone's paternal uncle, Scipio Cottone, is described in the document as "olim Principe Ville armose [at that time Principe di Villermate]." ASP, Lionti, 5520, ff. 262r–262v.

121. ASP, Notaio DF. Lionti, sala VI, busta 5520, ff. 262r–282r. See Sola, "Decorazione marmorea." I am grateful to Chris Brunelle and Jonathan Clark for their help in interpreting the document.

122. ASP, Notaio f. Lionti, 5520, f. 263r. In her absence, responsibility was to devolve to the current Prioress of the convent, "et in eorum et cuiusl[ib]e[t] eorum defecta?u d[icta]e Rev[erenda]e Priorisse que p[ro] temp[or]e erit." Ibid., f. 264r.

123. "In illis rebus et operibus ad d[icta]m Sorore[m] Felice[m] Vittoria[m] oretenus comun[ica]tis p[ro] execq[utio]ne voluntatis d[ict]i q[uo]nd[am] Ill[ustr]e de Cottone d[ict]e Rev[eren]de Sororis Hier[oni]me qua mortua." Ibid., f. 267v.

124. "I d[ett]i mobili oro et argento che resterà doppo la sua morte habbia da

pervenire in potere di detta Soro Ger[oni]ma Felice sua sorella, p[er] servirsene p[er] uso proprio." Ibid., f. 279r.

125. Ibid., f. 279v.

126. Ibid., f. 263v, 265v.

127. "Pro elemosina Pauperum egentiu[m] et precise illorum qui non possunt pro eorum reputatione ambulare mendicantes ac pro elemosina pauperum carceratoru[m]." Ibid., f. 263v.

128. Ibid., ff. 262v, 266r.

129. Ibid., ff. 263v–264r.

130. Ibid., 264r–264v.

131. Ibid., ff. 264v, 265v, 267v.

132. For this church and its iconographic program, see Hills, "Iconography and Ideology," 16–31, and Marmi Mischi, 145–164.

133. See, Hughes, "Representing the Family," 7–38.

134. This was the case in Venice. Chojnacki, "'Servir a Dio.'"

135. See Terpstra, *Lay Confraternities.*

136. ASN, Mon. sop., S. Giuseppe dei Ruffi, 4922, f. 52.

137. Anon, *Vita della serva di Dio sor Celestina Raineri*, 20–21.

138. ASN, Mon. sop., S. Maria Donn'Albina, 3307, ff. 287r–288r; 689r.

139. ASN, Mon. sop., S. Maria Donn'Albina, 3307, f. 765r.

140. "D Francesco mio la curiosité non amette dilazione, l'avviso come q[ue]sta matina e venuto da me D. Liborio q[ua]le desiderava parlarli, ma io per non incomodando con farlo scendere mi q. pigliato il carico di scriverli, in tanto a portato a voce il parere del Sig[no]re D. Antonio Carnavale q[ua]le non a voluto dalo in scritto per non dare gelosia, tanto piu che N[ost]ro pezzo fu a trovarlo e lui disse che era stato al monastero, ma non sapeva q[ue]lla che doveva fare, li dice pero che V.S. procura amichevolmente accordare il detto come a incominciato e si potra estendere sino a millequattro cento ducati; non volendosi il detto accordare allora si parlará d'altra maniera io domani a Dio piacendo doppo la Santa messa saró a parlarli benche mi sia ben espressata il detto non a trovato altro divario che io(?) appoggi sia 30 carlini e non venti e il legmame/seginam dato per l'intaglio q[ua]nto li disse del resto tutto andava bene; e viva mille anni il suo affetto giustizia, ed attenzione che usa a q[ues]to Santo luogo il Sig[no]re ce lo rimunerará mentre non ho talenti per ringraziarlo q[ua]nto devio p[er] D: Cioe/Cice e la riv: io ho detto 1400 p[er]che mi pare che v.s. stava intenzionato alli 1340 [che] lui vuole che vi potete astendere secondo il n[ost]ro conto." ASN, Mon. sop., S. Maria Donn'Albina, 3307, f. 1028r.

141. A dispute followed when sister Maria Costanza fell ill and moved to the convent of Donnaregina where she renewed her vows. Both convents claimed her money. Colombo, *Il Monastero*, 34.

142. Ibid., 56–57.

143. Quoted in ibid., 57–58.

144. ASN, Mon. Sop, S. Giuseppe dei Ruffi, 4933, unfoliated.

145. Rizzo, *Cinquantadue affreschi*, 34.

146. Ibid., 43.

147. Ibid., 37.

148. ASN, Mon. sop., S. Giuseppe dei Ruffi, 4926, n.f.

149. Ibid., n.f.

150. On 14 July 1688 sister Chiara Maria Ruffo completed payments to the goldsmith Matteo Treglia of 3,000 ducats for this pyx: "A Sig[no]r Matteo Treglia Orefice ducati dittanta [sic] cinque, quali sono à complim[en]to di ducati trecento atteso q[ua]li altri l'hà ricev[u]ti . . . quali somo p[er] li intiero prezzo di materiali, come di magistero della cassetta, seu custodia tutta di rame indorata fatta da esso p[er] la chiesa di d[ett]o no[st]ro Mon[aste]rio secondo la forma del modello et ordine datoli dal Sign[no]re Cavaliere Dionisio Lazzari," Ibid., n.f.

151. Ibid., n.f.

152. Celano, *Notitie del Bello,* 3:425.

153. Bulifon, *Giornali,* 88.

154. Peccerillo, *I Ragioni,* 9.

155. This was in spite of attempts by Church authorities to limit such expenditure (e.g., *Lettera circolare per li monasteri e conservatorii di questa Città di Palermo,* addressed to Reverend Mothers and other female superiors by the Sacra Congregazione dei Regolari, published in Palermo in July 1708).

156. That the Good Friday dinner was getting out of hand in this way emerges from an edict issued by the Archbishop of Palermo in 1654: "la Cena del Giovedi Santo si faccia con semplicità Religiosa senza forgio, ò apparati, ma in tutto si conformino con le rubriche, and ordinationi della Santa Chiesa." *Editto,* Palermo, 1654, n.p.

157. Russo, *Monasteri femminili,* 98.

158. Ibid., 110.

159. Quoted in ibid., 74.

160. ASN, Mon. sop., S. Maria della Consolazione, 4672, f. 111.

161. ASN, Mon. sop., Regina Coeli, 1975, fasc. 12, n. 14, unfoliated.

162. Russo, *Monasteri femminili,* 88.

163. ASN, Mon. sop., Regina Coeli, 1975, fasc. 12, n. 10, unfoliated.

164. Ibid., fasc. 12, n. 4, unfoliated. I think it dates from the 1640s, to judge from its relative position, handwriting, etc.

165. Ibid., fasc. 12, n. 10. Valuable goods were generally given or sold on to family members or to other nuns; battered goods and old clothes were usually given as alms.

166. Ibid., fasc. 12, n. 9, unfoliated.

167. "Già disponeva farsi una cella molto bene adobbata, di sedie, quadri, scrittorj, ed altre superfluità curiose, ed in particolare introdurvi un ricco, e prezioso orologio." Marchese, *Vita,* 69.

168. Quoted by Strazzullo, *Edilizia e Urbanistica,* 223.

169. ASN, Mon. sop., S. Gregorio Armeno, 3435, "Esemplare delle nobili memorie della Reverenda D. Fulvia Caracciola," f. 125r.

170. Rizzo, *Cinquantadue affreschi,* 37.

171. Vittorelli, *Vita di suor Maria Aurelia Cecilia,* 96.

172. Thus in 1629 the Sacra Congregazione dei Regolari attempted to limit this problem by monitoring it.

CHAPTER 5

1. For example, in 1541 Paul III bought up, demolished, and rebuilt houses so as to construct a street line submissive to the corner of his Palazzo Farnese. Its corner stands tall and proud, elbowing its way into via Monserrato, apparently indomitable in the urban environment. For a discussion of urbanistic strategies in baroque Rome see Joseph Connors's remarkable essay "Alliance and Enmity," 207–294.

2. Celano, *Notitie del Bello*, 1:65.

3. For aristocratic jostling in the newly opened Pizzofalcone quarter, see Labrot, "Naissance et croissance," lv.

4. ASN, Mon. sop., S. Giuseppe dei Ruffi, 4919, f. 48v.

5. "Dal quale per ogni angolo si vede monti, e mare, con gran parte della Città." ASN, Mon. sop., Donn'Albina, 3211, f. 5.

6. Chiarini, *aggiunzioni* to Celano, *Notitie del Bello*, 3:425.

7. Celano, *Notitie del Bello*, 4:666.

8. Ibid., 3:779.

9. Vittorelli, *Vita di Suor Maria Aurelia Cecilia*, 96.

10. Anon., *Vita della Serva di Dio Sor Celestina Raineri*, 38.

11. Ibid.

12. Ibid., 38–39.

13. Ibid., 39.

14. Ibid.

15. Celano, *Notitie del Bello*, 2:634–636.

16. "Come si è pratticato in altre chiese, dando li Campanili unione, e simetria alle facciate delle Chiese, e molto più alla chiesa di Donna Regina, per havere una piazza, e largo grandissimo avanti, e con la prospettiva al Palazzo di V.E. in modo che nella pianta fatta l'anni passati si lasciò il detto luogo vacuo, perche dovea servire per il campanile." Sacra Congregatione Episco[po]rum and regularium Emin. and Reverendiss. D. Card. Carpieno Praefecto Neapolitana Campanilis pro RR. Monialibus D. Reginae. Summarium, Roma, 1682. ASN, Mon. sop., S Giuseppe dei Ruffi, 4919, f. 96r.

17. Ibid., f. 33r.

18. Ibid.

19. Ibid., ff. 46r–445r.

20. "Non era necessario, ma puramente voluntario, per magnificenza." Ibid., f. 46r.

21. "Domandando tener bisogno d'alzare il muro della clausura, anco quello all'incontro del Monastero di S. Giuseppe, coll'apparente pretesto di far loggia, ed altre officine necessarie da dentro il lor monastero, per poter aver la licenza di fabricare, ma il vero loro disegno era di far un'altro ben grande belvedere, tentato più volte con altri Superiori, e sempre denegato, per ragion dell'incongruità del luogo, e per il pregiudizio del Monastero di S. Giuseppe." Ibid., f. 46r.

22. Ibid., ff. 53r–56v, "Reverendissimo D. Albergato Decano Neapolitano Campanilis. Opinio cuiusdem Architecti seù mathematicis pro vener. monasterio Donnae Reginae." Rome, 1685.

23. "Ad aequilitatem muri antiqui." Ibid., f. 46r.

24. "Per pura emulatione, e certissimo, consciosacosa che per fare le dette officine,

dormitorii, o altro, non tengono di bisogno ne tanpocho di alzare il muro della clausura infino al vecchio anzi di diminuirlo; però volere la libertà di poterlo alzare quanto le sia agrado, e per fare al monastero di san Giuseppe un grandissimo danno senza verun loro utile, ma danno, poiche alzando più del anticho, vengono ad oscurare, non solo un unico, e ben piccolo belvedere, che tiene il Monastero di San Giuseppe, ma qualche più importa, e dispiace al detta Monastero di s. Giuseppe, il fenestrone del Choro, in guisa tale, che anco in giorno più luminoso s'avrebbero da recitare gli Divini Oficii con candele accese." Ibid., f. 47r.

25. "Non era necessario, ma puramente volontario, per magnificenza . . . per pura emulatione." Ibid., ff. 46r, 47v.

26. "Questa decisione della Sacra Cong[regazio]ne non pose argine all'attentati del Monistero di D. Alvina, mentre da tempo, in tempo tentorono delle altre innovazioni." ASN, Mon. sop., Donn'Albina, 3323, f. 3r.

27. Ibid., ff. 5v, 25r–25v.

28. Quoted in Colombo, *Monastero*, 24.

29. Ibid.

30. That wing looked over the road of S. Pietro a Maiella, on which stood the rear of the Palazzo Conca. Ibid., 24–25.

31. Ibid., 26, 26 n. 2.

32. ASN, Mon. sop., S. Francesco, S. Francesco delle Cappuccinelle a Pontecorvo, 4540, ff. 1r–1v.

33. Ibid., f. 2r.

34. Ibid., ff. 2r, 4v.

35. Shortly afterward Silvia Ricci returned to her first convent for reasons that remain unclear. Ibid., f. 3r.

36. Dowries were used in this process. Ibid., f. 4v.

37. After staying at S. Francesco, Mother Teresa gave it 132 Spanish dubloons (594 ducats) before returning to her convent in Palermo in June 1628. Ibid., f. 3v.

38. "L'alzamento da farsi della cupola, li veniva ad impedire il beneficio non meno del sole, che de li venti." Ibid., f. 6v.

39. "Per prima, che ogn'uno nel proprio suolo ben può erigere gli Edificj sin' alle stelle. Per seconda, che alli predetti Conservatorio, e monistero veniva frammezzata la Strada Regia. E terzo . . . per la gran distanza, che v'era tra l'uni e l'altro luogo, non poteva recar ombra di pregiudizio al Conservatorio." Ibid., f. 6v. As Tommaso Astarita has reminded me, *ombra di pregiudizio* might simply mean here "any prejudice at all," but I have translated it more literally to pick up the point advanced by the Maddalena about light.

40. Ibid., ff. 6v–7r.

41. Ibid., f. 7r.

42. "La compra si era fatta dal Mon[astero] del Giesù non perché gli fusse utile, ne necessaria, ma solo per causa, che stando vicino di sito a questo Mon[astero], pretendeva sotto detto pretesto esiggere dal med[esim]o alcune convenienze circa l'altezza de la fabrica da questo facienda." ASN, Mon. sop., S. Maria della Consolazione, 4672, f. 9.

43. Ibid., ff. 9–10.

44. Generally speaking, houses belonging to one religious order were not clustered

together in Naples. For instance, the Franciscans were scattered between S. Maria delle Consolazioni, S. Francesco Cappuccinelle in Pontecorvo, S. Antonio di Padova, and S. Chiara; even the smaller Basilian order was not centralized, having houses at S. Gregorio Armeno, S. Maria Donnaromita, and S. Maria Donnaregina. Something of a clustering of Dominicans does occur, however, in the northwest of Naples, where, expressive both of their interconnectedness and their separateness, S. Maria della Sapienza and S. Giovanni Battista delle Monache, a subsidiary foundation, stand almost opposite each other.

45. "Per liberarsi dà pericoli di altre controversie, nelle quali con essi altre volte si erano trovate." ASN, Mon. sop., SS. Marcellino e Festo, 2882. Printed document dated 19 August 1720, n.p.

46. They were granted the concession for 166.66 ducats.

47. ASN, Mon. sop., SS. Marcellino e Festo, 2882, published document dated 18 December 1758, n.p.

48. Ibid., published document dated 19 August 1720, n.p.

49. "La qual strada sarà di grandissimo commodo al publico, & al trafico, possendo per detta strada communicarsi le robbe dallo quartiere della Marina del Vino al quartiero di sopra giacchè non vi è altra che dia detta commodità, se non la strada di Mezzocanone, e la strada delle ferri vecchi." Ibid., undated pamphlet, n.p.

50. "Comodo grande, vaghezza, ed abellimento alla Città." Ibid., f. 322r–322v.

51. "Si mascherano e fanno scudo del finto zelo dell'utilità publica." Ibid., undated pamphlet, n.p.

52. Ibid., published pamphlet, undated (c. 1720), n.p.

53. "Tanto però è lontano che la nuova strada sia di publico beneficio, anzi che più toste sarebbe dannevole al commune, sì perche rinferrandosi le case nel Collegio, diverrebbe sempre più angusta la Città, e dovrebbero quei abitatori ritrovars'altra stanza più lontana al lor mestiere." Ibid., undated pamphlet, c. 1720, n.p.

54. "Nel Mon[aster]o di s. Marcellino vivono le donne del primo ordine di questa Città, le quali per servir' à Dio, e publico bene, havendosi eletto menare la lor' vita in perpetua clausura, post'in non cale i diletti del mondo, e commodo delle proprie case, sono meritevoli di tutta la maggior' equità, ed attenzione, acciò non si pentono del loro stato, e per l'innanzi non s'arrestino dal professarvi." Ibid., undated printed pamphlet, c. 1720, n.p.

55. The rents of 166 ducats and 6 carlini paid by the Benedictines to date for the disputed properties was returned to them. Ibid., n.p.

56. "Per renderlo di maggiore ampiezza," Ibid., undated pamphlet (c. 1714), n.p.

57. Ibid., n.p.

58. Especially a document published 18 December 1758. Ibid., n.p.

59. "IMP. CAES CAROLO VI AUSTRIACO AUG. EX. AUCTORITATE. VII VIRIUM MUR. AQ. VIIS. CURANDIS PATRES SOCIETATIS JESUS. DETERRIMUS SEMITIS QUA AEDIUM AMBITUM LAXARENT OCCLUSIS VIAM HANC PRO DIGNITATE URBIS FACILOOREM AMPLIOREMQUE LATAM IN PORRECTUM PAL XVI IN ANFRACTO PAL.XXII. DE SUA PECUNIA FACIENDUM SILICEQUE STERNENDAM, CURARUNT IDEMQ.VII VIRI PROBABUNT ANNO MDCXXXIII." Celano (ed. Chiarini), *Notizie del Bello*, 3:678. The inscription is still legible, though not easily accessible.

60. On 5 November 1720. ASN. Mon. sop., SS. Marcellino e Festo, 2882, published pamphlet dated 18 December 1758, n.p.

61. Ibid., undated pamphlet (c. 1750), n.p.

62. Ibid., undated pamphlet (c. 1750), n.p.

63. Ibid., f. 419r.

64. On 18 June 1728 the Barlettane, followers of the Neapolitan preacher Barletta, finally reached a point of no return in their frustration at the Jesuits' blocking the enlargement of their convent of the Vittoria. A procession of twenty-eight professed nuns and eight maidservants, following their superior bearing a crucifix, departed from the convent. In their hands they carried rosary beads; but under their habits each had hidden a stick. And they made for the neighboring Jesuit college. The royal governor and the bishops of Trani and Bisceglie failed to placate them. The Jesuits fled their college to avoid scandal, but eventually managed to co-opt the energetic intervention of the marshal, Carafa, who ordered a halt to the new building as constituting a *pregiudizio al castello*. Although the Barlettane were unsuccessful in their attempts to expand, this case indicates that quite scandalous strategies were open to female religious, protected as they were by the fundamental contradiction of the functions of female orders. Strazzullo, *Edilizia e Urbanistica*, 201–202.

65. Ibid., 202–204.

66. ASN, Mon. sop., S. Francesco delle Cappuccinelle a Pontecorvo, 4540, f. 6r.

67. Ibid., f. 5r.

68. For the sum of 2,703.1.13 ducats. Ibid., f. 5r.

69. ASN, Mon. sop., SS. Marcellino e Festo, 2812, f. 141r.

70. Ibid., ff. 148r–149r.

71. Ibid., f. 150r.

72. "Si è sempre goduto." Ibid., f. 150r.

73. Nuns' response of 6 December 1738. Ibid., ff. 157v–158r.

74. ASN, Mon. sop., SS. Marcellino e Festo, 2812, f. 2.

75. Maggio, *Vita*, 40–41; Savarese, *Francesco Grimaldi*, 181.

76. Savarese, *Francesco Grimaldi*, 181.

77. Ibid.

78. Quoted in ibid., 182. See also above, 97–98.

79. Colombo, *Monastero*, 15; Savarese, *Francesco Grimaldi*, 182. A small part of this street remains in Vicoletto di S. Pietro.

80. Colombo, *Monastero*, 18–21.

81. Ibid., 21–22.

82. Ibid., 22.

83. Ibid., 23.

84. De Lellis, *Aggiunta*, 1:248.

85. Savarese, *Francesco Grimaldi*, 183.

86. Colombo, *Monastero*, 47.

87. Savarese, *Francesco Grimaldi*, 183.

88. I am grateful to Tim Benton for the observation that the façade is emphatically

secular and to John Pinto for suggesting that the references to the garden loggia of the Villa Mandragone in Frascati or the Loggia dei Lanzi in Florence may have been intended to recall the tradition of grand urban loggias.

89. See Gleijeses, *Chiese e Palazzi*, 247.

90. Celano tells us that the facade was unfinished in its upper stage; and Blunt suggests that Fanzago may have planned an elaborate upper story, with an open loggia. Blunt, *Neapolitan Baroque*, 72. Fanzago's task here was to add a facade and a vestibule to Grimaldi's church. Payments to the builders are recorded between 1638 and 1641, and a terminus ante quem is provided by a document of 1653. Ibid., 71. Fanzago's role has been disputed by Ulisse Prota-Giurleo on the basis of a 1653 contract made by Giacinto and Dionisio Lazzari and two marble workers, Francesco Valentini and Simone Tacca, to end their association, listing the works they had executed together, including "la facciata e chiesa del Monasterio della Sapienza." Prota-Giurleo argued that Grimaldi, not Fanzago, was the architect. It seems likely that, as Blunt suggests, Fanzago was indeed the architect, as Celano and Parrino claimed, and that Prota-Giurleo's document sheds light on the builders and marblers responsible for the facade of La Sapienza. Ibid., 71–72, n. 50. Gaetana Cantone, while emphasizing the role of Orazio Gisolfo in directing the execution of the facade, affirms Fanzago's role by noting that the marble workers documented at La Sapienza, including Francesco Valentino, Giacono Lazzari, and Matteo Pelliccia, along with Paolo Gallo, recorded as working on the floor, and Orazio Pacifico who supplied the *piperno* stone, were all frequent coworkers of Fanzago's. Cantone, *Napoli Barocca e Cosimo Fanzago*, 191–200, 232. Silvana Savarese has offered a modification to Blunt's interpretation. She suggests that the facade remained rough, perhaps because of shortages of money, until 1649 (which would explain the second consecration in 1649, following the first in May 1641), but it was not complete when Celano saw it before the publication of his book in 1692. She interprets the exactitude of "la facciata e la Chiesa del Monastero della Sapienza" in the 1653 document, contrasting it to that of 1640 ("l'opera del Monasterio della Sapienza di questa Città"), when the partnership of the three men was established, as further indication that the facade was added in the later period. Savarese, *Francesco Grimaldi*, 189. See also Nappi, "Giovan Giacomo Conforto," 113–134.

91. Blunt, *Neapolitan Baroque*, 72.

92. Cantone, *Napoli barocca*, 203–204.

93. Such an approach matches, too, the dedication to Wisdom.

94. Blunt, *Neapolitan Baroque*, 72.

95. Cantone, *Napoli barocca*, 204.

96. Borromeo, *Instructiones*, 3:12. See also Antinori, *Scipione Borghese*, 114–115.

97. This genealogical line descends from St. Peter's and includes Bernini's S. Bibiana (1624); S. Gregorio al Celio (1633), where the entablature supported by coupled columns recalls Martino Longhi the Elder's solution in the restoration of S. Maria Maggiore for the Jubilee of 1575; and S. Caterina a Magnanapoli (1624–1640). However, the Sapienza owes most to S. Sebastiano fuori le mura (1609–1613) by Flaminio Ponzio and Giovanni Vasanzio, where the use of arches rather than a straight entablature over coupled columns, what Alessandro Antinori calls the "pseudo-

serliane," was unprecedented in ecclesiastical architecture in Rome. Hibbard, *Palazzo Borghese*, 69; Antinori, *Scipione Borghese*, 31–223, esp. 115, 118–119.

98. Connors, "Alliance and Enmity," 219–220.

CHAPTER 6

1. For Archbishop Filomarino's stipulations with regard to Neapolitan convent churches, see Russo, *Monasteri femminili*, 74. In Palermo, Archbishop Rubio ordered that conventual church doors must be locked before two o'clock at night and must not be opened on Good Friday before dawn. *Editto*, Palermo, 1658, n.p.

2. Quoted by Patetta, "L'Età," 14.

3. For a brief, illuminating discussion of parlors in seventeenth-century Roman convents, see Dunn, "Spaces Shaped."

4. Sixtus V stipulated in 1590 that permission of the Sacra Congregazione dei Regolari was required by regulars who wished to talk to nuns (of whatsoever order) in their parlatories (a rule which Urban VIII in 1623 and many archbishops all over Italy were forced to reiterate). For example, the archbishop of Palermo rehearsed the threats in April 1654 (*Editto*, Palermo, 1654). Enforcing the regulation was bound to be difficult, but it was made more so by Urban VIII's granting to ordinaries the exceptional right to grant a license giving permission four times a year to a regular monk wishing to talk to a nun to whom he was related first or second degree.

5. See Amirante, *Architectura Napoletana*, 90–94. Compare the organization of men and women's bodies at the celebrated Cistercian monastery of S. Martino in Naples, where women had a separate small church to avoid the Cistercian monks (and the lay brethren had their own choir separate from the monks' choir behind the main altar). Celano, *Notitie del Bello*, 4:96.

6. The wheel for receiving goods was in the *stanza della Rota* between the atrium and the women's parlatory on the right of the entrance.

7. The inscription on the stone placed in the hallway leading into the church reads: "Sacram hanc aedem cum sepolcrali cripta tres et sexanta sacerdotes sub Immacolatae Conceptionis Mariae auspiciis congregati aere suo a fundamentis posuere anno MDCXL idem laxata cripta sedem conventui condiderunt." The plague of 1656 and the consequential economic difficulties caused interruptions and put a brake on building until 1678, when Guglielmelli received the task of finishing the existing small church. Amirante, *Architettura Napoletana*, 54.

8. Another plan (Fig. 10; ASN, Mon. sop., S. Maria di Gesù delle Monache, 3168, pta. 2) shows the kitchen farther away from the coach entrance (at "16"). This plan probably antedates Fig. 4 (S.M. della Consolazione 4672), because the area at top right is marked as separate small spaces, "old houses which were of the convent of S. Maria della Consolatione," while in Fig. 4 (SM. della Consolazione 4672) these spaces are rationalized and incorporated into the convent as kitchen and bakery. On the other hand, the fact that the proposed belltower is shown only in Fig. 10 (ASN, Mon. sop., S. Maria di Gesù delle Monache, 3168, pta. 3) might indicate a later date for this drawing.

9. Celano, *Notitie del Bello*, 3:59.

10. Ibid., 3:60.

11. Social-spatial practice within the church contributed to the production of sacred space, as did theological discourses, liturgical prescription, and the decoration, banners, *ex votos*, processional floats, and paintings in the church space.

12. In the writings of, for example, Isidore of Seville, the Venerable Bede, Hrabanus Maurus, and Dante. Randolph, "Regarding Women," 28. Roberta Gilchrist found that the cloister was more likely to be on the north in medieval nunneries than it was in male monastic houses (where cloisters were on the south). Gilchrist, *Gender and Material Culture*, 133–135.

13. The exact mechanics of dividing the sexes in church are impossible to reconstruct, and the ephemerality of the textile barriers themselves makes interpretations based on these objects alone particularly rash. Randolph, "Regarding Women," 27.

14. Jerome, "Commentariorum in Epistolam ad Ephesos libri III," quoted by Randolph, "Regarding Women," 28.

15. Savonarola inveighed against the practice of advertising nubile daughters in church space: "Look at the customs of Florence—how the Florentine women marry their daughters, they put them on display, and attire them so that they appear to be nymphs; and the first thing they do is to take them in to Santa Reparata. These are your idols, which you have placed in my temple." Savonarola, *Prediche*, 387.

16. Dante Alighieri *Vita nuova*, trans. M. Musa (1973), 8. Quoted in Randolph, "Regarding Women," 36.

17. Ibid., 36, 38.

18. Gonzaga, *Alcuni avvertimenti*, 108.

19. Gilchrist's suggestion that the form of medieval conventual churches was determined by the fact that nuns could not perform masses is inadequate. *Gender and Material Culture*, 97.

20. It is arresting in this respect that early Italian *vitae* of female saints sometimes stress seeing the Eucharist over eating it. Bynum, *Holy Feast*, 140.

21. The principle of the panopticon is an annular building with a watch tower at its center and cells around its periphery. Backlighting allows the supervisor to watch the prisoners in the cells, but they cannot see whether they are being observed or not. Thus the architecture participates in the system of surveillance. See Foucault, *Discipline and Punish*, 200.

22. Boureau, "L'Imene," 794–795. Adrian Randolph has argued that female sight was associated with seduction in fourteenth- and fifteenth-century Florence: "Sight, figured as the sensory linchpin, controls the entire body." He quotes Francesco Barbaro, who called the gaze "the most acute of all senses . . . [from which] all motions of the person [body] arise." Randolph, "Regarding Women," 36.

23. For the post-Tridentine linking of government of the soul with good household management and other female virtues, see Casali, "Economia e Creanza," 555–583. For models of female aristocratic behavior, see Visceglia, *Bisogno di eternità*, 141–174.

24. For instance, it receives careful attention in *Constitutioni delle Monache . . . di S. Andrea*, 3.

25. Borromeo, *Instructiones* 32 and 33, 87.

26. Ibid., 87, 91. The window of the main altar had been discussed in the First

Provincial Council of 1565, but Borromeo extended regulations further than that council. Voelker, "Borromeo's Influence," 187, n. 30.

27. Camiz, "Virgo Non-Sterilis," 142. Camiz appears to be unaware of the wide discrepancy between prescription and practice.

28. Such an observation connects to the useful accounts of the sexualization or charisma of sacred space, by Bornstein, Hamburger, and Randolph, although those scholars were not concerned with the organization of interior spaces of female convents in relation to the sexualized dynamics driven by the eroticizing force of the gaze. The very purity and enclosure of young virgins made convents irresistible to certain sexual appetites.

29. Scarano, "La chiesa," 52. Sadly, limitations of space prevent me from citing the quoted documents here.

30. Ibid.

31. For the social significance of music to nuns, see Monson, "Disembodied Voices," 191–209.

32. "Portavano la barà quattro Diaconi del Capitolo et di quattro Cavalieri accompagnandola tenevano la mano sopra la bara sino alla Chiesa dove si posava p[er] farnesi l'Esequie delli R[everen]di Can.ci restando le Moniche in la Chiesa sopra nel Choro." ASN, Mon. sop., S. Gregorio Armeno, 3435, Caracciolo, "Borro ó sia Esemplare," ff. 124v–125r.

33. "Si monacavano per mano dell'Abbadessa. Un giorno doppo detto le Vesperi, ove troncava alle Monache le trezze à curto, e dopò alcuni mesi, ò Anni secondo l'età pigliavano il secondo ordine, che'erano alcune dignità nel Choro." ASN, Mon. sop., S. Gregorio Armeno, 3435, Caracciola, "Borro ó sia Esemplare," f. 126r.

34. Vittorelli, *Vita di Suor Maria Aurelia Cecilia*, 87.

35. Ibid., 5.

36. Strictly speaking, it was founded as a conservatory in 1674 and became a convent in 1702. Cantone, "I conservatorii," 212.

37. "A forza di relevante suon di Campana non saprebbero raggiungere la divin contemplazione." ASN, Mon. sop., S. Francesco delle Cappuccinelle a Pontecorvo, 4540, f. 9.

38. Anthony Blunt noted this development in 1975, but his observation has not been pursued. Blunt, *Neapolitan Baroque*, 43, 100–101. See Hills, "Cities and Virgins," 29–54.

39. This type was well established among Cistercian female monasteries throughout Europe well before Tridentine reform. Patetta, "L'Età di Carlo," 169–170.

40. Ibid., 170.

41. Patetta, "Tipologia," 11–71.

42. The Clarissans had such churches in Bergamo, Chieri, Cuneo, Ferrara, Foligno, Modena, Mondoví, Naples (S. Chiara), Porto Maurizio, Reggio Emilia, Venice, and Vicenza; and the Dominicans at Bergamo, Chieri, and Florence; and the Augustinians in Florence, Modena, and Venice. Patetta, "L'Età di Carlo," 170.

43. In Milan S. Radegonda, a thirteenth-century Benedictine church, was rebuilt along those lines to accommodate enclosure in the late fifteenth century; fifteenth-century Dominican "double" churches include S. Maria della Vittoria, S. Maria delle Vetere, and the convent of the Dame Vergini della Vattabbia; and the fourteenth- and

fifteenth-century Franciscan churches of S. Chiara, S. Apolinnare, and S. Orsola; and the fourteenth-century Humiliate at S. Maddalena al Cerchio. Patetta, "L'Età di Carlo," 170–171.

44. S. Maurizio was founded in the seventh or eighth century, but the church (begun 1503), attributed to Bramantino or Zenale, was probably the result of a radical rebuilding of an earlier double church. Fiorio, *Le chiese di Milano,* 84. The church was remodeled between 1503 and 1510 or 1519, probably from a preexisting double church, which in turn perhaps dated back to the convent's adoption of claustration in 1444. Patetta, "L'Età di Carlo," 172. Certainly the division of the church by the transversal wall was complete before 1523, when Bernardino Luini began to decorate it on both the public and nuns' sides with frescoes. Winkelmes, "Taking Part," 104. Frescoes on the intrados of the nuns' choir-platform have been dated to c. 1510–1515, indicating a slightly earlier date. Patetta, "L'Eta di Carlo," 172.

45. Winkelmes, "Taking Part," 102.

46. Patetta, "L'Età di Carlo," 173–174; for S. Vittore a Meda, see Grassi, "Iconologia," 38.

47. Patetta, "L'Età di Carlo," 174.

48. Quoted in Weddle, "Enclosing Le Murate," 250, n. 351.

49. Such an interpretation is at odds with Luciano Patetta's. He conceives of architectural reforms as responding to prescription from ecclesiastical hierarchies. Patetta, "L'Età di Carlo," 169–183, esp. 170, 173–174.

50. Patetta, "L'Età di Carlo," 175–176.

51. Ibid., 177.

52. Ibid.

53. There is uncertainty about the precise date and authorship of this church, as Grimaldi died in the same year that the church was begun. The plans of this church were prepared shortly before Grimaldi's death in 1613, but building probably did not begin until after 1621; and it continued into the 1630s. After July 1625 Giovan Giacomo is recorded at the site, assisted by Nicolò Francesco Cuomo. Blunt, *Neapolitan Baroque,* 71; Colombo, "S. Maria della Sapienza," 59, 67; and Savarese, *Francesco Grimaldi,* 187.

54. The attribution of the church design to Grimaldi stems from Celano, but given the differences between this church and Grimaldi's other churches, it seems sensible to assume that his design was radically changed after his death. Celano, *Notitie del Bello,* 3:54. Giovan Giacomo Conforto, who directed the building of the church between 1625 and 1628, may have been responsible. Nappi, "Giovan Giacomo Conforto," 114.

55. The church was formally opened and blessed on 25 May 1641. Colombo, "S. Maria della Sapienza," 56.

56. By contrast, Grimaldi breaks the entablature no fewer than four times over each group of clustered pilasters in the nave at S. Paolo Maggiore, Naples.

57. Savarese, *Francesco Grimaldi,* 187.

58. Sister Eufrosina da Silva belonged to a noble family of the Capuana Seggio. Although destined to marry Emilio Caracciolo, count of Biscari and son of Ferrante Duke of Airola, while an *educanda* in the Franciscan convent of S. Girolamo, she decided to dedicate her life to God. Having taken her vows in S. Girolamo, she determined, together with Ippolita Caracciolo, daughter of the same duke of Airola, to

establish a convent adopting the strict rule of the Third Order. Celano, *Notitie del Bello,* 4:662.

59. Ibid.

60. Ibid., 4:663.

61. Fracanzano received 524 ducats for this work. Colombo, *Monastero,* 54.

62. I am grateful to Bruce Boucher for this observation.

63. Blunt, *Neapolitan Baroque,* 100–101.

64. Ibid., 44.

65. See Bruzelius, "Hearing Is Believing," 87–89; "Queen Sancia," 78, 80–81.

66. Bruzelius, "Hearing Is Believing," 88.

67. Bruzelius interprets the change in the position of the nuns' choir at S. Chiara in Naples as reflecting a change in women's veneration of the Eucharist, including an emphasis on the importance of seeing the altar and the host on it. Ibid., 83–91.

68. Del Pesco, *L'Architettura del Seicento,* 227.

69. "Buttare a terra le lamie, tanto della Chiesa di Fuora quanto di dentro e ivi farvi l'intempiature di tabule a modo di gaveta, stucchiate bianche, per alleviamento delle mure d'esse Chiese." ASN, Mon. sop., S. Francesco dell'Osservanza, 4511, f. 53.

70. "Farvi una gelosia per il Choretto di dentro per l'officio della notte, e commodità d'inferme." Ibid., f. 52.

71. Celano regards the distance from the dormitories to the nuns' night choir at SS. Trinità as a sign of their piety. Celano, *Notitie del Bello,* 4:666.

72. ASN, Mon. sop., S. Francesco delle Cappuccinelle a Pontecorvo, 4540, 7v.

73. "Vicino al quale [l'altar maggiore] è altro coro dà officiare, ed intagliata, à guisa dell'altro Coro già descritto, e posto a frontiera di questo." Ibid., f. 7r.

74. "Ma perché questo [il coro antico] ave l'ingresso dal piano del Claustro, che p[er] la situazione della nostra Città vien' ad essere il pian terreno del monistero, in tempo d'inverno volendo usare le Signore p[er] il matutino, ed altre ore notturno, vi usciva ad esse, ed alle S[uore] avanzate di qualche incomodo, motivo p[er] cui anticamente avendo voluto a questo riparare, si era formato al piano del primo Dormitorio un Coretto dalla parte d'Oriente, quale quantumque bislungo, a d'ogni modo p[er] l'angustia rendeva incomodo alle Signore nella recita de' Divini Ufficj p[er] la confusione della voce, e p[er] il calore che questo acquistava in istato, che alle S[uor]e veniva a vacillare la testa, non essendo altro intervallo tra l'una Sig[nor]a dirimpetto all'altra. che palmi sei. Di più, a tal inconvenienza di sopra espressato si aggiungeva ancora, che la recita sud[ett]a de' Divini Ufficj non veniva a farsi avanti il ven[erabi]le a tenore de' Statuti Pontificij, e questo anche operava in modo che volendo far la visita al ven[erabil]e qualche sig[nor]a inferma, non li riusciva, p[er] non calare all'ampiente." ASN, Mon. sop., S. Gregorio Armeno, 3430, ff. 116r–117r.

75. "Si ritrovavano in d[ett]o Mon[aste]rio circa cinq[uan]ta Monache et ciascheduna haveva serve, camere, ristretti, cucine, cantinem et altre commodità, tenevano molte serve per loro servigi delle q[ua]li ciascheduna Monaca teneva il peso doppo alcuni Anni della loro servitù, dotarle et collocarle honoratam[en]te, non come

serve, ma con molta amorevolezza." ASN, Mon. sop., S. Gregorio Armeno, 3430, Caracciola, "Borro. ol sia Esemplare," f. 125r.

76. Roberto Pane plausibly suggests that among Fulvia Caracciolo's motivations for writing her account of this "gran mutatione," or "great transformation," was the fact that she herself played an active part in it, as administrator of the building works. Pane, *Il monastero*, 48.

77. Ibid., 47.

78. Chapters 32 and 33 of Charles Borromeo's *Instructiones fabricae et supellectilis ecclesiasticae* (1577) follow the spirit of the Council of Trent in insisting on strict enclosure for female convents. Unlike Trent, the instructions are explicit and attempt to fuse monastic discipline to architectural design. They consist of precautionary measures to be taken in the design of female convent churches. The church should not have a chancel choir (*cappella maior*), but a transverse wall should separate the inner church from the outer church in which the priest must celebrate mass. "Cappella maior nulla in ea insit, sed paries in transverso fiat, quo interior ecclesia ab exteriori, ubi sacerdos sacrum facit, dividatur." Borromeo, *Instructiones*, 87.

79. "E conspectu altaris in transverso eo pariete fenestra fiat, unde moniales Missae sacrum spectent et audiant. . . . Cautio sit, ut fenestra altaris clathrata ita constituatur, ne inde in viam publicam, praesertim ubi spectacula aguntur, aut multitudinis frequens transitus est, prospici possit." Ibid., 87, 91. Voelker, "Borromeo's Influence," 187, n. 30.

80. *Canons and Decrees*, sess. 13, caps. 1–8.

81. Jungmann, *The Mass*, 93–104; Bossy, "The Mass," 29–61.

82. Bynum, *Holy Feast*, 204, and Bynum, "The Female Body," 178–182. References to cravings for frequent communion are common in *Vite* of individual nuns of the baroque period. See, for instance, Anon., *Vita della Serva di Dio Sor Celestina Raineri*; Anon., *Vita della Serva di Dio Suoro Teresa Benedetta*; Mongitore, *Compendio*. On female devotion and the Eucharist in Palermo, see Mongitore, *Palermo Divoto*. For female religiosity and the Eucharist in the baroque period more generally, see especially Matter, "Interior Maps," 60–73; Rapley, "Women and the Religious Vocation," 613–631.

83. Bynum, *Holy Feast*, 58–59. "As encounter with the Eucharist came to mean binding unto oneself either the inebriating joys of mystical union or the unspeakable pain of God's suffering, hunger became a powerful metaphor for desire." Ibid., 66.

84. Celano, *Notitie del Bello*, 4:623.

85. "Rimanendo p[er]ciò la Chiesa, come una casa vedovata, e le povere monache come smarrite pecorelle, non havendo luogo dove riposare potessero, giache l'uso loro era sempre di frequentare il S[antissi]mo Sacramento." ASN, Mon. sop., S. Gregorio Armeno, 3435, f. 134v.

86. McGinness, "Roma Sancta," 108–116.

87. Ibid., 108–109. Vittorelli, *Lettere Spirituoli*, 6.

88. Rodriguez, *Practice of Perfection*, 2:569–572. I am grateful to Frederick McGinness for his help in thinking about the relationships between the Eucharist and chastity and for recommending Alfonzo Rodriguez to me.

89. Ibid., 2:570.

90. Ibid.

91. Rodriguez, *Practice of Perfection*, 2:552.

92. Quoted in McGinness, "Roma Sancta," 109.

93. Rodriguez, *Practice of Perfection*, 2:570.

94. McGinness, "Roma Sancta," 108–109.

95. Quoted in ibid., 111.

96. McGinness, "Roma Sancta," 114–116.

97. Scholars drew on ascetical writers in the Desert Fathers' tradition, such as John Cassian, John Climacus, and Gregory Nazianzen, to support these notions. McGinness, "Roma Sancta," 109.

98. Celano, *Notitie del Bello*, 3:61.

99. Blok, "Notes," 29. See also Fiume and Scaraffia, "Premessa," 703–704.

100. Fiume and Scaraffia, "Premessa," 704.

101. Celano, *Notitie del Bello*, 3:777.

102. For instance, at S. Francesco a Pontecorvo gilt metal adorned both choirs and the *coretti*: "Sopra di detta porta è il sudetto coro da officiare con sua gelosia intagliata, e posta in oro . . . vicino [all'altare Maggiore] è altro coro dà officiare, ed intagliata, à guisa dell'altro Coro già descritto . . . Dalla parte di sotto il cornicione di detta Chiesa vi sono sei coretti con loro gelosie indorate." ASN, Mon. sop., S. Francesco delle Cappuccinelle a Pontecorvo, 4540, f. 7v.

103. "Sopra di detta porta è il sudetto coro dà officiare con sua gelosia intagliata, e posta in oro . . . Dalla parte di sotto il cornicione di detta Chiesa vi sono sei coretti con loro gelosie indorate." This appears in the "Iscrizione di questa nuova Chiesa principiata à fabbricarsi in Gennaro 1712." ASN, Mon. sop., S. Francesco delle Cappuccinelle a Pontecorvo, 4540, f. 7v.

104. Blok, "Notes," 29.

CONCLUSION

1. I am using architecture as metaphor in a material sense, distinguishing it from its more frequent employment as abstract metaphor, as in Rabelais's Abbey of Thélème, Montaigne's tower, or Teresa of Avila's interior castle. The best discussion of metaphor remains Ricoeur's "Metaphorical Process," but see also Turner, "Social Dramas and Ritual Metaphors," 23–59.

2. "The metaphor," writes Ricoeur, "is not the enigma but the solution of the enigma." Ricoeur, "Metaphorical Process," 144.

3. See Sennett, *Flesh and Stone*, for a path-breaking attempt to tell a city's history through people's bodily experiences.

4. More research is needed on the social uses of Neapolitan palaces, but see Labrot, *Baroni in città* and "Comportement collectif," 22. For Roman palaces in this period, see Waddy, *Seventeenth-Century Roman Palaces*, 25–31.

5. The presence of an apartment of women attendants was the principal feature distinguishing female from male apartments. The women had individual rooms, a common kitchen and dining room, and a *rota* to allow them to receive food and supplies without having contact with men. Men, meanwhile, often had small private staircases

and exits, such as the spiral staircase that allowed Giovanni Battista Borghese to come and go from Palazzo Borghese's northwest wing unobserved. Waddy, *Seventeenth-Century Roman Palaces,* 29–30.

6. I owe this characterization to Weddle, "Enclosing Le Murate," 40.

7. Brown, "Late Antiquity," 267–270.

8. De Luca, *La Dama e il Cavaliere,* 487–505. Gilchrist makes the same point in relation to medieval nuns and secular women of the upper classes. Gilchrist, *Gender and Material Culture,* 167–169.

9. The space of public worship was one of the few public spaces open to women. Randolph, "Regarding Women," 17.

10. ASN, Mon. sop., S. Francesco delle Cappuccinelle a Pontecorvo, 4540, f. 4v.

11. " 'Ad oggetto che j due Palazzi comprati dal detto Monistero per la sudetta causa, non erano capaci di commoda residenza per le sue Religiose, le quali, in occasione della nuova Clausura seguita, s'andavano accrescendo, si pensò dal med[esim]o attendere alla compra d'un altro." Ibid., f. 5r. Such aggressive expansion was possible only with the support of the Royal Council, a good deal of wrangling, and the systematic exploitation of incoming dowries.

12. Ibid., ff. 5v, 6r, 10r.

13. For the different patterns that developed after Trent in France, see Rapley, *The Dévotes,* 7–8.

14. "La clausura è cosa principale per conto del voto della castità." Alessandro de' Medici, Trattato sopra il governo de' monasteri, 16.

15. Foucault argues that architecture changes late in the eighteenth century: "A fear haunted the latter half of the eighteenth century: the fear of darkened spaces, of the pall of gloom which prevents the full visibility of things, men and truths. It sought to break up the patches of darkness that blocked the light, eliminate the shadowy areas of society, demolish the unlit chambers where arbitrary political acts, monarchical caprice, religious superstitions, tyrannical and priestly plots, epidemics and the illusions of ignorance were fomented. The chateaux, lazarets, bastilles and convents inspired even in the pre-Revolutionary period a suspicion and hatred exacerbated by a certain political overdetermination." From being concerned with making manifest power, divinity, and might through palace, church, and stronghold, architecture began to tackle new problems, using the disposition of space for economic-political ends. In this regard, especially in schools, Foucault argues that control over sexuality becomes inscribed in architecture. Foucault, *Power / Knowledge,* 148, 150, 153. I find Foucault's discussion stimulating, but many of the ideas which he locates as eighteenth-century developments reach back much earlier, even if the architectural forms he individuates as being their fullest articulation occurred in the eighteenth century.

16. Ardia, *Tromba Catechista,* 2:103–104.

17. Douglas, *Purity and Danger,* 121.

18. Zarri, "Recinti sacri," 381–386.

19. Chiesa, *Riflessioni religiose,* 12.

20. For the tension between conceptions of virginity as moral and physical (exemplified above all by St. Augustine and St. Jerome), see Fiume and Scaraffia,

"Premessa," 701–714; Boureau, "L'Imene e l'ulivo," 791–803; and Sissa, "La Verginità materiale," 739–756. See also Bugge, *Virginitas*; and Atkinson, "Precious Balsam," 131–143.

21. For a useful discussion of the ideology of enclosure, including several of the following examples, see Weddle, "Enclosing Le Murate," 29–39.

22. Bernardino da Siena, *Prediche volgari*, 2:859–888.

23. Ibid., 862.

24. Alberti, *On the Art of Building*, 28.

25. Ibid., 141.

26. Ibid., 139–140.

27. Convent architecture resembled that of prisons in other ways also, just as their organization and functions paralleled contemporary prisons. It is striking that the first time prisons were used for punishment, and long-term punishment at that, in France was in relation to women guilty of fornication, adultery, or prostitution (that is, sins of concupiscence). Not only did Louis XIV's 1684 ordinance link prostitution with sin, requiring physical penance and spiritual conversion, but it also established the connections between sin, punishment, and imprisonment in relation to women found guilty of prostitution, fornication, and adultery. In itself the refashioning of imprisonment to police women's chastity is significant. It is even more noteworthy that the women's prison of the Salpêtrière was run along lines reminiscent of a convent. Seventy-five lay *soeurs*, assisted by eight priests, ran the prison. Prayer, devotional reflection, and spiritual exercises were allotted in fifteen-minute intervals between cleaning, weaving, and carding wool. The sisters (chaste, unmarried, and widowed women who received a pension and lifelong employment within the prison) administered discipline, led the prayers, and recorded the prisoners' penitential progress. Borromeo's *Istructiones* was among the literature used to determine whether women were truly contrite. Riley argues that female imprisonment at the Salpêtrière, where penance, conversion, and spiritual instruction were linked, was overridingly religious in character. At Bon Pasteur, a private refuge in Paris for 120 women, lust (not sloth) was the capital sin. Those women chose to expiate their sins by accepting a life of mortification, silence, obedience, and work. Riley, "Michel Foucault," 41, 43. The picture is complicated by the fact that a considerable number of convents were converted to prisons, especially in France after the Revolution. Evans, *Monastic Architecture*, 4.

28. Foucault, *Discipline and Punish*, 136–137. Foucault argues that "the classical age discovered the body as object and target of power." He acknowledges that even before the eighteenth century the body had become the object of imperious investments, but identifies concern with the body as focused on "elements of behaviour or the language of the body" rather than "the economy, the efficiency of movements, their internal organization" which it later became. What was earlier restricted to monasteries, armies, and workshops came to be extended in the seventeenth and eighteenth centuries to be general formulas of domination. For Foucault this is "an uninterrupted, constant coercion, supervising the processes of the activity rather than its result," which is exercised according to a codification that partitions time, space, and movement as closely as pos-

sible. These "disciplines" made possible attentive control of the body's operations, allowing the constant subjection of its forces and imposing upon them a relation of "docility-utility." These controls were different from slavery, from service and vassalage. The eighteenth-century regulation of bodies is different from asceticism or monastic discipline, in that the latter sought to achieve renunciations rather than increases in utility and had as their principal aim "an increase of the mastery of each individual over his own body." Ibid.

29. Gadamer, *Truth and Method,* 159.

30. For a stimulating discussion of the relationship between architectural decoration and body adornment, see Scott, *The Rococo Interior.*

31. Russo, *Monasteri femminili,* 67.

32. Lefebvre, *The Production of Space,* 220.

33. Anon., *Vita della serva di Dio sor Celestina Raineri,* 40.

34. *Regola e Constitutioni,* Turin, 1671, 33.

35. "La quale veste era la prerogativa che donava alle Monache la voce attiva, e passiva, e le faceva partecipi delli beni del Mon[aster]io." ASN, Mon. sop., S. Gregorio Armeno, 3435, f. 126v.

36. "Li giorni feriali s'ufficiava in choro con un manto negro, senza di cui non si posseva dire un piccolo verso in quel luogo." Ibid., "Esemplare delle nobilii memorie," f. 126v.

37. Russo, *Monasteri femminili,* 221. For plays performed in convents, see Weaver, "The Convent Wall in Tuscan Convent Drama," in Monson, *Crannied Wall,* 73–83.

38. These were inveterate abuses that had been ruled against by Alfonso Carafa in 1564.

39. Maggio, *Vita,* 455. Although the official author is F. M. Maggio, the text makes clear that priorers Angelica Caterina Carafa was also responsible.

40. Ibid.

41. "Sicut enima Altare debet esse omnino coopertum, sic Monialis and Mulier Deo sacra and dicata." Ibid., 456.

42. Maggio, *Vita,* 452.

43. Ibid.

44. Ibid., 457.

45. Weddle, "Enclosing Le Murate," 235.

46. Russo, *Monasteri femminili,* 99.

47. These practices were widespread throughout Italy. See Lowe, "Secular Brides," 41–65.

48. Russo, *Monasteri femminili,* 90.

49. Conspicuous consumption and luxury furnishings were also very much the case in mundane wedding celebrations. This needs further exploration, but see P. Allerston, "Wedding Finery in Sixteenth-Century Venice," in Dean and Lowe, *Marriage in Italy,* 25–40. Kate Lowe has observed something of the parallels between the ceremonies of marriage and of consecration. Lowe, "Secular Brides," 41–65.

50. Vargas Macciucca, *Dissertazione,* vi.

51. Turner, *Ritual Process,* 97.

52. Vargas Macciucca, *Dissertazione,* vii.

53. Ibid.

54. ASN, Mon. sop., S. Maria Donn'Albina, 3307, f. 633r.

55. Ibid.

56. ASN, Mon. sop., S Giuseppe dei Ruffi, 4922, f. 161.

57. Ibid., f. 172.

58. "Non solo portò la sua musica ma ce fece venire altri forastieri et molte solenne fece lui la funtione e si parò tutta la Chiesa e fora." Ibid., f. 170.

59. Vittorelli, *Vita di suor Maria Aurelia Cecilia,* 94.

60. Vargas Macciucca, *Dissertazione,* vi.

61. "Solamente nell'ingresso un'onesta ricreazione volontaria, che non ecceda in tutto la somma di Carlini 5 per ciascuna monaca." ASN, Mon. sop., S. Francesco Cappuccinelle a Pontecorvo, 4540, ff. 3v–4r.

62. *Bullarum privilegiorum,* vol. 4, part 4, p. 195.

63. See Hills, "Cities and Virgins," 29–54.

64. "Quale quantumque bislungo, a d'ogni modo p[er] l'angustia rendeva incomodo alle Signore nella recita de' Divini Ufficj p[er] la confusione della voce, e p[er] il Calore che acquistava in istato, che all SS[uo]re veniva a vacillare la testa, non essendo altro intervallo tra l'una Sig[nor]a dirimpetto all'altra, che palmi sei." ASN, Mon. sop., S. Gregorio Armeno, 3430, f. 116v.

65. *Editto,* [April 1658], n.p.

66. For instance, an *editto* issued by Archbishop Rubio in Palermo in February 1664 threatens nuns who speak to anyone apart from their mothers, fathers, brothers, or sisters without written permission from the vicar general with the deprivation of active and passive voice for four months. *Editto,* Palermo, 1664, p. 1.

67. *Constituzioni delli Convertite degli Incurabili,* quoted in Russo, *Monasteri femminili,* 103–104, n. 281.

68. Russo, *Monasteri femminili,* 104.

69. Quoted in ibid., 84.

70. Ibid., 104.

71. Gregory XIII prescribed regular episcopal visitations to inspect convents.

72. Russo, *Monasteri femminili,* 73.

73. Quoted in Weddle, "Enclosing Le Murate," 253 n. 359.

74. Alberti, *On the Art of Building,* 140.

75. Likewise, attempts were made to guard against the widespread practice whereby nuns made gifts to their confessors. Any priest who received such presents risked having his license to hear confessions revoked. Cardinal Filomarino was charged in 1652 by the Sacra Congregazione dei Regolari with checking the accounts of convents of Regina Coeli and the Sapienza in this regard. Russo, *Monasteri femminili,* 91.

76. Ibid., 103.

77. Quoted in Weddle, "Enclosing Le Murate," 252, n. 357.

78. "Dietro l'Altare maggiore vien costrutto il Communicatorio tutto di marmo bianco con sua portellina d'ottone," ASN, Mon. sop., S. Francesco delle Cappuccinelle a Pontecorvo, 4540, f. 7v.

79. *Constitutioni delle povere Capuccine,* 26.

80. See Bynum, *Holy Feast,* 260–269. Other scholars argue that manipulation of food is a rejection of societal expectations, an assertion of their autonomy (Bell, *Holy Anorexia*), and others see eating in sexual terms (Schutte, "Inquisition," 110).

81. Russo, *Monasteri femminili,* 116.

82. Ibid., 93, n. 259.

83. *Editto,* 1654, n.p.

84. "Una gran parte delli predetti zuccari va per l'esattioni delle entrate del monastero, e si fanno notabili presenti a diversi per havere il pagamento della Corte e Città, avendone il monastero 124,000 scudi di capitale. Di più parte de zuccari si da per le liti e ad altre persone che servano il monastero, come ad avvocati, procuratori, scrivani, officiali, esattori, chierici, servitori del monasterio, Medici, chirugi, sagratori, ed altre persone simili." ASN, Mon. sop., S. Maria la Sapienza, 1590, f. 78.

85. Ibid.

86. The most famous such discussion is Foucault's of the panopticon. Foucault, *Discipline and Punish,* 195–228.

87. Agostino Valier, *La istituzione,* 3:18.

88. Celano, *Notitie del Bello,* 3:68–70.

89. Ibid., 3:70.

Glossary

SOURCES: Catella Salvati, *Misure e pesi nella documentazione storica dell'Italia del Mezzogiorno*, Naples, 1970; R. Villari, *The Revolt of Naples*, trans. J. Newell, Cambridge, 1993; Tommaso Astarita, *The Continuity of Feudal Power*, Cambridge, 1992.

Arrendamento: Tax farm.
Bizocca: House nun.
Camera della Sommaria: See Sommaria.
Canna: Unit of measurement equivalent to 8 *palmi* or 2.109 meters.
Canone: Land lease.
Carlino: One-tenth of a ducat; 10 *grani*.
Carro: Surface measure, equivalent to 60 *tomoli*, about 24.5 hectares; dry measure equivalent to c.40 kg.
Catasto: A direct tax or the land survey drawn for fiscal purposes.
Cona (Conetta): Image or icon; small glass reliqmaries.
Consiglio Collaterale: Instituted by Ferdinand of Aragon in 1507, the highest political-administrative council of the kingdom, with administrative, legislative, and judiciary functions.
Conversa: Lay sister.
Corista: Choir nun.
Donativo: Fiscal contribution to the king; originally voluntary and voted by parliament, but by the late sixteenth century an ordinary tax of 600,000 ducats a year, to which *donativi* were added.
Dotario: One-third of the husband's feudal goods or their monetary value.
Ducat: Unit of money equivalent to 5 *tarí*, 10 *carlini*, 100 *grani*.

Educanda: A boarder in a convent.

Eletti: The "Elect," the elected representatives of the five aristocratic Seggi, plus the representative of the People (Popolo) in Naples. The *Eletti* therefore constituted the city council.

Gabella: An indirect tax.

Grano: One-hundredth of a ducat. 1 *grano* = 12 *sestini* = 24 *cavalli*.

Legato perpetuo: Perpetual bequest.

Luogo di Monte: Government bond.

Maritaggio: Dowry contribution assigned by any public or private Monte.

Moggio: Surface area measurement, 900 square *passi* of 7.5 *palmi* each, equivalent to 0.336 hectares.

Monte di Maritaggi: Dowry fund.

Oncia: Unit of money equivalent to 6 ducats.

Palma: Unit of measurement equivalent to 0.26 meters.

Paraggio: Minimum dowry guaranteed by feudal law to all barons' daughters who married.

Passo / Trapasso: Unit of measurement equivalent to 7 *palmi* or 1.85 meters.

Pinzochera: House nun.

Prammatica: Royal law.

Rosciato or Rosato: Pink or purple cloth.

Relationes ad Limina: Reports to Rome of episcopal visits.

Rotolo: A measure of weight, equivalent to 0.89 kg.

Sacro Regio Consiglio: Sacred Royal Council, the royal tribunal and the highest appeal court in the Kingdom of Naples. It also functioned as the first court for civil cases involving feudal patrimonies.

Salma: Unit of dry measurement, equivalent to 8 *tomoli*, c. 320 kg.

Scrivania di Razione: A high financial office responsible for authorizing all government payments.

Seggio or Piazza: One of the five district subdivisions of the aristocracy of the city of Naples. Their membership was closed at the beginning of the sixteenth century.

Sommaria: The highest fiscal and financial court of the Kingdom of Naples.

Tantum: 500 ducats.

Tarí: Unit of money, equivalent to 2 *carlini* and 20 *grani*; one-fifth of a *ducat*.

Togati: Lawyers and magistrates, mostly of the Neapolitan tribunals.

Tomolo: Measure of grain, equivalent to 40 kg; measure of surface, 20 square *passi* equal to 0.4089 hectares.

Vicar-general: The prelate appointed by the bishop to assist him in the administration of the diocese by exercising ordinary jurisdiction in his name.

Vicaria: The central civil and criminal court in Naples. Appeals on its decisions could be taken to the Sacred Royal Council.

Vicario: Official representing the monarch and presiding over the Court of the Vicaria.

Vitalizio: Life-long annuity.

Vita milizia: Annual subsidy for cadet sons, consisting of a share of feudal revenues.

Zecca: A feudal right to enforce laws regulating standard weights and measures, and resulting fees and fines.

Bibliography

ARCHIVAL SOURCE ABBREVIATIONS

ASN: Archivio di Stato, Naples
ASP: Archivio di Stato, Palermo
BNN: Biblioteca Nazionale, Naples
Mon. sop.: Monasteri soppressi (suppressed monasteries/convents); archive section

PUBLISHED WORKS AND DISSERTATIONS

Accati, L. "Simboli maschili e simboli femminili nella devozione alla Madonna della Controriforma: Appunti per una discussione." In E. Van Kessel, ed., *Men and Women in Spiritual Culture.* The Hague, 1986.

Ago, R. *Carriere e clientele nella Roma barocca.* Rome, 1990.

Alberti, L. B. *On the Art of Building in Ten Books.* Trans. J. Rykwert, N. Leach, and R. Tavernor. Cambridge, Mass., 1988.

Ambrose, Saint. *Verginità e Vedovanza.* Ed. and trans. F. Gori. 2 vols. Milan, 1989.

———. *On Virginity.* Trans. D. Callam. Toronto, 1989.

Ambrosius, Saint, Saint Hieronymus, and Saint Augustinus. *De virginitate opuscula.* Rome, 1562.

Amirante, G. *Architettura napoletana tra Seicento e Settecento: L'opera di Arcangelo Guglielmelli.* Naples: Edizioni Scientifiche Italiane, 1990.

Andretta, Saint. *La Venerabile Superbia: Ortodossia e trasgressione nella vita di Suor Francesca Farnese (1593–1651).* Turin, 1994.

Anon. *Vita della Serva di Dio Sor Celestina Raineri palermitana.* Palermo, 1734.

Anon. [a Neapolitan priest]. *Vita della venerabile madre D. Maria Carafa sorella di Paolo IV. Pap. e fondatrice del monasero di S. Maria della Sapienza con aggiunta delle Vite della ven. suor Francesca del SS. Sacramento e di S. Caterina di Genova ristrette, da un sacredote Napoletano per ajuto delle S. Anime Purganti.* Naples, 1778.

Anon. *Vita della Serva di Dio Suoro Teresa Benedetta Monaca Professa del Ven. Monastero di S. Gio. Battista detto lo Riglione nel secolo, D. Caterina Gerbino. Composta da un Carmelitano Scalzo suo confessore. Dedicata alla Rev. madre Suor Maria Nazarena Grugno, e Parisi Degniissima Abbadessa del sudetto Monastero.* Palermo, 1744.

Antinori, Aloisio. *Scipione Borghese e l'Architettura.* Rome, 1995.

Ardia, A., S.J. *Tromba Catechistica: Cioè spiegazione della Dottrina Cristiana, fatica, e dono a tutti i fedeli e dedicata all'Altezza Serenissima di Maurizio Emanuele di Lorena, Principe d'Elbeuf.* Naples, 1713.

Astarita, T. *The Continuity of Feudal Power.* Cambridge: Cambridge University Press, 1992.

Atkinson, C. "Precious Balsam in a Fragile Glass: The Ideology of Virginity in the Later Middle Ages." *Journal of Family History* 8 (1983): 131–143.

Augustine, Saint. *De bono coniugali: De sancta virginitate.* Trans. P. G. Walsh. Oxford, 2001.

Aymard, Maurice. "L'Europe Moderne: Féodalité ou Féodalités?" *Annales: Economies, Sociétés, Civilisations* 3 (1981): 426–435.

———. "Une famille de l'aristocratie sicilienne aux XVIe et XVIIe siècles." *Revue historique* 247 (1972): 29–66.

Bacco, E. *Naples an Early Guide by Enrico Bacco.* Ed. E. Gardiner. New York, 1991.

Barbagallo, F. *Mezzogiorno e questione meridionale, 1860–1980.* Naples, 1980.

Barberi, F. *Paolo Manuzio e la stamperia del popolo romano, 1561–1570.* Rome, 1985.

Battaglia, S. *Grande Dizionario della Lingua Italiano,* vol. 3. Turin, 1964.

Bell, R. M. *Holy Anorexia.* Chicago, 1985.

Beloch, Julius. *Bevölkerungsgeschichte Italiens.* Berlin, 1965.

Beltrano, Ottavio. *Breve Descrittione del Regno di Napoli.* Naples, 1640.

Bendiscioli, M. "Il Quietismo a Roma e in Italia." *Studi Romani* 9 (1961): 168–179.

Benigno, Francesco. *Una casa, una terra: Ricerche su Paceco, paese nuovo nella Sicilia del Sei e Settecento.* Catania, 1985.

———. *L'Ombra del re. Ministri e lotta politica nella Spagna del Seicento.* Venice, 1992.

———. "La questione della capitale: Lotta politica e rappresentanza degli interessi nella Sicilia del Seicento." *Società e Storia* 13, no. 47 (January–March 1990): 27–63.

———. "The Southern Italian Family in the Early Modern Period: A Discussion of Coresidential Patterns." *Continuity and Change* 4 (1989): 165–194.

———. "Vecchio e nuovo nella Sicilia del Seicento: Il ruolo della colonizzazione feudale." *Studi Storici* 27, no. 1 (1986).

Benvenuti Papi, Anna. "Il 'patronage' nell'agiografia femminile." In Lucia Ferrante, Maura Palazzi, and Gianna Pomata, eds., *Ragnatele di Rapporti: Patronage e reti di relazione nella storia delle donne,* 201–218. Turin: Rosenberg and Sellier, 1988.

Berengo, M. *Nobili e mercanti nella Lucca del Cinquecento.* Turin, 1974.

Bernardino da Siena. *Prediche volgari sul campo di Siena* (1427). Ed. C. Delcorno. 2 vols. Milan, 1989.

Besoldo, C. *Historiae et regni Hierosolynitani, regum item Siculorum et Neapolitanorum.* Strasburg, 1636.

Bevilacqua, Mario. *Santa Caterina da Siena a Magnanapoli.* Rome, 1993.
Bibliotheca Sanctorum. Istituto Giovanni 23. Rome, 1968.
Bilinkoff, Jodi. "Navigating the Waves (of Devotion): Toward a Gendered Analysis of the Counter-Reformation." Unpublished paper discussed at the North Carolina Research Group on Medieval and Early Modern Women, Chapel Hill, 16 November 1997.
Billacois, F. "La Crise de la noblesse européenne (1550–1650)." *Revue d'histoire moderne et contemporaine* 23 (1976): 258–277.
Blok, A. "Notes on the Concept of Virginity in Mediterranean Societies." In E. Van Kessel, ed., *Men and Women in Spiritual Culture,* 22–39. The Hague, 1986.
Blunt, A. *Neapolitan Baroque Architecture.* London, 1975.
———, ed. *Baroque and Rococo.* London, 1978.
Boccadamo, G. "Una riforma impossibile? I papi e i primi tentativi di riforma dei monasteri femminili di Napoli nel '500." *Campania Scara* 21 (1990): 96–122.
Boesch-Gajano, Sofia, and L. Scaraffia, eds. *Luoghi sacri e spazi della santità.* Turin, 1990.
Boesch-Gajano, Sofia, and L. Sebastiani, eds. *Culto dei santi, istituzioni e classi sociali in età preindustriale.* Rome, 1984.
———. *Luoghi sacri e spazi della santità.* Turin, 1990.
Bologna, C. "L''Invenzione' dell'interiorità (spazio della parola, spazio del silenzio: Monachesimo, cavalleria, poesia cortese)." In Sofia Boesch-Gajano and Lucetta Scaraffia, eds., *Luoghi sacri e spazi della santità,* 243–266. Turin, 1990.
Bolton, B. "Mulieres Sanctae." In S. M. Stuard, ed., *Women in Medieval Society,* 141–158. Philadelphia, 1976.
Bonazzi, F. *Dei veri Autori di alcuni Dipinti della Chiesa di S. Maria della Sapienza in Napoli.* Naples, 1888.
Bornstein, Daniel. "Women and Religion in Late Medieval Italy: History and Historiography." In Daniel Bornstein and Roberto Rusconi, eds., *Women and Religion in Medieval and Renaissance Italy,* 1–27. Chicago, 1996.
Bornstein, D., and R. Rusconi, eds. *Women and Religion in Medieval and Renaissance Italy.* Chicago, 1996.
Borrelli, G. "La chiesa e il convento di S. Maria della Stella." In *Napoli Nobilissima* (1983): 22, pp. 24–33.
Borromeo, Carlo. *Instructiones fabricae et supellectilis ecclesiasticae* (1577).
Boscarino, S. "Architettura e Urbanistica dal Cinquecento al Settecento." In *Storia della Sicilia.* Naples, 1981.
———. *Sicilia Barocca, Architettura e Città, 1610–1760.* Rome, 1986.
Bösel, R. "Cosimo Fanzago a Roma." *Prospettiva* 15 (1978): 29–40.
Bossy, John. "The Counter-Reformation and the People of Catholic Europe." *Past and Present* 47 (1970): 55.
———. "The Mass as a Social Institution, 1200–1700." *Past and Present* 100 (August 1983): 29–61.
Bourdieu, P. *La Distinction. Critique sociale du jugement.* Paris, 1979. In English: *Distinction: A Social Critique of the Judgement of Taste,* trans. R. Nice. London, 1986.
———. *Outline of a Theory of Practice.* Trans. R. Nice. Cambridge, 1977.
———. *Practical Reason: On the Theory of Action.* Stanford, 1998.

Boureau, A. "L'imene e l'ulivo. La verginità femminile nel discorso della chiesa nel XIII secolo." *Quaderni Storici* n.s. 75, 25, no. 3 (1990): 791–803.

Branca, Vittore. *Mercanti scrittori: Ricordi nella Firenze tra Medioevo e Rinacimento di Paolo da Certaldo [et al.]*. Milan, 1986.

Brett, E. T. "Umbert of Romans." *Memorie Domenicane,* n.s. (1981): 12–25.

Breve Narrazione della Vita, Martirii, e Miracoli dell'Invittissimo, S. Gregorio Martire Apostolo, Arcivescovo, e Primate della Grand'Armenia [.] Raccolta da diversi Authori, ed autorizzato per la Sacra Scrittura dal P.M.F. Angelo Volpe. Naples, 1636.

Brown, J. C. *Immodest Arts: The Life of a Lesbian Nun in Renaisance Italy.* New York, 1986.

———. "Monache a Firenze all'inizio dell'età moderna. Un'analisi demografica." *Quaderni Storici* 85 (April 1994): 117–152.

Brown, P. *Augustine of Hippo: A Biography.* London, 2000.

———. *The Body and Society: Men, Women, and Sexual Renunciation in Early Christianity.* New York: Columbia University Press, 1988.

———. *The Cult of the Saints.* Chicago: University of Chicago Press, 1981.

———. "Late Antiquity." In P. Veyne, ed., *A History of Private Life,* vol. 1: *From Pagan Rome to Byzantium,* 239–311. London, 1987.

———. *The Making of Late Antiquity.* Cambridge, Mass.: Harvard University Press, 1978.

Brundage, J. A., and E. Makowski. "Enclosure of Nuns: The Decretal *Periculoso* and Its Commentators." *Journal of Medieval History* 20 (1994): 143–155.

Bruzelius, C. "Art, Architecture and Urbanism in Naples." In E. Gardiner, ed., *Naples An Early Guide by E. Bacco,* lxv–lxxix. New York, 1991.

———. "Hearing Is Believing: Clarissan Architecture, ca. 1213–1340." *Gesta* 31, no. 2 (1992): 83–91.

———. "Queen Sancia of Mallorca and the Convent Church of Sta Chiara in Naples." *Memoirs of the American Academy in Rome* 50 (1995): 69–100.

Bruzelius, Caroline, and Constance Berman. "Monastic Architecture for Women." *Gesta* 31, no. 2 (1992): 73–75.

Bugge, J. *Virginitas: An Essay in the History of a Medieval Ideal.* The Hague, 1975.

Bulifon, A. *Giornali di Napoli dal MDXLVII al MDCCVI,* vol. 1 (1547–1691). Ed. N. Cortese. Naples, 1932.

Bullarum diplomatum et privilegiorum sanctorum Romanorum pontificum Neapolitana editio. Naples, 1885.

Burke, P. *The Historical Anthropology of Early Modern Italy: Essays on Perception and Communication.* Cambridge, 1987.

———. *Popular Culture in Early Modern Europe.* London, 1978.

Burnet, Gilbert. *Voyage de Suisse, d'Italie, e de quelques endtroits d'Allemagne and de France,* 2nd ed. Rotterdam, 1688.

Burr Litchfield, R. "Demographic Characteristics of Florentine Patrican Families from the Sixteenth to the Nineteenth Centuries." *Journal of Economic History* 29, no. 2 (1969): 191–205.

Butler, D. C. *Benedictine Monasticism: Studies in Benedictine Life and Rule.* Cambridge, 1961.

Bynum, C. W. "The Female Body and Religious Practice in the Late Middle Ages." In

M. Feher, ed., *Zone 3: Fragments for a History of the Human Body,* part 1, pp. 160–219. New York, 1989.

———. *Fragmentation and Redemption: Essays on Gender and the Human Body in Medieval Religion.* New York, 1991.

———. *Holy Feast and Holy Fast: The Religious Significance of Food to Medieval Women.* Los Angeles, 1987.

———. *Jesus as Mother: Studies in the Spirituality of the High Middle Ages.* Los Angeles, 1982.

———. "Religious Women in the Later Middle Ages." In J. Raitt, ed., *Christian Spirituality: High Middle Ages and Reformation.* New York, 1987.

Cabibbo, Sara. "La Santità femminile dinastica." In L. Scaraffia and G. Zarri, eds., *Donne e Fede: Santità e vita religiosa in Italia,* 399–418. (Laterza) Rome, 1994.

Cabibbo, S. , and M. Modica. "Identità religiosa e identità di genere: Scritture di famiglie nella Sicilia del Seicento." *Quaderni Storici* 83 (1993): 415–42.

———. *La Santa dei Tomasi: Storia di Suor Maria Crocifissa (1645–1699).* Turin, 1989.

Caiazza, Pietro. "Nunziatura di Napoli e Problemi Religiosi nel Viceregno Post-Tridentino." *Rivista di Storia della Chiesa in Italia* 42 (1988): 24–48.

Camillocci, Solfaroli. "L'obbedienza femminile tra virtù domestiche e disciplina monastica." In L. Scaraffia and G. Zarri, eds., *Donna e Fede,* 269–284. Rome, 1994.

Camiz, F. T. "*Virgo non-sterilis*: Nuns as Artists in Seventeenth-Century Rome." In G. Johnson and S. Matthews Grieco, eds., *Picturing Women in Renaissance and Baroque Italy,* 139–164. Cambridge, 1997.

Camporesi, P. "The Consecrated Host: A Wondrous Excess." In M. Feher, ed., *Fragments for a History of the Human Body,* part 1, 220–237. New York, 1989.

Canones, et Decreta Sacrosancti Oecumenici et Generalis Concilii Tridenti, sub Paulo III, Iulio III, Pio IIII, Pontificibus Max. Rome, 1564. Trans. J. Waterworth: *The Canons and Decrees of the Sacred and Oecumenical Council of Trent.* New York, 1848.

Canosa, R. *Il velo e il cappuccio: Monacazioni forzate e sessualità nei conventi femminili in Italia tra Quattrocento e Settecento.* Rome, 1991.

Cantone, Gaetana. "I Conservatorii dell'Imbrecciata di Gesù e Maria." *Napoli Nobilissima* 7, parts 5–6 (September–December 1968): 204–218.

———. *Napoli barocca.* Rome, 1992.

———. *Napoli barocca e Cosimo Fanzago.* Naples, 1984.

Capaccio, G. C. *Il Forastiero.* Naples, 1630.

———. "Napoli descritta ne' principii del secolo XVII," ed. B. Capasso. *Archivio Storico per le Province Napoletane* 7 (1882): 68–103, 531–554, 776–797.

Capasso, B. "La Vicaria vecchia." *Archivio Storico per le province napoletane* 15 (1890): 659–695.

Caracciolo, E. *Misteri del chiostro napoletano.* Florence, 1864.

Caracciolo, Francesco Paolo. *Le Couvent de Baïano. Chronique du seizième siècle, extraite des archives de Naples et traduite littéralmente de l'Italien par M. J. Co.; précédée de recherches sur les Couvens au seizième siècle par M. P.-L. Jacob, Bibliophile.* Paris, 1829.

Caracciolo di Torchiarolo, Ambrogino. "I Monti di previdenza della famiglia Caracciolo." *Atti dell'Accademia Pontaniana,* n.s. 6 (n.d.): 337–371.

Caridi, G. *La Spada, la seta, la croce: I Ruffo di Calabria dal XVIII al XIX secolo.* Turin, 1995.

Carletti, N. *Topografia Universale della Città di Napoli in Campania Felice e Note Enciclopediche Storiografiche di Niccolò Carletti, filosofo, professore delle Architetture Accademico di Merito di S. Luca di Roma.* Naples (Raimondiana), 1776.

Carratelli, G. P., ed. *Storia e Civiltà della Campania. Il Rinascimento e L'Età Barocca.* Naples, 1994.

Casali, E. "Economia e creanza cristiana." *Quaderni Storici* 41 (1979): 555–83.

Castelnuovo, E., and C. Ginzburg. "Centre and Periphery." In *History of Italian Art,* trans. E. Bianchini and C. Dorey. Cambridge, 1979.

Catena, C. *Le Carmelitane: Storia e Spirtualità.* Rome, 1969.

Catholic Encyclopedia. New York, 1910 (vol. 9), 1913 (vol. 11).

Cecchetti. *La Republica di Venezia e la corte di Roma nei rapporti della religione,* vol. 1. Venice, 1874.

Celano, C. *Notitie del Bello dell'antico e del curioso della città di Napoli,* 4 vols. 10 pts. Naples, 1692.

———. *Notizie del Bello, dell'antico e del curioso della città di Napoli con aggiunzioni del Cav. G. B. Chiarini* (1856–60). Ed. G. B. Chiarini. New edition with introduction by P. Macry, 5 vols., Naples: Edizioni dell'Anticaglia, 2000.

Chaunu, P. *L'église, culture et société: Essais sur réforme et contre-réforme.* 2d ed. Paris, 1984.

Chiappa, Paola Vismara. "De Monialibus (Secoli XVI–XVII–XVIII)." *Rivista di Storia e Letteratura Religiosa* 33, no. 3 (1997): 643–715.

———. "Per la storia del monachesimo femminile nell'Italia del Settecento." *Rivista di Storia e Letteratura Religiosa* 33 (1997): 694–715.

Chiesa, G. N. *Riflessioni Religiose e Critiane* [sic] *per tutte le Domeniche, ferie, ed alcune più principali solennità dell'Anno.* Naples, 1737.

Chojnacki, S. "Dowries and Kinsmen in Early Renaissance Venice." In s. M. Stuard, ed., *Women in Medieval Society,* 173–89. Philadelphia, 1976.

———. "Servir a Dio": Choice, Coercion, and Chastity in Renaissance Venetian Convents." Paper delivered at the Eighth Berkshire Conference on the History of Women, Douglass College / Rutgers University, 1990.

Christian, W. "The Delimitation of Sacred Space and the Visions of Ezquioga, 1931–1987." In S. Boesch Gajano and L. Scaraffia, eds., *Luoghi sacri e spazi della santità.* Turin, 1990.

Chrysostom, J. *De virginitate.* Trans. *On Virginity; Against Remarriage.* Trans. S. Riger Shore and E. A. Clark. Lewiston, N.Y., 1983.

Ciuffreda, A. "Lo scambio dei ruoli: Primogeniti-e e cadetti-e tra Quattrocento e Settecento nel Mezzogiorno d'Italia." *Quaderni Storici* 83 (1993): 507–525.

Clark, Elizabeth A. Introduction to John Chrysostom, *On Virginity.* Trans. S. R. Shore. New York, 1983.

Clark, P., ed. *The European Crisis of the 1590s.* London, 1985.

Coakley, J. "Friars as Confidants of Holy Women in Medieval Dominican Hagiography." In R. Blumenfeld-Kosinski and T. Szell, eds., *Images of Sainthood in the Middle Ages,* 71–131. Ithaca, N.Y., 1991.

Cochrane, E. "Southern Italy in the Age of the Spanish Viceroys: Some Recent Titles." *Journal of Modern History* 58, no. 1 (March 1986): 194–217.

Cohen, Sherrill. "Asylums for Women in Counter-Reformation Italy." In s. Marshall, ed., *Women in Reformation and Counter-Reformation Europe,* 166–188. Bloomington, Ind., 1989.

Coleman, D. et al., eds. *Architecture and Feminism*. Princeton, 1996.
Colombo, A. *Il monastero e la Chiesa di S. Maria la Sapienza*. Trani, 1901.
———. "S. Maria della Sapienza." *Napoli nobilissima* 11 (1902).
Colomina, Beatriz, ed. *Sexuality and Space*. New York, 1992.
Confuorto, D. "Notizie di alcune famiglie popolari della Città e Regno di Napoli divenute riguardevoli per causa di ricchezza e dignitate" (1693). Manuscript, BNN, I-D-5.
Connors, Joseph. "Alliance and Enmity in Baroque Urbanism." *Römisches Jahrbuch der Biblioteca Herziana* 25 (1989): 207–94.
Consolino, Franca Ela. "Modelli di santità femminile nelle più antiche Passioni romane." *Augustinianum* 24 (1984): 83–113.
Constitutioni delle Monache del Monastero di S. Andrea di Napoli dell'Ordine Eremitano fatte per facolta concessa dela felice memoria di Papa Gregorio XIII. and confirmate da N.S. Sisto V. Naples, 1589.
Constitutioni delle povere Capuccine Monache della prima Regola di S. Chiara del Monastero di S. Carlo di Piacenza. Piacenza, 1683.
Cooper, J. P. "Patterns of Inheritance and Settlement by Great Landowners from the Fifteenth to the Eighteenth Centuries." In J. Goody, J. Thirsk, and E. P. Thompson, eds., *Family and Inheritance: Rural Society in Western Europe, 1200–1800*, 192–327. Cambridge, 1976.
Creytens, Raimondo. "La giurisprudenza della Sacra Congregazione del Concilio nella Questione della Clausura delle Monache (1564–1576)." *Apollinaris* 37 (1964): 251–285.
———. "La Riforma dei monasteri femminili dopo i Decreti Tridentini." *Il Concilio di Trento e la riforma tridentina: Atti del Convegno Storico Internazionale Trento (1963)*: vol. 1, 45–84. Rome, 1965.
Croce, Benedetto. "Il Palazzo Cellamare a Chiaia: I." *Napoli Nobilissima* 10, fasc. 4 (1901): 165–174.
———. "Il Palazzo Cellamare a Chiaia: II." *Napoli Nobilissima* 10, fasc. 6 (1901): 148–151.
———. "Il Palazzo Cellamare a Chiaia: III." *Napoli Nobilissima* 10, fasc. 11 (1901): 161–165.
———. *Storia del Regno di Napoli*. Ed. H. Stuart Hughes and trans. F. Frenaye: *History of the Kingdom of Naples*. Chicago, 1970.
Cyprian, Saint. *De bono patientiae*. Trans. G. E. Conway. Washington, 1957.
D'Addario, A. *Aspetti della controriforma a Firenze*. Rome, 1972.
Dagens, J. *Bérulle et les origines de la Restauration catholique (1575–1611)*. Paris, 1952.
D'Amelia, Marina. "La Conquista di una dote. Regole del gioco e scambi femminili alla Confraternita dell'Annunziata (secc. XVII–XVIII)." In Lucia Ferrante, Maura Palazzi, and Gianna Pomata, eds., *Ragnatele di Rapporti: Patronage e Reti di Relazione nella Storia delle Donne*, 305–343. Turin: Rosenberg and Sellier, 1988.
———. "Scatole cinesi: Vedove e donne sole in una società d'ancien régime." *Memoria* 18 (1987).
Davis, N. Z. *Society and Culture in Early Modern France*. Stanford, Calif.: Stanford University Press, 1975.

Davis, N. Z., and A. Farge, eds. *A History of Women in the West: Three Renaissance and Enlightenment Paradoxes.* Cambridge, Mass., 1993.

Dean, Trevor, and Lowe, K. J. P., eds. *Marriage in Italy, 1300–1650.* Cambridge: Cambridge University Press, 1997.

De Certeau, Michel. *The Practice of Everyday Life.* Berkeley, Calif., 1988.

de Fontette, M. *Les religieuses à l'âge classique du droit canon: Recherches sur les structures juridiques des branches féminine des ordres.* Paris, 1967.

De Giorgio, Michela, and Christiane Klapisch-Zuber. *Storia del matrimonio.* Rome, 1996.

De la Ville sur Yllon, L. "Il ponte di Chiaia." *Napoli nobilissima* 1 (1892): 142–147.

———. "La Strada di S. Giovannia Carbonara." *Napoli Nobilissima* 15, fasc. 2 (1906): 17–23.

De Lellis, C. *Aggiunta alla Napoli Sacra di D. Cesare d'Engenio Caracciolo, Napolitano.* Ed. F. Aceto. 2 vols. Naples, 1977.

Delille, G. *Famille et propriété dans la Royaume de Naples (XVe–XIXe siècle).* Paris, 1985.

Delille, G., and A. Ciuffreda. "Lo scambio dei ruoli: Primogeniti-e e cadetti-e tra Quattrocento e Settecento nel Mezzogiorno d'Italia." *Quaderni Storici,* n.s. 83 (1993): 507–525.

Dell'Aja, P. Gaudenzio. *Il Restauro della Basilica di Santa Chiara in Napoli.* Naples, 1992.

Della Torre, S. "Il problema dei referimenti classicisti nell'architettura post-tridentina." *I Tempi del Concilio. Atti del Convegno: Società, religione e cultura agli inizi dell'Europa moderna, 1994. Economia trentina,* suppl. to no. 1 (1995).

Delooz, P. "The Social Function of the Canonization of Saints." In C. Duquoc and C. Floristan, eds., *Models of Holiness,* 14–24. New York, 1979.

———. "Towards a Sociological Study of Canonised Sainthood in the Catholic Church." In S. Wilson, ed., *Saints and Their Cults: Studies in Religion, Sociology, Folklore and History,* 189–216. Cambridge, 1983.

del Pesco, Daniela. "L'Architettura della Controriforma e i cantieri dei grandi ordini religiosi." In G. Pugliese Carratelli, ed., *Il Rinascimento e l'età barocca,* 327–386. Naples, 1994.

De Luca, Giovanni Battista. *La Dama e il cavaliere.* Rome, 1657.

Delumeau, J. *Catholicism between Luther and Voltaire: A New View of the Counter-Reformation.* Philadelphia, 1977.

———. *La Peur en Occident (XIVe–XVIIIe siècles).* Paris, 1978.

De Maio, Romeo. *Religiosità a Napoli (1656–1799).* Naples: Edizioni Scientifiche Italiane, 1997.

———. *Società e vita religiosa a Napoli nell'età moderna, 1656–1799.* Naples, 1971.

De Seta, Cesare. *Napoli: Le Città nella storia d'Italia.* Naples, 1981; reprint, 1995.

———. "The Urban Structure of Naples: Utopia and Reality." In H. Millon and V. M. Lampugnani, eds., *The Renaissance from Brunelleschi to Michelangelo: The Representation of Architecture.* London, 1994.

De Seta, C., and L. Di Mauro. *Palermo: Le Città nella storia d'Italia.* Bari, 1988.

Devos, Roger. *Vie religieuse féminine et société: L'origine sociale des Visitandines d'Annecy aux XVIIe et XVIIIe siècles.* Annecy, 1973.

Ditchfield, Simon. "Sanctity in Early Modern Italy." *Journal of Ecclesiastical History* 47, no. 1 (January 1996): 98–112.

Dizionario degli Istituti di Perfezione. Rome, 1975.

Doria, P. M. "Il regno di Napoli, descritto nel 1713 da P.M Doria." Ed. M. Schipa. *Archivio Storico Napoletano* 24 (1899): 329–350.

Douglas, M. *Purity and Danger: An Analysis of Concepts of Pollution and Taboo.* London, 1966.

Dunn, Marilyn. "Nuns as Art Patrons: The Decoration of S. Marta al Collegio Romano." *Art Bulletin* 70 (1988): 451–477.

———. "Piety and Patronage in Seicento Rome: Two Noblewomen and Their Convents." *Art Bulletin* 76 (December 1994): 644–663.

———. "Spaces Shaped for Spiritual Perfection: Convent Architecture and Nuns in Early Modern Rome." In Helen Hills, ed., *Architecture and the Politics of Gender.* Ashgate, U.K., forthcoming 2003.

———. "Spiritual Philanthropists: Women as Convent Patrons in Seicento Rome." In C. Lawrence, ed., *Women and Art in Early Modern Europe,* 154–188. University Park, Pa., 1997.

Durning, L. *Gender Perspectives in Architectural History: A Working Bibliography.* Oxford, 1995.

Eade, J., and M. J. Sallnow, eds. *Contesting the Sacred: The Anthropology of Christian Pilgrimage.* London, 1991.

Editto. "Don Pietro Martinez Rubio." 1 February 1664.

Editto. "Per il Regolari." Palermo, 18 April 1654.

Editto. "Reverenda Madre, andC." Palermo, 11 April 1658.

Elling, C. *Rome: The Biography of Her Architecture from Bernini to Thorvaldsen.* Trans. B. and I. Gosney. Boulder, Colo., 1975.

Elliott, J. H. *The Count-Duke of Olivares: The Statesman in an Age of Decline.* New Haven, 1986.

———. "The Twilight of Habsburg Spain." In E. J. Sullivan and N. A. Mallory, eds., *Painting in Spain 1650–1700 from North American Collections.* Princeton, 1982.

Enciclopedia Cattolica. 12 vols. Rome, 1948.

D'Engenio, D. Cesare. *Napoli Sacra: Ove oltre le vere origini e fondationi di tutte le Chiese, Monasterij, Cappelle, Spedali, e d'altri luoghi sacri della Città di Napoli, e de' suoi Borghi, si tratta di tutti i corpi, e reliquie de' santi e beati.* Naples: Ottavio Beltrano, 1624.

Evangelisti, S. "Wives, Widows, and Brides of Christ: Marriage and the Convent in the Historiography of Early Modern Italy." *Historical Journal* 43, no. 1 (March 2000): 233–248.

Evans, J. *Monastic Iconography in France: From the Renaissance to the Revolution.* Cambridge, 1970.

Facchiano, A. "Monasteri benedettini o capitoli de canonichesse? L'esempio di S. Patrizia di Napoli." *Benedictina* 38 (1991): 35–60.

———. *Monasteri femminili e nobiltà a Napoli tra medioevo ed età moderna. Il Necrologio di S. Patrizia (secc. XII–XVI).* Salerno, 1992.

Feher, M., ed. *Fragments for a History of the Human Body,* parts 1 and 3. New York, 1989.

Ferraironi, F. *Il Santuario di S. Brigida in Napoli.* Rome, 1931.

Ferrante, Lucia, Maura Palazzi, and Gianna Pomata, eds. *Ragnatele di rapporti: Patronage e reti di relazione nella storia delle donne.* Turin: Rosenberg and Sellier, 1988.

Ferrara, M. P. *Arte napoletana in Puglia dal XVI al XVIII secolo: Pittori, scultori, marmorari, architetti, ingegneri, argentieri, riggiolari, organari, ferrari, ricametri, banderari, stuccatori.* Naples, 1983.

Filopatro, E. [pseud. Giuseppe Sanfelice]. *Riflessioni Morali e Teologiche sopra l'Istoria Civile del Regno di Napoli esposte al Publico in più lettere familiari di due Amici da E.F.* 2 vols. Colonia [Rome], 1728.

Fiorani, L. "Monache e monasteri romani nell'età del Quietismo." *Ricerche per la Storia Religiosa* (Rome) 1 (1977): 63–111.

Fiorio, M. T. *Le chiese di Milano.* Milan, c. 1985.

Fitzpatrick, E. A., ed. St. *Ignatius and the Ratio Studiorum.* New York, 1933.

Fiume, Giovanna, and L. Scaraffia. "Premessa." *Quaderni Storici,* n.s. 75, vol. 25, no. 3 (1990): 701–714.

Foucault, M. *Discipline and Punish.* Trans. A. Sheridan. London, 1977.

———. *A History of Sexuality,* vol. 1. Harmondsworth, U.K., 1976.

———. "Of Other Spaces: Utopias and Heterotopias." In J. Ockman, ed., *Architecture Culture, 1943–1968,* 419–426. New York, 1993.

———. *Power / Knowledge: Selected Interviews and Other Writings, 1972–1977.* Ed. C. Gordon. New York: Pantheon, 1980.

Frigo, D. "Dal caos all'ordine: Sulla questione del 'prender moglie' nella trattatistica del sedicesimo secolo." In M. Zancan, ed., *Nel cerchio della luna: Figure di donna in alcuni testi del XVI secolo,* 82–98. Venice, 1983.

Fuidoro, I. *Giornali di Napoli dal MDCLX al MDCLXXX.* 3 vols. Naples: Lubrano, 1934–39.

Furnivall, F. J. *Hali Meidenhad: An Alliterative Homily of the Thirteenth Century.* London, 1922.

Gadamer, Georg. *Truth and Method.* Trans. J. Weinsheimer and D. G. Marshall. London, 1989.

Galasso, Giuseppe. *Il Mezzogiorno nella storia d'Italia.* Florence, 1977. Rev. ed., Florence, 1984.

———. *Napoli spagnola dopo Masaniello, politica, cultura, società.* 2 vols. Naples: ESI, 1967–72. Reprint, Florence: Sansoni, 1982.

Galasso, Giuseppe, and Carla Russo. *Per la storia sociale e religiosa del Mezzogiorno d'Italia.* Naples, 1980.

Gardiner, E., ed. *Naples an Early Guide by Enrico Bacco.* New York, 1991.

Garzya, G. "Reclutamento e sacerdotalizzazione del clero secolare della diocesi di Napoli. Dinamica di una nuova politica pastorale nella seconda metà del Seicento." In G. Galasso and C. Russo, eds., *Per la Storia Sociale e Religiosa del Mezzogiorno d'Italia.* Naples, 1980.

Gennep, A. van. *The Rites of Passage.* Trans. M. B. Vizedom and G. L. Caffee. London, 1960.

Giannone, Pietro, *Istoria Civile del Regno di Napoli.* 4 vols. Palmyra, 1762–1763.

Gilchrist, Roberta, *Gender and Material Culture. The Archaeology of Religious Women.* London: Routledge, 1994.

Gill, K. "Open Monasteries for Women in Late Medieval and Early Modern Italy: Two Roman Examples." In C. Monson, ed., *The Crannied Wall: Women, Religion, and the Arts in Early Modern Europe,* 15–47. Ann Arbor, Mich., 1992.

Gilmour, D., ed. *Honor and Shame and the Unity of the Mediterranean.* Washington, D.C., 1987.

Gleijeses, V. *Chiese e palazzi della città di Napoli.* Naples, 1978.

Goddard, V. *The Anthropology of Europe: Identity and Boundaries in Conflict.* Oxford, 1994.

Gonzaga, Bonaventura. *Alcuni avvertimenti nella vita monacale, utili, et necessari a ciaschedura Vergine di Christo.* Venice, 1568.

Goody, J. *The Development of the Family and Marriage in Europe.* Cambridge, 1983.

Gramsci, A. *Prison Notebooks.* Trans. J. A. Buttigieg. Chichester, 1996.

Grassi, L. "Iconologia delle chiese monastiche femminili dall'alto medioevo ai secoli XVI–XVII." *Arte lombarda* 9 (1964): 131–150.

Greaves, R. L., ed. *Triumph over Silence: Women in Protestant History.* Westport, Conn., 1985.

Gregory of Nyssa. *De virginitate.* Basel, 1567.

Hamburger, Jeffrey. "Art, Enclosure and the *Cura Monialium*: Prolegomena in the Guise of a Postscript." *Gesta* 31, no. 2 (1992): 108–134.

———. *Nuns as Artists: The Visual Culture of a Medieval Convent.* Berkeley, Calif., 1997.

———. "The Use of Images in the Pastoral Care of Nuns: The Case of Heinrich Suso and the Dominicans." *Art Bulletin* 71 (1989): 20–46.

Harris, Barbara. "A New Look at the Reformation: Aristocratic Women and Nunneries, 1450–1540." *Journal of British Studies* 32 (1993): 89–113.

———. "Power, Profit, and Passion: Mary Tudor, Charles Brandon, and the Arranged Marriage in Early Tudor England." *Feminist Studies* 15, no. 1 (1989): 59–88.

———. "Women and Politics in Early Tudor England." *Historical Journal* 33 (1990): 259–281.

Herlihy, David. "Did Women Have a Renaissance? A Reconsideration." *Medievalia et Humanistica,* n.s. 13 (1985): 1–22.

Herlihy, D., and C. Klapisch-Zuber. *Tuscans and Their Families.* New Haven, 1978.

Hibbard, Howard. *The Architecture of the Palazzo Borghese.* London, 1962.

Hillier, B. *Space Is the Machine: A Configurational Theory of Architecture.* Cambridge, 1996.

Hills, Helen. "Cities and Virgins: Female Aristocratic Convents in Early Modern Naples and Palermo." *Oxford Art Journal* 22, no. 1 (1999): 29–54.

———. "Iconography and Ideology: Aristocracy, Immaculacy and Virginity in Seventeenth-Century Palermo." *Oxford Art Journal* 17, no. 2 (1994): 16–31.

———. *Marmi mischi siciliani: Invenzione e identità.* Messina, 1999.

Hirschon, R. *Women and Property—Women as Property.* London: Croom Helm, 1984.

Howell, Martha. "Marriage, Property, and Patriarchy: Recent Contributions to a Literature." *Feminist Studies* 13, no. 1 (Spring 1987): 203–224.

Hughes, Diane Owen. "From Brideprice to Dowry in Mediterannean Europe." *Journal of Family History* 3 (1978): 262–296.

———. "Representing the Family: Portraits and Purposes in Early Modern Italy." In T. K. Rabb and J. Brown, eds., *The Evidence of Art: Images and Meaning in History,* 7–38. Cambridge, 1988.

Jantzen, G. M. *Power, Gender and Christian Mysticism.* Cambridge, 1995.

Jedin, H. *History of the Council of Trent.* Trans. E. Graf. London, 1961.

Jerome, Saint. *Select Letters.* Trans. F. A. Wright. Cambridge, Mass.: Harvard University Press, 1991.

Jodice, M. *Suor Orsola: Cittadella monastica nella Napoli del Seicento.* Milan, 1987.

Johnson, A. M. "Custodias for the Processionals of Corpus Christi." *Notes Hispanic* 1 (1941): 63–85.

Johnson, G., and S. Matthews Grieco, eds. *Picturing Women in Renaissance and Baroque Italy.* Cambridge, 1997.

Jordan, C. "Renaissance Women and the Question of Class." In J. G. Turner, ed., *Sexuality and Gender in Early Modern Europe,* 90–106. Cambridge, 1993.

Jungmann, J. A. *The Mass of the Roman Rite: Its Origins and Development.* London, 1959.

Kealy, T. *Dowry of Women Religious. A Historical Synopsis and Commentary.* Washington, D.C., 1941.

Kelly Gadol, Joan. "Did Women Have a Renaissance?" In Renate Bridenthal and Claudia Koonz, eds., *Becoming Visible: Women in European History,* 137–64. Boston, 1977.

Kent, S. *Domestic Architecture and the Use of Space.* Cambridge, 1990.

Kertzer, D., and C. Brettell. "Recenti sviluppi nella storia della famiglia italiana e iberica." *Rassegna italiana di Sociologia* 28, no. 2 (1987): 249–289.

Klapisch-Zuber, C. "The 'Cruel Mother': Maternity, Widowhood, and Dowry in Florence in the Fourteenth and Fifteenth Centuries." In *Women, Family, and Ritual in Renaissance Italy,* trans. L. Cochrane, 117–131. Chicago, 1985.

———. "The Griselda Complex: Marriage Dowries and Gifts in the Quattrocento." In *Women, Family, and Ritual in Renaissance Italy,* trans. L. Cochrane, 215–218. Chicago, 1985.

———. *Women, Family, and Ritual in Renaissance Italy.* Trans. L. Cochrane. Chicago, 1985.

Knox, Dilwyn. "Civility, courtesy and women in the Italian Renaissance." In L. Panizza, ed., *Women in Italian Renaissance Culture and Society,* 2–10. Oxford, 2000.

———. "Disciplina: Le origini monastiche e clericali del buon comportamento nell'Europa cattolica del Cinquecento e del primo Seicento." In P. Prodi, ed., *Disciplina dell'anima, disciplina del corpo e disciplina della società tra medioevo ed età moderna: Annali del'Istituto Storico italo-germanno Quaderno* 40, pp. 63–99. Bologna, 1994.

Labrot, Gerard. *Baroni in città. Residenze e comportamenti dell'aristocrazia napoletana, 1530–1734.* Naples: Società Editrice Napoletana, 1979.

———. *Collections of Paintings in Naples 1600–1780.* Munich, 1992.

———. "Le comportement collectif de l'aristocratie napolitaine du seizième au dix-huitième siècle." *Revue historique* 101, no. 258 (1977): 45–71.

———. "Images, tableaux et statuaire dans les testaments napolitains (XFIIe–XVIIIe siècle)." *Revue hsitorique* 268 (1982): 131–166.

———. "Naissance et croissance d'un quartier de Naples: Pizzofalcone 1530–1689." *Urbi* 1 (September 1979): xlvii–lxvi.

Laqueur, T. *Making Sex: Body and Gender from the Greeks to Freud.* Cambridge, Mass.: Harvard University Press, 1990.

Lawrence, Cynthia. Introduction to *Women and Art in Early Modern Europe,* 1–20. University Park: Pennsylvania State University Press, 1997.

Leander of Seville. *De institutione virginum et contemptu mundi.* English version: "The Training of Nuns and the Contempt of the World." Trans. C. W. Barlow. In R. J. Deferrari, *The Fathers of the Church: Iberian Fathers: I,* 175–238. Washington, D.C., 1969.

Leanti, G. *La Stato presente della Sicilia.* Palermo, 1761.

Lefebvre, Henri. *The Production of Space.* Trans. D. Nicholson-Smith. Oxford, 1991.

Le Goff, J. "Apostolat mendiant et fait urbain dans la France médiéval: L'implantation des Ordres mendiants. Programme-questionnaire pur une enquete." *Annales ESC* 23 (1968): 335–348.

———. "Head or Heart? The Political Use of Body Metaphors in the Middle Ages." In M. Feher, ed., *Fragments for a History of the Human Body,* part III. New York, 1989.

Lepre, A. "Rendite di monasteri nel Napoletano e crisi economica del Seicento." *Quaderni storici* 15 (1970): 844–865.

Liebowitz, R. P. "Virgins in the Service of Christ: The Dispute over an Active Apostolate for Women during the Counter-Reformation." In R. Ruether and E. McLaughlin, eds., *Women of Spirit: Female Leadership in the Jewish and Christian Traditions,* 132–152. New York, 1979.

Ligresti, D. *Sicilia moderna: Le città e gli uomini.* Naples: Guida, 1984.

Lojacono, G. "La Chiesa di Casa Professa: La sua architettura; la sua decorazione marmorea." Unpublished tesi di laurea, University of Palermo, 1937.

Lowe, Kate. "Nuns and Choice: Artistic Decision-Making in Medicean Florence." In E. Marchand and A. Wright, eds., *With and Without the Medici: Studies in Tuscan Art and Patronage, 1430–1530,* 129–153. Aldershot, 1998.

———. "Secular Brides and Convent Brides: Wedding Ceremonies in Italy during the Renaissance and Counter-Reformation." In T. Dean and K. Lowe, eds., *Marriage in Italy,* 41–65. Cambridge, 1998.

Maggio, F. M. *Vita della Venerabile D. Maria Carafa Napoletana, sorella del Santiss. Pontefice Paolo IV e fondatrice del sacro monistero di S. Maria della Sapienza di suore Domenicane.* Naples, 1670.

Makowski, E. M. *Canon Law and Cloistered Women: Periculoso and Its Commentators, 1298–1545.* Studies in Medieval and Early Modern Canon Law 5. Washington, D.C.: Catholic University of America Press, 1997.

Mâle, Emile. *L'Art Religieux après le Concile de Trente.* Paris, 1932.

Mann, J. W. "The Annunciation Chapel in the Quirinal Palace, Rome: Paul V, Guido Reni, and the Virgin Mary." *Art Bulletin,* Vol. 75, no. 1, March (1993): 113–134.

Mantelli, R. *Il pubblico impiego nell'economia del Regno di Napoli: Retribuzioni, reclutamento e ricambio sociale nell'epoca spagnola (sec. XVI–XVIII).* Naples, 1986.

Marchese, D. M. *Vita della Ven. serva di Dio Suor Maria Villani dell'ordine de'Predicatori, fondatrice del monastero di S. Maria del Divino Amore di Napoli.* 1673. Reprint, Naples: Vincenzo Orsino, 1778.

Marshall, S., ed., *Women in Reformation and Counter-Reformation Europe,* 166–188. Bloomington, Ind., 1989.

Matter, E. Ann. "Interior Maps of an Eternal External." In U. Wiethaus, ed., *Maps of Flesh and Light: The Religious Experience of Medieval Women Mystics,* 60–73. Syracuse, 1993.

———. "The Personal and the Paradigm: The Book of Maria Domitilla Galluzzi." In C. Monson, ed., *The Crannied Wall: Women, Religion, and the Arts in Early Modern Europe,* 87–103. Ann Arbor, Mich., 1992.

———. *The Voice of My Beloved: The Song of Songs in Western Medieval Christianity.* Philadelphia, 1990.

Matthews Grieco, Sara. "Modelli di santità femminile nell'Italia del Rinascimento e della Controriforma." In L. Scaraffia and G. Zarri, eds., *Donne e fede: Santità e vita religiosa in Italia*, 303–325. Laterza, 1994.

Mazza, I. *I Carafa e S. Gaetano Thiene*. Naples, 1938.

Mazzucchelli, Mario. *La monaca di Monza (suor Virginia Maria de Leyve)*. Milan, 1993.

McGinness, F. "Preaching Ideals and Practice in Counter-Reformation Rome." *Sixteenth Century Journal* 11, no. 2 (1980): 109–128.

———. "Roma Sancta and the Saint: Eucharist, Chastity, and the Logic of Catholic Reform." *Historical Reflections* 15, no. 1 (1988): 99–116.

Medioli, F. "Le monacazioni forzate: Donne ribelli al proprio destino." *Clio* 30 (1994): 431–454.

———. "To Take or Not to Take the Veil: Selected Italian Case Histories, the Renaissance and After." In L. Panizza, ed., *Women in Italian Renaissance Culture and Society*, 122–131. Oxford, 2000.

———, ed. *L'"Inferno Monacale" di Arcangela Tarabotti*. Turin, 1990.

Metaphrastes, Simeon. *Vita di S. Gregorio Archivescovo Armenia*. Ed. Fr. F. Gravina, *Hanc Vitam cum miraculis s. Gregorij collectam ex Metaphraste, exemplari Longobardo, & relationibus Christianitatis Armeniae*. Naples, 1630.

Methodius, Saint. *The Symposium. A Treatise on Charity*. Trans. H. Musurillo. New York, 1958.

Miele, Michele. "La Riforma dei conventi nel Cinquecento: Osservazioni e istanze di un teologo napoletane dell'epoca." *Memorie Domenicane*, n.s., no. 3 (1972): 76–113.

———. *La Riforma domenicana a Napoli nel periodo post-tridentino, 1583–1725*. Rome, 1963.

———. "Sisto V e la Riforma dei monasteri femminili di Napoli." *Campania Sacra* 21 (1990): 123–209.

Moneta, L. [C. Borromeo]. *Instructionum fabricae et supellectilis ecclesiasticae libri duo*. Milan, 1577.

Mongitore, Antonino. *Compendio della vita e virtù della serva di Dio Suor Rosaria Caterina*. Palermo, 1718.

———. *Palermo divoto di Maria Vergine*, vol. II. Palermo, 1720.

Monson, C. "Disembodied Voices: Music in the Nunneries of Bologna in the Midst of the Counter-Reformation." In Monson, ed., *The Crannied Wall: Women, Religion, and the Arts in Early Modern Europe*, 191–209. Ann Arbor, Mich., 1992.

———, ed. *The Crannied Wall: Women, Religion, and the Arts in Early Modern Europe*. Ann Arbor, Mich., 1992.

Monter, William. *Frontiers of Heresy: The Spanish Inquisition from the Basque Lands to Sicily*. Cambridge, 1990.

———. "Protestant Wives, Catholic Saints and the Devil's Handmaid: Women in the Age of Reformations." In *Becoming Visible: Women in European History*, ed. Renate Bridenthal and Claudia Koonz, 2d ed. (Boston: Houghton Mifflin, 1987).

Monti, G. M. *Ricerche su Papa Paolo IV Carafa*. Turin, 1980.

Moore, Henrietta. *Space, Text and Gender: An Anthropological Study of the Marakwet of Kenya*. Cambridge, 1986.

Morris, J. *The Lady Was a Bishop: The Hidden History of Women with Clerical Ordination and the Jurisdiction of Bishops*. London, 1973.

Morrogh, Andrew D. *The Early History of the Cappella de' Principi. Florence*. Ph.D. diss., Courtauld Institute, University of London, 1983.

Mortari, L. S. *Maria Maddalena*. Rome, 1987.

Motta, Giovanna. *Strategie Familiari e Alleanze Matrimoniali in Sicilia nell'età della transizione (secoli XIV–XVII)*. Biblioteca dell'Archivio Storico Italiano 23. Florence, 1983.

Mugnos, F. *Teatro Genologico delle famiglie Nobili Titolate Feudatarie ed Antiche Nobili del Fidelissimo Regno di Sicilia Vivente ed Estinte*. Palermo, 1647.

Musi, A. "Il patriziato a Salerno in Età moderna." In M. A. Visceglia, ed., *Signori, patrizi, cavalieri*, 122–145. Rome, 1992.

Muto, G. "Come leggere il Mezzogiorno spagnolo." In G. Signorotto, ed., *L'Italia degli Austrias: Monarchia cattolica domini Italiani nei secoli XVI e XVII*, 55–80. Brescia, 1993.

Nappi, Eduardo. "Giovan Giacomo Conforto e la Chiesa di S. M. della Sapienza di Napoli." *Ricerche sul '600 Napoletano* (Milan) (1989): 113–134.

———. "I Viceré e l'Arte a Napoli." *Napoli Nobilissima* 22, fasc. 1–2 (1983): 41–57.

Narkis, B. "The Story of Jonah." *Gesta* 28, 1 (1979).

New Catholic Encyclopedia. London, 1969–73.

Niccoli, Ottavia. *Rinascimento al femminile*. Rome, 1991.

Nicolini, F. "La murazione di don Pietro Toledo." *Napoli Nobilissima* 15 (1905): 129–135.

———. *Sulla vita civile, letteraria e religiosa napoletana alla fine del Seicento*. Naples, 1929.

Norberg, Kathryn. "The Counter Reformation and Women: Religious and Lay." In J. O'Malley, S.J., ed., *Catholicism in Early Modern History: A Guide to Research*, 133–146. St. Louis, Mich., 1988.

Novi Chavarria, Elisa. "L'Attività missionari dei Gesuiti nel Mezzogiorno d'Italia tra XVI e XVIII secolo." In G. Galasso and C. Russo, eds., *Per la storia sociale e religiosa del Mezzogiorno d'Italia*. Naples, 1980.

———. *Monache e gentildonne: Un labile confine. Poteri politici e identità religiose nei monasteri napoletani secoli XVI–XVII*. Milan: FrancoAngeli, 2001.

———. "Nobiltà di Seggio, nobiltà nuova e monasteri femminili a Napoli in Età moderna." *Dimensioni e problemi della ricerca storica* 2 (1993): 84–111.

———. "Pastorale e devozione nel XVI e XVII secolo." In G. Galasso and R. Romeo, eds., *Storia del Mezzogiorno* 9, no. 2, pp. 369–413.

Odorisio, Ginevra Conti. *Donna e società nel Seicento*. Rome, 1979.

Ordinationi per le monache Regolari della Città di Palermo, e sua Diocesi fatti per Comandamento dell'Eminentissimo, e Reverendissimo Signor, D. Giannettino Doria Cardinale di S. Chiesa and Arcivescovo di Palermo. Palermo, 1536.

Ortner, S. B. "The Virgin and the State." *Feminist Studies* 4 (1978): 19–35.

Oulton, J. E. L. *Alexandrian Christianity: Selected Translations of Clement and Origen*. London, 1954.

Ozment, Steven. *The Reformation and the Family*. New Haven, 1984.

Pacichelli, Giovan Battista. *Memorie de' Viaggi per l'Europa Christiana*. Naples, 1685.

Palermo, F., ed. "Narrazioni e documenti sulla storia del regno di Napoli dall'anno 1522 al 1667." *Archivio Storico Italiano* 9 (1846): 147–190.

Pane, Roberto. *Il monastero di S. Gregorio Armeno*. Naples, 1957.

Panizza, L., ed. *Arcangela Tarabotti: Che le donne siano della spezie degli uomini*. London: Institute of Romance Studies, 1994.

———. *Women in Italian Renaissance Culture and Society*. Oxford, 2000.

Paolo da Certaldo. *Mercanti Scrittori*. Ed. V. Branca. Milan, 1986.

Papi, Anna B. "'Velut in sepulchro': Cellane e recluse nella tradizione agiografica italiana." In S. Boesch-Gajano and L. Sebastiani, eds., *Culto dei santi*, 365–455. Rome, 1984.

Paschini, P. *I Monasteri femminili in Italia nel Cinquecento*. Padua, 1960.

Patetta, Luciano. "L'Età di Carlo e Federico Borromeo e gli sviluppi delle chiese 'doppie' conventuali nella diocesi di Milano." In G. Spagnesi, ed., *L'Architettura a Roma e in Italia (1580–1621)*, Atti del 23d Congresso di Storia dell'Archittetura, 160–189. Rome, 1989.

———. "La Tipologia delle chiese doppie (dal Medioevo alla Controriforma)." In *Storia e tipologia: Cinque Saggi sull'architettura del passato*, 11–71. Milan, 1989.

Pearson, A. P. "Gender, Image, and Ideals at the Cistercian Convents of Flines, 1500–1575." Ph.D. diss., University of California, Santa Barbara, 1995.

Peccerillo, F. *I Ragioni per la Fedelissima, ed Eccellentissima Città di Napoli circa l'Impedire la Fabbrica delle Nuove Chiese e l'acquisto, che gl'Ecclesiastici fanno de' beni de' Secolari*. Naples, 1719.

Peers, E. Allison, ed. and trans. *The Complete Works of St. Teresa of Jesus*. 3 vols. New York, 1946.

Penco, Gregorio. *Storia della Chiesa*. 2 vols. Milan, 1978.

Peristiany, J. G. *Honour and Shame: The Values of Mediterranean Society*. London, 1966.

Pio, G. M. *Della Nobile Et Generosa Progenie del P.S. Domenico in Italia*. Bologna, 1615.

Pontieri, Ernesto. "Le origini della riforma cattolica-tridentina a Napoli." *Problemi di vita religiosa in Italia nel Cinquecento: Atti del Convegno*, 289–313. Padua, 1960.

Prima Regola delle Monache di santa Chiara, Datale dal Padre, S. Francesco e confirmato da Papa Innocentio III. Con il modo di ricever le Novitie all'Ordine, and alla professione. Revista, e corretto dal Rev. Padre Procuratore di Corte de' Frati Capuccini. Con l'aggiunta nel margine del Concilio Tridentino. Naples, 1655.

Putnam, E. J. *The Lady, Studies of Certain Significant Phases of Her History*. New York, 1910.

Radke, G. M. "Nuns and Their Art: The Case of San Zaccaria in Renaissance Venice." *Renaissance Quarterly* 54, no. 2 (2001): 430–459.

Randolph, A. "Regarding Women in Sacred Space." In Geraldine A. Johnson and Sara F. Matthews Grieco, eds., *Picturing Women in Renaissance and Baroque Italy*, 17–41. Cambridge: Cambridge University Press, 1997.

Rapley, Elizabeth. *The Dévotes: Women and Church in Seventeenth-Century France*. Montreal, 1990.

———. *A Social History of the Cloisters: Daily Life in the Teaching Monasteries of the Old Regime*. Montreal: McGill-Queen's University Press, 2001.

———. "Women and the Religious Vocation in Seventeenth-Century France." *French Historical Studies* 18, no. 3 (1994): 613–631.

Regola e Constitutioni delle, M. Rever. Monache del Terzo Ordine di S. Francesco. dette Convertite del Monastero di S. Maria Maddalena nella Città di Torino. Turin, 1671.

Renna, T. "Virginity and Chastity in Early Cistercian Thought." *Studia Monastica* (1984): 26, 43–54.

Rice, Eugene. *Saint Jerome in the Renaissance*. Baltimore, 1985.

Ricoeur, Paul. "The Metaphorical Process as Cognition, Imagination, and Feeling." In S. Sacks, ed., *On Metaphor*, 141–157. Chicago: University of Chicago Press, 1979.

Riley, Philip. "Michel Foucault, Lust, Women and Sin in Louis XIV's Paris." *Church History* 59 (March 1990): 35–50.

Rizzo, Vincenzo. *I cinquantadue affreschi di Luca Giordano a, S. Gregorio Armeno: Suoi allievi noti ed ignoti.* Naples: Arte Tipografica, 1992.

Rodriguez, Alfonso, S.J. *The Practice of Perfection and Christian Values.* Trans. J. Rickaby. 2 vols. Chicago, 1929.

Rosa, Mario. "The Nun." In R. Villari, ed., *Baroque Personae,* trans. L. Cochrane, 195–238. Chicago, 1995.

———. "L'onda che ritorna: Interno ed esterno sacro nella Napoli del '600." In S. B. Gajano and L. Scaraffia, *Luoghi sacri e spazi della santità,* 397–416. Turin, 1990.

Rosenthal, M. "Venetian Women Writers and Their Discontents." In J. G. Turner, ed., *Sexuality and Gender in Early Modern Europe: Institutions, Texts, Images,* 107–132. Cambridge, 1993.

Ruether, R., and E. McLaughlin, eds. *Women of Spirit: Female Leadership in the Jewish and Christian Traditions.* New York, 1979.

Rusconi, R. "Women Religious in Late Medieval Italy: New Sources and Directions." In D. Bornstein and R. Rusconi, *Women and Religion in Medieval and Renaissance Italy,* 305–326. Chicago, 1996.

Russo, Carla. *I monasteri femminili di clausura a Napoli nel secolo XVII.* Naples, 1970.

Sallmann, Jean-Michel. *Naples et ses saints à l'age baroque.* Paris, 1994.

———. "La sainteté mystique féminine à Naples au tournant des XVIe e XVIIe siècles." In S. Boesch-Gajano and L. Sebastiani, *Culto dei Santi, istituzioni e classi sociali in età preindustriale,* 638–710. Rome, 1984.

Sanfelice, G. [under the patriotic pseudonym Eusebio Filopatro]. *Riflessioni Morali e Teologiche sopra l'Istoria Civile del Regno di Napoli.* Rome, 1728.

Sardella, T. "Agli inizi dell'ascetismo femminile. Sicilia e Italia suburbicana." In S. Pricoco, F. Nervo, and T. Sardella, eds., *Sicilia e Italia suburbicaria tra IV e VIII secolo.* Catania, 1991.

Sarnelli, Pompeo. *Guida de' Forestieri, curiosi di vedere, e d'intendere le cose più notabili della Regal Città di Napoli, e del suo amenissimo Distretto Ritrovata colla lettura de' buoni Scrittori.* Naples, 1688.

Savarese, S. *Francesco Grimaldi e l'architettura della Controriforma a Napoli.* Rome, 1986.

———. *Palazzo Cellamare: La stratificazione di una dimora aristocratica (1540–1730).* Naples, 1996.

Savonarola. *Prediche e scritti.* Ed. M. Ferrara. Milan, 1930.

Scarano, C. "La chiesa e il monastero di S. Francesco dell'Osservanza" *Napoli Nobilissima* 25, fasc. 1–2 (1986): 52–61.

Scavo, M. *Vita della Venerabile Suor Benedetta Reggio, Abbadessa Perpetua e Fondatrice del Monistero dell'Immacolata Concezione della Città di Palermo.* Palermo, 1742.

———. *Religiose Difonte con odore, o fame di santità nel ven. Monastero della Concezione di Palermo Dal principio della sua fondazione fino al presente.* Venice, 1743.

Schipa, M., ed. "Il Regno di Napoli, descritto nel 1713 da P. M. Doria." *Archivio Storico Napoletano* 24 (1899): 329–350.

Schmitt, J.-C. *La raison des gestes dans l'Occident médiéval.* Paris, 1990.

Schneider, Jane. *La vigilanza delle vergini.* Palermo, 1987.

Schulenburg, Jane Tibbetts. "The Heroics of Virginity: Brides of Christ and Sacrificial

Mutilation." In M. B. Rose, ed., *Women in the Middle Ages and the Renaissance,* 29–72. Syracuse: Syracuse University Press, 1986.

Schulte van Kessel, Elisja. "Virgins and Mothers between Heaven and Earth." In Natalie Zemon Davis and Arlette Farge, eds., *A History of Women in the West: III Renaissance and Enlightenment Paradoxes,* 132–166. Cambridge, Mass.: Harvard University Press, 1993.

Schutte, A. J. "Inquisition and Female Autobiography: The Case of Cecilia Ferrazzi." In C. Monson, ed., *The Crannied Wall: Women, Religion, and the Arts in Early Modern Europe,* 105–114. Ann Arbor, Mich., 1992.

———, ed. *Autobiografia di una santa mancata.* Bergamo, 1990.

Scott, Katie. *The Rococo Interior: Decoration and Social Spaces in Early Eighteenth-Century Paris.* New Haven, 1995.

Sennett, Richard. *Flesh and Stone: The Body and the City in Western Civilization.* London: Faber and Faber, 1994.

Sicola, Sigismondo. *La Nobiltà Gloriosa nella Vita di S. Aspreno Primo Cristiano, e Primo Vescovo della Città di Napoli.* Naples, 1696.

Sissa, G. "La Verginità materiale. Evanescenza di un oggetto." *Quaderni Storici,* n.s. 75, vol. 25, no. 3 (1990): 739–756.

Sola, Valeria. "La decorazione marmorea della chiesa di S. Caterina del Cassaro in Palermo." *B.C.A. Sicilia,* n.s. AA, 3, 7, 4, fascs. 1–4 (1993–1994): 11–33.

Sparano, G. *Memorie istoriche per illustrare gi Atti della S. Napoletana Chiesa.* Naples, 1768.

Sposato, P. "Dati statistici sulla popolazione civile ed eccclesiastica nel viceregno di Napoli tra la prima e la seconda metà del Seicento." *Annali della Scuola speciale per archivisti e bibliotecari dell'Università di Roma* 5 (1965): 156–166.

Stone, Lawrence. *The Crisis of the English Aristocracy, 1558–1641.* Oxford, 1965.

———. *Family, Sex, and Marriage.* Oxford, 1965.

Storr Cohen, E. "La verginità perduta: Autorappresentazione di giovani donne nella Roma barocca." *Quaderni Storici* 67 (1988): 169–192.

Strazzullo, F. *I Diari dei Cerimoni della Cattedrale di Napoli: Una fonte per la storia napoletana.* Naples, 1961.

———. *Edilizia e urbanistica a Napoli dal '500 al '700.* 1968. 2d ed., Naples, 1995.

———. "Il monastero e la chiesa dei SS. Marcellino e Festo." In *Archivio Storico per le province napoletane,* n.s., 35 (1955): 433–469.

———, ed. *Settecento Napoletano. Documenti,* vol. 1. Naples, 1982.

Tarabotti, Arcangela. "L'Inferno Monacale." In Ginevra Conti Odorisio, ed., *Donna e società nel Seicento.* Rome, 1979.

———. *Lettere familiari e di complemento* (1650)." In Ginevra Conti Odorisio, ed., *Donna e società nel Seicento,* 215–230. Rome, 1979.

———. *La Semplicità Ingannata* (1663)." In Ginevra Conti Odorisio, ed., *Donna e società nel Seicento,* 199–214. Rome, 1979.

Teresa of Jesus. *The Complete Works of St. Teresa of Jesus.* Ed. and trans. E. Allison Peers. 3 vols. New York, 1946.

Terpstra, Nicholas. *Lay Confraternities and Civic Religion in Renaissance Bologna.* Cambridge, 1995.

Tertullian. *Ad uxorem.* Trans. W. P. Le Saint, *Treatises on marriage and remarriage.* Westminster, 1951.

———. *Apologetic and practical treatises.* Ed. C. Dodgson. Oxford, 1854.
Thomas Aquinas, Saint. *Summa theologica.* Trans. W. D. Hughes. London, 1969.
———. *Summa Theologiae: Vol. 43: Temperance.* Trans. T. Gilby. New York, 1963.
Thompson, S. "The Problem of the Cistercian Nuns in the Twelfth and Early Thirteenth Centuries." In D. Baker, ed., *Medieval Women,* 227–252. Oxford, 1978.
Tolley, T. "States of Independence: Women Regents as Patrons of the Visual Arts in Renaissance France." *Renaissance Studies* 10, no. 2 (1996): 236–257.
Trattato di Accommodamento tra la S. Sede, e la Corte di Napoli, Conchiuso in Roma tra li Plenipotenziarj della Santità di Nostro Signore Papa Benedetto XIV e della Maestà di Carlo Infante di Spagna Re delle Due Sicilie. Naples, 1741.
Trexler, R. "Le célibat à la fiin du Moyen Age: Les religieuses de Florence." *Annales ESC* (November–December 1972): 1329–50.
Turner, J. G., ed. *Sexuality and Gender in Early Modern Europe: Institutions, Texts, Images,* 107–132. Cambridge, 1993.
Turner, Victor. *Image and Pilgrimage in Christian Culture: Anthropological Perspectives.* Oxford, 1978.
———. *The Ritual Process: Structure and Anti-Structure.* London, 1969.
———. "Social Dramas and Ritual Metaphors." In *Dramas, Fields and Metaphors,* 23–59. Cornell, 1974.
Valier, Agostino. *La istituzione d'ogni stato loderale delle donne cristiane.* Ed. Gaetano Volpi. Padua, 1744.
Valone, Carolyn. "Mothers and Sons: Two Paintings for San Bonaventura in Early Modern Rome." *Renaissance Quarterly* 53, no. 1 (Spring 2000): 108–131.
———. "Roman Matrons as Patrons: Various Views of the Cloister Wall." In C. Monson, ed., *The Crannied Wall: Women, Religion, and the Arts in Early Modern Europe,* 49–72. Ann Arbor, Mich., 1992.
———. "Women on the Quirinal Hill: Patronage in Rome, 1560–1630." *Art Bulletin* 76, no. 1 (1994): 129–146.
Vargas Macciucca, Francesco Vargas. *Dissertazione attorno alla riforma degli abusi introdotti ne' Munasterij delle Monache per le doti e per le spese che vogliono dalle donzelle.* Naples, 1745.
Vickery, A. "Golden Age to Separate Spheres? A Review of the Categories and Chronology of English Women's History." *Historical Journal* 36 (1993): 383–414.
Vigorelli, G.. *Vita e processo di suor Virginia Maria de Leyva, monaca di Monza.* Milan, 1986.
Villari, Rosario. "Masaniello: Contemporary and Recent Interpretations." *Past and Present* 108 (1985): 117–132.
———. *La rivolta antispagnola a Napoli: Le origini 1585–1647.* Bari, 1994.
———, ed. *Baroque Personae.* Trans. L. Cochrane. Chicago, 1995.
Visceglia, Maria Antonietta. *Il Bisogno di eternità. I Comportamenti aristocratici a Napoli in età moderna.* Naples, 1988.
———. "Corpo e sepoltura nei testamenti della nobiltà napoletana (XVI–XVIII secolo)." *Quaderni Storici* 50 (1982): 583–614.
———. "Linee per uno studio unitario dei testamenti e dei contratti matrimoniali dell'aristocrazia feudale napoletana tra fine Quattrocento e Settecento." *Mélange de l'Ecole Française de Rome: Moyen Age et Temps Modernes* 95 (1983): 393–470.
———. *Territorio feudo e potere locale. Terra d'Otranto tra medioevo ed età moderna.* Naples, 1988.

———, ed., *Signori, patrizi, cavalieri in Italia centro-meridionale nell'età moderna* (Laterza), Rome, 1992.

Vita della Venerabile Madre, D. Maria Carafa Sorella di Paolo IV. Pap e fondatrice del monastero di S. Maria della Sapienza con aggiunta delle Vite della ven. suor Francescca del SS. Sacramento e di S. Caterina di Genova ristrette da un sacerdote Napoletano per ajuto delle SS. Anime Purganti. Naples, 1778.

Vittorelli, P. Ignazio Maria, S.J. *Lettere Spirituali ed istruttive dirette ad alcune religiose claustrali.* Naples, 1748.

———. *Vita e Virtù di Suor Maria Aurelia Cecilia di S. Giuseppe dell'Ordine delle Eremitane di S. Agostino; detta nel secolo, D. Teodora Costanza Caracciolo, degli Eccellentissimi Duchi di Martina.* Naples, 1743.

———. *Della Vita e Virtù della Duchessa di Martina, D. Aurelia Imperiali nelli Caracciolo.* Naples, 1743.

Voelker, E. C. "Borromeo's Influence on Sacred Art and Architecture." In J. Headley and J. B. Tomaro, eds., *San Carlo Borromeo: Catholic Reform and Ecclesiastical Politics in the Second Half of the Sixteenth Century*, 172–187. London and Mississauga, 1988.

Waddy, Patricia. *Seventeenth-Century Roman Palaces: Use and Art of the Plan.* Cambridge, Mass., 1990.

Warner, Marina. *Alone of All Her Sex: The Myth and Cult of the Virgin Mary.* London, 1976.

Weaver, E. "The Convent Wall in Tuscan Convent Drama." In C. Monson, ed., *The Crannied Wall*, 73–86. Ann Arbor, Mich., 1992.

Weber, A. *Teresa of Avila and the Rhetoric of Femininity.* Princeton, 1990.

Weddle, Saundra. "Enclosing Le Murate: The Ideology of Enclosure and the Architecture of a Florentine Convent, 1390–1597." Ph.D. diss., Cornell University, May 1997.

Weinstein, D., and R. Bell. *Saints and Society: The Two Worlds of Western Christendom 1000–1700.* Chicago, 1982.

Wiesner, Merry E. *Women and Gender in Early Modern Europe.* Cambridge, 2000.

Williams, Gerhard Scholz. "Music and Dancing with Mary Magdalen." In C. Monson, ed., *The Crannied Wall: Women, Religion, and the Arts in Early Modern Europe.* Ann Arbor, Mich., 1992.

Winkelmes, Mary-Ann. "Taking Part: Benedictine Nuns as Patrons of Art and Architecture." In G. Johnson and S Matthews Grieco, *Picturing Women in Renaissance and Baroque Italy*, 91–110. Cambridge, 1997.

Wood, Jeryldene. *Women, Art, and Spirituality: The Poor Clares of Early Modern Italy.* Cambridge: Cambridge University Press, 1996.

Wright, Anthony D. "The Religious Life in the Spain of Philip II and Philip III." In W. J. Sheils, ed., *Monks, Hermits and the Ascetic Tradition* (Studies in Church History, vol. 22), 252–274. Oxford, 1985.

———. "Venetian View of Church and State: Catholic Erastianism?" *Studi secenteschi* 19 (1978): 96–97.

Zanette, E. *Suor Arcangela Trabotti monaca del Seicento Veneziano.* Rome, 1960.

Zanetti, D. *La demografia del patriziato milanese nei secoli XVII, XVIII, XIX.* Pavia, 1972.

Zannini, G. L. Masetti. "Donna Marianna de Leyva dal monastero di Soncino a quella di Monza." *Studi Borromaica* 4 (1990): 250–276.

Zardin, D. *Donna e religiosa di rara eccelenza: Prospera Cornoa Bascapè, i libri e la cultura nei monasteri milanesi del Cinque e Seicento.* Florence, 1992.

Zarrabini, Onofrio M.R.D. [M.R.D. Onofrio Zarrabini da Cotignola]. *Della Nobiltà Civile et Christiana: Libri Quattro et de gli Stati Verginale Maritale et Vedovile.* Venice, 1586.

———. *Dello Stato Verginale, Maritale et Vedovile. Libri Tre.* Venice, 1586.

Zarri, Gabriella. "Christian Good Manners: Spiritual and monastic rules in the Quattro- and Cinquecento." In L. Panizza, *Women in Italian Renaissance Culture and Society*, 76–86. Oxford, 2000.

———. "'De Monialibus' (Secoli XVI–XVII–XVIII)." *Rivista di Storia e Letteratura Religiosa* 33, no. 3 (1997): 643–669.

———. *Donna e fede: Santità e vita religiosa in Italia.* Rome, 1994.

———. "The Marriage of Virgins in the Sixteenth Century." In E. A. Matter and J Coakley, eds., *Creative Women in Medieval and Early Modern Italy*, 237–278. Philadelphia, 1994.

———. "Il monachesimo femminile in Italia dall'alto medioevo al secolo XVII." *Convegno del Centro di Studi farfensi* (Verona) 6 (1995).

———. "Monasteri femminili e città (secoli XV–XVIII)." In G. Chittolini and G. Miccoli, eds., *Storia d'Italia, Annali 9. La Chiesa e il potere politico dal Medioevo all'Età contemporanea* (Einaudi), 420–429. Turin, 1986.

———. "Note su Diffusione e Circolazione di testi Devoti (1520–1550)." In G. Zarri, ed., *Libri, idee e sentimenti religiosi nel Cinquecento italiano*, 131–154. Turin, 1987.

———. *Recinti: Donne, clausura e matrimonio nella prima'Età moderna.* Bologna, 2000.

———. "Recinti sacri: Sito e forma dei monasteri femminili a Bologna tra '500 e '600." In S. Boesch Gajano and L. Scaraffia, eds., *Luoghi sacri e spazi della santità.* Turin, 1990.

———. *Le Sante Vive: Cultura e religiosità femminile nella prima età moderna, Annali dell'Istituto storico italo-germanico in Trento* (1980). Vol. 6, pp. 371–445. Turin, 1990.

———, ed. *Donna, disciplina, creanza crisiana dal XV al XVII secolo: Studi e testi a stampa.* Rome, 1996.

Zarri, Gabriella, F. Medioli, and P. M. Chiappa. "De Monialibus (Secoli XVI–XVII–XVIII)." *Rivista di Storia e Letteratura Religiosa* 33, no. 3 (1997): 643–715.

Ziegler, Joanna. "Reality as Imitation: The Role of Religious Imagery among the Beguines of the Low Countries." In U. Wiethaus, ed., *Maps of Flesh and Light: The Religious Experience of Medieval Women Mystics*, 112–126. Syracuse, 1993.

———. *Sculpture of Compassion: The Pieta and the Beguines in the Southern Low Countries.* Brussels and Rome, 1992.

Zito, R. *Alcune Notizie intorno al Monastero di S. Maria Donnaregina.* Naples, 1862.

Zucchi, A. *Roma Domenicana.* Florence, 1938.

INDEX

Abate, Antonia, nun, 101
Abbate, Lucrezia, nun, 101
Acquaviva family, 78
  Isabella, nun, 80
  Reparata, nun, 78–79
active voice, 140, 175, 226n66. *See also* passive voice
A Lapide, Cornelis, SJ, 157
Alberti, Leon Battista, 41–42, 167, 176
Alexander VII, Pope, 174, 177
Amato, Giacomo, architect, 109
Ambrose, Bishop of Milan, 46, 47, 48, 49, 59, 195n105
Angevins (or Anjou), 35
Arcamone
  Filippo, 99
  Lucia, nun, 99
  Margarita, nun, 205n55
archiepiscopal curia. *See* Curia; visitations of convents
Ardia, Antonio, SJ, 165
Arezzo d', cardinal archbishop, 55
Argenzio, Candida Maria d', nun, 104
aristocracy
  and bequests to convents. *See* convents, aristocratic bequests to
  and *Serrata*, 36
  feudal
    and feudal jurisdiction, 5, 6, 30, 43, 62–76, 184n5, 190n99, 196n5, 197n22
    and convents, 5, 7, 11, 16–17, 22, 33–44, 62–81, 96, 106–107, 137, 160, 161, 162, 169, 196n17, 198n37. *See also* entail; feudal inheritance and gender; primogeniture
  See also aristocracy, Neapolitan; aristocracy, nonfeudal; Seggi
aristocracy, Neapolitan, 4, 5, 6, 13–14, 20, 22, 30, 33–44, 62–89, 187n38, 187n41, 189n76, 189n79, 197n20, 200n94, 200n93, 202n143
  di piazza and *fuori piazza*, 39, 43
  and power blocks within convents, 99–103
  See also Seggi
aristocracy, nonfeudal
  rise of, 5, 6, 7, 30, 31, 68, 137, 198n40, 200n94
  and convents, 7, 11, 17, 20, 30, 43, 81–89, 96, 137, 160, 161, 169
  See also Seggi
aristocratic patrimony and convents, 4, 5, 7, 20, 40–44, 65–81, 89, 161, 162, 164, 200n103, 207n96. *See also* aristocracy, feudal; aristocracy, nonfeudal; enclosure and aristocratization

art patronage and nuns. *See* gender and art patronage; nuns and art patronage
Asprenus, Saint, bishop of Naples, 79
Augustine, Bishop of Hippo and saint
feast of, 178
on body /soul relation, 195n82
on chastity as a virtue of the soul, 49, 195n92
on reading matter for nuns, 101
on virginity, 46, 49, 56, 57, 192n18, 193n50, 223n20
Augustines and Augustinian order, 20, 21, 99, 124, 125, 148, 149, 151, 186n14, 218n42. *See also* names of individual convents and monasteries
Austria (and Vienna), 7, 133, 186n2
Avignon
S. Chiara, 144

Banco della Pietà (Monte di Pietà). *See* Naples, financial institutions, Banco della Pietà
Barberini, Taddeo, 107, 108. *See also* Urban VIII, Pope
Barchi, Giovanni Pietro, 56
Basilians and Basilian order, 124, 213n44. *See also* Benedictines and Benedictine order; names of individual convents
beguines, 52
Benedictines and Benedictine order, 20, 21, 38, 40, 95, 111, 128–129, 130, 133, 140, 149, 150, 152, 186n14, 213n55, 218n43. *See also* names of individual convents and monasteries
Benincasa, Orsola (1547–1618), 157. *See also* Naples, Suor Orsola Benincasa convent
Bentham, Jeremy, 145
Bergamo, 218n42
Bernardino da Siena, 167
Bernini, Gian Lorenzo, 215n97
Bisignano, prince of, 126
bizocche (house nuns). *See pinzochere*
Blunt, Anthony, 135
Boccaccio, Giovanni, 144
Boncompagni
Francesco, Cardinal, 104, 105, 146
Maria Cecilia, nun at S. Giuseppe dei Ruffi, 173
Maria Geronima, nun at S. Giuseppe dei Ruffi, 109, 114, 173
Ugo, duke of Sora, husband of Maria Ruffo, 107,173
Bonet, Ludovica, 39
Boniface VIII, Pope, 53, 149, 193n69, 200n96
Bonifacio de'Colli (da Colle), Theatine, 101
Borromeo, Carlo, cardinal archbishop of Milan, 58, 136, 146, 150–151, 156, 194n69, 218n26, 221n78
Bourbons, 7
Bozzuto family, 37
Brancaccio family, 37
Anna, nun, 94
Brunengo family, 80
Burali d'Arezzo, Bl. Paolo, Cardinal Archbishop of Naples, 40
Burnet, Gilbert, 20

Candia, Cesare Maria, 133
Candido, Tommasina, 204n23
Cangiano, Andrea, 135
Cantelmo family, 72
Giacomo, Cardinal Archbishop of Naples, 79
Capano, Teresa, nun at S.Maria Regina Coeli, 116
Capece family and clan, 37, 74, 78
Violante, 84
Capece-Bozzuto, Geronima, 73
Capece Galeotto
Dorotea, nun (in secular Ippolita), 000
Ludovico, 95
Capece Minutolo, Maria, nun at S. Gregorio Armeno, 78
Caposcacco, Virginia, nun at S. Geronimo, 93–94
Cappella, Paola, nun at S. Maria del Gesù and S. Antonio, 187n24
Capua, convent of S. Giovanni, 102, 103
Capuchins. *See* Franciscan order
Caracciolo, Innico, Cardinal archbishop of Naples, 173
Caracciolo
clan, 38, 65, 69, 70, 74, 76, 77–78, 86, 114, 199n60, 200n99
di Brienza family and clan, 67, 72, 196n17, 199n69, 200n95, 200n103
family patronage at S. Giuseppe dei Ruffi, 106
family patronage at S. Gregorio Armeno, 55, 100, 114

Adriana, duchess of Bagnara, 173
Alfonso, count of Brienza, 38, 77
Anna, nun at S. Gregorio Armeno, 100, 114
Annibale, 134
Aurelia, nun at Donnaromita, 174, 203n152
Aurelia Cecilia, nun at S. Giuseppe, Martina, 122, 148, 174
Baldassare, husband of Giulia Monadoi, 106
Carlo Caracciolo of Sant'Eramo, 65
Diana (Sicignano), wife of Giovan Battista, 2nd marquis of Brienza, 72
Dianora, nun, 86
Domenico VII, marquis of Brienza, husband of Cristina Gambacorta, 72
Domizio, 77
Eleonora, nun at S. Gregorio Armeno, 100
Emilio, count of Biscari, 219n58
Francesco, II Duke of Martina, 42, 74
Fulvia, nun at S. Gregorio Armeno, 55, 100, 118, 147, 148, 157, 221n76
Giovan Battista, 2nd marquis of Brienza, 65, 72, 199n69
Giovanni Antonio, count of Oppido, 69
Giulia, daughter of Giuseppe Caracciolo VIII marquis of Brienza, 74, 75, 80
Giulia, nun at S. Arcangelo in Bajano, 117–118
Giuseppe, VIII marquis of Brienza, husband of Teresa Pinto, 73
Ippolita, daughter of duke of Airola, 219n58
Ippolita, mother of Fulvia, 100
Isabella, sister of Francesco II Duke of Martina, 42
Laura, nun, 86
Laura, wife of Giovanni Angelo Muscettola, 204n58
Lucrezia, nun at Croce di Lucca, 86
Lucrezia, nun at S. Gregorio, 100
Luisa, nun at S. Gregorio Armeno, 78, 114
Maria Aurelia Cecilia, nun (in secular, Teodora) at S. Giuseppe, Martina, 42
Maria, nun (in secular, Teodora Costanza)
Maria, prioress at S. Giuseppe dei Ruffi, 106
Pasquale, husband of Francesca Sersale, 75
Petraccone, son of Francesco, 74
Scipione, 135
Teodora, nun at Donnaregina, 42
Teodora Costanza, nun at S. Giuseppe, Martina, 42, 118
Tommasa, nun at S. Gregorio Armeno, 78, 114
Carafa, clan and family, 35, 37, 67, 71, 73, 74, 78, 171
and Divino Amore convent, 206n73
and the Sapienza, 97–98, 100–101, 134–136, 171, fig. 6, fig. 23
Carafa della Spina family, princes of Stigliano, 207n96, 71
Alfonso, cardinal bishop of Naples, 55
Alfonso, count of Montorio, 100
Angelica Caterina, prioress at the Sapienza, 171
Antonio, marquis of Monteballo, 100
Beatrice, daughter of marquis of S. Lucido, 71
Clarice, daughter of Antonio II, prince of Stigliano, 71
Cornelia, nun, 100
Diomede, count and duke of Maddaloni, 71, 100, 197n27
Eleonora, nun at S. Gregorio Armeno, 78, 118
Fabio, son of Luigi Carafa, prince of Stigliano, 71
Ferdinando, duke of Nocera and count of Soriano, 71
Francesco Domenico, husband of Maria Ruffo di Scilla, 74
Gerolama, sister of Diomede, 71
Gian Pietro, 97–98, 101, 135, 206n66, fig. 6
Giovanni, count of Montorio, father of Diomede, 100
Lucrezia, 80
Luigi, II prince of Stigliano, 71
Marco Antonio, prince of Stigliano, 71
Maria (1468–1552), abbess and nun, 97–98, 100, 101, 134, 135, 171, 206n66, fig. 6
Maria Domenica, nun and abbess, 78
Oliviero, cardinal archbishop of Naples, 101, 134
Paola, nun, 100
Roberta, daughter of Luigi Carafa prince of Stigliano, 71
Roberto, dei Maddaloni, 73
Sancia, nun at Donnaromita, 101
Tommaso, dei Maddaloni, 73
Cardinez (or Cardines) family and clan, 35
Carini, Sicily
S. Vincenzo Ferreri, convent, 91
Carmelites and Carmelite order, 32, 83, 108, 127, 186n14

Carmignani, Camilla, 39
Carnavale, Antonio, 112
Cassian. *See* John Cassian
Cavagna, Giovanni Battista (architect), 152
Cecca
  Caterina, nun, 91
  Giulia, 91
Cecinelli, Galeazzo, 39
Celano, Carlo, 19, 122, 142, 152
Charles V, 67
Charles Bourbon, King of Naples, 7
chastity. *See* virginity
Chieri, 218n42
choir nuns (*coriste*), 95–96, 104, 147, 153, 160, 168. *See also* nuns' choirs
Chrysostom, John. *See* John Chrysostom
Cistercians, 216n5, 218n39
cittadelle sacre, 19–44
Clarissans (Poor Clares of the Franciscan order), 127, 134, 151, 153, 218n42. *See also* Franciscans and Franciscan order
claustrum, 165, 184n13, 195n92
Climacus, John. *See* John Climacus
clothes and clothing of nuns. *See* veils and clothing of nuns
Colbert, Jean, 28
Colonna family, 107–108
  Anna (Barberini), 106, 107–108
  Filippo, *conestabile* of Naples, 107
  Ippolita Maria, 107
  Vittoria, 107
confessors and confession, 13, 42, 56, 58, 103–104, 114, 226n75
Conforto, Giovan Giacomo, 219n53, 219n54
conservatories, 19, 20, 21, 91, 94, 127. *See also* under names of conservatories
convent churches
  architecture and decoration of, 7–8, 17–18, 112–117, 127. *See also* nuns' choirs
  site of nuns' patronage, 118–119
  and optics of power, 137–138, 139–160, 168–181
  See also names of convents
convent reform and discipline. *See* reform and discipline of convents
convents
  architecture of, 4, 7, 9, 17–18, 22, 24, 32, 54–55, 64, 95–96, 112–114, 120–138, 139–160, 161–181
    circulation routes within, 166–167
    and optics of power, 137–138, 139–160, 168–181
  and aristocratic bequests, 31–32, 76–81, 203n4
  and aristocratic families, 4, 7, 62–89, 100–103, 110–113, 118, 130–131, 161, 162
  and *feste*, 171–172, 178, 180, 210n155
  foundation of, 41, 100–108, 127, 186n11
  incomes of, 90–104, 172. *See also* dowries, conventual; vitalizi, conventual
  increase in number of in Naples, 186n11
  offices in held by nuns, 95, 96, 100–103
  population of, 186n10, 186n14, 186n15, 186n18
  as protectors of the city, 4, 23, 51, 130, 132, 138. *See also* conventual urbanism and public good
  sites of, 42–43, 120–121, 123, 187n27, 187n28, 187n30, 212n44
  and scandal, 10, 37, 40, 58, 174–176, 191n135. *See also* reform and discipline of convents
  See also conventual urbanism; names of convents
conventual urbanism
  and access to light and air, 128–129, 130, 132, 162
  and belltowers, 128, 148, 168, 216n8
  and belvederes, 121–123, 124, 126, 128, 134, 162, 168
  and expansion of convents, 8–9, 16, 17–44, 77, 78, 95, 96–97, 98, 120–160, 182n24, 187n24
  and fortification, 125, 165–168
  and policy of occupying blocks, 22, 24, 123, 141, 17n41
  and public good, 130–133, 179, 181
  and rivalries, 5, 120–138, 214n64
  vertical city, 121–124, 126, 128, 139, 162, pl. 7
  See also names of convents
Coppola
  Luca, 176
  Violante, 39
  Vittoria, nun, 99
Corcione, Father, SJ, 103
Corenzio, Baldassare, painter, 98, 152
Corono, Giacomo, 171
Cottone family, 208n120
  Carlo, prince of Castelnuovo, 110
  Geronima Felice, prioress, 109,110
  Scipio, prince of Villermate, 110, 208n120
  Vittoria Felice, nun, 109–110, 120n208

Council of Trent. *See* Trent, Council of
Cuomo, Nicolò Francesco, 219n53
Curia, Neapolitan archiepiscopal, 39, 55, 133. *See also* names of archbishops
Cyprian, Bishop of Carthage
  on virginity, 47

D'Alessandro family, 37
Dante Alighieri, 143, 217n16
d'Aquino family, 78
  Chiara Maria, nun at the Sapienza, 78
  Giovanna, nun at Donnalbina, 93
  Maria, 144
da Silva, Eufrosina, nun at SS. Trinità, 152, 219n58
da Varese, Cirillo (Fra`), 170
de Cordua, Maria, nun, 127
de Franchis. *See* Franchis, de
de Gennaro family (counts of Martirano), 37
Del Chiano, Diana, personal servant at S. Gregorio Armeno, 118
De Leyva
  Mariannina, nun (Monaca di Monza), 92
  Martino, 92
della Leonessa, Giuseppe Maria, prince of Supino, 133, 134
dell'Aquila, Gennaro, 141
delle Castelle, Giovanni Andrea, 134
Del Tufo, Elisabetta, nun at Regina Coeli, 116
De Mauro
  Giulia, nun, 91
  Vittoria, nun, 91
De Mura, Francesco, 159
Dentice family, 101
  Lucrezia, 101, 134
De Ponte
  Anna Maria, 202,n134
  Giovanni Francesco, 202n134
  Marc'Antonio, 202n134
De Popoli, Giacinto, painter, 113
de Quiros
  Francesco Bernardo, 202n134
  Maria, 202n134
de Rago family, 78
De Rosa, Carlo, painter, 98
De Rossi
  Giovanni Antonio, architect, 137
  Nicoletta, nun at Regina Coeli, 116
de Sancio, Bonifacio (Bonifacio de Sanctis), 122
De Stefano
  Beatrice, nun, 202n134
  Cristina, nun, 83
  Vittoria, nun, 202n134
de Urso, Luigi, canon, 194–179
di Capua, dukes of Termoli and Altavilla family and clan, 35, 67, 72, 73, 74
  Maria Costanza, nun at the Sapienza, 78
Di Costanza, Eleonora, 206n73
di Enrico, Teodoro. *See* Teodoro di Enrico
Diez y Gomez
  Antonio, 87
  Maria Brigida del SS. Crocefisso, nun (Giuseppina in secular), 203n160
  Maria Teresa del Gesù, nun (Maria, in secular), 203n160
  Paola dell'Incarnazione, nun (Emanuela, in secular), 203n160
dimesse (virgins in the home), 51. *See also* pinzochere
di Notarnicola
  Antonio, architect, 131, 132
  Marco, 113
di Somma, Domenico, prince of Colle, 74
Dominicans and Dominican order, 20, 21, 95, 102, 103, 109, 110, 134, 135, 149, 151, 186n14, 213n44, 218n42, 218n43. *See also* names of individual convents
dotario, 75
"double churches," 149–151, 156, 218n43, 219n47, 221n78. *See also* nuns' choirs
dowries, conventual, 4, 7, 26, 38, 59, 79–81, 91–99, 116, 164, 174, 184n17, 187n21, 199n87, 200n96, 204n14, 204n15, 204n18, 204n23, 204n27, 205n55, 205n56, 212n36
dowries, marriage, 7, 11, 38, 62–81, 196n5, 197n20, 197n121, 199n86. *See also* dowry funds, common
dowry funds, common, 198n41, 199n60

educande (convent boarders), 202n134, 204n56
Eletti of Naples, 36
enclosure, 33, 37, 39–40, 50–52, 53–61, 79, 118, 120, 124, 127, 128, 132, 134, 142–160
  and active cloister, 140, 175, 226n66
  alleviated during plague and revolt, 194n79
  and architecture, 136–137, 139–160, 163–181
  and aristocratization of convents, 162, 164–165, 184n17
  and passive cloister, 140, 175, 226n66

enclosure (*continued*)
and virginity, 130, 34–135, 144–160, 165–168, 194n85
See also dowries, spiritual; reform and discipline of convents; Trent, Council of; visitations
entail and entails, 17, 30, 65, 69, 71, 75, 76, 198n40, 198n46, 198n49, 199n54, 200n93
Eucharist
gendered veneration of, 17, 147, 157, 217n20, 220n67, 221n82, 221n83
regulations regarding, 177–179
relationship to virginity and chastity, 153–160, 174, 221n88
and communion window, 177–178
and enclosure, 127, 142, 144–145, 146–147, 155, 157, 174–175, 177–179, 221n78
and nuns' patronage, 111–112, 114, 119
See also nuns' choir and eucharist
excommunication, 133

Falcone family house, 132
Fanzago, Cosimo, 135, 136, 137, 215n90
Fazio, Antonia, *educanda*, 91
Federici, Federico, 82
Ferrera, 218n42
feste in convents. *See* convents and *feste*
feudal inheritance and gender, 67–76, 197n20, 197n21, 197n25, 197n30, 197n35
feudalism. *See* aristocracy, feudal; entail; feudal inheritance and gender; primogeniture
Feulo, Camillo de, 39
Filomarino family, 78
Ascanio, Cardinal archbishop of Naples, 27, 33, 55, 83, 84, 107, 116, 123
and conventual reform, 27, 55, 115, 116, 176, 194n79, 216n1, 226n75
and monacation feste, 173
and widows in convents, 93
Flanders and Flemish, 6, 43
Florence, 6, 150, 165, 171, 176, 177, 186n18, 191n120, 191n14, 208n109, 217n15, 217n22, 218n42
S. Maria Novella, 196n15
Loggia dei Lanzi, 215n88
Foligno, 218n42
Fonte, Moderata, 12
Foucault, Michel (and Foucauldian concepts), 18, 5, 144, 145, 171, 196n18, 223n15, 224n28, 227n86
foundation of convents. *See* convents, foundation of
Fracanzano, Cesare, da Bisceglie, painter, 98, 152
France, 27–28, 86,184, 204n33, 223n13, 224n27
Franchis, de, family, 87
Isabella, nun, daughter of the marquis of Taviano, 84
Franciscans and Franciscan order, 20, 21, 24, 95, 127, 128, 133, 142, 147, 148, 149, 154, 186n14, 187n32, 213n44, 219n58. *See also* under names of individual convents and monasteries
Frascati, Villa Mandragone, 215n88
Frederick II of Swabia, emperor of Naples and Sicily (1198–1250), 66
Frezza, Giulia, nun at S. Gregorio Armeno, 78

Gaetani, Portia, 197n27
Gaetano da Thiene, 206n66, fig. 6
Gallo, Paolo, 215n90
Galluccio family, 37
Gambacorta
Cristina, wife of Domenico VII marquis of Brienza, 72
Elisabetta, 39
Gargiulo, Domenico (Micca Spadaro), painter, 98
Gaudiosi
Aniello, 27
Candida, 27
Domenico, 27
Orsola, 27
gelosie and grilles, 144, 145, 146, 147, 149, 150, 153, 154, 155, 156, 159, 166, 168, 171, 174, 175, 177, 179
gender
and architecture, 7–8, 13–16
and art patronage, 4–5, 7–8, 13–16, 119–120
and dowries. *See* dowries
and the gaze, 137–138, 139–160, 166–167, 168–181, 217n22, 218n28
and marriage. *See* marriage
and religious practice, 9–13, 15–16. *See also* Eucharist and gender
and sanctity, 10–11
and sexuality, 7,45, 163, 168, 217n22. *See also* virginity and sexuality
and social class, 7–8, 64–69. *See also* aristocracy
and virginity. *See* virginity and gender

Gennaro, Saint, 26
Genoa (and the Genoese), 6, 34, 43, 68, 81, 82, 87
Gesualdo
  Alfonso, cardinal archbishop of Naples, 81, 97
  Maria Costanza, nun at the Sapienza, 113
Giannone, Pietro (1676–1748), 19, 22, 25, 31, 32, 186n2
Giglio, Giovanni Luca, 23, 127
Ginnasi, Caterina, 51
Giordano family of duke of Montecorice
  Maria Illuminata dello Spirito Santo, nun (in secular Angela), 80
Giordano da Rivalto (Fra`), 196n15
Gisolfo, Orazio, 215n90
Giudazzo family, 37
Giudice family, 81–86
  Antonio, prince of Cellamare, duke of Giovanazzo, 86, 202n148
  Aurelia, nun, 83–84, 8
  Chiara, 86, 203n150
  Cornelia, 86, 203n150
  Domenico, husband of Costanza Pappacoda, 86, 202n148
  Elena, nun, 83–84, 85
  Eleonora, nun, 83–84
  Isabella, nun, 83–84
  Marcantonio, 81
  Maria, *educanda*, 83–84
  Nicolò, prince of Cellamare, 81–86, 88, 126
  Teresa, 86
  Zenobia, 86
Gonzaga
  Francesco Bonaventura, 56, 144
  Ippolita, 71
  Isabella, 71
Grano, Antonino, architect, 109–110
Gravina, Duke of. *See* Orsini
Gregory XIII, Pope, 40, 226n71
Gregory Nazianzen, 222n97
Gregory of Armenia, 38
Gregory of Nyssa, Greek Church Father, 46, 48
grilles. *See* gelosie and grilles
Grimaldi, Francesco, Theatine architect, 151, 152, 153, 215n90, 219n53, 219n54, 219n56
Guarini, Giovanni (Fra`), Theatine architect, 153
Gubbio, 187n18
Guevara family and clan, 35
  Giuseppe, Theatine, 42
Guglielmelli, Arcangelo, architect, 141, 159, 216n7
Guise, duke of (Henri of Lorraine), 7
Guzman, Eleonora Maria Guzman, vicereine. *See* vicereine
Guzman, Manuel de, count of Monterey (1631–1637). *See* Viceroy Monterey

honor. *See* virginity and honor

Immaculate Conception, 33, 159
Imperiali, Aurelia, wife of Petraccone Caracciolo, 74
Innocent X (Pamphilj), Pope (1644–1655), 187n21
integritas, 157, 158, 221n88. *See also* virginity

Jerome
  on chastity, 46, 49, 158, 193n50
  on death as consequence of marriage, 46
  letters to aristocratic women, 49
  on virginity, 50, 171, 193n50, 223n20
Jesuits, 21, 110, 128–129, 138, 157
  and policy of making a block, 24
  versus Theatines, 26
  and urbanism, 22, 24, 27, 128–133, 214n64
  See also names of individual Jesuit buildings
John Cassian, 222n97
John Chrysostom
  on marriage, 48
  on virginity, 46, 47, 48, 58
John Climacus, 222n97
John the Baptist, Saint, relics of, 40

Kingdom of Naples, 30, 34, 198n46
Kingdom of the Two Sicilies, 6

Lafréry, A., map of Naples (1566), 21, 23, fig. 1
La Grua, Maria Geronima, nun at S. Giuseppe dei Ruffi, 114
Lazzari
  Dionisio, sculptor and architect, 109, 114, 153, 210n150, 215n90
  Iacopo, sculptor and marble worker, 98, 215n90
Leander of Seville, 49, 59
Leo X, Pope, 149
Lepanto, battle of, 6
Loffredo family, 37, 78
Longhi the Elder, Martino, 215n97
Louis XIV, King of France, 28, 224n27
Lubrano family
  Angelica, nun, 84

Lubrano family (*continued*)
Cecila, nun, 84
Cesare, duke of Ceglie, 87
and Croce di Lucca convent, 87
Lucchese, Giuseppe, royal engineer, 131
Luini, Bernardino, 219n44

Macario, Paolo, 133, 164
Maggio, Francesco Maria, 171
Magliuoli family
Geronimo, 133
Nicola, 133
Maiorano family, 80
Patrizia, nun (in secular Virginia, daughter of Carlo Maria Mairano and Lucrezia Carafa), 80
male celibacy and monasticism, 163, 191n147, 195n102, 200n94
and domination of the Chiaia, 187n29
malmaritate, 12
Malta, 207n99
Manlio, Ferdinando, architect, 151
Manni, Giovanni Battista, 131
Manuzio, Paolo, 60
Marinoni, Giovanni, 206n66, fig. 6
marriage
secular, 10, 11, 13, 35, 38, 41, 48, 49, 51–52, 58, 59, 64–65, 68, 69, 71–76, 77, 78, 80, 89, 100, 143, 162, 172, 173, 185n20, 196n15, 198n37, 198n48, 225n49
spiritual. *See* Sponsa Christi
Martina, S. Giuseppe convent, 42, 122, 148
Marullo, Giuseppe, painter, 113
Mary, Virgin
and conception of Christ , 47
divinity and virginity, 48, 167
and Marian cults, 196n120
as model for virgins, 48, 143, 167
as virgin and mother, 47, 196n120
Mary of Austria, 115
Masaniello, revolt of. *See* revolt of Masaniello
Mass. *See* Eucharist
Mastellone, Angela, nun, 98
Meda, S. Vittore, 150
Mendoza, de, Gerolamo Alercon, marquis of the Valle Siciliana, 72
Mercaldo, Francesco, 30
Messanello, Ottavio, baron of Teana, 135
Methodius of Olympus on virginity, 47, 50
Mezzogiorno, the, and historiography, 5
Milan, 6, 149–151
double churches in, 149–151, 156
churches/monasteries
convent of Dame Vergini della Vattabbia, 218n43
S. Apollinare, 219n44
S. Barbara, 151
S. Caterina alla Chiusa, 151
S. Chiara, 219n43
S. Margherita, 149
S. Maria della Vittoria, 218n43
S. Maria delle Vetere, 218n43
S. Maurizio Maggiore, 149–150, 219n44, fig. 34
S. Orsola, 219n44
S. Paolo Converso
S. Radegonda, 218n43
S. Vincenzino, 150, 151
Minutolo
family, 36
Maria Capece, nun at S. Gregorio Armeno, 78
Miroballo
family, 11
Beatrice, nun at S. Maria Donnalbina, 000
Cesare, 81
Modena, 218n42
modestia, 48
monacation
forced, 200n109, 201n112
rituals of, 26, 93, 107, 111, 148, 172–174, 193n69
See also veils and clothing
Mondoví, 218n42
monks. *See* male celibacy and monasticism; monks' choirs
monks' choirs, 152, 216n5
Montalto, Teresa dello Spirito Santo, nun, formerly duchess of Montalto, 127
Montoja de Cardona (Montoya de Cardona) family and clan, 35
Maddalena, nun, 94
Monza, convent of S. Margherita, 92
Muscettola Leporano family, 37, 190n118
Giovanni Angelo, 204n14
Lucrezia, nun at S.Maria Donnalbina, 112
Scolastica, nun, 92, 204n14
music in convents, 173–174, 178, 181, 218n31. *See also* monacation rituals; nuns' choirs, functions of

Naples
and the Mezzogiorno, 5–6
Castel Sant'Elmo, 3, 29
churches, conservatories, and convents
Annunziata, 77
the Cappuccinelle. *See* S. Francesco delle Cappuccinelle
della Concezione (le Crocelle), 000
Concezione in S. Giacomo, 21
Convertite all'Incurabili (pentite), 21, 78
Convertite all'Incurabili (Riformate) (Santa Casa degli Incurabili), 132, 175, 187n28
Convertite of S. Giorgio, 21
Convertite Spagnuole, 21
Croce di Lucca, 22, 81, 87, 93, 127, 135, fig. 3, fig. 14
conventual dowries at, 83, 92, 95
dispute with the Sapienza, 126–127
and Giudice family, 81–86, 88
reputation of, 95, 83
Gesù delle Monache (S. Maria del Gesù / S. Giovanni in Porta), 22, 23, 40, 134, fig. 10, fig. 11, fig. 12, fig. 30, fig. 39
belvedere, fig. 12
and Carafa family, 86, 134
dispute with S. Maria della Consolazione, 128
and nuns' choir, 159, fig. 39
and S. Antonio di Padova, 187n24
and urbanism, 123, 124, 128
Gesù e Maria, 19, fig. 15
Gesù Nuovo, 21, 22
college at, 22, 27
Gesù Vecchio, 129, 131
college at, 129, 130, 131, 132, figs. 16–22
the Girolamini (s. Filippo Neri), 106
Monteoliveto monastery, 189n71
Periclitanti. *See* S. Maria delle Periclitanti
romitorio of suor Orsola Benincasa, 32
S. Agata, 40, 55
S. Agnello de' Grassi, 129, 131, 132
S. Agnello Maggiore, 33, 40
S. Andrea delle Dame, 23, 40, 90, 139
constitutions of, 6
location, 197n28
reputation of, 95
S. Angelo de' Cardamoni, 132
S. Antonio Abate, 105
S. Antonio di Padova, 21, 22, 108, 187n4, 187n28, 135n191, 213n44, fig. 3
SS. Apostoli, 179
S. Arcangelo a Baiano, 39, 40, 55, 117, 191n135
lax conditions of, 117–118
suppression of, 55
S. Benedetto, 55
SS. Bernardo e Margherita, 20
S. Caterina da Siena, 21, 186n11
S. Chiara, 21, 22, 115, 145, 170, 178, 213n44, fig. 31
conventual dowries at, 95
finances of, 96, 115, 186n15
location of, 187n27
nuns' choir at, 153, 156, 220n67, fig. 31
population of, 186n15
reputation of, 95
rivalry with S. Maria Donnalbina, 125–126, fig. 14
S. Domenico Maggiore, 207n96
S. Festo, 39. *See also* SS. Marcellino e Festo
S. Filippo Neri. *See* Girolamini
S. Francesco delle Cappuccinelle a Pontecorvo, 21, 22, 23, 25, 80, 87, 127, 133, 203n4, 213n44, fig. 15
dowries at, 92, 164, 204n33, 127
enclosure and expansion, 127, 164, 135, 146
finances of 127
foundation, 23, 127, 186n11
new church, 127, 128, 154
nuns' choir at, 148, 154–155, 159–160, 222n102
and urbanistic disputes, 127–128, 133, 148
vitalizi at, 208n113
S. Francesco (dell'Osservanza) delle Monache
church of, 146–147, 154–155
dowries at, 98, 99
expansion of, 98, 99, 146–147
location of, 187n27
S. Gaudioso, 23, 37, 55, 187n28
S. Geronimo, 219n58
dowries at, 92, 93–94, 95
location of, 187n27
reputation of, 95
S. Giacomo degli Spagnoli, 151
S. Giovanni Battista delle Monache, 4, 79, 90, 104, 105, 117, 207n89

Naples (*continued*)
foundation of, 102–103, 186n11
location of, 187n28, 213n44
S. Giovanni in Porta. *See* Gesù delle Monache
S. Giuseppe dei Ruffi (delle Eremitane), 22, 80, 90, 109, 111, 113–114, 116, 124–125, fig. 7, fig. 11, fig. 26, fig. 29, fig. 32, fig. 36
and Caracciolo family, 106
church of, 107, 109, 114, 153, pl. 6, fig. 7, fig. 26, fig. 29, fig. 32, fig. 36
conflict with S. Maria del Gesù, 124
conflict with S. Maria Donnaregina, 124–125
dowries and *vitalizi* at, 92, 95, 98, 108, 109, 114, 204n14
expansion of, 98, 107, 109, 113–114, 124
fasting at, 178
foundation of, 100, 105–107, 186n11
location of, 187n28
monacations at, 173
and Oratorians, 106
and Ruffo clan, 100, 105–107, 108, 109, 114, 173
S. Giuseppe delle Scalze a Pontecorvo, 32, 136, 186n11, fig. 24
S. Gregorio Armeno, 22, 24, 37, 38, 40, 41, 55, 78, 79, 80, 86, 114, 118, 147–148, 151–152, 213n44, fig. 40, fig. 41, fig. 42, fig. 44, pl. 4, pl. 5, pl. 7, pl. 9, pl. 10
archiepiscopal regulation of, 157
and Caracciolo family, 114
church and main altar, 114, 159, 180, pl. 4, pl. 5, pl. 9, pl. 10
covered bridge at, 166
dowries at, 92, 95
and enclosure, 118, 155–156, 157
funeral of abbess at, 147–148
income of, 90
nuns' choirs at, 151–152, 153, 154–155, 174–175, 180, pl. 9, pl. 10
reputation of, 95, 118
scala santa at, 159
S. Lorenzo, 24, 38, 144
SS. Marcellino e Festo (S. Donato, S. Festo, S. Marcellino), 21, 22, 24, 55, 99, fig. 5, figs. 16–22
dispute with Jesuits, 128–132, figs. 16–22
dowries at, 92, 95
income of, 90, 99
reputation of, 95, 176
urbanism of, 128–132, 133–134
S. Maria d'Agnone, 38, 77
S. Maria degli Angeli, 38, 111, 191n135
S. Maria degli Angeli alle Croci, 136
S. Maria dei Vergini, 38
S. Maria del Carmine Maggiore, 32
S. Maria del Divino Amore, 22, 24, 122
decoration of, 159
dowries at, 92, 94, 95
foundation of, 100, 102, 103–105, 159, 186n11
reputation of, 95
S. Maria del Gesù. *See* Gesù delle Monache
S. Maria della Concezione, 21
S. Maria della Conciliazione, 187n28
S. Maria della Consolazione degli Afflitti, 24, 90, 91, 116, 123, 127, 128, 141, 203n3, 213n44, fig. 4
dispute with S. Maria del Gesù, 128
dowries and *vitalizi* at, 92, 96–97, 98–99, 108
expansion of, 96–97, 98–99, 128, 203n3
income of, 203n3
plan of convent, 177, 216n8
S. Maria della Misericordia, 38
S. Maria della Sanità, 38
S. Maria della Sapienza, 21, 22, 40, 78, 102, 103, 127, 134–137, 151, 152, 213n44, p.8, fig. 3, fig. 23, fig. 35
and Carafa family, 86, 100, 102, 108, 134–135, 172
church of, 113, 135–137, 215n97, 215n90, pl. 8, fig. 23, fig. 35
confessors at, 134–135, 172, 226n75
dispute with Croce di Lucca convent, 126–127
dowries and *vitalizi* at, 92, 95, 97–98, 108, 204n18
expansion at, 98, 134–137
nuns' choir at, 151, 152, 156, fig. 35
population of, 186n4
reputation of, 95, 98, 103
sugar economy at, 179
and Theatines, 86, 100, 102, 108, 134–135, 172, 206n66
S. Maria delle Grazie a Caponapoli, 132, 133

S. Maria delle Periclitanti (di S. Pietro e Paolo), 23, 25, 148
S. Maria di Betlem, 21
S. Maria di Costantinopoli, 23
S. Maria di Gerusalemme, 40, 142, 158, 176, 187n28
S. Maria Donnalbina, 22, 37, 40, 55, 96, 128, 140, 173, fig. 13, fig. 25, fig. 43
  decoration of, 112
  dowries at, 92, 93, 95, 96
  parlatories at, 140–141, fig. 25
  reputation of, 95
  rivalry with S. Chiara, 125–126, fig. 14
  urbanism and, 125–126
S. Maria Donnaregina (Nuova), 21, 27, 42, 78, 90, 153, 209n141, 213n44, fig. 27, fig. 28, fig. 37, fig. 38
  belvederes at, 121
  church architecture of, 153, fig. 27, fig. 28
  conflict with S. Giuseppe dei Ruffi, 124–125
  dowries at, 92, 95
  nuns' choir at, 153, fig. 37
  reputation of, 95, 176
  and urbanism, 121, 123–124
S. Maria Donnaromita, 21, 2, 37, 55, 86, 101, 213n44, pl. 3
S. Maria Egiziaca a Pizzofalcone, 92, 115, 178, 186n11, 201n112
S. Maria Maddalena, 21, 23, 91, 17, fig. 15
  dispute with S. Francesco delle Cappuccinelle, 127–128
  foundation of, 186n11
  location of, 187n27
S. Maria Regina Coeli, 23, 79, 116, 151, fig. 33
  confessors at, 226n75
  location of, 187n28
  nuns' choir at, 153, fig. 33
  nuns' possessions at, 116–117
  population of, 186n14
  sweets at, 178
  visitations at, 176
S. Martino (Certosa di), 216n5
S. Monica, 20, 27
  building and expansion at, 99
  communal fund at, 96
  dowries and *vitalizi* at, 94, 96, 99, 108–109
  and enclosure, 94
S. Nicolò al Molo, 33
S. Paolo Maggiore, 179, 219n56
S. Patrizia, 23, 24, 37, 55, 187n28
  double church at, 180
  dowries at, 95
  reputation of, 95
S. Pietro a Maiella, fig. 3
S. Pietro Martire, 91
SS. Pietro e Sebastiano, 187n28
S. Potito, 37, 40
  dowries at, 92
S. Sebastiano, 21, 22, 27, 101
SS. Severino e Sossio, 129
S. Severo, 38
S. Teresa a Chiaia, 32
S. Teresa del SS. Sacramento, 186n11
SS. Trinità delle Monache, 40, 115, 122, 152, 186n11, 220n71
  dowries at, 92
  suor Orsola Benincasa *romitorio*. *See romitorio* of suor Orsola Benincasa
financial institutions
  Banco della Pietà (Monte di Pietà), 93
government, 35–37. *See also* Seggi
palazzo
  Andria, 134
  Archiepiscopal palace, 123–124
  Caracciolo (Capuana), 69–70
  Caracciolo di Brienza at S. Giovanni a Carbonara, 198n49
  Carafa di Stigliano. *See* Palazzo Cellamare
  Cellamare (Carafa di Stigliano), 202n148
  Conca, 22, 126–127, 187n24, 212n30
  Salerno. *See* Palazzo Sanseverino
  Sanseverino (Salerno), 21, 22
population of. *See* population of Naples
quarters (districts) of
  Borgo of S. Antonio Abate, 187n30
  Capodichino, 187n30
  Chiaia, 29, 86, 187n29, 189n71
  Chiatamone, 29
  Marina del Vino, 130
  Mortelle hills, 189n71
  Olimpiano, 22
  Pizzofalcone, 29, 189n71, 211n3
  Porto, 129, 131
  quartieri or Spanish quarters, 29–30, 187n30
streets (*vie, vicoli, strade*)
  di Angelillo, 129
  della Campana, 24

Naples (*continued*)
Cisterna dell'Olio, 21
Costantinopoli, 21, 22, 103, 122, 135, 136, 152
Ferri Vecchi, 130
Mezzocanone, 130
di Nido, 129
di Pistaso, 24
Pontecorvo, 22
de' Sanguini, 24
S. Gregorio Armeno, 166, fig. 42
di S. Pietro, 214n79
S. Pietro a Maiella, 135, 212n30
Sebastiano, 21
Sole e Luna, 134
Toledo, 28, 30
topography, 3, 129, 131
viceregal court. *See* viceregal court in Naples
viceroy. *See* viceroys
Nauclerio, Michelangelo, architect, 127
nobles, nobility. *See* aristocracy
Notario (Notariis), Giovanella da, 39
nuns
as brides of Christ. *See* nuns as *Sponsae Christi*
consecration of, 58, 93. *See also* monacation
as patrons, 90–119, 185n33, 207n108
property and possessions of, 90–98, 101, 104–105, 108, 109–119, 199n87, 210n165. *See also vitalizi*
as protectors of the city. *See* convents as protectors of the city
as relics, 179–181
as *Sponsae Christi*, 5, 48, 51, 58–60, 63, 65, 79, 123, 157, 165, 169, 170, 171, 172–174, 195n105, 225n49
and dramatic productions in convents. *See* plays (theatrical) in convents
nuns' choirs (architectural spaces)
architecture and decoration of, 152, 153–160, 166
function and status of, 145, 146, 147–148, 153–154, 155, 158, 159, 162, 168, 180, 220n67
location of, 145, 146, 148–160, 220n67, 220n71
and Mass, 146, 147, 148–149, 153–154, 155, 156, 158, 159
regulations regarding, 147, 153–154, 168, 170
See also choir nuns; monks' choirs

Oliva, Alberico, 39, 191n129
Onorata, Serafina, nun, 91
Oratorians (Congregation of S. Filippo Neri), as confessors to nuns, 106–107
Origen, 58
Oriundo, Nunzia, *educanda* at the Incurabili, 78
Orsini family and clan, 35
duke of Gravina, 125
Maria Giovanna, nun, 92
Ottavio, count of Piacenza, 92

Pacifico, Orazio, 215n90
Palagano
Dianora, nun, 85
Ippolita, daughter of Zenobia della Marra, princess of Cellamare, 84, 85, 86
Lucio, 85
Palermo, 63, 175, 178, 210n156, 212n37, 216n1, 216n4, 226n66
churches
Casa Professa (Jesuit church), 110
S. Caterina, 109–111, fig. 8
S. Maria del Cancelliere, 111, 122–123
S. Maria dell'Immacolata Concezione, 111
See also Sicily
Palladio, Andrea, 152
Palmieri family property, 131, 132
Panciroli, Cardinal, 93
Pandone, Camillo, count of Venafro, 101
Paolucci, Maria Felice, abbess at S. Giovanni Battista, 105
Pappacoda family, 86
Costanza, 86
Elena, wife of Giuseppe, 86
Giuseppe, prince of Triggiano, 86
Paris, 27–28, 86, 224n27
parlatories, 54, 139, 142, 170, 175, 205n55, 216n3, 216n4, 216n6
passive voice, 140, 175, 226n66. *See also* active voice
Patricia, Saint, 180
Paul, Saint, 48, 49
Paul III, Pope, 211n1
Paul IV, Pope. *See* Carafa, Gian Pietro
Peccerillo, Francesco, 24, 26, 27
Pelliccia
Matteo, sculptor and marble worker, 98, 215n90
Pietro, sculptor and marble worker, 98
Periculoso, bull of Boniface VIII, 53, 200n96. *See also* enclosure
Philip III, king of Spain, 25, 71

Philip IV, king of Spain, 70
Philip V, king of Spain, 121–122
Piazza. See Seggi
Piccole Ancelle del Sacro Cuore, 151
Pietro Berettini da Cortona, at the Girolamini, 106
Pignatelli family and clan, 35, 71, 78
  Agnese, nun, daughter of Carlo duke of Bisaccia, 86
  Andrea, archbishop, 128
  Carlo, duke of Bisaccia, 203n150
  Eleonora, nun, daughter of duke of Bisaccia, 86
  Ettore, 71
  Fabrizio, prince of Noia, marquis of Cerchiara, 71
  Francesco, cardinal archbishop, 133
  Giovanna, 71
  Ippolita, 203n152
  Lucrezia, abbess at S. Gregorio Armeno, 78
  Marcello, 104
  Zenobia, 203n152
Pignone family, 78
Pinto family, 73, 74
  Emanuele, prince of Ischitella, 73
  Teresa, wife of Giuseppe Caracciolo, VIII marquis of Brienza, 73, 74
pinzocchere (bizocche), 52, 91
Piscicelli family, 37
Pius IV, Pope, 53
Pius V, Pope, 53, 175, 193n69, 200n96
plague, 26, 28, 31–32, 194n79
plays (theatrical) in convents, 170–171
Poderico, Giovan Francesco, 38
Pomarancio. *See* Roncalli, Cristoforo
Ponzio, Flaminio, 215n97
population of Naples, 20–23, 28–29, 188n62, 188n65, 189n79
Porto district of Naples. *See* Naples, quarters (districts) of
Portogallo, Beatrice, Abbess of S. Chiara, 186n15
Porto Maurizio, 218n42
Portuguese, 6
Prato, 186n18
primogeniture, 17, 65–66, 68, 69–71, 76, 162, 198n37, 198n40, 198n46
prostitutes and prostitution, 12, 21, 23, 89, 187n30, 224n27
Protestantism and gender, 9, 60
pudicitia, 51. *See also* virginity

Quaranta, Geronimo, canon, 194n79

Rago, de. *See* de Rago
Raineri
  Anna, nun, 111
  Celestina, nun, 122–123, 170
  Giuseppe, 111
Ravaschieri family, 35
"recinti sacri" (sacred enclosures), 163–164
reform and discipline of convents, 27, 33, 37, 39–40, 41–43, 53–61, 63, 96–98, 101–102, 115, 116, 176, 194n79, 216n1, 226n75
  and silence, 175–176, 226n66
  See also convents and scandal; Trent, Council of; visitations
Reggio Emilia, 218n42
Regio Consiglio. *See* Sacro Regio Consiglio
Regular Canonesses of the Lateran, 20, 186n14
relics and reliquaries
  in convents' possession, 40, 116, 117, 180
  nuns as. *See* nuns as relics
  S. Gennaro, 26
  S. Gregorio Armeno, 38, 41, fig. 44
  St. John the Baptist, 40
religious orders
  rivalries between, 5
  See also under names of specific orders and convents
revolt of Masaniello (1647–1648), 7, 26, 33, 82, 179, 194n79
Ricca (Richa), Giovanni, painter, 98
Ricci, Silvia, nun, 127, 212n35
Ristaldo, Maria Giacinta, prioress of S. Giuseppe dei Ruffi, 114
Rocchi family, 37
Rocco
  Lucrezia, 116
  Maria Egiziaca, nun at the Consolazione, 116
Rodriguez, Alfonso, 157
Rome, 5, 6, 26, 33, 4, 107, 120, 126, 137, 211n1. *See also* names of popes
Rome
  churches and convents
    S. Bibiana, 215n97
    S. Caterina a Magnanapoli, 215n97

Rome (*continued*)
S. Gregorio al Celio, 215n97
S. Maria Maggiore, 215n97
S. Maria Regina Coeli, 108
S. Sebastiano fuori le mura, 215n97
palazzi
Borghese, 223n5
Farnese, 211n1
Muti-Bussi, 137
Rome, Sacra Congregazione dei Regolari. *See* Sacra Congregazione dei Regolari, Rome
Roncalli, Cristoforo (Pomarancio), 106
Rosalia, Saint, *festino* of, 122
Rossi family, 37
Margherita, 39
Rubio, Archbishop of Palermo, 175, 16n1, 226n66
Ruffo family and clan, 35, 67, 71, 72, 74, 100, 114, 199n86, 207n96
family and convent of S. Giuseppe dei Ruffi, 100–101, 105–107, 113–114, 173
Anna Maria Ruffo di Scilla, wife of Carlo Ruffo, duke of Bagnara, 74
Arcangela (in secular Ippolita), nun at S. Giuseppe dei Ruffi, daughter of Carlo Ruffo and Adriana Caracciolo, 173
Carlo II, duke of Bagnara, 72, 74, 173
Catarina Ruffo, 106, 207n96
Chiara Maria, nun at S. Giuseppe, 114, 210n150
Enrico Ruffo di Scilla, 74
Fabrizio, 107, 114, 207n96, 207n99
Feliciana, wife of Fabrizio Villani, 105
Francesco, duke of Bagnara, 72
Giovanna, princess of Scilla, 70, 74
Imara, wife of Giuseppe Spatafora, 70
Ippolita Caterina, 109, 114
Ippolita, daughter of Paolo Ruffo, count of Sinopoli, 106, 109
Lucrezia, 72
Margarita Caterina, 71
Maria Margarita, nun at the Sapienza, 78
Maria, princess of Scilla, 70, 71, 74
Maria, wife of Ugo Boncompagni, duke of Sora, 107, 173
Marino, 38
Ottavio, 106, 207n96
Paolo, count of Sinopoli, 106
Tiberio, 75
Vincenzo Ruffo-Santapau, marquis of Licodia, 71, 74
Vincenzo, prince of Scilla, 106, 207n96

Sacra Congregazione dei Regolari, Rome, 26, 27, 92, 99, 108, 125, 126, 129, 174, 179, 205n56, 210n155, 226n75, 177, 210n172, 216n4
Sacro Regio Concilio (Sacred Royal Council), Naples, 29, 135, 202n134
Sancia of Mallorca, queen (b. Clare Morì), 153, 186n15
sancta voluntas, 49
sanctitas corporis, 49
Sanfelice family, 37
Camilla, 38
Camillo, 38
Giuseppe, 186n3
Vincenzo, 38, 40
Sangro, de, family, 36–37, 78
Anna, 7
Eleonora, 78
Lucrezia, 78
San Marco, Porzia, 201n112
Sanseverino, clan and family, 7, 68, 75, 197n35, 199n86, 200n91
Giuseppe Leopoldo, 75
Luigi, 75
Maria, 75
Savonarola, Girolamo, 101, 217n15
Sbarra, Andrea, 82
Scarpato, Eleanor, 23, 127
Scrivá, Pedro Luis, 29
Sebastiano
Giovanni Francesco, Rationale of the Reale Camera del Sommaria, 87, 204n23
Ippolita, nun, 204
Sedili. *See* Seggi
Seggi (Piazze, Sedili), 16, 20, 21, 35–41, 43, 137, 190n104, 190n106
Seggio del Popolo (of the People), 36
Seggio of Capuana, 36, 37, 38, 40, 41, 70, 73, 77, 86, 106–107, 219n58
Seggio of Montagna, 26, 36, 37, 38, 39, 40, 102
Seggio of Nido, 36, 37, 38, 39, 40, 41, 77, 86, 207n96
Seggio of Portanova, 36
Seggio of Porto, 36, 37, 40, 130

Semer, Enrico, painter, 98
Serrata. See aristocracy and *Serrata*
Serriana, Antonia, daughter of count of Casaduni, 93
Sersale family, 37, 75
Francesca, 75
sexuality
and convent architecture, 174–175, 176, 177–181
See also gender and sexuality; virginity and sexuality
Sicily, 6, 7, 31, 184, 196n5, 198n37, 198n46, 199n54. *See also* Palermo
signaculum. See virginity, material versus corporeal
Sixtus IV, Pope, 193n69, 194n69
Sixtus V, 216n4
Somaschi fathers, 200n99
Somma, di family. *See* di Somma
Sommaria, Court of, 29, 87
Sorgente family, 37
Spadaro, Micco, painter. *See* Gargiulo, Domenico
Spain (and the Spanish), 6–7, 34, 68, 81, 86, 87, 88, 198n46, 200n94, 204n3
Spanish rule in Naples, 5, 6–7, 26, 30–31, 32–34, 34–36, 55, 64, 86, 88, 200n94, 190n106
Spanish nuns, 21, 186n14
Spano, Olimpia, 95
Spatafora
Camilla, 70
Giuseppe, marquis of San Martino, 70
Muzio, 70
Pietro, 70
Spinelli family, 78
Caterina, 106
Cremona, 82
Giacinta, nun at the Sapienza, 113
Spinola, Giuseppe, 75
Sponsa Christi. See nuns, as *Sponsae Christi*
Stendardo
Gianpiero, 134
Marino, 39, 134
Stopendael, B., map of Naples, 21, fig. 2
Strambone family, 37
sugar and sweets, 174, 178–179
suppression of convents, 40, 55, 191n135. *See also* reform and discipline of convents

Tacca, Simone, 215n90
Teodoro di Enrico, 180
Teresa of Avila, Saint, 60, 222n1
tertiaries, 52, 91, 204n10
Tertullian, 58
Theatines and Theatine order, 42, 101, 103, 151, 152, 153, 179, 206n66, 215n90, 219n53, 219n54, 219n56
and female convents, 101, 103, 134, 135, 151, 153, 179, 206n66
versus Jesuits, 26
See also names of individual Theatines
Thomas Aquinas, Saint, on virginity, 49–50, 60, 145, 158, 193n48, 193n50
Tocco family, 72
Tomacelli family, 106
Chiara, nun (in secular, Caterina), 106
Girolamo Tomacelli, 106
Maria Giacinta, nun and abbess at S. Maria Regina Coeli, 116, 117
and S. Giuseppe dei Ruffi, 106
Trent, Council and Decrees of, 9, 11, 31–40, 53–61, 78, 92, 114, 124, 139, 141, 144, 146, 149, 150, 153, 155, 156–157, 158, 160, 162, 164–167, 184n17, 188n42, 193n69, 194n85, 200n96, 200n109, 217n23, 218n39, 223n13
and regulation of convents, 11, 53–55, 124, 221n78, 141, 157, 194n85, 201n110
See also reform and discipline of convents
Tribunal of fortification, Naples, 129, 131, 132
Turin, 86
S. Maria Maddalena convent, 57
Turks, 6, 207n99

Udine, 194n78
Ulcano
Marc'Antonio, 90–91
Bernardina, 91
Lucrezia, 91
Vittoria, 91
Urban VIII (Barberini), Pope, 77, 107–108, 216n4

Vaaz family, 64–65
Vaccaro, Andrea, painter, 98
Valentini, Francesco, sculptor and marble worker, 98, 215n90
Valier, Agostino, Cardinal and bishop of Verona
on states of women, 51, 179
Vasanzio, Giovanni, 215n97

veils and nuns' clothing, 148, 162–163, 169–170, 171–174, 178. *See also* monacation feste
Venice, 6, 191n120, 218n42
S. Giorgio, 152
Vicaria, Court of, 29
Vicenza, 218n42
viceregal court in Naples, 5, 6, 7, 30, 31, 68, 137, 200n94
vicereine countess of Monterey, Eleonora Maria Guzman, 104
Viceroy Monterey (Manuel de Guzman, count of Monterey) (1631–1637), 189n71
Viceroy Olivares (Enrique de Guzman Count of Olivares) (1595–1599), 55
Viceroy Oñate (Iñigo Velez y Tassis de Guevara, Count of Oñate) (1648–1653), 33
Viceroy Peñaranda (Gaspare de Bracamante Peñaranda), 32
viceroys, 30, 32, 33, 55, 104
Viceroy Toledo (Pedro Alvarez de Toledo), 29, 30–31, 172, 189n71
Vienna. *See* Austria
Villani family, 159
Dorotea, nun at Sapienza, 102, 105, 206n89
Fabrizio, husband of Feliciana Ruffo, 105
Francesco del Balzo, 79
Giovanna Maria, nun (in secular Cornelia, daughter of Franceo Villani), 79
Giovanni, marquis of Polla, 102, 103, 206n73
Maria, nun and prioress (in secular Beatrice), 100, 101–105, 117, 159, 206n89
Maria, nun, daughter of Francesco Villani
Ottavia, nun, 94
Virgin. *See* Mary, Virgin
virginity
and enclosure, 45–61, 63, 79, 145–160, 161–181, 174–175
and eucharist, 156–158, 159–160, 174, 177–179, 221n88
and family honor, 5, 7–8, 16, 40, 45–61, 63, 76, 160, 161, 174
and gender, 5, 6, 12, 42, 47, 144, 145, 158, 162, 163, 167, 195n102
hermaphroditic, 48
male. *See* male celibacy
material virginity versus perfect, 49–50, 57, 144, 193n48, 223n20
and nuns' appearance, 148, 162–163, 169, 171–173
and other forms of chastity, 12, 16, 51–52, 144–145, 193n50
and Paradise, 45–46, 158, 166, 179, 181, 192n18
reemphasized, 9
and sexuality, 45–50, 144–145, 158, 160, 165–166, 167, 175, 193n48, 218n28, 223n20
and shame. *See* virginity and family honor
and sight, 145–160
and social class. *See* virginity and family honor
and touch, 145–146
See also male celibacy
visitations, episcopal visitations to convents, 16, 55, 175, 176, 194n79
vitalizi
of cadets, 73, 208n110
of nuns, 92, 94, 96, 100, 108–109, 114, 205n37, 208n110, 208n113
Vittorelli, Ignazio, SJ, 60
vows (solemn), 59

widows, 12, 21, 51, 93, 200n109, 224n27

Zarrabini, Onofrio
on virginity, 50, 51–52, 57–58
Zufia, de, family, 87
Zuñica (Zuniga), Eleonora, nun, 96